FROM PLUNDER TO PRESERVATION
Britain and the Heritage of Empire, *c.*1800–1940

PROCEEDINGS OF THE BRITISH ACADEMY · 187

FROM PLUNDER TO PRESERVATION
Britain and the Heritage of Empire, *c.*1800–1940

Edited by
ASTRID SWENSON
AND PETER MANDLER

Published for THE BRITISH ACADEMY
by OXFORD UNIVERSITY PRESS

Oxford University Press, Great Clarendon Street, Oxford OX2 6DP

Oxford New York

*Auckland Cape Town Dar es Salaam Hong Kong Karachi
Kuala Lumpur Madrid Melbourne Mexico City Nairobi
New Delhi Shanghai Taipei Toronto*

*With offices in
Argentina Austria Brazil Chile Czech Republic France Greece
Guatemala Hungary Italy Japan Poland Portugal Singapore
South Korea Switzerland Thailand Turkey Ukraine Vietnam*

*Published in the United States
by Oxford University Press Inc., New York*

*© The British Academy 2013
Database right The British Academy (maker)*

First published 2013

*British Library Cataloguing in Publication Data
Data available*

*Library of Congress Cataloging in Publication Data
Data available*

*Typeset by
New Leaf Design, Scarborough, North Yorkshire
Printed and bound by CPI Group (UK) Ltd, Croydon, CR0 4YY*

*ISBN: 9 78–0–19–726541–3
ISSN: 0068–1202*

Contents

List of Figures

Notes on Contributors

Mary Beard is Professor of Classics at the University of Cambridge. She has wide research interests in the history of the Roman world and its reception in the nineteenth and twentieth centuries. She is author of *The Roman triumph* (2007) and *Pompeii: the life of a Roman town* (2008). She is currently working on a book on Roman laughter.

Robin Cormack is Emeritus Professor of the History of Art, Courtauld Institute of Art, University of London and teaches in the Faculty of Classics, University of Cambridge. His books include *Writing in gold* (1985), *The Byzantine eye* (1989), *Painting the soul* (1997), *Byzantine art* (2000), *Icons* (2007), and *Byzantium 330–1453* (1998).

David Gange is Lecturer in History at the University of Birmingham. He is the author of *Dialogues with the dead: Egyptology in British culture and religion* (2013) and editor with Michael Ledger-Lomas of *Cities of God: the Bible and archaeology in nineteenth-century Britain* (2013). He has published a number of essays in journals and collected volumes on reception of the ancient world and archaeology in the nineteenth century.

Simon Goldhill is Professor of Greek at the University of Cambridge and Fellow of King's College, Cambridge. He is also Director of the Cambridge Research Centre for Arts, Social Sciences, and Humanities, and Director of the Cambridge Victorian Studies Group. His most recent books are *Victorian culture and classical antiquity: art, opera, fiction and the proclamation of modernity* (2011) and *Sophocles and the language of tragedy* (2012). He has published widely on Greek literature, and on the relation between Victorian culture and antiquity.

Melanie Hall is Associate Professor and Director of Museum Studies in the Department of History of Art and Architecture at Boston University. Her research interests lie in British and American preservation, particularly as a form of cultural diplomacy. She is the author of a number of essays in collective volumes on this topic and recently edited *Towards world heritage: international origins of the preservation movement 1870–1930* (2011). She has also written seventeen statutory *Lists of buildings of historic or architectural interest*. Her current work is on the origins of the National Trust in a transatlantic context. She is Fellow of the Society of Antiquaries of London.

Peter Mandler is Professor of Modern Cultural History at the University of Cambridge and Bailey College Lecturer in History at Gonville and Caius College. His writing on heritage and history in modern British culture includes the books *The fall and rise of the stately home* (1997) and *History and national life* (2002). Most recently he is the author of *Return from the natives: how Margaret Mead won the Second World War and lost the Cold War* (2013).

Sadiah Qureshi is Lecturer in Modern History at the University of Birmingham. She is the author of *Peoples on parade: exhibitions, empire and anthropology in nineteenth-century Britain* (2011). This followed on from a postdoctoral research fellowship with the Cambridge Victorian Studies Group on a Leverhulme-funded project that explored Victorian notions of the past, at the University of Cambridge. She is currently working on her next book, which will examine notions of human endangerment within the context of modern settler colonialism in Britain, America, South Africa, and Oceania.

Donald Malcolm Reid is Professor of History Emeritus at Georgia State University and Affiliate Faculty, Department of Near Eastern Languages and Civilization, University of Washington. He is the author of *Whose pharaohs? archaeology, museums, and Egyptian national identity from Napoleon to World War I* (2002) and *Cairo University and the making of modern Egypt* (1990). His current research centres on issues of archaeology and Egyptian identity since the First World War.

Edmund Richardson is Lecturer in the Department of Classics at the University of Leeds. He is the author of *Classical Victorians: scholars, scoundrels and generals in pursuit of antiquity* (2013). He is currently exploring the ways in which forgetfulness and absence can structure relationships with the past.

Indra Sengupta is Academic Coordinator and Head of the Transnational Research Project – India of the German Historical Institute London and Max Weber Foundation, Germany. She is the author of *From salon to discipline: state, university and Indology in Germany, 1821–1914* (2005) and editor (with Daud Ali, University of Pennsylvania) of *Knowledge production, pedagogy and institutions in colonial India* (2011). She has also edited *Memory, history, and colonialism: engaging with Pierre Nora in colonial and postcolonial contexts*, Bulletin of the German Historical Institute London, Supplement 1 (2009) and authored a number of articles on German orientalism and India, and on colonial monument-making practices in British India. She is currently completing a book entitled *Colonial monumentality: religious sites, conservation and heritage-making in colonial India*.

Sujit Sivasundaram is Cambridge University Lecturer in World and Imperial History since 1500 and Fellow of Gonville and Caius College, Cambridge. He is the author of *Nature and the Godly Empire: science and evangelical mission in the Pacific 1795–1850* (2005) and also *Islanded: Britain, Sri Lanka and the bounds of an Indian Ocean colony* (2013). His written articles consider the history of modern empires in relation to race, culture, nature, science, the environment, and geography, amongst other broad themes. He is beginning a new project on the nineteenth-century Pacific and Indian Ocean worlds.

Astrid Swenson is Lecturer in European History at Brunel University, London, following fellowships with the Cambridge Victorian Studies Group and Darwin College, Cambridge. Her research and publications focus on uses of the past since the eighteenth century. Her book *The rise of heritage: preserving the past in France, Germany and England, 1789–1914* is forthcoming with Cambridge University Press. She is currently conducting a study on imperial preservation of crusader sites across the Mediterranean.

Donna Yates is Leverhulme Early Career Fellow at the Scottish Centre for Crime and Justice Research, University of Glasgow. Her current research is focused on providing a better understanding of the criminal networks involved in the trafficking of illicit cultural objects from Latin America. The ultimate goal of this work, a component of the ERC-funded 'Trafficking Culture' project, is to help develop effective national and international policy for the protection and preservation of archaeological sites.

Acknowledgements

We are extremely grateful to the contributors to this book, to the participants in the conference 'From Plunder to Preservation: Britain and the Heritage of Empire' held in Cambridge in March 2009, where many of these papers were first presented, and to our colleagues in the Cambridge Victorian Studies Group for comments on various drafts of this book. Brigid Hamilton-Jones and Elizabeth Stone are due many thanks for their editorial work. For their generous financial support we thank the Leverhulme Trust, the British Academy, the Paul Mellon Centre for Studies in British Art, King's College, Cambridge, and Darwin College, Cambridge.

Part I

Introduction

1

The Heritage of Empire*

ASTRID SWENSON

WILLIAM MORRIS'S CAMPAIGN to save St Mark's Cathedral in Venice from 'restoration' was one of the most notorious cases of British intervention in foreign heritage during the Victorian period. When, in 1879, Morris received information about plans for a major restoration of the western front of the cathedral, his recently founded Society for the Protection of Ancient Monuments (SPAB) decided to appeal to the British public. Letters to the press were published in all the major British newspapers and meetings were held throughout the country. 'The Morris dance round St. Mark's', as the satirical journal *Punch* dubbed it, readily gained momentum among Victorian elites.[1] The official letter of protest sent to the Italian minister of public works counted more than 2,000 prominent signatories, including both Gladstone and Disraeli.[2] Yet the campaign remains best remembered for its blunders. The letter of protest was sent to the wrong minister and claims of success were precipitate. Moreover, the unsolicited interference, coupled with a patronizing demeanour and lack of knowledge about the local situation (the petition counted no Italian signatories), alienated Italian public opinion and enhanced Morris's and the Society for Ancient Buildings' image as unabashed Radicals. But despite this amateurism, the campaign enhanced rather than deflated their ambition to care for heritage globally.

In the same year, the SPAB set up a permanent Foreign Committee, not least because 'we must consider that in trying to stimulate people elsewhere we shall get a reaction towards ourselves'.[3] However, the Society reframed the

*I would like to thank my colleagues from the Cambridge Victorian Studies Group, David Motadel, Tamson Pietsch, and especially my co-editor Peter Mandler, for comments on various drafts of this chapter.
[1] 'The Morris dance round St. Mark's', *Punch*, 10 Jan. 1880, pp. 2–3.
[2] C. Miele, 'The first conservation militant: William Morris and the Society for the Protection of Ancient Buildings', in M. Hunter, ed., *Preserving the past: the rise of heritage in modern Britain* (Stroud, 1996), pp. 17–37, at p. 27; F. C. Sharp, 'Exporting the revolution: the work of the SPAB outside Britain, 1878–1914', in C. Miele, ed., *From William Morris: building conservation and the Arts and Crafts cult of authenticity, 1877–1939* (Studies in British Art, vol. 14, New Haven, CT, and London, 2005), pp. 187–212.
[3] Society for the Protection of Ancient Buildings (SPAB), *Annual Report*, 2 (1879), p. 23, speech by M. Leonard Courtney, MP.

Proceedings of the British Academy, **187**, 3–28. © The British Academy 2013.

methods and also the territories in which it would operate. Henceforth SPAB consulted local correspondents for campaigns in Europe, but also considered a shift of focus towards the British colonies, where intervention could be more wide-ranging.[4] As one member of the Society, a conservative MP, pointed out, it was unlikely that the Society would obtain the cooperation and influence of the governments of countries such as France or Spain in their endeavours to put a stop to works of renovation and restoration:

> But there is a country where, if we are allowed, we may be of some assistance—in India. In one part of India there are the most wonderful works of art built under the orders of the great Mogul king. In Agra, in Delhi, and in Futtehpore Sikkri, you will find triumphs of art very different from our own, but triumphs of a very precious character, which ought to be carefully treasured.[5]

'The Morris dance round St. Mark's' captures how entangled the preservation of heritage in Britain was with attempts to save monuments in Europe and the empire. The episode reminds us that the Victorian idea of heritage was not confined to an island story; British preservationists actively intervened in preservation policies across the globe. Their notion of heritage included more than the nostalgic rediscovery of stately homes and timbered cottages, and went beyond London churches and Lake District meadows. It forces us to rethink the still dominant view of heritage consciousness as primarily local, 'inward-looking and rather separate from Empire and the world'.[6] On the contrary, all the major heritage-makers in Britain (like their counterparts in other imperial powers such as France) were simultaneously involved in domestic and imperial ventures. In the voluntary sector, domestic and colonial preservation were closely intertwined. Like the SPAB, who, after the St Mark's episode, campaigned for preservation in continental Europe, North Africa, the Near East, and the Indian subcontinent, the other epitome of Victorian preservationism, the National Trust, founded in 1895, was also keenly interested in preservation beyond the confines of the British Isles. Although its holdings ultimately remained limited to England, it established an American Council (1901–04) and the executive committee expressed its readiness to hold properties across the British empire, from Cyprus to the West Indies. Many of its most prominent members also pursued preservationist causes across several territories of the British world in a variety of capacities.[7] Britain,

---

[4] For interventions see SPAB Archives, London, case files: 'Ancient monuments in India'; 'Old Indian capital of Bijpur'; 'Arab monuments'; 'Cairo Coptic churches Egypt'; 'Ottoman antiquities'; 'The Dome on the Rock Jerusalem'.

[5] SPAB, *Annual Report*, 2 (1879), p. 23.

[6] See the similar argument that Billie Melman makes about the literature on historical culture, B. Melman, *The culture of history: English uses of the past, 1800–1953* (Oxford, 2006), p. 323.

[7] Swindon, National Trust Archives, Executive Committee Minutes, passim. On some of the activities of individual members such as the designer C. R. Ashbee, or the Earl of Dufferin and

moreover, teamed with a range of more specialized societies that focused on the heritage of imperial areas, including several exploration funds, created to raise money for the study and acquisition of artefacts from particular territories. In terms of state involvement, imperial ventures preceded active engagement on behalf of domestic heritage by almost a century. While the British state committed resources to obtain foreign antiquities from as early as the turn of the eighteenth century, state protection for domestic monuments only dates from the 1880s.[8] The British Museum had filled its galleries with Italian, Greek, Assyrian, and Indian antiquities long before it could be persuaded to care for British artefacts.[9] 'The Morris dance round St. Mark's' thus impels us to explore how far the rise of heritage was marked by preservationists operating in a global context, and the ways in which sometimes coexisting, sometimes conflicting, local, national, international, European, universal, and imperialist visions shaped the idea of heritage we know today.

I

The invention of heritage has become an important, yet highly fragmentary, field of enquiry in the humanities. *From plunder to preservation* is premised on the central importance of imperialism to histories of British (as well as many other) heritage movements. Presently, most research on preservation in Britain has been largely unaffected by the growing body of work showing how Britons were 'at home' with the empire, and demonstrating that colonialism was central for the very emergence of the notion of 'culture'.[10] While a claim has been made to reinstate empire in the formation of a number of disciplines from anthropology to art history,[11] and histories of collecting increasingly pay

Ava, the Trust's second president, see, for instance, Simon Goldhill's and Melanie Hall's chapters in this book.

[8] C. Chippindale, 'The making of the first Ancient Monuments Act, 1882, and its administration under General Pitt-Rivers', *Journal of the British Archaeological Association*, 136 (1983), pp. 1–55, at pp. 3–8. Foreign involvement preceding national involvement was most pronounced in, but not limited to, Britain. In the German empire for example, some preservationists repeatedly complained that federal funds were employed to finance excavations in Greece and the Near East while no institutions were established for the preservation of German monuments on the national level. See *Verband deutscher Architekten und Ingenieur-Vereine* to *Ministerium für landwirtschaftliche Angelegenheiten zu Berlin*, Feb. 1878, Geheimes Staatsarchiv Preußischer Kulturbesitz (GStA PK), I. HA Rep. 87 B Ministerium für Landwirtschaft, Domänen u. Forsten, Nr. 3131, fol. 5.
[9] See C. Manias, 'Learned societies and the ancient national past in Britain, France and Germany, 1830–1890' (Ph.D. thesis, Birkbeck College, University of London, 2008).
[10] C. Hall, *Cultures of empire: a reader* (London, 2000); idem, *At home with the empire: metropolitan culture and the imperial world* (Cambridge, 2006).
[11] For instance N. Dirks, 'Introduction: colonialism and culture', in idem, ed., *Colonialism and culture* (Ann Arbor, MI, 1992), p. 3; T. Barringer, G. Quilley, and D. Fordham, eds., *Art and the British empire* (Manchester, 2007), especially pp. 1–19.

attention to imperial provenance,[12] a comprehensive 'history of art imperialism has yet to be written'.[13] The history of preservation remains largely rooted in national historiographic contexts. Most overviews still treat the history of heritage mainly within the confines of the British archipelago.[14] Plunder and preservation in former colonies, on the other hand, are dealt with in an entirely separate literature. Although growing, historical accounts remain fragmentary and largely replicate the national paradigm.[15]

This book takes a different approach. For the first time, it brings together specialists on preservation in Britain and the empire from a range of disciplines to map a more entangled picture of plunder and preservation in the British empire between the late eighteenth and the mid-twentieth centuries. Presenting original research on a variety of regional contexts, it offers the possibility of comparing different parts of the world under British domination, to

[12] See, for example, A. E. Coombes, *Re-inventing Africa: museums, material culture and popular imagination in Edwardian England* (New Haven, CT, and London, 1994); N. Thomas, *Colonialism's culture: anthropology, travel and government* (London, 1994); T. Barringer and T. Flynn, eds., *Colonialism and the object: empire, material culture and the museum* (London, 1997); M. Jasanoff, *Edge of empire: conquest and collecting in the East, 1750–1850* (London, et al., 2006); H. Hoock, 'The British state and the Anglo-French wars over antiquities, 1798–1858', *The Historical Journal*, 50 (2007), pp. 49–72; idem, *Empires of the imagination: politics, war, and the arts in the British world, 1750–1850* (London, 2010); L. Patrizio Gunning, *The British consular service in the Aegean and the collection of antiquities for the British Museum* (Aldershot, 2009).

[13] J. H. Merryman, 'Introduction' in idem, ed., *Imperialism, art and restitution* (Cambridge, 2006), p. 3.

[14] See, for instance, general works such as Hunter, ed., *Preserving the past*; J. Delafons, *Politics and preservation: a policy history of the built heritage, 1882–1996* (London, 1997); D. Lowenthal, *The heritage crusade and the spoils of history* (Cambridge, 1998); B. Cowell, *The heritage obsession: the battle for England's past* (Stroud, 2008). However, recent attempts to popularize the history of heritage, such as the BBC and Open University series on *Whose heritage: stories of Britain's changing attitudes to heritage* (2009), and recent textbooks such as R. Harrison, ed., *Understanding the politics of heritage* (Manchester, 2009), take into account the legacies of empire.

[15] See, for example, M. Hall, 'Great Zimbabwe and the lost city: the cultural colonization of the South African past', in P. Ucko, ed., *Theory in archaeology: a world perspective* (London, 1995), pp. 28–45; M. Larsen, *The conquest of Assyria: excavations in an antique land, 1840–1860* (London, 1996); D. M. Reid, *Whose pharaohs? Archaeology, museums and Egyptian national identity from Napoleon to World War I* (Berkeley, CA, 2002); T. Guha-Thakurta, *Monuments, objects, histories: institutions of art in colonial and postcolonial India* (New York, 2004); U. Singh, *The discovery of ancient India: early archaeologists and the beginnings of archaeology* (Delhi, 2004); S. Sivasundaram, 'Buddhist kingship, British archaeology and historical narratives in Sri Lanka c.1750–1850', *Past & Present*, 197 (2007), pp. 111–42. Jasanoff's stimulating *Edge of empire* and Hoock's 'The British state and the Anglo-French wars over antiquities' are among the rare works that trace British policies in several geographical areas, namely Egypt and India. Works on art plunder with a geographically broader focus such as Merryman, ed., *Imperialism, art and restitution* tend not to address the question of preservation. The same area-focused nature also dominates the historiography of other European empires. For the French context see, for instance, P. M. E. Lorcin, 'Rome and France in Africa: recovering colonial Algeria's Latin past', *French Historical Studies*, 25 (2002), pp. 295–329; N. Oulebsir, *Les usages du patrimoine: Monuments, musées et politiques coloniale en Algérie, 1830–1930* (Paris, 2004).

understand the mechanisms of cultural transfer within the empire and to situate preservation in the British empire within the wider history of imperial competition, especially with France and the United States of America.

Our leading and most general questions are these: what response did an imperial authority take towards the heritage of a dependent area and how did this vary chronologically and spatially? How did imperial and indigenous preservationism interrelate and how did this come to affect or interact with attitudes towards heritage in the metropole? Finally, how important were the practices of other imperial powers to the development of heritage in the British empire? By focusing on the relationship between metropolitan and dependent heritages, the book looks both backwards and forwards—backwards, in showing how indigenous knowledge from the pre-colonial period was invariably appropriated (while at the same time often transformed) by the efforts of imperial powers to define and preserve a local heritage; forwards, in showing how these imperially defined heritages were often amongst the first resources claimed by anti-colonial nationalisms.

Throughout the book, both 'heritage' and 'empire' will be used in a loose, open way. While 'heritage' is now believed to be 'expressed in many different forms, both tangible (monuments, landscapes, objects) and intangible (languages, know-how, the performing arts, music, etc.)',[16] during the period covered in this book there was no single word to refer at once to the built, the natural, the genetic, or the ideal.[17] The use of the word 'heritage' in a generic sense only started in recent decades. In part, the widening of meaning and the replacing of the hitherto more common term 'monument' by 'heritage' reflected a wish to overcome a definition based on the monumental that, in the second part of the twentieth century, increasingly seemed elitist, colonial, and Eurocentric. And yet, in this book, we do not use 'heritage' only for want of a better word, but to draw attention to how the plunder and the preservation of different kinds of 'heritage' were often linked during the period, and to inscribe the history of heritage into wider histories of dispossession and appropriation. For instance, during the conference that preceded this book, Maya Jasanoff raised the issue of how far (or not) we should see the human plunder of empire, in the form of slaves, as analogous to the plunder in the form of artworks, while, in this volume, Sadiah Qureshi's contribution draws attention to the connections that were made between natural and human extinction. Crucially,

---

[16] K. Matsuura, 'United Nations year for cultural heritage', UNESCO (2002), <http://portal. unesco.org/culture/en/ev.php-URL_ID=15418&URL_DO=DO_TOPIC&URL_SECTION= 201.html>.

[17] On the semantics of heritage see A. Swenson, 'Heritage, Patrimoine, Kulturerbe: Eine vergleichende Historische Semantik', in D. Hemme, M. Tauschek, and R. Bendix, eds., *Prädikat Heritage: Wertschöpfungen aus kulturellen Ressourcen* (Berlin, 2007), pp. 53–74; Oulebsir, *Les usages du patrimoine*, pp. 13–16.

those who reacted against this plunder increasingly saw the destruction of culture, nature, and humans as connected. Keeping the definition of 'heritage' broad also allows non-European understandings of tradition to be included. Hence, although a good part of the book is on 'ancient monuments', as this category was so central to the European definition of civilization and most ostensibly formed imperialist ideas about peoples with and without history, different chapters consider the ways that these monumental notions were enhanced, challenged, and extended through other forms of 'heritage'.

Similarly, our use of 'empire' is flexible and refers to both formal and informal forms of domination. We try to avoid writing the history of British imperialism in isolation, as the history of the British empire was not only profoundly shaped by the Anglo-French rivalry over antiquities (which made it 'very much a history of the French Empire too')[18] but interacted with other European imperialisms and, increasingly, with the cultural and imperial ambition of the United States. Thus, while the focus is on the British empire, it is not restricted to it. Rather, we suggest the need for a framework that explores the importance of imperial spaces within other forms of international and transnational exchange. Although far from attempting exhaustive geographical coverage, the volume follows protagonists from (present-day) Britain to France, Germany, Italy, Greece, the Crimea, Turkey, Israel, Palestine, Egypt, Sudan, Sri Lanka, India, Pakistan, South Africa, Kenya, Guatemala, the United States of America, Canada, and the South Pacific (and a few side forays into China and Brazil). In doing so, it attempts to analyse the entanglements of the British empire, but also seeks to shed light on broader questions regarding the cultural construction of empire, trans-imperial entanglements, and the place of empire in European cultures.

II

Studies that see the roots of the modern 'heritage obsession' only in nationalism and nostalgia overlook the importance of transnational and imperial entanglements. It is important to understand how, during the nineteenth and early twentieth centuries, historic preservation and imperialism were increasingly used for mutual legitimation, and how they constantly enhanced and strengthened each other.

All over Europe, preservationism was reinforced by being declared an imperial necessity. In Britain, in particular, the idea that imperial cohesion could be created through the identification of all citizens of the empire with the 'national heritage' of the British Isles was a chief argument employed to

---

[18] Jasanoff, *Edge of empire*, p. 6.

convince opponents of preservation of the importance of state intervention. First brought forward in the Commons debate over the Ancient Monuments Bill in 1875, this rationale underpinned the foundation of the National Trust in 1895. It also opened the most influential book on the necessity of state intervention, Gerald Baldwin Brown's 1905 seminal study, *The care of ancient monuments*,[19] and was reiterated time and again after the First World War.[20] As Baldwin Brown, Britain's first professor of art history, observed in his plea for the introduction of preservation legislation, if all citizens were aesthetes, the need for 'heritage' legislation would be removed: 'If we be sensible of the charm [of monuments] the question of preservation is for us settled—we would sacrifice anything rather than let these scenes and monuments be lost to modern life.'[21] However, as Baldwin Brown laconically continued, 'we cannot make others sensible of the charm'. Instead, arguments 'which are of a more practical kind' were needed.[22] Such arguments had to be strong enough to overcome the view of certain legislators and a good proportion of public opinion that state institutions would only 'gratify the antiquarian tastes of the few at the public expense'.[23] Hence, Baldwin Brown suggested that preservationists should stress the way in which British monuments could foster a sense of belonging across the empire:

> Great Britain in relation to the Empire at large ... must always remain the soil in which are rooted all the traditional memories of the race. In the tangible evidence of a storied past, this island possesses what is necessarily wanting to our colonies and to the offshoots from those colonies ... The interest which these memorials excite in the minds of our kinsfolk from across the seas is very great, and will probably increase as the generations advance. The feelings thus kindled help to keep alive throughout the Empire the sense of the unity of the stock ... [Monuments] are imperial assets, and on economic, almost on political, grounds, the duty of safeguarding them might well be recognized even by the least artistic and least antiquarian of the population.[24]

The preservation of monuments (as well as landscapes and traditions) in Britain was thus primarily legitimized by the feelings that these monuments could create among British settlers across the colonies. This tactical invocation of preservation as a means for achieving imperial cohesion was much stronger in Britain than in other European empires. Similar arguments were

---

[19] G. Baldwin Brown, *The care of ancient monuments* (Cambridge, 1905), pp. 3–4, 31, 152–3.
[20] See, for instance, 'Address by Miss Lena Ashwell at the General Meeting of the Society for the Protection of Ancient Buildings', SPAB, *Annual Report*, 44 (1921).
[21] Baldwin Brown, *Care of ancient monuments*, p. 28.
[22] Ibid.
[23] Parl. Debs. (series 3) vol. 273, col. 15 (28 July 1882) (speech by Marquess of Salisbury in the House of Lords).
[24] Baldwin Brown, *Care of ancient monuments*, pp. 3–4, also pp. 30–1.

not found in the public debates about state intervention in France or Germany, for instance. In these two countries, arguments focused on the benefits of national rather than imperial cohesion.[25] This might suggest that 'empire' was a straw to which the ever-struggling British preservationists clung desperately. However, it also implies that 'empire' was more important in overcoming opposition and establishing domestic preservation policies in Britain than in other European countries.

Conversely, across Europe, the protection of monuments explicitly became a symbol of a nation's ability to rule overseas—a measurement of civilization. As a German preservationist put it: 'The care of ancient monuments, in the way we understand it today, so that it can be regarded as a yardstick for a people's cultural attainment, is a modern concept and a modern activity.'[26] In Britain, as well as in all other European countries, this link between preservation and civilization was constantly used to convince opponents of state intervention.[27] Treatises and bills time and again referred to superior monument legislation abroad, urging the legislator to 'catch up' with the other 'civilized countries', namely the chief European powers. To be surpassed by 'less civilized' countries in such a civilizing task was declared to be even less acceptable: the General Assembly of the Historical Associations of Germany expounded in 1899 the necessity to improve monument legislation in Germany, as, 'with regard to the legal protection of monuments, the North African states are at the present moment way superior to Prussia, Saxony, Wurttemberg: that is a dishonourable and untenable state of affairs'.[28]

Declaring the preservation of monuments—rather than the monuments themselves—to be an index of civilization was a noticeable and crucial turn in British, but also other Western, attitudes. Whereas early to mid-nineteenth century 'heritage-makers' defined their countries' international standing in terms of the quality and quantity of actual monuments (home-grown as well as looted or otherwise imported),[29] in the era of new imperialism expansion, the *preservation* of heritage took priority. In part, this has to do with advances

---

[25] See A. Swenson, *The rise of heritage: preserving the past in France, Germany and England, 1789–1914* (Cambridge University Press, forthcoming).

[26] A. von Oechelhaeuser, *Wege, Ziele und Gefahren der Denkmalpflege: Festrede bei dem Feierlichen Akte des Rektoratswechsels an der Großherzoglich- Technischen Hochschule Fridericiana zu Karlsruhe am 20. November 1909* (Karlsruhe, 1909), p. 5.

[27] See A. Swenson, 'Conceptualising heritage in nineteenth- and early twentieth-century France, Germany and England' (Ph.D. thesis, University of Cambridge, 2007), pp. 292–413.

[28] 'Die Verhandlungen über Denkmalschutz und Denkmalpflege auf der Hauptversammlung des Gesamtvereins der deutschen Geschichts- und Alterthumsvereine in Straßburg', *Die Denkmalpflege*, 1 (1899), pp. 106–7.

[29] On competition about domestic monuments see, for instance, P. Mérimée, *Rapport au Ministre de l'Intérieur* (Paris, 1843). On Anglo-French rivalry over antiquities see Hoock, 'The British state and the Anglo-French wars over antiquities', pp. 49–72.

in disciplines such as archaeology and art history. As scholars from different countries had to abandon the idea that their most 'national' style, the Gothic, resulted from complex forms of interaction, the preservation rather than the invention of heritage became a criterion for national distinction.

Yet, this shift also happened because a Herderian distinction between Europe and the 'peoples without history' was increasingly being challenged in the face of majestic ancient monuments. In the first instance, Westerners often developed many strategies to negate indigenous creations. They were particularly inventive when it came to African artefacts. In the case of Great Zimbabwe, for instance, until the 1920s Europeans could not conceive that the magnificent fortress had been constructed by Africans and tried to prove its Western origins, alternatively declaring it to be a lost biblical city or the product of bypassing crusaders. Similar reasoning was applied to African sculptures, from the Benin Bronzes to the brass heads from Ife, until the late 1930s.[30] As Donna Yates discusses in her contribution to this book, archaeologists also ascribed 'North American earthworks to a white race of "mound builders", Mesoamerican pyramids to travelling Egyptians and just about everything to lost tribes of Israel'.

However, this form of appropriation was less easily applicable to the 'Old World'. As imperial authorities from North Africa to the Middle East and the Indian subcontinent were moving towards a clearer acceptance that these *were* peoples *with* history, the civilizing achievement was redefined as a European ability to preserve, and was opposed to a neglect of the ancient heritage by the 'native' population.[31] The necessity to remedy supposed local neglect and ignorance already underpinned Lord Elgin's justification for the acquisition of the Parthenon Marbles.[32] It was even more strikingly propagated with regard to Austen Henry Layard's Assyrian discoveries in the late 1840s, which were captured and popularized through a range of illustrations. *The Illustrated London News*, for instance, contrasted Layard's depictions of

[30] See M. Hall, 'Great Zimbabwe and the lost city'; idem, 'The legend of the lost city; or, the man with golden balls', *Journal of Southern African Studies*, 21 (1995), pp. 179–99; David Beach, M. F. C. Bourdillon, James Denbow, Gerhard Liesegang, Johannes H. N. Loubser, Innocent Pikirayi, David Schoenbrun, Robert Soper, and Ann B. Stahl, 'Cognitive archaeology and imaginary history at Great Zimbabwe [and comments and reply]', *Current Anthropology*, 39 (1998), pp. 47–72; S. T. Carroll, 'Solomonic legend: the Muslims and the Great Zimbabwe', *International Journal of African Historical Studies*, 21 (1988), pp. 233–47; M. Hall and R. Stefoff, *Great Zimbabwe* (Oxford, 2006). For a discussion of the reception of the Benin Bronzes and Ife Head see N. MacGregor, *A history of the world in 100 objects* (London, 2010), pp. 404–9 (esp. 406–7) and 497–502 (esp. 501).
[31] Baldwin Brown, *Care of ancient monuments*, pp. 232–5.
[32] On the Elgin Marbles see M. Beard, *The Parthenon* (London, 2002); J. H. Merryman, 'Whither the Elgin Marbles?' in idem, ed., *Imperialism, art and restitution*, pp. 98–113; W. St Clair, 'Imperial appropriations of the Parthenon', ibid., pp. 65–97.

bewildered Arabs inspecting with great caution and uneducated suspicion the colossal head that had appeared in one of Layard's trenches, with the educated observant gaze of the English visitors at the British Museum.[33]

During the French Revolution, the Abbé Grégoire had already established a strong link between preservation and civilization, arguing that 'only Barbarians and slaves destroy works of art and science. Free men love and preserve them.'[34] He had advanced this argument mainly to put a stop to Revolutionary iconoclasm, but it was soon extended to legitimize rather than stop the looting of art by the Revolutionary armies across Europe and Egypt. As only free men could love and preserve art, and France was the homeland of free men, all art should, so the argument went, find its home there, 'repatriated' and freed from tyrannical feudal lords. Although the right to plunder was challenged by the return of most of the art looted from Europe by the Congress of Vienna, the discursive link between preservation and freedom endured in the colonial context. In 1815, Egypt was the only country that did not receive its antiquities back. What is more, a connection between preservation, civilization, and the right to independence was highlighted increasingly towards the end of the century. For instance, two years before the British occupation of Egypt, the French journalist Gabriel Charmes expounded that only European control could properly preserve Cairo's monuments, and that a nation that neglected its antiquities did not deserve independence:

> It is clear that if Egypt wants to escape the shocks with which the Orient is menaced, [the Khedive of Egypt's] first duty is to link up the new power of the Muhammad Ali dynasty to a long and glorious national tradition … The Greeks spare nothing to make one believe they are the descendants of Pericles and Phidias; why don't the Egyptians try to persuade the world that they are the descendant of Saladin, of Qait Bey, and of Sultan Hasan? The Acropolis has done more for the independence of Greece than all the exploits … of Canaris and Lord Byron; it is the best title of the small Hellenic kingdom to the protection and the favors of Europe; why shouldn't the mosques of Cairo render the same kind of service for Egypt? The day when they are restored it will be impossible to deny the right to independence to a country capable of understanding and conserving such works.[35]

While this hints at a promise of independence through preservation, and does indeed foreshadow the use of ancient monuments for resistance by nascent anti-colonial nationalisms (as Donald Malcolm Reid's chapter in this volume discusses in detail), in the meantime the colonial powers sought to enhance

---

[33] E.g. Austen Henry Layard, *Nineveh and its remains*, i (London, 1849), p. 66 versus *Illustrated London News*, 26 Oct. 1850. See, for a more detailed discussion, Larsen, *The conquest of Assyria*, pp. 91, 126.
[34] Abbé Grégoire, *Patrimoine et cité*, ed. D. Audrerie (Bordeaux, 1999).
[35] G. Charmes, 'L'Art arabe', qu. in D. M. Reid, *Whose Pharaohs*, p. 222.

the care of colonial heritage in order to establish credence as ruling powers. This claim was particularly strident in the case of India. Viceroy Lord Canning had already declared, in 1862, that neglecting the care of ancient monuments 'will not be to our credit as an enlightened ruling power'. In a climate of imperial competition, he argued, it seemed shameful that in the jewel of Britain's empire, all existing attempts had been 'done by private persons, imperfectly and without system' and not by the government. 'It is impossible,' he continued, 'not to feel that there are European Governments, which if they had held our rule in India, would not have allowed this to be said.'[36] His successor, Lord Lytton, reaffirmed the fact that the care of national antiquities was an 'essentially imperial' duty,[37] while Lord Curzon, during his time as viceroy (1898–1905), created the role of directorate-general of archaeology, multiplied the restoration budget by a factor of eight, and personally oversaw repairs to monuments. He rejoiced in the restoration of the Taj Mahal and the other monuments of Agra: 'If I had done nothing else in India,' he told his wife, 'I have written my name here.'[38] In an address to the Bengal Asiatic Society at Calcutta in 1900, which presents one of the most comprehensive pleas for colonial preservation, Curzon asserted that:

> I regarded the conservation of ancient monuments as one of the primary obligations of the Government ... [It] is one of an even more binding character in India than in many European countries. There abundant private wealth is available for the acquisition or the conservation of that which is frequently private property ... Here all is different. India is covered with the visible records of vanished dynasties, of forgotten monarchs, of persecuted and sometimes dishonoured creeds. These monuments are for the most part, though there are notable exceptions, in British territory and on soil belonging to Government. Many of them are in out of the way places, and are liable to the combined ravages of a tropical climate, an exuberant flora, and very often a local and ignorant population, who see only in an ancient building the means of inexpensively raising a modern one for their own convenience. All these circumstances explain the peculiar responsibility that rests upon Government in India. If there be any one who says to me that there is no duty devolving upon a Christian Government to preserve the monuments of a pagan art or the sanctuaries of an alien faith, I cannot pause to argue with such a man. Art, and beauty, and the reverence that is owing to all that has evoked human genius or has inspired human faith are independence [sic] of creeds, and in so far as they touch the sphere of religion, are embraced by the common religion of all mankind ... what is beautiful, what

---

[36] Qu. in Baldwin Brown, *Care of ancient monuments*, pp. 231–2. The Egypt Exploration Fund expressed similar fears that the lack of care in Egypt might lead to 'righteous judgement of indignant Europe'. Qu. in David Gange's chapter, this volume.

[37] Qu. in Baldwin Brown, *Care of ancient monuments*, p. 233.

[38] Qu. in D. Gilmour, 'Curzon, George Nathaniel, Marquess Curzon of Kedleston (1859–1925)', *Oxford Dictionary of National Biography* (Oxford, 2004; published online Oct. 2005), <http://www.oxforddnb.com/view/article/32680>.

tears the mask off the face of the past, and helps us to read its riddles, and to
look it in the eyes—these, and not the dogmas of a combative theology, are the
principal criteria to which we must look.[39]

Curzon went on to contrast this universal definition of art with the 'work of
"Iconoclasts"' in India, where he claimed that: 'Every, or nearly every succes-
sive religion that has permeated or overswept this country has vindicated its
own fervour at the expense of the rival whom it had dethroned ... Each fresh
conqueror, Hindu or Moghal or Pathan, marched, so to speak, to his own
immortality over his predecessor's grave.' He concluded that such local, parti-
san definitions of heritage compared unfavourably with his own universal
definition, and hence justified imperial intervention:

> The British Government are fortunately exempt from any such prompting,
> either of religious fanaticism, or restless vanity or dynastic and personal pride.
> But in proportion as they have been unassailed by such temptations, so is their
> responsibility the greater for inaugurating a new era and for displaying that
> tolerant and enlightened respect to the treasures of all, which is one of the main
> lessons that the returning West has been able to teach to the East.[40]

III

Preservationism and imperialism were thus fundamentally linked on an ideological level. The likening of preservation with civilization, first established
during the French Revolution to put a stop to iconoclasm and art looting, was
increasingly fostered in the imperial age as a means to legitimize European
domination, and as a way to position different European states to their advantage among their competitors. As such, this rhetoric is highly significant,
because the competition contributed in a major way to the institutionalization
of preservation, not just in colonies, but in metropolitan Europe.[41]

However, while this rhetoric elucidates the dynamics of preservation inside
Europe, it tells us little about the practices of plunder and preservation in an
imperial context. As has been increasingly pointed out in the literature engaging with Edward Said's *Orientalism*, colonial hegemony is an insufficient framework for understanding what were often more complex processes of interaction.[42]

---

[39] Lord Curzon, 'Address to the Bengal Asiatic Society', 6 Feb. 1900, repr. in Dilip K. Chakrabarti,
A history of Indian archaeology: from the beginning to 1947 (New Delhi, 1988), pp. 227–36, at
227–8.
[40] Ibid., pp. 230, 231.
[41] Swenson, 'The rise of heritage', passim.
[42] See, for a concise summary of debates in relation to art: Barringer, Quilley, and Fordham,
'Introduction', in idem, eds., *Art and the British empire*, pp. 3–6. On methods to uncover hidden
histories of collaboration and appropriation see, for instance, L. Schiebinger, 'Focus colonial

Across all our case studies, empire appears much 'more piecemeal, contingent, uncertain—and in many ways collaborative—than the familiar language of an "imperial project" would suggest'.[43]

Many responses to the imperial preservation project lacked Curzon's missionary certainty. For instance, H. H. Cole, first Curator of Ancient Monuments in India (and son of the 'Great Exhibitor' and Director of the South Kensington Museum, Henry Cole), warned in his reports to the public about the dangers that Western archaeology posed to Indian treasures, as 'the keenest investigators have not always had the greatest respect for the maintenance of monuments'.[44] Imperial soldiers also developed a concern about the damage that war was doing to the historic fabric of invaded areas, as Edmund Richardson's account of the Crimean War shows. The British public could read about it in *The Times*. Melting down ancient statues to make new teapots or destroying a museum built by the Russians did not receive public support for long.[45] In the British Isles the 'inter-relationship between empire and archaeology was much more complicated than it is often assumed to be', not least, as Mary Beard argues, because those imbued with classical culture grappled with the Romans' own ambivalences about imperial expansion.[46] Regrets and ambiguities were also not limited to the destruction of artefacts. Already, in the late eighteenth century, naturalists deplored the 'tyranny', which had extirpated indigenous peoples and 'together with them lost the result of their useful experience'.[47] Although in a minority, some voices also recognized that local populations 'such as the Egyptian fellaheen are not in a position to pay for the care which these monuments of the past deserve, for the funds of the Egyptian treasury represent simply what are extorted from a very poor people',[48] and called for Britain and America to ensure the return of treasures to the people as a source for future development and humanizing influence.[49]

Moreover, while many preservationists still called for European intervention, the same individuals commented on the superior skills of local craftsmen,

science. Forum introduction: the European colonial science complex', *Isis*, 96 (2005), pp.52–5; F. Driver and L. Jones, *Hidden histories of exploration: researching the RGS-IBG collections* (London, 2009).

[43] Jasanoff, *Edge of empire*, p. 10.

[44] H. H. Cole, *Preservation of national monuments: first report of the curator of ancient monuments in India for the year 1881–82* (Simla, 1882), p. 11.

[45] See Edmund Richardson's chapter, this volume.

[46] Mary Beard's chapter, this volume.

[47] A. Sparrman, *A voyage to the Cape of Good Hope, towards the Antarctic Polar Circle and round the world* i (London, 1786), p. 144., qu. in Sivasundaram's chapter, this volume.

[48] Robert Hamilton-Lang to Poynter, undated, VIIIa.38, qu. in Gange's chapter, this volume.

[49] Cope Whitehouse, 'The Raiyan Moeris', *Journal of the American Geographical Society of New York*, 21 (1889), p. 536, qu. in Gange's chapter, this volume.

especially with regard to Arab buildings in Egypt and Mughal structures in India. As craftsmen still used the same methods as the generations before them, preservationists argued that it was they rather than European restorers who should carry out the repairs of temples, mosques, and palaces. Europeans often struggled to reconcile their nostalgic longing for this continuous tradition—deploring that it had been interrupted by modernity in Europe—with their expressed wish to extend their modernity to the rest of the world.[50]

The writings of imperialists such as Curzon tried to suggest that preservation was an entirely European invention. They negated all prior existence of indigenous ideas about heritage, and existing preservation policies,[51] as well as their appropriation and transformation by imperial powers. Yet, as Sujit Sivasundaram's chapter (this volume) shows, 'British definitions of tradition did not emerge from a tabula rasa.' The British not only used local guides to 'discover' many ancient temples in the jungles of Asia and America, they also appropriated pre-existing concepts of tradition from the South Pacific to Southeast Asia and southern Africa.[52]

During the eighteenth and early nineteenth centuries, collaboration and appropriation were often acknowledged. British naturalists, for instance, acknowledged Khoisan assistance in the Cape to authenticate their findings. As the Liberal and abolitionist politics that emphasized the civilizational potential of the Khoisan gave way to the increasing bureaucratization of the colony (and the establishment of science institutions), 'exchange and entanglement of traditions of heritage mutated into attitudes of detachment'.[53] Although this example is representative of a broader trend across the nineteenth century, in some contexts the search for local knowledge continued to be openly lauded. Imperialists might have been haughty about Egyptians' lack of interest in their built heritage (developing various strategies to prevent those who wanted to reclaim it from entering the Egyptological ranks), but explorers and engineers interested in the heritage of irrigation and reservoir systems hunted out every piece of local villagers' knowledge because they believed the oral tradition could reconstruct the knowledge of the biblical Joseph, who had supposedly built the first reservoir.[54]

On the other hand, colonial authorities were closely watched by the colonized, as Indra Sengupta's analysis of the preservation of religious structures in India highlights. Indigenous groups employed colonial ideas of heritage to strengthen their own interests and impose limits to colonial authority, for instance by using the clauses on religious monuments in the Indian legislation

---

[50] See SPAB Archives, case files on India and Egypt.
[51] For counterexamples see Singh, *Discovery of ancient India*, pp. 290–336.
[52] See also Sivasundaram, 'Buddhist kingship', pp. 111–42.
[53] Sivasundaram's chapter, this volume.
[54] See David Gange's chapter, this volume.

of 1904. By appropriating the universalist language of history and aesthetics, and combining it with an appeal to local religious traditions, they not only obtained funding for maintenance from the colonial government, but at the same time managed to restrict British access to temples and mosques. As Morris had found in Europe earlier, in India the cooperation of local religious elites increasingly became vital for the success of any monument policy, and the colonial state found itself much less powerful than the rhetoric would indicate.

Subversive uses also instrumentalized intra-Western competition. Lindsay Allen's work on the Iranian shah's use of Persepolis, for instance, suggests ways in which 'heritage' and the competition among Western powers were employed to safeguard a fragile independence during the interwar years. The shah invited American archaeologists to be in charge of archaeological sites in Iran in order to position them as a counterweight to the British presence and control over oil.[55] Anti-colonial nationalisms thus often appropriated colonial ideas for their own ends. This is not to say, however, that the reclaiming of imperially defined heritages by anti-colonial and postcolonial nationalisms was primarily derivative, as ideas about heritage were constantly shaped by the exchange between imperial and indigenous knowledge.

IV

The constant exchange between metropole, colonies, and other territories in turn requires us to re-evaluate how far practices in colonial sites and informal areas of influence shaped approaches to heritage in the metropole. Curzon's address, quoted above, suggested that preservation measures, and especially state intervention, needed to be more wide-ranging in India than in Britain because of the absence there of private initiatives. He equipped his Ancient Monuments Act for India (1904) with compulsory clauses, prohibitions, and penal sanctions that he thought inappropriate for legislation that concerned England. As a prominent Tory he was unwilling to join the Liberal drive for state control as far as English soil was concerned, and he did not want his own holdings to be controlled by the government. Insistence on property rights made any form of state intervention extremely difficult in the metropole. Establishing preservation in Britain was so difficult precisely because the definition of civilization based on preservationism clashed with a definition of civilization based on the respect of private property. Hence, many preservationists

---

[55] L. Allen, 'Appropriations of imperial space at Persepolis', paper presented at 'From Plunder to Preservation—Britain and the "Heritage" of Empire, c.1820–1940', University of Cambridge, 21–22 Mar. 2009.

like Baldwin Brown regretted that 'really drastic' preservation could only exist 'where the personal rights of the highly civilised man are almost unknown'.[56] As a result they saw the colonies as laboratories for measures that could not be experimented with in Europe, as the example of Morris and the SPAB above indicated. To view the colonies as playgrounds for preservation—and associated activities such as city planning and archaeology more widely—was a theme not confined to the British empire, however. In their work on French colonial urbanism, Paul Rabinow and Gwendolyn Wright have drawn attention to the importance of the idea of the colonies as a laboratory of ideas for French urbanism,[57] captured in a phrase by the Parisian art critic Léandre Vaillat, who observed when visiting Casablanca: Morocco is 'a laboratory of western life and a conservatory of oriental life'.[58] The principle of using the colonies for practices not possible in the mother country also extended beyond European imperialism and characterized Japanese archaeological policies in Korea.[59]

The idea of the laboratory was thus common, but whether many practices tried out in the colonies were applied to the heritages of European metropoles is another question. Gwendolyn Wright's findings on urban planning suggest little re-transfer before the Vichy government used colonial experience for its regionalist ideas. Preservationist legislation, however, is an area where re-transfer can be seen more clearly. From the late nineteenth century onwards, when legal bills were drafted in Europe, colonial administrative practices and colonial legislation often served as an inspiration. Such a direct transfer can, for instance, be seen when the provisions of the Ancient Monuments Act for Ireland (1892) were applied to England and Wales in 1900. More generally, it appears that (because of the above-discussed qualms about treating 'highly civilized men' in the same way as one's colonized subjects) re-transfer often occurred via other empires. For instance, when consulting foreign evidence to draft a new Monument Bill in 1913, the French dismissed all 'English' legislation as too permissive, but took inspiration from Curzon's Ancient Monument Act for India.[60] Curzon's idea then returned to the UK when French law

---

[56] Baldwin Brown, *Care of ancient monuments*, p. 235.

[57] P. Rabinow, *French modern: norms and forms of the social environment* (Cambridge, MA, 1989); G. Wright, *The politics of design in French colonial urbanism* (Chicago, 1991); see also H. Vacher, *Projection coloniale et ville: rationaliser le role de l'espace colonial dans la constitution de l'urbanisme en France, 1900–1931* (Aalborg, 1997). For a review of recent writings on colonial city planning in a comparative perspective see J. L. Cohen, 'Architectural history and the colonial question: Casablanca, Algiers and beyond', *Architectural History*, 49 (2006), pp. 349–72.

[58] L. Vaillat, *Le Périple marocain* (Paris, 1934), p. 55.

[59] Hyung Il Pai, 'The creation of national treasures and monuments: the 1916 Japanese laws on the preservation of Korean remains and relics and their colonial legacies', *Journal of Korean Studies*, 25 (2001), pp. 72–95.

[60] Paris, Médiathèque de l'Architecture et du Patrimoine (MAP), 80/1/32–33, 'Législation étrangère sur les monuments historiques'.

served as a model for further reform in Britain.[61] The precise extent of re-transfers deserves further study, but a better knowledge of the interaction between colonial and indigenous actors in and across different contexts is necessary first.

V

It is a major aim of this book to explore the variety of experiences across the British empire. Throughout the period, the institutional framework for colonial preservation lacked any coordinated nature and varied widely for different areas. Whereas, in the French empire, certain measures were put in place to extend metropolitan institutions to colonial settings,[62] and Algeria was integrated into the metropolitan administration,[63] British state involvement was more piecemeal, reflecting the fact that, unlike France, which had had a Monument Commission since the 1840s, Britain had no metropolitan agency or legislation on which to model such an administration before the Edwardian period. Before the twentieth century, the state was involved in heritage through institutions such as the navy, the royal engineers, and the consular system. However, all of them were better equipped to facilitate the policies of plunder than the policies of preservation. Among the areas under British influence, India and Egypt stand out, as they possessed the most institutionalized frameworks for the preservation of heritage. In India this happened through the establishment of the archaeological survey in 1861, the creation of a curatorship in the 1880s, and far-reaching monument legislation from 1904. In Egypt it was due to a cultural administration that remained in French hands throughout the British period. New bodies that had a multinational membership, such as the Comité de l'Art Arabe, also played an important role here. Before the slow establishment of legislative frameworks in the twentieth century, in most of the other areas discussed in this book the administrative framework was less fixed, and was marked by the interaction of diplomatic missions, voluntary associations, and expanding university excavations financed by the different imperial powers.

---

[61] London, The National Archives (TNA), WORK 14/ 2278, 'Systems adopted in foreign countries for preservation of ancient monuments. 1911–1954'.

[62] The first French Monuments Law of 1887 also applied to Algeria and Tunisia, while the 1913 legislation was further applied to Indochina (with some delay because of the advent of the First World War), see MAP, 80/1/119–123 'Le Service des monuments historiques en Algérie, 1844–1939', and 81/098/0022 'Indochine'.

[63] On the development of monument administration in North Africa see Oulebsir, *Les usages du patrimoine*.

In an attempt to understand entanglements within and beyond the confines of British power, the chapters in this book are not grouped according to
geographical location, but in relation to imagined spaces that shaped the way
different forms of heritage (which often shared a geographical space) were
encountered. The volume starts by looking at the classical world (Part II) as
the interaction with remains from ancient Greece and Rome (and their
Byzantine successor) constituted the most long-standing engagement with
artefacts that were in foreign territory yet claimed as an integral part of British
culture—captured so succinctly in Shelley's phrase, 'we are all Greeks'.[64]
These chapters ask how this familiarity shaped approaches to territories as
diverse as the Crimea and Sudan, and whether the colonial gaze was then in
turn applied to Roman structures back in Britain. As the biblical world played
an equally crucial part in the Victorian cultural imagination—or, as the archbishop of York put it, 'Palestine is ours'[65]—Part III analyses the preservation
of religious sites under British domination in Egypt and Palestine, arguing
that historical interest in the region was 'rarely a simple product of Empire,
but more often a product of religion which Empire began to amplify and
embellish with new providential twists'.[66] Part IV, 'Empires and Civilizations',
then examines how imperialists dealt with the heritage of non-European civilizations, from the South Pacific to India, which often had been empires themselves, but which were not always seen as direct antecedents to the British
empire in the way the classical and the biblical world were. Finally, the last
section considers how interactions with the New World further challenged the
monument-centred concept of heritage to include endangered nature and
peoples. These chapters link the violent processes of extermination, dispossession, and othering that were synonymous with empire, with transatlantic
attempts to preserve the built and natural heritage of the English-speaking
world at a time when the United States was rising from former colony to an
empire in its own right.

These juxtapositions reveal that a variety of definitions of 'common heritage' existed in the late nineteenth and early twentieth centuries, and that the
boundaries between 'us' and 'them', between 'centre' and 'periphery', were
flexible and shifting. The past's distance often 'collapsed by historical imagination into the experience of the present'.[67] Commonalities were defined in
classical, religious, racial, or universal terms, to advocate nationalist and
internationalist aims, and to achieve imperialist expansion and anti-colonial
resistance.

---

[64] See Edmund Richardson's chapter, this volume.
[65] See Simon Goldhill's chapter, this volume.
[66] See David Gange's chapter, this volume.
[67] See Simon Goldhill's chapter, this volume.

A coherent narrative of identity politics is further complicated by the interplay of imperial reasoning with other forms of international and transnational collaboration. The intra-European and Western competition so apparent in the scramble for antiquities coexisted with an intense cooperation. Bénédicte Savoy's work highlights how the Rosetta stone—the epitome of the Anglo-French War over antiquities, which the British inscribed with 'captured from the French' on its side—also incited the learned world to collaborate in its deciphering.[68] Almost a century later, the Egyptologist Gaston Maspero still saw the fair division of archaeological findings among Western archaeologists as a sign of enlightened French stewardship.[69]

Big imperial interventions in heritage, such as the construction of the Aswan Dam in fin-de-siècle Egypt, also took place on a world stage and had consequences for future reservoir projects on different continents.[70] Moreover, archaeological sites and cultural institutes in the Mediterranean and the Middle East—from Pompeii and Herculaneum to Rome and Jerusalem—served as a meeting ground for international preservationists. Contacts made in an imperial context often led to broader international collaborations through congresses and conventions, as well as to campaigns for particular sites in Europe and beyond. For example, contacts between the British Society for the Protection of Ancient Buildings and its French counterpart L'Ami des Monuments were first established over Egyptian monuments, resulting in a decade-long cooperation to intervene in British, French, and Italian domestic cases.[71] In turn, ties that were fostered through common actions on European sites often led to coordinated interventions outside the continent. To come back to the ever-present SPAB: work with the German attaché Hermann Muthesius to save buildings from Heidelberg to Peterborough provided a link that made it possible for them to ask the German foreign office to save antiquities in Turkey, despite a climate of intense rivalry between Germany and Britain over informal control within the Ottoman empire.[72] The imperial framework therefore needs to be seen in conjunction with international and transnational networks, to understand the way 'common heritages' were defined.

[68] B. Savoy, ' "Objet d'observation et d'intelligence": La pierre de Rosette entre Paris, Londres et le Caire, 1799–1805', in A. Bandau and R. von Mallinckrodt, eds., *Les mondes coloniaux à Paris au XVIIIe siècles: circulation et enchevêtrement des saviors* (Paris, 2010), pp. 75–96.
[69] B. Savoy, *Nofretete: Eine deutsch-französische Affare, 1912–1931* (Cologne, 2011), and Reid's chapter, this volume.
[70] See Gange's chapter, this volume.
[71] SPAB Archives, 3rd Committee Minute Book, 25 Nov. 1880.
[72] SPAB Archives, case file 'Ottoman antiquities (1901)'.

VI

How then, did ideas about common heritage affect the practices of plunder and preservation? Were 'common' heritage sites less often plundered than those regarded as alien? The title of this book does not mean to suggest a whiggish path from plunder to preservation during the period covered, although the nineteenth century undoubtedly opened with the most publicly practised and widespread art plunder seen in Europe for a long time.[73] Between the 1790s and the Congress of Vienna, the French armies took whatever they could carry from conquered territories from Flanders to Rome. Following the Napoleonic invasion of Egypt in 1798, Britain and France became fierce competitors as collectors of objects. While the Louvre became a treasure house filled with conquered works of art illustrating the grandeur of the little Corsican, the British state, although not following quite such extreme collection policies, committed resources to fill the British Museum with ancient treasures too. Logistical support, naval vessels, and diplomatic efforts were all mobilized to assure large-scale acquisitions from Lycia, Assyria, Halicarnassus, and Cnidus.[74]

As a result of Napoleon's fall, however, international treaties increasingly outlawed the looting of art.[75] These provisions primarily applied to Europe and did not directly affect colonial plunder; they did, however, help decrease the rhetorical purchase of the discourse of 'plunder'. Even before the Congress of Vienna, plunder was rarely called by its name. Although the Revolutionary and Napoleonic troops openly emulated the ancient Romans in their theft of Greek art, and even restaged Titus's pillage of the Temple of Jerusalem in a procession in Paris, at the same time they proclaimed themselves superior: their plunder was no greedy theft, but a liberation and 'repatriation' of art from feudalism. In turn the British captures during the same period were justified as saving art from potential French tyranny.[76] A century later, when Egypt came under British influence in 1882, however, overall attitudes were radically different from those of the French in 1798. Britain's Consul-General Evelyn Baring, later Lord Cromer, fearing complaints from other European

---

[73] On the Napoleonic art plunder see D. Mackay Quynn, 'The art confiscations of the Napoleonic Wars', *American Historical Review*, 50 (1945), pp. 437–60; W. Treue, *Art plunder: the fate of works of art in war, revolution and peace* (London, 1960); E. Pommier, *L'Art de la liberté: doctrines et débats de la Révolution française* (Paris, 1991); B. Savoy, *Patrimoine annexé: Les biens culturels saisis par la France en Allemagne autour de 1800* (2 vols., Paris, 2003).

[74] See Hoock, 'The British state and the Anglo-French wars over antiquities'; Larsen, *Conquest of Assyria*; Patrizio Gunning, *The British consular service in the Aegean*.

[75] R. O'Keefe, *The protection of cultural property in armed conflict* (Cambridge, 2006).

[76] See Pommier, *L'Art de la liberté*; R. Tombs and I. Tombs, *That sweet enemy: the French and the British from the Sun King to the present* (London, 2006), pp. 234–6.

powers, warned 'that the occupation of Egypt by the British ought not to be made an excuse for filching antiquities from the country'.[77]

Yet in many ways the trajectory from plunder to preservation was not quite as linear as Baring's comment suggests. Many British officers (and some generals) did not share his feelings, and continued to use the military infrastructure to export antiquities. The British Punitive Expedition against Benin in 1897 is also testament to the fact that, at the end of the nineteenth century, colonial aggression was still linked with the plunder of art objects. The famous Benin Bronzes, a collection of more than a thousand brass plaques from the royal palace of the kingdom of Benin, were triumphantly brought to Britain.[78] In her analysis of the capture of the gates from the tomb of Ghazni's legendary eleventh-century sultan Mahmud, following the worst defeat in the history of Britain's eastern empire, Maya Jasanoff has suggested that in some instances 'trophy-taking disguised the lack of imperial power'.[79] The variety of cases discussed in our book supports the idea that where a shift from plunder to preservation occurred, it often correlated with the securing of imperial control.

This shift was further facilitated by better technologies of reproduction. When announcing the invention of the daguerreotype at the Academy of Sciences in Paris in 1839, François Arago had already foreseen how photography might change the advance of preservation:

> Everyone will imagine the extraordinary advantage which could have been derived from so exact and rapid a means of reproduction during the expedition to Egypt; everybody will realise that had we had photography in 1798 we would possess today faithful picture records of that which the learned world is forever deprived of by the greed of the Arabs and the vandalism of certain travellers. To copy the millions of hieroglyphics which cover even the exterior of the great monuments of Thebes, Memphis, Karnak and others would require decades of times and legions of draughtsmen. By daguerreotype one person would suffice to accomplish this immense work successfully.[80]

Alongside the slowly developing art of photography, less expensive ways of taking plaster casts and increasing international exchange of copies supported in situ preservation. Although the trustees of the British Museum had been advocating in situ preservation from the 1830s onwards, it was international

---

[77] Qu. in Reid's chapter, this volume.

[78] Merryman, 'Introduction', in idem, ed., *Imperialism, art and restitution*, pp. 6–7.

[79] Jasanoff, *Edge of empire*, p. 313.

[80] D. F. Arago, 'Report', in Josef Maria Eder, *History of photography*, trans. E. Epstean (New York, 1945), p. 235. On the use of photography in exploring ancient civilizations see C. L. Lyons, 'The art and science of antiquity in nineteenth-century photography', in *Antiquity and photography: early views of ancient Mediterranean's sites* (Los Angeles, 2005), pp. 22–65. In both Britain and France, photography was used to survey foreign monuments long before it was used for domestic ones.

competition that helped to turn the tide, as exemplified by an international
quarrel over the Sanchi Stupa in the Bhopal. After both the French and the
British had been scheming endlessly during the 1850s and 1860s to obtain the
begum's permission to ship the original Stupa to Paris and London respectively, the case went to the viceroy's council, who decided that the remains
should stay in Sanchi. But, as it also decided that casts were sent to the British
and French capitals (as well as to Berlin), everybody felt they had won.[81] In
other contexts, leaving buildings in situ happened more by default than by
design. As Donna Yates discusses in Chapter 10, some Maya archaeologists
initially thought it more feasible to transport a Maya temple to New York
City across thousands of miles by sea, than for tourists to visit it in the
Honduran jungle. Yet the density of vegetation made both plunder and in situ
care impossible, leaving publication as the only form of preservation.

   Practices remaine varied despite the evolving international law context,
the securing of control, and better modes of reproduction. This was not least
the case as, most of the time, one person's preservation was somebody else's
plunder.[82] The disagreements about the return of the Elgin Marbles are sufficient reminder of this. Debates about the best forms of preservation in the
colonies interacted with older European debates about preservationist
practice, from Quatremère de Quincy's campaigns against Revolutionary art
looting to the 'conservation versus restoration' debate between John Ruskin,
William Morris, and the Anglican church restorers.[83]

   Just as Lord Byron had fiercely disagreed with Lord Elgin, and Quatremère
de Quincy with Louvre director Vivant Denon about the right to remove
objects from their original location in the late eighteenth and early nineteenth
centuries, so too the cultural administrations of different imperial powers
were often divided on whether artefacts should be shipped to the metropole
or preserved in their place of origin. Donald Malcolm Reid's chapter shows
how the question of where antiquities should remain led to conflict both in
the French empire (where the Director of Antiquities in Egypt, Gaston

---

[81] See Singh, *Discovery of ancient India*, pp. 230–9; T. Guha-Thakurta, 'Careers of the copy:
travelling replicas in colonial and postcolonial India', Firth Lecture, Annual Conference of the
Association of Social Anthropologists of the UK and Commonwealth, 'Archaeological and
Anthropological Imaginations', Bristol University, 8 Apr. 2009, <http://www.theasa.org/publications/
firth/firth09.pdf>.

[82] For a more extended discussion of terminology see Melanie Hall's chapter, this volume.

[83] On these debates see A. Quatremère de Quincy, *Lettres à Miranda sur le déplacement des
monuments de l'art de l'Italie*, ed. E. Pommier (Paris, 1989); S. Mellon, 'Alexandre Lenoir: the
museum versus the revolution', *Proceedings of the Consortium on Revolutionary Europe*, 8 (1979),
pp. 75–88; S. Tschudi-Madson, *Restoration and anti-restoration* (Oslo, 1976); J. Jokilehto, *A
history of architectural conservation* (Oxford, et al., 1999); A. McClellan, *Inventing the Louvre: art
politics and the origins of the modern museum in eighteenth-century Paris* (Berkeley, CA, and
London, 1994).

Maspero, opposed the Louvre) and in the British empire (where Baring opposed the desires of the representative of the British Museum). In another Egyptian case, discussed in David Gange's chapter, disagreements about the proper nature of preservation even ended in a fistfight between the American lawyer Francis Cope Whitehouse, a champion of Egyptian hydraulics, and the Pre-Raphaelite artist Henry Wallis, over the new Society for the Preservation of the Monuments of Ancient Egypt's attitude towards spoliation. The removal of objects to museums was not the only plunder that was seen as preservation. The removal of indigenous populations was justified as the preservation of wilderness. The forceful conquest of Jerusalem was sold as an act of preservation, and the flooding of Egyptian temples as a resurrection of the biblical irrigation system.[84]

Despite the multiplicity of practices towards plunder and preservation, we can also see four overarching themes that point to a difference in attitudes towards domestic and imperial sites. The first is unsurprising: in an imperial context, the removal of works of art from their original site was seen as legitimate for much longer than it was in Europe. The justification given for the practice of imperial removal was that objects could be better conserved and studied in Europe. It was underpinned by the ideas that 'all the monuments of antiquity belonged to the learned of Europe ... because they alone know how to appreciate them'.[85]

The second non-simultaneity is more intriguing and concerns restoration rather than transportation. From the late nineteenth century onwards, the idea of authenticity was on the rise in Europe, and restoration alongside plunder was decried as 'vandalism' and the 'worst form of destruction'.[86] Many national and international campaigns (such as Morris's intervention for St Mark's) slowly convinced the public that it was impossible to restore anything without destroying something else. In the interwar years these principles translated into the international Athens Charter for conservation. And yet, some of the individuals who had fought against restoration for many decades, completely ignored the 'conservation principle' in their work away from the metropole. The most prominent case in point is the Arts and Crafts architect C. R. Ashbee (a close friend of Morris), discussed in Simon Goldhill's chapter, who 'restored' Jerusalem in the 1920s according to a model that he himself had objected to when it concerned St Mark's in Venice almost half a century

---

[84] See Qureshi's, Goldhill's, and Gange's chapters, this volume.

[85] Captain E. de Verninac Saint-Maur, *Voyages de Luxor* (n.p., 1835), qu. in Reid, *Whose pharaohs?*, p. 1.

[86] J. Ruskin, *The seven lamps of architecture* (1880; repr. New York, 1989); W. Morris, 'Manifesto of the Society for the Protection of Ancient Buildings' (London, 1877), reproduced on the website for the Society for the Protection of Ancient Building's, <http://www.spab.org.uk/what-is-spab-/the-manifesto>.

earlier. On occasion, the empire thus became a preserve of old ideas rather than a laboratory for new ones.

The wider imperial perspective shows many other familiar faces from the British preservation movement in a less purist light. It also challenges assumptions about the traditional 'anti-heroes' of British preservation. Holger Hoock has suggested that by taking the empire into account, state involvement in the arts in Britain appears much stronger than is generally thought. Throughout the chapters of this book, we encounter many other groups not traditionally thought of as concerned with preservation. Military men appear, as well as doctors such as Duncan McPherson, who went to the Crimea as the Inspector-General of Hospitals for the Turkish Continent and returned as the champion of classical monuments. In David Gange's analysis of the fights over the creation of the Aswan Dam, the usual roles are reversed: not archaeologists and biblical scholars, but engineers, lawyers, and politicians stand out as the strongest defenders of historical preservation.

Finally, many European debates about preservation were greatly magnified in the imperial context. While in Europe debates focused on whether present generations had the right to reinvent lost traceries or scrape façades, in an imperial context stakes were often higher. Here the question was whether entire nations and empires might be resurrected. After Greece had been reborn once, the temptation persisted to resurrect it again, for instance on the Crimea. In the context of Jerusalem, 'restoration' referred both to the return of the Jews and to the repair of the city. In Egypt, plans for re-creating the biblical Lake Moeris as an alternative to the Aswan Dam were voiced as a 'restoration' project on the vastest geographical scale. In America and Africa, on the other hand, the 'conservation–restoration' question was transformed into whether land should be preserved according to the status quo as a park for 'man and beast', or whether 'original' wildernesses should be restored by removing indigenous groups—as if human beings were nothing more than the later architectural additions that restorers so frequently removed from buildings to restore them to their original state.[87]

VII

From the chapters of this book a deeply entangled world thus emerges. Although many more case studies are necessary to reveal the density of encounters, it is safe to assert that the making of heritages emerged from an intense exchange within and beyond the British empire. People, objects, and ideas flowed in multiple directions between metropole, colonies, and foreign

[87] See Richardson's, Goldhill's, Gange's, and Qureshi's chapters, respectively.

states. Many metaphors expressed the resulting proximities: Hadrian's Wall was equated to the North West Frontier, Silchester became the 'Pompeii of Hampshire', while Lake Moeris and the Raian Delta in Egypt was 'the Yorkshire of the Pre-Christian world'.[88] This should not, however, lead us to see every preservationist in Britain as 'enthusiastic supports of the imperialist project' or even as 'imperial'—as Mary Beard reminds us. As her chapter in this book argues, Hadrian's Wall might have been a metaphor for the North West Frontier, but the key figures who promoted the study and tourist potential of the English–Scottish border were members of the local northern antiquarian elite without any direct experience of service overseas.

Sometimes heritage policies were transferred from one context to another through a systematic compilation of foreign examples. In other areas individual biographies provide connections between distant lands. We often encounter the same individuals throughout the chapters in different capacities and contexts. The plundering of sites by show-business entrepreneur Phineas Barnum, for instance, connects debates about the commodification of Maya temples to Shakespeare's Birthplace in Stratford-upon-Avon and Niagara Falls.[89] The two main heroes of Richardson's Crimean chapter, Duncan McPherson and Robert Westmacott, link the Black Sea to China, Australia, Mauritius, Illawarra, and Brazil respectively. The spread of Arts and Crafts ideas across the globe becomes particularly apparent in individual biographies too. Architects and designers such as Robert Weir Schultz, Sidney Barnsley, Walter George, and C. R. Ashbee, for instance, interwove the Cotswolds with Athens, Cairo, Khartoum, New Delhi, Jerusalem, and Montreal. As Robin Cormack shows, their imperial journeys resulted in new heritages that fused a variety of traditions from a variety of territories, and which make for a 'provocative case study for any debate on colonialism and hybridity' and an 'instructive example of cultural syncretism'.

The comparison of different individual trajectories also reveals the importance of personal choices. For instance, the three architects Cormack examines all started their careers in classical lands, and subsequently worked on prestige buildings in the British empire, yet only one of them, Robert Weir Schultz, chose to make imperial claims through Greek forms. The translation of the Arts and Crafts principles to new contexts also varied widely.[90] Most designers maintained the original emphasis on local material, but chose different solutions regarding the role of local craftsmanship: Ashbee, for example, worked on reviving dying crafts in Jerusalem, but Weir Schultz imported the furniture for his Sudanese cathedral directly from Britain.

[88] See Beard's and Gange's, chapters, this volume.
[89] See Yates's and Hall's chapters, this volume.
[90] See, for example, the case of Sidney Barnsley (1865–1925) discussed in Cormack's chapter, this volume.

Although this introductory chapter indicates many broad themes and connections that are ripe for further investigation, what stands out from all the chapters is the contingency and the importance of encounters, personal tastes, ambitions, idiosyncrasies, and passions, which escape a single coherent narrative and simple statements about an 'imperial project'.[91] Instead, the invention of heritage between the eighteenth and the twentieth centuries was the product of entangled connections that combined in a range of complex and shifting ways.

---

[91] Contrary to Jasanoff's assertion (*Edge of empire*, p. 12), these complicated ways of living, loving, fighting, and identifying with empire continued well beyond the 1850s during the 'chauvinist phase of imperialism'.

Part II

The Classical World

The example of the classical world, and especially the Roman empire, was obviously central to the self-image of the British empire, certainly to its sense of mission and probably also to its understanding of its due relations with its dependent peoples and their histories. Although the Mediterranean was not a principal cockpit of British imperial power, throughout the period studied it remained constantly in play with regard to informal influence and imperial rivalries. It was extensively exploited for archaeological purposes, yielding a continuous stream of new findings and new ideas; besides, its romance was deeply embedded (and made ever more romantic) in elite British education.

As this section shows, however, Britain's use of the classical world for understanding its responsibilities was not as simple as emulation. The Roman empire stood as a warning as well as a model. Its tendency to overreach itself was a proverbial explanation for its decline. Britons excavating their own Roman heritage could see themselves as colonized as well as colonizers. Even where they did emulate the Romans, British imperialists might discover for themselves the tragedies of conquest, learning that archaeology, especially in the context of war, could destroy as much as it preserved. At the fringes of empire, Britons could also discover hybrid forms that even an all-conquering, all-assimilating power had failed to master. Here the Greeks offered an interesting counterpoint to the Romans, blending strongly with indigenous civilizations in Central Asia, or with primitive Christianity in the Byzantine empire.

Undoubtedly, the British elite's 'possession' of classical literature and its civilization fuelled appetites for the possession of peoples and their lands. On the ground, however, it proved more difficult to master vast material legacies than to master texts in the classroom or oratory in parliament.

2

Of Doubtful Antiquity:
Fighting for the Past in the Crimean War*

EDMUND RICHARDSON

ROBERT WESTMACOTT CAME home in the winter of 1852 to a city that his father had filled with the past. His career in the army had been undistinguished; his life in Australia as a settler and occasional painter had ended in financial ruin. For decades, Robert had drifted from one place to another—from London to Mauritius to Illawarra—rarely remaining anywhere long. Some thought him prickly and disagreeable—'the little tyrant'—others called him the most charming person in all of Australia.[1] In 1852, returning to London, his life was at a low ebb: his wife had run away with a sailor, and his prospects seemed grey indeed. His father, by contrast, was enjoying an illustrious retirement.

Sir Richard Westmacott had been 'Great Britain's premier official sculptor'[2] for more than a generation. His work was defined by the classical past. In Bloomsbury Square, his *Charles James Fox* sat in a toga. His *Duke of York* peered down on Carlton House Terrace from a towering column.[3] His *Achilles* bestrode Hyde Park with bronze sword and bronze fig leaf—a muscular monument to the Duke of Wellington, beloved of cartoonists and paid for 'entirely from funds donated by patriotic British Women'[4] (*Achilles* was swiftly dubbed the 'Ladies' Fancy-Man'). As one French critic put it, in 1856, 'one cannot take a step in the great city, one cannot visit Westminster or Windsor, without

* I would like to thank all the participants of the 'Plunder to Preservation' conference for their insightful comments on my chapter—and Astrid Swenson and Peter Mandler, in particular, for their invaluable suggestions and editorial work. I have previously discussed the soldier-archaeologists of the Crimean War in E. Richardson, *Classical Victorians: scholars, scoundrels and generals in pursuit of antiquity* (Cambridge, 2013)—and I am grateful to Cambridge University Press for their permission to reproduce material from that book here.
[1] See N. S. King, *History of Austinmer and Robert Marsh Westmacott in Australia* (Wollongong, 1964), for a full account of Westmacott's time in Australia.
[2] M. Busco, *Sir Richard Westmacott, sculptor* (Cambridge, 1994), p. 1.
[3] Ibid., p. 63 for a discussion of the echoes of Trajan's Column, which this monument was intended to evoke.
[4] Ibid., p. 51.

bumping into some monument, some bas-relief, of Westmacott's'.[5] This was the city that Robert had left, and the one to which he returned; his travels had taken him from the heights of nineteenth-century classicism to a farm in the Australian outback and to the middle of the Indian Ocean. Now, back in the marble-filled family home on South Audley Street, Robert Westmacott was ready to embrace the past once more. For him, the next few years would bring Russian winters and uncertain heroism: a search for the ancient world full of longing and disappointment.

I

The Crimean War, for which he would soon be bound, was fought between March 1854 and February 1856.[6] Its place in military history is not glorious: it was known for its frustrations, its mud and disease, its indecisive campaigns. As Ingram puts it, 'nobody shows up well during the Crimean War'.[7] Britain, France, and Turkey allied against Russia in a conflict where triumphs were few and far between—but where ambitions, nevertheless, were almost boundless.

The battle for the Crimea took place in the shadow of the ancient world. British soldiers on their way to the front lines dined in the Parthenon. Poets compared contemporary skirmishes to the greatest battles of antiquity. Generals took their cues from Homer—and excavations took precedence over military duties. Not content to fight for the present, Britain fought for the past as well—and pursued the Crimea's ancient heritage obsessively. The search swept up officers, doctors, and private soldiers alike—many of whom set about it with high ideals and swashbuckling enthusiasm. In London, the war minister directed the disposition of their finds. Wartime efforts to recover the ancient Crimea, however, were often slipshod and fragile: more artefacts were destroyed or looted than were recovered—and those that remained were carried away to London with the departing army at the end of the campaign. This, then, will be a story of plunder haphazardly carried out—and the swift wreckage of good intentions.

Examining this army in search of the past—asking why British soldiers became obsessed with recovering the ancient Crimea, and how they often

---

[5] 'On ne peut faire un pas dans la grande ville, on ne peut visiter Westminster ou Windsor sans heurter à quelque statue, à quelque bas-relief de Westmacott': Paul Mantz, 'Robert Westmacott', *L'Artiste*, 6 (1856), p. 141.

[6] On 28 Mar. 1854 Britain declared war on Russia (though troops did not land in the Crimea until 29 Sept. of that year); military operations were formally concluded by the signing of the armistice on 29 Feb. 1856.

[7] E. Ingram, 'Review of *Raglan: from the Peninsula to the Crimea* by John Sweetman', *Journal of Military History*, 59 (1995), pp. 150–1.

fumbled in their attempts to do so—not only sheds new light on the depth of Victorian Britain's commitment to the ancient world, it shows up its fragility and its slippery utilitarianism. Rare was the archaeologist whose principles did not have to bend with shifting circumstances during the war. Snow, mud, a general's whims, hospitals full of the sick and dying, and the small matter of a hostile Russian army—all pressured the excavators. Rarely has antiquity been sought with such great fallibility. Britain's pursuit of the Crimea's ancient heritage ultimately found expression in ransacked museums, collapsed excavations, smashed artefacts: in disillusion and failure—yet also in enduring hope. It reveals how greatly the ancient world was desired, and how self-destructively it could be pursued.

The Crimea was not the first nineteenth-century campaign to be enmeshed in the ancient past. The chaotic Greek War of Independence, fought against the occupying Turkish army in the 1820s, was portrayed by many as a battle to bring the glories of ancient Greece back to life. The prospect stirred up gigantic enthusiasm: 'Could any man suppress his desire to see reborn again in Greece the days of liberation of Marathon and Salamis, and if possible the blessed time when Plato listened to Socrates, and when the songs of Homer and the choruses of Sophocles resounded through the court of Pericles and the temple of Phidias?'[8] The Greeks were encouraged to 'pour into their hearts the spirits of departed heroes'[9]—as one famous song (translated into English by Byron) ran, 'Hellenes of past ages, / Oh, start again to life!'[10] Volunteers from all over Europe descended on Greece, hoping to play a part in its battle for the past. Before Byron took ship for the war, he had a Homeric helmet—complete with horsehair crest—custom-made for himself. While few Greeks had much enthusiasm for this project of 'regeneration', they humoured the Philhellenes. As William St Clair puts it, 'The Greek leaders in Greece itself who joined the conspiracy were content to adopt the propaganda of the expatriates.' However, 'they had no wish to set up European political institutions, to assume Western or ancient dress, or to speak ancient Greek'.[11]

Upon their arrival in Greece, many foreign volunteers expected to be commissioned as officers in the Greek army—and thereafter to play a leading role in the campaign. But things did not go according to plan. Few spoke modern Greek. Several did not have maps. Volunteers wandered from place to place,

[8] J.-G. Schweighauser, *Discours sur les Services que les Grecs ont rendus à la Civilization* (Paris, 1821), p. 56.
[9] W. Burckhardt Barker, *A short historical account of the Crimea, from the earliest ages and during the Russian occupation* (London, 1822), p. 15.
[10] W. St Clair, *That Greece might still be free: the Philhellenes in the War of Independence* (London, 1972), p. 21; also cf. ibid., p. 20: 'At Odessa a Greek theatre put on plays with such patriotic titles as *The Death of Demosthenes* and *Harmodius and Aristogeiton*.'
[11] St Clair, *That Greece might still be free*, p. 22.

looking for a chance to become heroes. Many ended up robbed, shot, tied to trees—or waiting desperately for the first ship away from Greece.[12] To make a difference in this war, something more than schoolroom Greek and a well-thumbed volume of Homer were needed. Every kind of opportunism came to haunt the conflict—and the classical heritage of Greece was despoiled more frequently than it was preserved. Many foreigners found their devotion to antiquity becoming quite flexible after a time:

> Since the arrival of the English many objects of antiquity have been found in the tombs [in the Ionian]. Unfortunately, however, they were of silver, gold, or bronze, such as idols, cups, bracelets, necklaces, rings, small vases, &c ... These objects were scattered among the English ... and were for the most part melted down for the purpose of forming into the shapes of tea-pots, spoons, knives and forks, &c. Nothing of all that has been found, is to be met with in the Ionian islands, nothing was carried to London to the British Museum, nor any where else.[13]

Overwrought ambitions collided with the day-to-day reality of the conflict—and quickly proved to be impossible to sustain. Fighting for the past could be an unexpectedly sobering—and mercenary—thing.

Nevertheless, the Greek War's promise that the ancient world might 'start again to life' had incredible resonance. It turned many into passionate supporters of the cause of the Greeks—and three decades later in the 1850s, before the outbreak of the Crimean War, it was lovingly spoken of still. In 1852, for instance, an anonymous 'Scottish Philhellene'[14] published a volume of poetry seeking 'to promote, among classical scholars, a more intimate acquaintance with the existing language and literature, as well as the social condition, of regenerated Greece'.[15]

This Philhellenic template was undeniably attractive to supporters of the Crimean War. It was no easy task to persuade an often-sceptical public that this was a war worth fighting. As John Vincent put it, 'the central issue in most wars is how to win. The central issue in the Crimean War was whether there should be a war.'[16] The rhetoric of the earlier Greek War of Independence, which had urged young men to go into battle for the sake of the ancient past they loved—and held out the promise of Homeric glory to those who suc-

---

[12] St Clair, *That Greece might still be free*, p. 34.
[13] C. Müller, *Journey through Greece and the Ionian islands, in June, July and August 1821* (London, 1822), p. 41.
[14] Anon. (pseud. A Scottish Philhellene), *Poetic translations, with an introduction on the conditions and prospects, social, religious, and literary, of the Greek nation* (Edinburgh, 1852).
[15] Ibid., p. 7.
[16] J. R. Vincent, 'The parliamentary dimension of the Crimean War', *Transactions of the Royal Historical Society*, 5th ser., 31 (1981), pp. 37–49, at p. 37. This was a debate that the war's supporters never succeeded in closing down.

ceeded—had been one of the era's most effective rallying calls. Might it not, many wondered, once more prove effective? As Britain's army prepared to sail for the Crimea to engage the Russians, the coming campaign began to be cast as another battle to bring the glories of the ancient world back to life. The ancient beacon was lit—for volunteers, funds, and public enthusiasm.

II

Where, though, could the ancient past be found in the Crimea? Certainly, by comparison to Greece, notable classical landmarks were few and far between. What kind of past would 'start again to life' here? Newspapers made much of the monuments that were present in their narratives of the landscape: 'There you saw a mighty but solemn temple; yonder a ponderous line of classic buildings and terraces.'[17] And scholars stepped forward to claim the Crimea as a classical land. They did so with brazen inventiveness.

Some played creative games with geography—transferring numerous episodes from the *Odyssey* to the Black Sea, for instance.[18] Others took a more sophisticated approach—arguing that the ancient Crimea had grown into 'civilization' through its trading relationship with Greece. According to one British commentator, Thomas Miller, thanks to the 'enterprising Greeks', the ancient Crimea grew to become one of the richest and most sophisticated areas of Europe. 'While the Thames and the Seine long remained ... paddled by naked barbarians ... the Crimea had its cities, temples, galleys, harvests, fisheries, export and import, trade, and was the scene of events upon which the orators and tragedians of the Piraeus expatiated.'[19] 'Trade' is the key word here—it was a constant preoccupation for these wartime histories of the ancient Crimea.[20] All evidence of commerce between ancient Greece and the Crimean region, no matter how scanty (or mythological), was set down and expanded upon. 'The tradition of the Argonauts would seem to imply that a trade in valuable furs ... was carried on with countries north-east of the Euxine.'[21] Ancient artefacts may well have been found in the Crimea, but these

---

[17] *Illustrated London News*, 27 Oct. 1855, p. 498; cf. also *Illustrated London News*, 8 Dec. 1855, p. 673, for a sketch of the 'Remains of an ancient building found near the head-quarters, Sebastopol.'

[18] Cf. D. McPherson, *Antiquities of Kertch, and researches in the Cimmerian Bosphorus* (London, 1857), pp. 3–4; T. Miller, *The Crimea, its ancient and modern history* (London, 1855), p. 85.

[19] Ibid., p. 83.

[20] H. Strachan, 'Soldiers, strategy and Sebastopol', *The Historical Journal*, 21 (1978), pp. 303–25, emphasizes the importance of trade in discourses of the Crimean War.

[21] Barker, *A short historical account of the Crimea*, p. 16.

'Greeks' are unabashedly contemporary creations—constructed to mirror Britain's wartime ambitions.[22]

Britain had entered the war hoping to extend its particular brand of 'civilization' to the Crimea—and thereby make a handsome profit. Civilization, according to many contemporary writers, was founded on the development of commerce. For W. Burckhardt Barker, 'the day is not far distant when civilized Europe may point to ... the Crimean peninsula ... and to its ports, again become the commercial entrepôts of the East;—as evidence that it was actuated by no selfish ambition ... when it wrested from the tenacious grip of the Russian Czars the fair territory which they had ruled only to blight'.[23] This project was justified through its purported reflection of the deeds of the ancient Greeks—who had brought (in two very contemporary, very loaded, couplings) 'civilization and wealth' to the Crimea, through their pursuit of 'commerce and colonization'.[24] Reviving and preserving the Crimea's ancient civilization meant, here, reviving its ancient prosperity—and opening up new markets for Britain:

> All the ancient poets and historians seem to have chosen the Black Sea ... as the point whence civilization and wealth proceed ... the discovery of the rich countries on the shores of the Black Sea opened up a new and vast field for commerce and colonization to this bold and enterprising people [the Greeks of the *Iliad*].[25]

Spurring on Britain's concern for the Crimea's ancient past—and professed determination to 'regenerate' its ancient civilization—was the profit-hungry determination of colonial enterprise.

Initially, it seemed as if the war's supporters had not misjudged their audience—the rhetoric that claimed it as a war fought to revivify the ancient past took hold of the public imagination swiftly and convincingly. Infinite numbers of poets piled up classical allusions —and sent the British fleet sailing off into a golden past to overpass the glories of the Greeks:

---

[22] The interdependency of the classical and the commercial, an obvious trope in these narratives, was echoed in some contemporary British educational discourses (see Rev. C. Badham, *Thoughts on classical and commercial education* (London, 1864), p. 22, for example).

[23] Barker, *A short historical account of the Crimea*, p. 236. The way in which these historians—and their contemporaries—narrated the Russian occupation of the Crimea is also noteworthy: its effects were said to be antithetical to the British aims. Miller stressed that 'the work of spoliation with reference to lands and buildings marked the first exercise of Russian authority in the Crimea' (Miller, *The Crimea*, pp. 282–3); see also Barker, *A short historical account of the Crimea*, pp. v–vi. By ruining the region's trade, these writers argued, the Russians had halted the Crimea's advance towards (a very British form of) civilization (cf. ibid., pp. viii–ix).

[24] See *Daily News*, 21 Sept. 1854, p. 4.

[25] McPherson, *Antiquities of Kertch*, p. 6.

Never before did the far-echoing sea
Lift such proud fleets upon his buoyant wave
Never did billow curl more joyously
Around the floating bulwarks of the brave!
By many a classic spot, which is the grave
Of chiefs in Hellas and Ausonia known—
By isles which yet the Ægean waters lave,
So gallantly they pass'd.[26]

Unsurprisingly, in the British expedition—amongst close-knit communities of officers confined aboard ship for weeks, with little to pass the time and calm their worries—this rhetoric found fertile ground. Officers kept diaries bubbling with excitement—and full of the conviction that the army was sailing into a classical landscape, and into a new closeness with the ancient world. John Bostock, a military doctor attached to the expedition,[27] rarely mentions his location without referring to some landmark from the ancient world: Troy, the Pillars of Hercules, and a snow-capped Mount Olympus cram onto the pages.[28] A letter home from another junior officer—published in *The Glasgow Herald*—gushed:

> We soon arrived amongst the Grecian islands, and anchored in the Bay of the Piraeus, probably the very same place from whence the Grecian ships sailed ... to Troy. I could plainly see modern Athens, classic Athens! Oh, what school-boy recollections did the gazing on thee bring to my memory.[29]

Britain's senior commanders were no less preoccupied by the past—but they approached it with a rather different agenda to some of their subordinates. Not content to be swept along by the excitement of the 'regeneration' of the Crimea, they staged deliberate, self-aggrandizing ancient performances of their own. At the time, it was argued that the Crimea's first contact with the 'civilized' world had occurred when it was visited by the Greeks of the *Iliad*, after the Trojan War.[30] Perhaps, therefore, it should be unsurprising that the British commander-in-chief, Lord Raglan, approached the Crimea for the first time in a ship named for the commander of the Trojan expedition, HMS *Agamemnon*: 'Lord Raglan and the heads of the Engineers' department went away in the "Agamemnon" steam line-of-battle ship to reconnoitre the coast.'[31]

---

[26] R. Haxell, *Alma and Inkermann: a heart-offering to the brave* (London, 1855), p. 8.
[27] See J. Ashton Bostock, *Letters from India and the Crimea* (London, 1896).
[28] Cf. ibid., p. 161—'Sailed towards Ceuta, the other "Pillar of Hercules"'; p. 169—'We coasted along the plains of Troy'; p. 171—'To the south ... Mount Olympus, covered with snow.'
[29] *Glasgow Herald*, 12 Dec. 1855, p. 7.
[30] McPherson, *Antiquities of Kertch*, p. 6.
[31] Bostock, *Letters from India and the Crimea*, p. 197.

Not long afterwards, the French commander-in-chief, St. Arnaud, remarked that: 'Lord Raglan is like a hero of antiquity.'[32]

While some soldiers were lost in latter-day Homeric dreams, others became fascinated by the physical remains of the ancient Crimea. Many officers spent every free hour hunting for the most promising sites to excavate—and a string of reports on their finds was published in the London press. The *Illustrated London News* focused, in particular, on the exploits of one Colonel Monroe, who 'being himself an antiquary ... received permission from head-quarters to employ every day fifty men of his regiment in excavating'.[33] Monroe's discoveries (Figure 2.1)—which were featured in a number of articles—generated 'no small degree of attention and interest'.[34] He was painstaking by nature, and this paid off in his archaeological work: 'Under the directions of Colonel Monroe,' remarked the *News*, 'the situation has been excavated with great care.'[35] Monroe was soon placed on official leave from his regiment, and sent on a lecture tour in Britain: 'Bristol Institution. Liet.-Col. Munro [*sic*] will deliver for the benefit of the Institution, on Thursday Evening Next ... a Lecture on "An Ancient Building lately Excavated in the Crimea, containing Greek Pottery, Coins, and other Remains", illustrated by numerous interesting Specimens and Drawings. Admission One Shilling each person.'[36]

Robert Westmacott was also in the Crimea. On the outbreak of war, twenty thousand Turkish troops were placed under British command—and he had volunteered for a post in what came to be known as the Turkish Contingent. Given the rank of major,[37] and placed in charge of one of the regiments, he was ordered to garrison the town of Kertch in eastern Crimea, which had been captured by the allied armies. It was a region with deep connections to the ancient world; the colony of Panticapaeum had been founded there by settlers from Miletus, in the seventh century BC. Westmacott struck up a friendship with a military doctor, Duncan McPherson, who was the Inspector-General of Hospitals for the Turkish Contingent. Their fascination with the region's ancient history steadily grew, and together they began to plan the grandest of all the war's excavations.

---

[32] Qu. in C. E. Vulliamy, *Crimea: the campaign of 1854–56* (London, 1939), p. 160. See also *Glasgow Herald*, 9 Oct. 1854, p. 5: 'Lord Raglan, with his ancient courage.' While Britain embraced ancient Greece, France tended towards Rome. The French emperor, Louis Napoleon, when addressing the returning French army in Paris, cast himself in an equally classical role to Lord Raglan: 'Soldiers,—I come to meet you, as the Roman Senate of old came to the gates of Rome to meet their victorious legions' (*Illustrated London News*, 12 Jan. 1856, p. 42).

[33] *Illustrated London News*, 19 Jan. 1856, p. 80.

[34] *Illustrated London News*, 8 Dec. 1855, p. 674.

[35] Ibid.

[36] *Bristol Mercury, and Western Counties Advertiser*, 22 Mar. 1856, p. 5.

[37] See *United Service Magazine*, 1855, part 2, p. 355. Westmacott had never risen higher than captain's rank in the regular army.

Figure 2.1: 'Antiquities found near head-quarters, before Sebastopol'. *The Illustrated London News*, 19 January 1856, p. 80.

For years, the Westmacott family had been arguing that archaeology ought to be approached—and practised—as an exact science. As Robert's brother Richard (known as Richard Westmacott III, to distinguish him from his father) put it in 1850, in a speech sometimes incorrectly attributed to Robert himself,[38] preservation ought to be the overriding goal of all archaeological work: 'Though there always have been a few unobtrusive, painstaking, and devoted students who have dedicated themselves to the interesting work of preserving ... the remains of the past; yet, unrecognised and unhonoured by the world at large, their only reward has too often been found in the gratification that has attended the pursuit.'[39] The archaeologist had a duty to safeguard all that was discovered with the utmost care: 'He but holds it in charge, as it were, for the instruction of those who are able to appreciate it, and who alone can give it its real value.'[40] Richard condemned 'the vagueness of speculation often indulged in by collectors of objects of antiquity'.[41] 'The collector who is totally uninformed respecting the history of his possessions,' he remarked acidly, 'or whose sole satisfaction is in acquiring, ranks indeed but little higher, intellectually, than the cabinet in which his treasure is secured.'[42] Robert Westmacott began his pursuit of the ancient Crimea loaded with

---

[38] Hoselitz attributes it to Richard—but then remarks that he 'did some excavating while in the Crimea'. It was Robert Westmacott, not Richard, who served in the Crimea (V. Hoselitz, *Imagining Roman Britain: Victorian responses to a Roman past* (Rochester, NY, 2007), p. 13).

[39] R. W. Westmacott, 'Progress of archaeology', *Archaeological Journal*, 7 (1850), pp. 1–7.

[40] Ibid., p. 3.

[41] Ibid., p. 2.

[42] Ibid.

ideals. For him, as for many at the start of the campaign, the past seemed close enough to touch—and was to be approached with reverence.

III

Westmacott and McPherson began to slip away from Kertch, whenever their duties allowed, in search of antiquity. They commenced excavations on the hills surrounding the town—and their ambitions steadily increased.

McPherson was by turns irritable, brilliant, and infuriating. His career had taken him to India for several decades, and to China during the First Opium War. There, he had hovered on the edges of diplomatic meetings, and hidden under mattresses with escaping envoys, as they fled from angry Chinese forces.[43] His fierce dedication to his work—and to the health of his patients— did not stand on ceremony. He left a trail of imperial officials, stretching across Asia, fairly speechless with fury. As his obituary in *The Lancet* ruefully put it: 'It is hardly necessary to add that his [McPherson's] career was not a peaceful one ... The plain truth is, he was a man repugnant to official men.'[44] McPherson could be as prickly and as open-hearted as Westmacott—and the two soon became close.

Their excavations began to bear fruit. In McPherson's account of his service in the Crimea, which he wrote upon returning to Britain,[45] he spoke of the excitement and fulfilment of those early times; it seemed as if he was making the classical past visible on the Crimean landscape after a gap of at least two millennia: 'All the objects remained as they had been placed twenty centuries ago ... I had come upon an unexplored field.'[46] The newspapers were fascinated, calling his *Antiquities of Kertch* 'a work of much elegance and interest'.[47]

The excavations grew ever more elaborate (see Figure 2.2 for a section of one of the largest digs)—and a detachment of the British army's engineers, under the command of Major Crease, was persuaded to assist. But amidst the chaos of the campaign, and their other pressing obligations, Westmacott and McPherson found their excavations steadily diverging from the precise, scholarly pursuit that Westmacott's brother had endorsed. Keenly conscious of the limitations of their archaeological knowledge, they were often obliged to proceed by guesswork and improvisation—when not thwarted by the bitter weather. (For months, 'the duration and intensity of the frost ... rendered the

---

[43] See D. McPherson, *Two years in China* (London, 1842), pp. 196–7.
[44] *Lancet*, 13 July 1867, p. 57.
[45] McPherson, *Antiquities of Kertch*.
[46] Ibid., pp. 87–8.
[47] *Blackwood's Edinburgh Magazine*, 83 (1858), p. 553.

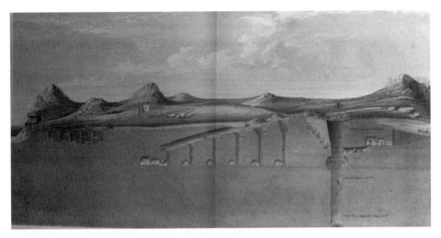

Figure 2.2: Plan of one of Duncan McPherson's excavations in the Crimea. McPherson, *Antiquities of Kertch*, insert before title page.

soil as hard as rock, to a depth of many feet, [and] no excavations could be proceeded with'.)[48] 'The task which I have attempted to perform,' McPherson remarked, 'would worthily occupy undivided attention, profound scholarship, and archaeological skill. Lacking these, but with the weighty responsibility of superintending the health of an army in a hostile country ... the alternative lies between doing nothing and doing one's best.'[49] High ideals were forever being accosted by inconvenient details: the local workmen frequently went on strike;[50] the tunnels were hastily constructed, and were forever collapsing, almost burying McPherson on several occasions.[51] Yet the excavations advanced.

Uncertainty was mingled with a kind of awe, in the presence of the past. 'There in the stillness of this chamber, lay the unruffled dust of the human frame, possessing still the form of man ... The position of the features could still be traced on the undisturbed dust.'[52] McPherson speaks with wonder of finding a decanter of wine in a tomb: 'In this decanter there was about a table-spoonful of wine, and, from the lees encrusted on the glass that stood close to it, the glass must have been filled with wine when placed there; both vessels being conveniently situated, as if the deceased might be inclined to partake of the contents of the glass and replenish it from the decanter.'[53] He poured a

[48] McPherson, *Antiquities of Kertch*, p. 53.
[49] Ibid., p. 129.
[50] Ibid., p. 93.
[51] Ibid., p. 90.
[52] Ibid., p. 88.
[53] Ibid., p. 89.

drop of wine for himself, and tasted it: 'the wine was of a red colour, and it had a distinctly vinous taste'.[54] Then, to his chagrin, he watched as 'the red and white portions [of the wine] separated, on being exposed to the air, and the fluid rapidly evaporated'.[55]

That decanter joined vases, statues, brooches, broken fragments of pottery, bones, glasses, and finds of every description, which were piling up in the army's encampment in Kertch (Figure 2.3). McPherson and Westmacott were beginning to wonder what to do with them all.

In Britain, too, covetous eyes were turning towards the Crimea, as more and more accounts of the archaeological discoveries began to be published. And, here, the nexus of official support and personal passion that drove the classical rhetoric of this campaign forward started to come into play once more. Influential members of the British elite—most notably Sir Richard Westmacott—began to lobby the War Office, asking them for assistance in carrying away the Crimean finds. As McPherson put it:

> The attention of that great sculptor, the late Sir Richard Westmacott, was early attracted to the favourable opportunity which the occupation of the Crimea by the Allied armies afforded of securing to England such remains as had escaped

Figure 2.3:   A selection of McPherson's finds, published in *Antiquities of Kertch* p. 102.

---

[54] McPherson, *Antiquities of Kertch*, p. 89.
[55] Ibid.

destruction in the Museum at Kertch, and his son, who commanded one of the Regiments of Infantry in the Turkish contingent, warmly seconded his laudable desires. Major Westmacott lost no time in bringing the subject to the notice of General Vivian, then in command at Kertch. But the General being unable to act on his own responsibility, a reference was made to the War Minister.[56]

The war minister, Lord Panmure, was delighted by this notion—and swiftly authorized McPherson and Westmacott to ship their discoveries wholesale to the British Museum on military transport ships:

> Lord Panmure promptly issued orders to secure everything of interest, and placed tonnage at the disposal of the General to convey them to England. On this the following order was issued:—'In consequence of a communication from the War Department, directing the removal to England of any sculptured marbles or valuable relics that have escaped destruction in Kertch, and are worthy of being placed in the British Museum, the Lieutenant-General has appointed Dr. McPherson, Major Crease, and Major Westmacott, a committee to decide on the value of such relics as may be remaining.'[57]

The classical past had found Robert Westmacott again, and he had embraced it. Yet even as the first crates were leaving the dockside on the Black Sea, this war's fusion of past and present, its claim on the classical past, was faltering.

IV

McPherson, in particular, was growing ever more doubtful about the merits of Britain's pursuit of the ancient Crimea. The search for it was very dear to him—but he could not help looking closely, and critically, at the true effects of the British presence in the region. For every fragment of antiquity that was recovered, he saw as many destroyed by looters. Before the war, Kertch had boasted a fine museum, built by the Russians. When the allied armies took the town, its collections were smashed to powder. His anger fairly boils off the page—and he quotes W. H. Russell's report in *The Times*:

> On a remarkable conical hill at the back of the town are two buildings, one of which is said to mark the resting-place of Mithridates, the other is built after the model of the Parthenon. It had been used as a museum ... The doors have been forced open, and the ancient Greek marbles and tablets which stood against the wall have been overturned. It is impossible to convey an idea of the scene within this place ... One might well wonder how the fury of a few men could effect such a prodigious amount of ruin in so short a time. The floor of the museum is covered for several inches in depth with the debris of broken glass, of vases,

[56] Ibid., p. 47.
[57] Ibid.

urns, statuary—the precious dust of their contents; and charred bits of wood and bone mingled with the fresh splinters of the shelves, desks and cases in which they had been preserved. Not a single thing that could be broken or burnt any smaller, had been exempt from reduction by hammer or fire. The cases and shelves were torn from the walls; the glass was smashed to atoms, and the statues pounded to pieces.[58]

The museum is prominently featured in the frontispiece to McPherson's *Antiquities of Kertch*, and in the section of the excavation that introduces the book; indeed, in the excavation section, it is almost the only building present in an otherwise depopulated landscape. McPherson may have been proud of his work, but he insists on granting Kertch's museum, destroyed by the allied forces, perhaps the most prominent place of any building in his book. The reproach to his fellow countrymen is telling. Yet the moral he draws from the looting is curious. If battles must be fought amidst the remains of the classical past, then British armies should make it their business to safeguard those remains—by carrying them away:

Our army passed within stone-throw of the Museum, the building stood prominently forward in their path, and must have attracted the attention of every officer and man. Will this not serve to convince us of the necessity of having attached to every force proceeding on service, an officer especially instructed to receive, and guard from pillage and destruction, relics of antiquity, and other works of art and science which may be prized by the nation?[59]

McPherson was far from alone in his doubts. The war—and its classical rhetoric—did not command widespread support for long. In the depths of winter, British soldiers were left 'houseless and tentless ... with no bed but the reeking puddle under the saturated blankets'.[60] In this landscape of mud and squalor, the prospect of reviving the glories of the ancient world seemed—to many who had entered the campaign filled with optimism—to be a wretched joke. The generals who had begun the war comparing one another to 'heroes of antiquity'[61] became objects of unforgiving ridicule. Their slipshod appropriation of the ancient past only threw their own inadequacies into more unfortunate relief: 'Napier ... / Like Caesar cries, "I came", "I saw", (but *not / Like him*) "I conquered!" Wherefore? ... / (To play the Braggart, were to play the fool!)'.[62] Soldiers bitterly wrote home about the past they had been in

---

[58] McPherson, *Antiquities of Kertch*, pp. 40–1.

[59] Ibid., p. 42.

[60] Qu. in E. Grey, *The noise of drums and trumpets: W. H. Russell reports from the Crimea* (London, 1971), pp. 67–8.

[61] Qu. in Vulliamy, *Crimea*, p. 160.

[62] Mrs Yorick Smythies, *Sebastopol: a poem* (London, 1854), p. 25. Judging the war's supporters by the very ancient standards that they had set up for their own self-aggrandizement seemed, for

search of, and the roles they had been asked to play. In December 1855, a family in Gloucester received this letter from a soldier at the siege of Sebastopol:

> It is no surprise that several learned renown-mongers have clothed it [Sebastopol] with prophetical glory, as I see by the advertisements they have done. It is essentially nothing but a palace of ruins ... you might fancy yourself in the ruins of Troy; but as far as waste and desolation go, this comparison of Sebastopol with its classical prototype is perfect ... But I cannot add more now. The snow is falling faster, and my hands are getting cold.[63]

The campaign slowly ground into stalemate. McPherson and Westmacott found their excavations running into one problem after another. They were forced to work so quickly that numerous artefacts were destroyed: 'Many articles of a fragile nature were unavoidably destroyed by the workmen. But indeed it was impossible to avoid this, for such relics were often turned out of the earth, there being nothing to indicate our approach towards them.'[64] Finds were stolen. Soldiers laughed at their ambitions.[65] A tomb was uncovered, late one day—and McPherson planned to open it on the following morning. Overnight, the door was prised open, and every object within removed; when McPherson returned the next day, only some matches, left by the robbers, awaited him.[66] Even those artefacts that were safely recovered did not often survive the journey home; 'the greater number of bones which I attempted to bring with me to this country [Britain] have crumbled into powder'.[67] McPherson was forever convinced that a golden burial chamber, full of treasure and splendour, awaited him—just below the next rock, just around the next corner. He dug and dug, until the conclusion of peace took the British army away from the Crimea—keeping up his excavations until the last possible day.[68] Packing to leave, he felt that he was only now starting to understand the practice of archaeology: 'I had, as it were, served my apprenticeship, and formed a good general notion where to begin.'[69]

In the years after peace was signed, historians turned once more to the ancient world to frame their accounts of Britain's campaign. The catalogue of British military cemeteries in the Crimea, produced by John Colborne

---

critics of the conflict, an irresistibly apt form of one-upmanship—and they did not stop at lampooning the generals. See Anon. (pseud. Nemo), *A word to the British public, before entering into hostilities with Russia* (London, 1855), p. 44, for an attack on the Cabinet in similar terms.
[63] *Morning Chronicle*, 27 Dec. 1855, p. 7.
[64] McPherson, *Antiquities of Kertch*, p. 103.
[65] Ibid., pp. 128–9.
[66] Ibid.
[67] Ibid., p. 98.
[68] Ibid., p. 96.
[69] Ibid., pp. 103–4.

and Frederick Brine in 1858, let the war retreat into a realm halfway between history and fable: 'The sound of the horses' hoofs has died away upon those far-off plains … Few traces of our presence in the Crimea remain to this day.'[70] The remains of the British presence—the cemeteries—and the region's ancient past are part of the same story: on the cover of their book, Colborne and Brine placed a British soldier and sailor, standing either side of a broken pillar, capped with a laurel wreath. As their epigraph they employed (without any trace of irony or bitterness) the line that was to become Wilfred Owen's 'old lie': '*Dulce et decorum est pro patria mori*.'[71] George Brackenbury's 1856 account of the war, *The campaign in the Crimea*,[72] likewise fuses the recent and the distant past. Ancient monuments (Figure 2.4) and battlefields from recent months (Figure 2.5) appear on equal terms—depicted in the same fragmentary manner: the remains of the past lie scattered haphazardly on the ground, with no effort made towards preservation; they are only spared, perhaps, a passing glance.

Figure 2.4: Fragments of the distant past: ancient ruins near Sebastopol. Brackenbury, *The campaign in the Crimea*, p. 129.

[70] J. Colborne and F. Brine, *Memorials of the brave; or resting places of our fallen heroes in the Crimea and at Scutari* (London, 1858), preface.
[71] Ibid., frontispiece.
[72] G. Brackenbury, *The campaign in the Crimea: an historical sketch* (London, 1856).

Figure 2.5: Fragments of the recent past: scattered cannonballs marking the site of the disastrous charge of the Light Brigade. Brackenbury, *The campaign in the Crimea*, p. 106.

Standing in the wreckage of the museum at Kertch, or in a ransacked tomb, or watching the winter months roll by outside the walls of Sebastopol, the soldiers who had been so eager to claim the past for their own found that it could slip away from them all too easily. The ancient world suddenly seemed more distant than ever. McPherson and Westmacott—so confident, initially, in their hopes—sailed away from the Crimea believing that they had ulti-mately left it with an impoverished heritage, rather than an enriched one. 'Had time admitted,' McPherson concluded, 'I entertained no doubt that a large measure of success would have rewarded my labours.'[73]

It was a painful homecoming. Nothing could hide the anger of many in Britain from the returning soldiers. In Oxford Street, on the day of the grandest homecoming parade, a sign had been hung out, reading: ' "Peace to the Remains of the Heroes who fell in the Crimea and the Victims of Mismanagement" ... Another tradesman, of a sombre and cynical turn of mind, had hung his shop with crepe; while two black flags were suspended from above; one bearing the word "Kars", and the other "Starvation". In one window was a design representing a widow mourning for her husband; and in another a mother weeping for her son.'[74] Westmacott's father had died while

---

[73] McPherson, *Antiquities of Kertch*, p. 104.
[74] Henry Tyrrell, *The history of the war with Russia* (London, 1855), p. 267.

Robert was in the Crimea, and he soon left London again, for an expedition to South America. It was an unhappy journey; his health was crippled by malaria, and he died some few years later. McPherson sailed for India—and years of mostly unrewarded service. Neither sought the ancient world again. For them, as Byron wrote in *Aristomenes*, 'the Gods of old are silent on their shore'. The past had turned to dust in their hands.

3

Officers and Gentlemen?
Roman Britain and the British Empire*

MARY BEARD

ON 11 MAY 1911 Francis Haverfield, Camden Professor of Roman History at
the University of Oxford and a leading figure in the archaeology of Roman
Britain, delivered the inaugural address at the first annual general meeting of
the newly formed Society for the Promotion of Roman Studies. If the published version of the speech, in the first volume of the *Journal of Roman
Studies*, is an accurate guide to what was said on the occasion, Haverfield gave
a packed manifesto for the new Society in little under an hour.[1] He opened by
considering the purpose of a 'learned society'; in fact he presciently foretold
the day when historians of the future would study this 'tendency to group
activity' that was so characteristic of the period. 'That historian, I fear, will
not wholly praise the result,' Haverfield frankly (or ironically) admitted.
'Many of these societies, he will note, have proved ineffective, many have
altogether perished, others have lingered on in a state little better than death,
and while good work has been published, a vast mass of rubbish has been
printed with it.'[2]

  The main point of the address, however, was to survey the current state of
Roman studies and to offer a manifesto for the future. This involved some
rueful, if not wholly original, reflections on the character of contemporary
British engagement with the Roman past. For Haverfield, it displayed too
much enthusiastic amateurism and not enough expertise, and there was a
positive distrust of the true specialist: 'I well remember reading an account of
a supposed Roman road in North Wales, compiled under state authority, and

---

* I am extremely grateful to Peter Mandler and Astrid Swenson for both comments and patience
in the preparation of this chapter; and to Richard Hingley, who, despite our disagreements and
very different approaches, has shared his expertise and, as yet, unpublished work.
[1] F. J. Haverfield, 'An inaugural address delivered before the first annual general meeting of the
Society, 11th May, 1911', *Journal of Roman Studies*, 1 (1911), pp. xi–xx. Haverfield's career is
extensively discussed by P. W. M. Freeman, *The best training-ground for archaeologists: Francis
Haverfield and the invention of Romano-British archaeology* (Oxford, 2007).
[2] Haverfield, 'Inaugural address', p. xi.

finding the confident conclusion "All the oldest inhabitants agree that it is a Roman road."' (How typically British, he implied, to imagine that the oldest inhabitants of the country were reliable guides to the Roman province!) In Germany, by contrast, Theodor Mommsen and his successors had re-established the study of ancient Rome on a much more rigorous, scientific footing—from the technical knowledge of Roman law to the detailed analysis of Roman inscriptions. This was the 'open road' that the new Roman society was to follow, with the archaeology and material culture of Roman Britain in a central and honoured place: 'The potsherd and the fibula and the ground-plan of house or fort are, or soon will be, among the most valuable aids to the Roman student.'[3]

Towards the end of the speech, Haverfield had a few remarks about the relevance of ancient Rome to the modern world. Most of these were directed to the impending conflict in Europe and the sense of European identity bequeathed by Rome:

> We know that [Rome] stayed for centuries the inrush of innumerable barbarian tribes and that the pause insured to European civilisation not only a survival but a triumph over the invading peoples ... Yet if the European nations fall to destroying each other, such dangers may recur ... The man who studies the Roman frontier system, studies not only a great work but one which has given us all modern western Europe.[4]

But he also made some remarks, in passing, about the relevance of the history of the ancient Roman empire to the understanding of British imperialism and the world in which he lived. The history of Rome, Haverfield suggested, offered to his contemporaries:

> stimulating contrasts and comparisons ... Its imperial system, alike in its differences and similarities, lights up our own Empire, for example in India, at every turn. The methods by which Rome incorporated and denationalised and assimilated more than half its wide dominions, and the success of Rome, unintended perhaps but complete, in spreading its Graeco-Roman culture over more than a third of Europe and a part of Africa, concern in many ways our own age and empire.[5]

Haverfield himself would, I suspect, be amazed and dismayed that this carefully crafted manifesto is now regarded as a *locus classicus* of the imperialist character of Romano-British archaeology, and cited as a clear example of the imperialist mindset that underlay the archaeological exploration and interpretation of Roman remains in Britain. His address, it is now argued,

[3] Haverfield, 'Inaugural address', p. xvii.
[4] Ibid., pp. xviii–xix.
[5] Ibid., p. xviii.

amounted to a plea for the 'imperial value of Roman archaeology'.[6] Yet, in truth, if there was an overriding modern message in his speech, it was a reflection on the dangers of forthcoming conflict—and, indeed, that is how his words were remembered in the years that immediately followed.[7]

Haverfield would, I hope, be gratified by the aim of this chapter, which is to challenge the simple connection between the British empire and Victorian and Edwardian studies of Roman Britain. My principal, but not only, focus will be what we now generally know as 'Hadrian's Wall' (although, as we shall see, it was only in the middle of the nineteenth century that this structure became recognized as the work of the emperor Hadrian, rather than of the later emperor Septimius Severus).

I

It has become a truism in the history of the study of Roman Britain that nineteenth- and early twentieth-century archaeologists of the province were driven by an imperialist agenda: a powerful combination of Roman and British imperialisms. To put this in its simplest and crudest form, Victorian excavators and their immediate successors, Victorian students and popular-izers of Romano-British antiquities and history were almost to a man—and they were almost exclusively men—public schoolboys, steeped in classical literature and operating with a vision of the Roman occupation of Britain drawn from their own imperial experience, particularly in British India. Their 'Hadrian's Wall' was a metaphor for the North West Frontier, and/or vice versa.[8] And from this position it has proved but a small step to an even more drastic view: that nineteenth-century students of the province not only drew on imperial analogies in their work on Roman Britain, but were enthusiastic

[6] R. Hingley, *Roman officers and English gentlemen: the imperial origins of Roman archaeology* (London, 2000), repeatedly stresses the imperialist agenda of this and other addresses given by Haverfield around the same time (qu. at p. 56); see also R. Hingley, 'Past, present and future: the study of the Roman period in Britain', *Scottish Archaeological Review*, 8 (1991), pp. 90–101; C. Stray, '"Patriots and Professors": a century of Roman studies, 1910–2010', *Journal of Roman Studies*, 100 (2010), pp. 1–31 (referring to the address, he writes (p. 2): 'In the empire of Classics, this was the final province waiting to be established.'). P. M. W. Freeman has attempted to defend Haverfield against these 'charges' (most succinctly in 'British imperialism and the Roman empire', in J. Webster and N. Cooper, eds., *Roman imperialism: post-colonial perspectives* (Leicester, 1996), pp. 19–34), though using a more strictly biographical approach than that adopted here.
[7] For example, H. H. E. Craster, 'Francis Haverfield', *The English Historical Review*, 35 (1920), pp. 63–70 (esp. p. 70).
[8] This approach is summarized by J. Webster, 'Roman imperialism and the "post imperial age"', in Webster and Cooper, *Roman imperialism*, pp. 1–17; for a French and North African colonial perspective, see D. J. Mattingly, 'From one colonialism to another: imperialism and the Maghreb', in Webster and Cooper, *Roman imperialism*, pp. 49–69.

supporters of the imperialist project. At the height of the British empire, in other words, Romano-British archaeology amounted to imperialism pursued by other means. Indeed, this argument goes on, the modern view of the province is still in part contaminated by the imperialist framework of the past. So, for example, with the archaeology of Roman Britain particularly in mind, Richard Hingley has claimed that 'the agenda for twentieth-century Roman studies was set within the context of a wildly, uncritically pro-imperial Britain'.[9]

Of course, that crude summary does an injustice to some fine and nuanced analyses of the discursive intersections between British and Roman imperialism, and of the chronological shifts in the search for historical analogues for the British empire. One outstanding example of this would be Duncan Bell's recent demonstration of an increasing focus in Victorian thought on the model of the United States, rather than either Greece or Rome.[10] It is also unfair to a number of recent studies that have re-examined the intersection between ancient classical texts and nineteenth-century reflections of empire. Mark Bradley, for example, has carefully explored the shifting modern interpretations of Tacitus' account of Britain, written in the second century CE, in his biography of his father-in-law, Agricola, who had been Roman governor of the province in the late first century (an account which contains that famously devastating description of Roman conquest: 'they make a desert and call it peace').[11] Nonetheless, in considering the strictly archaeological aspects of the subject, it remains true that many modern scholars, and even more students, sum up the historiography of Roman Britain as if there was a straightforward link between, on the one hand, the British empire and its partisans and, on the other, the development of Romano-British archaeology through the nineteenth century and the early years of the twentieth. It is a link blazoned, for example, in the title of Hingley's influential book, *Roman officers and English gentlemen: the imperial origins of Roman archaeology* (a formulation intentionally echoed in the title of this chapter),[12] and it is reflected in many recent sketches of the history of the archaeology and pres-

---

[9] R. Hingley, 'Britannia, origin myths and the British empire', in S. Cottam, D. Dungworth, S. Scott, and J. Taylor, eds., *TRAC 94: proceedings of the fourth annual Theoretical Roman Archaeology Conference* (Oxford, 1994), pp. 11–23, at p. 12.

[10] D. Bell, 'From ancient to modern in Victorian imperial thought', *The Historical Journal*, 49 (2006), pp. 735–59.

[11] M. Bradley, 'Tacitus' *Agricola* and the conquest of Britain: representations of empire in Victorian and Edwardian England', in idem, ed., *Classics and imperialism in the British empire* (Oxford, 2010), pp. 123–57; V. Hoselitz, *Imagining Roman Britain: Victorian responses to a Roman past* (Woodbridge, 2007) likewise captures many of the ambiguities of mid-Victorian engagement with the history of the Roman province. On the description of conquest, see below, p. 56, with n. 23.

[12] See note 6.

ervation of the remains of the Roman province. Haverfield is certainly not seen as the only culprit. 'Britain was at the height of its imperial age,' explains one historian of archaeology, 'and parallels were constantly being made between Roman Britain and the frontiers and civilizing mission of Victorian Britain.'[13]

This is the simple link that I want to challenge: the apparently clear waters that I wish to muddy. I shall be suggesting that the interrelationship between empire and archaeology was much more complicated than it is often assumed to be (just as is the relationship between empire and politics, political philosophy, or history more generally—though that is not my subject here). My point is that the nineteenth-century study of Roman Britain, and the presentation of the remains of the Roman province to an ever larger audience during that period, was not so straightforwardly driven, or so heavily coloured, by the imperialist agenda as we so often imagine. Romano-British archaeology did not, in other words, take its distinctive shape in 'the context of a wildly, uncritically pro-imperial Britain'.

This is not to say that in discussing the history of the Roman province, and in attempting to explain the nature of the relations between the Romans and the ancient British, or to conjure up the social, cultural, and historical background for the remains that were uncovered, comparisons were not sometimes drawn between the two empires, and between their various imperial wars. Of course they were, in a variety of ways. One early visitor to the Wall, John Skinner, writing in 1801, complained at the Roman use of the term 'barbarian' for the indigenous, non-Roman inhabitants of the province—comparing it unfavourably to the term 'native' used by the British in India.[14] A century later, Haverfield himself likened a Roman fort at Borrans Field near Ambleside to forts on the North West Frontier, 'a Chitral or a Gilgit', and he explicitly compared the military problems of the Romans to those of the modern British, 'such as we still have to face in guarding our Indian North-west frontier, and even in making safe our own east coast in Britain'.[15] Elsewhere, we find that the pre-Roman huts and settlements of the ancient British were conveniently compared to those of the modern New Zealanders.[16]

---

[13] S. L. Dyson, *In pursuit of ancient pasts: a history of classical archaeology in the nineteenth and twentieth centuries* (New Haven, CT, and London, 2006), p. 130.

[14] J. Skinner, *Hadrian's Wall in 1801: observations on the wall*, ed. H. and P. Coombs (Bath, 1978), p. 41; see also K. Painter, 'John Skinner's observation on Hadrian's Wall in 1801', *British Museum Quarterly*, 37 (1973), pp. 18–70.

[15] F. J. Haverfield and R. G. Collingwood, 'Report on the exploration of the Roman fort at Ambleside', *Transactions of the Cumberland and Westmorland Antiquarian and Archaeological Society*, 14 (1914), pp. 433–65, at pp. 433–5.

[16] See, for example, J. W. Grover, 'Verulam and Pompeii compared', *Journal of the British Archaeological Association*, 26 (1870), p. 46; J. Plummer, *Silchester or the 'Pompeii of Hampshire': how to get there and what to see* (Basingstoke, Reading, and London, 1879), p. 17.

And, in a memorable lecture given in 1856, and published a year later, John Collingwood Bruce, one of the two central figures in the opening up of Hadrian's Wall in the middle of the nineteenth century, suggested a close parallel between the Roman general Agricola's campaigns in Scotland and the British campaigns in the Crimea. Or rather, he criticized the recent British leadership precisely for not having learned the lessons that Agricola had to teach. The key to the successes of Agricola was roads and infrastructure. As Collingwood Bruce writes:

> Unfortunately, however, the Prime Minister of that day was too busy to study antiquities. It was not until after our army had suffered the severest calamities that a road was made from Balaklava to the camp. Again, we should probably after this have taken him to some of our Roman stations on the wall and shown him the care with which a Roman army was entrenched when it rested even for a night.[17]

These are the kinds of allusions often quoted to illustrate how embedded nineteenth- and early twentieth-century ideas of empire were in the archaeology of Roman Britain. But the truth is that such allusions are much less frequent in archaeological literature than the selective quotation and anthologizing of them suggests; indeed they form only one part of the available repertoire of comparisons (note, for example, how Haverfield appealed to the idea of the defence of the east coast of England in the same breath as the North West Frontier).

It is also the case that a more careful look at the original context of these remarks sometimes suggests a significantly different reading. The message and moral about the Crimea that I have just quoted has been wheeled out, with a straight face, as a prize specimen of 'imperial archaeology' (as 'an explicit argument for the direct significance of Roman military planning to the organisation of the British army following the battle of Balaclava in the Crimean War').[18] There is, however, as readers may already have guessed, more to it—or rather less to it—than meets the eye. For Collingwood Bruce's lecture was actually a light-hearted—almost joking—performance on 'The Practical Advantages accruing ... from Archaeology', in which he went to suggest first that Roman underfloor heating could have been useful in the Crimea, while later turning to the advantages of Roman mortar (much better, he claimed, than that used in building Durham Jail), and to the superiority of Roman kitchen equipment, pointing to a gravy strainer from Pompeii in the collection of the Duke of Northumberland:

[17] J. Collingwood Bruce, 'The practical advantages accruing from the study of archaeology', *The Archaeological Journal*, 14 (1857), pp. 1–7, at p. 3.
[18] R. Hingley, *The recovery of Roman Britain, 1586–1906: a colony so fertile* (Oxford, 2008), p. 310.

I am informed that when the master cook was introduced into the museum, he was struck with the admirable practical form of some cooking utensils. I have here a sketch of a sort of gravy strainer, which he pronounced better than any he had. The peculiarity of it consists in its rim being turned slightly inwards, so that it can be slightly shaken over the joint, without the risk of any unstrained gravy coming over the edge.[19]

To be sure, joking comparisons with the British imperial experience (or with British cooking practice) are still comparisons, even if of a different sort. But the overall tone of this article sits uneasily with modern arguments about the serious 'imperial lessons' that nineteenth-century archaeologists are said to have found in the remains of Roman Britain. Needless to say, Collingwood Bruce's more obvious jokes (such as the gravy strainer) are usually now passed by without comment, if read at all.[20]

We are dealing here, in part, with that common problem of decontextualized quotation, and the pattern of smash-and-grab scholarship, whose cumulative effect is to give a distinctly misleading impression of the imperial character of the archaeology of Roman Britain. But that is not all. There are two other, major points about the position of Romano-British archaeology within imperial discourse that are often overlooked. It is to these I wish to turn now, before finally reflecting on how some of the archaeological sites were presented 'on the ground'—including a rather more complex story of Hadrian's Wall than is usually told.

II

The first point is a simple classical one. Part of the argument about the imperialism at the heart of Romano-British archaeology in the nineteenth century goes directly back to classical texts. The public school (and Oxbridge) classical background of the key players in the exploration of Roman Britain underpinned, it is often assumed, their broadly positive assessment of Roman imperialism; it is as if they had internalized the positive assessment of the Roman authors themselves.

---

[19] Collingwood Bruce, 'Practical advantages', p. 6.
[20] Similar issues of tone and context are important in other connections drawn between Roman and British imperialism. In a discussion of (in part) Haverfield's inaugural address, Raymond F. Betts (in 'The allusion to Rome in British imperialist thought of the late nineteenth and early twentieth century', *Victorian Studies*, 15 (1971), pp. 149–59) lists in a lengthy footnote a number of explicit comparisons between Rome and modern empires by leading scholars of the period; though he finally concedes: 'In fairness it must be noted that all these persons were critical of Roman despotism' (p. 151). 'Straightforward' comparisons are rarely as 'straightforward' as they seem.

That is not, in principle, an implausible proposition. The problem is that many, if not most, ancient Roman historians had a profoundly ambivalent attitude to the vast expansion of Roman power, and they correlated Roman decline, in character and morals, with the spread of empire; in fact, they often concluded that the downward turn in Roman history began in 146 BCE (in the period of the so-called 'Republic', long before the advent of the Roman emperors), when in a single year Rome destroyed the cities of Corinth and Carthage, leaving no major rival for power in the Mediterranean.[21] But more than that, as Mark Bradley has insisted (with an eye to recent debates on postcolonial archaeology),[22] the main extended ancient account of the history of the province of Britain—Tacitus' biography of Agricola—is also the best-known Latin text to interrogate the nature, and the moral ambivalences, of Roman imperialism. Tacitus lists, for example, the apparently civilizing initiatives of Agricola in the province (the benefits of Latin, baths, and Roman dress, etc.), but goes on to describe them as a 'facet of the enslavement of the British'. And, in the final battle between Agricola's forces and the barbarians the balance of virtue is reversed; although the barbarians are defeated by superior Roman firepower, they fight heroically and voice the sentiments of freedom and liberty that the Romans have lost (and it is these barbarians who voice the famous phrase 'they make a desert and call it peace').[23]

In other words, if we are dealing with deeply classically educated students of Roman Britain, that deep classical learning and reading would have been much more likely to prompt a questioning response to the imperialist project, not—as is so often assumed—knee-jerk sympathy. In that light, it should come as no surprise that one of the questions that has always marked the study of the province is precisely 'whose side are we on?' Is the archaeologist speaking for, and about, the Romans or the Britons? That question is famously raised in studies and representations of Boadicea (Boudicca), where the image of the murderous terrorist is almost always held in tension with the image of the queen as a proto-imperialist, national hero: is she criminal or freedom fighter?[24]

---

[21] Sallust, *Catilinarian conspiracy* 6–13; idem, *Jugurthan war* 41; P. McGushin, ed., *Sallust, the histories*, volume 1 (Oxford, 1992), pp. 78–9; N. Purcell, 'On the sacking of Carthage and Corinth', in D. Innes, H. Hine, and C. Pelling, eds., *Ethics and rhetoric: classical essays for Donald Russell on his seventy-fifth birthday* (Oxford, 1995), pp. 133–48.

[22] Bradley, 'Tacitus' *Agricola*'.

[23] Tacitus, *Agricola* 21; 30—echoed by Byron ('He makes a solitude and calls it—peace', *The bride of Abydos: a Turkish tale* (London, 1813), Canto 2, 20). For a recent analysis of Tacitus' discussion of empire, see R. Rutherford, 'Voices of resistance', in C. S. Kraus, J. Marincola, and C. Pelling, eds., *Ancient historiography and its contexts: studies in honour of A. J. Woodman* (Oxford, 2010), pp. 312–30.

[24] M. Beard and J. Henderson, 'Rule(d) Britannia: displaying Roman Britain in the museum', in N. Merriman, ed., *Making early histories in museums* (Leicester, 1999), pp. 44–73; and, in general, R. Hingley and C. Unwin, *Boudica: an iron age warrior queen* (London, 2005).

There are hints of a similar ambivalence in a wide range of discussions of the Roman province, and in some unlikely places. Some of the most jingoistic children's novels in the late nineteenth century were those by the prolific G. A. Henty, who brought upstanding character and courageous adventure, combined with the 'glories' of empire, into the nursery. His giveaway titles include *By sheer pluck: a tale of the Ashanti War* (1884), *By right of conquest: with Cortez in Mexico* (1891), and *The dash for Khartoum: a tale of the Nile expedition* (1892). But, as Richard Hingley has rightly observed,[25] the preface to his novel *Beric the Briton: a story of the Roman invasion* (1893) includes a much more subtle discussion of the nature of British character and the virtues—or otherwise—of Roman imperial rule. Almost in Tacitean mode, Henty deplores the effects of Roman 'civilisation' on the Britons, so enervating them that they were unable, in the post-Roman period, to withstand Saxon invasions:

> The Roman conquest for the time was undoubtedly of immense advantage to the people—who had previously wasted their energies in perpetual tribal wars—as it introduced among them the civilization of Rome. In the end, however, it proved disastrous to the islanders, who lost all their military virtues. Having been defended from the savages of the north by the soldiers of Rome, the Britons were, when the legions were recalled, unable to offer any effectual resistance to the Saxons . . .[26]

For Henty (as is stated clearly in the slightly later foreword to *Wulf the Saxon: a story of the Norman conquest*), the true grit of character that was the driver behind the British empire came not from the Romans but from the Normans.[27]

The map of empire: centre and periphery

My second point concerns the territorial extent of the Roman and British empires. As C. P. Lucas pointed out in his famous discussion, *Greater Rome and Greater Britain*, there were striking geographic differences between the Roman and British empires—something that is now, as far as I can see, rarely stressed. For all the likeness that might be claimed between the two imperial powers, the extraordinary fact was that they hardly overlapped *territorially* at all. At least until the final dismemberment of the Ottoman empire, the only areas to be parts of both empires were Gibraltar, Malta, Cyprus, and Britain itself: 'otherwise the whole of the British Empire is in parts of the world which

[25] Hingley, *Roman officers and English gentlemen*, pp. 82–5.
[26] G. A. Henty, *Beric the Briton: a story of the Roman invasion* (London, 1893), p. 5.
[27] Idem, *Wulf the Saxon: a story of the Norman conquest* (London, 1895), pref.

Rome never knew and which never knew Rome'.[28] When Cowper wrote (in the verses later inscribed underneath the statue of Boadicea by Thomas Thorneycroft on the Thames Embankment in London)—'Regions Caesar never knew / Thy posterity shall sway', he was even more literally correct than we usually take him to be.[29]

There are some significant consequences of this. First, Roman archaeology did not develop on the ground, following the flag (in clear contrast to the French experience, for example, where the Roman archaeology of North Africa became, in effect, a branch of French rule).[30] It is true that in the late 1880s, a few years after the annexation of Cyprus, the usual late Victorian suspects (Sidney Colvin, Richard Jebb, George Macmillan, etc.) combined to establish a Cyprus Exploration Fund, but despite the considerable Roman material on Cyprus, the Fund sponsored only excavations on Greek and pre-historic Greek sites.[31] In the nineteenth century at least there was no Roman archaeology in the British empire; nor, to all intents and purposes, could there have been.

This put Britain itself in a particularly loaded position (which, again, Lucas pointed out). It was both the furthest outlying province of the ancient empire and the metropolitan heartland of the new; it was both periphery and centre. I would argue that it is this ambivalence (rather than some simple imperialist project, as is often claimed) that lies at the heart of the nineteenth-century archaeology of Roman Britain, and that governs its presentation.

This is clear from the treatment of the sites and excavations themselves. On the one hand, we find repeated attempts to 'metropolitanize' the British archaeological material. This is especially striking in the explicit reconstruction of Romano-British towns on the model of Pompeii. Almost every one of them, from Silchester to Wroxeter and St Albans, gained the popular (and sometimes academic) appellation of the 'British Pompeii'. This is nicely seen in a tourist pamphlet (one of a series rather dispiritingly entitled, 'Roving rambles around Basingstoke'), which parades Roman Silchester as 'the Pompeii of Hampshire'. This *vade mecum* guides the visitor around the British site as if it was Pompeii itself—starting, as visitors at the time always did at Pompeii, with the tombs lining the roads that led out of the city. Except in this case there were no roads and, *as yet*, no tombs had been discovered. And, with slight tongue in cheek, I assume, the writer observes on the site 'one or two houses which are evidently nineteenth-century homes, but Roman villas

[28] C. P. Lucas, *Greater Rome and Greater Britain* (Oxford, 1912), p. 140.
[29] W. Cowper, 'Boadicea: an ode', first published 1782; in H. S. Milford, ed., *Complete poetical works of William Cowper* (London, 1905), pp. 310–11.
[30] Mattingly, 'From one colonialism to another'.
[31] *Times*, 3 Mar. 1888, p. 11; 20 July 1888, p. 13; 29 July 1889, p. 6; *Standard*, 5 Mar. 1888, p. 3.

are conspicuous only by their absence'.[32] Even more thorough was the point-by-point comparison of Verulamium (St Albans) and Pompeii by J. W. Grover in the *Journal of the British Archaeological Association* for 1870, which stressed the similarity of the two towns:

> The dimensions are most strikingly similar in both cities. The length of Pompeii is 4,300 feet; of Verulam 4,488. The width of Pompeii is 2,400 feet; of Verulam, 2,541. The area of the former being 167 acres, and of the latter 190 acres.... The theatre at Verulam not only occupies the same relative position, but is, singularly enough, nearly the same size as that of its model, being 193 ft. 3 in, diameter, against 195 ft. approximately in Pompeii.[33]

The competing image of the province as imperial periphery can predictably enough be highlighted by Hadrian's Wall, which, in the middle decades of the nineteenth century, was studied, excavated, and made accessible to larger numbers of 'pilgrims' (as they were often called rather than 'tourists') than ever before. It was then an even more controversial monument than it is now. Current controversies centre on the function of the Wall—defensive, symbolic, or a line of communication?[34] But our Victorian predecessors were more concerned with exactly whose Wall it had been. Over the middle years of the nineteenth century, the prevailing view that it was the work of the emperor Septimius Severus (CE 193–211) gave way, not without a considerable struggle, to the now standard idea that the builder (or, at least, the mastermind) was the emperor Hadrian (CE 117–138).[35]

The key figures of this development of the study and the tourist potential of the Wall were two members of the local elite: Collingwood Bruce, who from 1849 led the regular series of 'pilgrimages' along the monument, and who argued strongly and, in the end, successfully, that the Wall was Hadrianic;[36]

---

[32] Plummer, *Silchester*, at p. 13. Hoselitz, in *Imagining Roman Britain*, reviews various aspects of these Pompeian comparisons, pp. 147–9, 174–5.

[33] Grover, 'Verulam and Pompeii compared', p. 50.

[34] D. J. Breeze and B. Dobson, 'Hadrian's Wall: some problems', *Britannia*, 3 (1972), pp. 182–208; J. J. Wilkes, 'Hadrian's Wall', in P. Ganster and D. E. Lorey, eds., *Borders and border politics in a globalizing world* (Lanham, MD, and Oxford, 2005), pp. 1–10.

[35] The most significant defence of Severus' role in establishing the Wall was a pamphlet by R. Bell, *The Roman Wall: an attempt to substantiate the claims of Severus to the authorship of the Roman Wall* (Newcastle-upon-Tyne, 1852). Further pamphlet warfare followed: J. Collingwood Bruce, *Hadrian: the builder of the Roman Wall* (London, 1853); Anon. (pseud. A Cumbrian), *Mural controversy: the question, 'Who Built the Roman Wall'* (London, 1857). The debate is discussed in R. Miket, 'John Collingwood Bruce and the Roman Wall controversy: the formative years, 1848–1858', in R. Miket and C Burgess, eds., *Between and beyond the walls: essays on the prehistory and history of north Britain in honour of George Jobey* (Edinburgh, 1984), pp. 243–63.

[36] Miket, 'John Collingwood Bruce', stresses the earlier role of John Hodgson, in his multi-volume *History of Northumberland* (Newcastle-upon-Tyne, 1820–58), in advocating Hadrianic authorship. Collingwood Bruce's career is also reviewed by D. J. Breeze, 'John Collingwood Bruce and the study of Hadrian's Wall', *Britannia*, 34 (2003), pp. 1–18.

and John Clayton, local landowner and, between 1830 and 1840, the town clerk of Newcastle.[37] They were both classically educated maybe, but they were much more part of the patriotic, local antiquarian, northern tradition (as the word 'pilgrimages' itself hints) than linked—in any capacity—with the outposts of the British empire, from the Crimea to the North West Frontier; for example, neither had any direct experience of service overseas.

To be sure, the Wall prompted discussion of frontier conflict—unlike the more comfortable vision of the Pompeian-style towns. But it was not simply seen in terms of the British imperial experience. Other imperial powers were brought into the picture: one writer, for example, saw the ancient conflicts around the Wall on the model of the Spanish in South America. Significantly, though, he and others also reflected, much closer to home, on the more recent conflicts between English and Scots, the 'imperial' conquests on England's doorstep.[38]

III

But there is a characteristically nineteenth-century sting in the tail. I have mentioned that the Wall was made accessible and excavated during the middle years of the nineteenth century. There was more to it than that. Like any ruin, the Wall had suffered centuries of looting and depredation; it was part collapsing and had been, in part, robbed; it was, in short, gradually disappearing. John Clayton was the man who put a stop to much of this, buying up much of the land on which the central section of the Wall stood. And he initiated a vast campaign of rebuilding it. Teams of local workmen, acting on Clayton's instructions but entirely unsupervised, gathered together what stones they could and built up the monument as drystone wall, in several courses, topping it with turf (quite different, in fact, from the original construction). It was a long process that took place over many miles, and many years, in the middle of the nineteenth century.

It is known locally as 'Clayton's Wall' and it is certainly more Clayton's than Hadrian's (or, for that matter, Septimius'). It has given us those most picturesque sections of the Wall—that grace the tourist posters, postcards, and, indeed, provide the illustrations for many academic accounts of the

[37] His contribution is discussed in R. Woodside and J. Crow, *Hadrian's Wall: an historic landscape* (London, 1999) and R. Hingley, R. Witcher, and C. Nesbitt, 'Life of an ancient monument: Hadrian's Wall in history', *Antiquity*, 86 (2012), pp. 760–71.

[38] W. Hutton, *The History of the Roman Wall, which crosses the island of Britain from the German Ocean to the Irish Sea* (2nd edn., Newcastle-upon-Tyne, 1814), reprinted as *The first man to walk Hadrian's Wall 1802* (Newcastle-upon-Tyne, 1990), p. 12.

Roman frontier. Yet this is a landscape artfully (re)constructed by Clayton's workers; it is only 'Roman' in a very limited sense.[39]

But there is a further irony. When, late in the nineteenth century and early in the twentieth, scholars and tourists came along and (as, it is true, some did) wondered at this powerful image of a frontier and compared it to their own frontiers—little did they know that the Wall at which they were marvelling had been built in its present form only a few decades earlier; that it had been (re)built in the image of what the Roman frontier should be. It is one of those classic ironies of (plunder and) preservation.

---

[39] More fully discussed in Richard Hingley, Robert Witcher, and Claire Nesbitt, 'Life of an ancient monument: Hadrian's Wall in history', *Antiquity* 86.333 (2012), 760–71.

4

Unity Out of Diversity?
The Making of a Modern Christian
Monument in Anglo-Egyptian Sudan

ROBIN CORMACK

THE ISSUES IN this chapter arise out of the character of one special building, the Anglican All Saints' Cathedral at Khartoum (Figure 4.1). Without the establishment of the Anglo-Egyptian Condominium of Sudan in 1898 this church would never have been commissioned and constructed.[1] One way of analysing it is to see its visual features as plunder from other architectural traditions imposed on a new colonial capital. The aim here is to probe much further into its genesis and character, and to argue that it can only be under-stood as part of a complex and positive cultural episode in architectural and intellectual thinking around 1900. This argument highlights the decisions that were made by a British architect in producing a prestigious colonial monu-ment in sub-Saharan Africa to serve the British community as a place of Christian worship according to Anglican rites. The dilemma faced by the architect, and the local committee in Khartoum that commissioned him (watched over by the governor-general at the time), was to decide on the nature and the evocations of the new Anglican church. Should its design resemble a nostalgic form of cathedral-building from the home country or should it fit into the traditions of Sudan (or even Egypt)? In the event it was none of these; instead the individual career of the architect resulted in the production of a unique solution. It is suggested here that only by an examination of the apparently piecemeal sources of the design can we recognize the ultimate homogeneity of the finished church at the centre of imperial Khartoum.

This investigation must first glance at the interests and attitudes of a number of late nineteenth-century/early twentieth-century British architects who, at the beginning of their careers, went to classical lands in the Mediterranean, and subsequently, in their maturity worked on prestige buildings in the British

---

[1] For a narrative of the historical context of this chapter, see M. W. Daly, *Empire on the Nile: the Anglo-Egyptian Sudan, 1898–1934* (Cambridge, 1986).

Proceedings of the British Academy, **187**, 63–90. © The British Academy 2013.

Robin Cormack

Figure 4.1: All Saints' Cathedral from the southwest, Khartoum, Sudan, January 2009.

empire. They were members of a group of Arts and Crafts enthusiasts who developed their subsequent colonial building projects in response to their first-hand exposure to classicism and medievalism in Greece itself. This chapter examines three men, Walter Sykes George, Sidney Barnsley, and, in particular, Robert Weir Schultz: who was the architect of the cathedral at Khartoum, and whose work forms the main part of this chapter.

These architects were all trained in London and had connections with the Norman Shaw practice there, but they widened their horizons through travel and study far afield. They grew up under the shadow of John Ruskin (who himself never went further east than Venice, and whose concept of the influence of the Arab world on Venice is thoroughly exaggerated and muddled through underestimating the contribution of European Gothic architecture),[2] and their interest in Byzantium was deepened by, in particular, the studies of William R. Lethaby.[3] This means that they were familiar with the rehabilitation in Great Britain of the previously scorned medieval architecture of the Church of San Marco and the Ducal Palace in Venice, as well as of the Church of St Sophia in Constantinople. The latter is provocatively described as 'a

[2] For an alternative assessment of the value of Ruskin's conception of the East, see Deborah Howard, *Venice and the East* (New Haven, CT, and London, 2000), passim.
[3] See Godfrey Rubens, *William Richard Lethaby: his life and work, 1857–1931* (London, 1986).

work surpassing every edifice in the world' (a quotation from William of Malmesbury) on the title page of Lethaby's best-selling book—*The Church of Sancta Sophia, Constantinople: a study of Byzantine building* by W. R. Lethaby and Harold Swainson (London, 1894). This book offered much more than a rebranding or a full and accurate account of the church and its decoration. It also set out a radical philosophy for the modern architect as conceived by Lethaby, one that was profoundly significant for the work and ambitions of the architects to be discussed in this chapter. This philosophy is expressed most succinctly by Lethaby in the preface (p. vi):

> A conviction of the necessity for finding the root of architecture once again in sound common-sense building and pleasurable craftsmanship remains as the final result of our study of S. Sophia, that marvellous work, where, as has so well been said, there is no part where the principles of rational construction are not applied with 'hardiesse' and 'franchise'. In estimating so highly the Byzantine method of building in its greatest example, we see that its forms and results directly depended on then present circumstances, and then ordinary materials. It is evident that the style cannot be copied by our attempting to imitate Byzantine builders; only by being ourselves and free, can our work be reasonable, and if reasonable, like theirs universal.[4]

The argument of this chapter is that this philosophy set out by Lethaby permeated the thinking of this group of architects, and explains both their emulation and absorption of Byzantine architecture and at the same time their resistance to producing nostalgic neo-Byzantine structures.[5] They did not work in a simple 'Byzantine style'. Their work needs to be examined and interpreted within a particular conceptual framework, which developed in the late nineteenth century, and which underlay their thinking throughout their careers. They developed a specific kind of progressive yet traditional modern architecture, which, however, disdained 'modernism'.

Walter Sykes George (1881–1962) is mentioned here first (and only very briefly) as the clearest example among them of a person who showed in his interests a total absorption in Byzantium, yet whose subsequent architectural projects show virtually no hints of Byzantine style or influence. What his mature work conspicuously exhibits is empathy both to the materials and to the circumstances of the environment in which he later operated: the virtue of the architecture and decoration of St Sophia, which Lethaby had praised. Although, in a private letter written on 14 March 1952, George says that

---

[4] The use of these French terms is due to the influence of the architect and historian Auguste Choisy (1841–1909), author of *L'art de bâtir chez les byzantins* (Paris, 1883); this book remains in many ways the best account of the structural procedures of Byzantine architects, and was well known to the architects considered in this chapter.

[5] J. B. Bullen, *Byzantium rediscovered* (London, 2003) surveys the phenomenon of the European revival of Byzantine forms in the nineteenth century as an antidote to Gothicism.

'the best years of my life were those in Greece', his subsequent career in India was conspicuous for its visual distance from medieval Byzantine forms and vocabulary.[6]

W. S. George studied under W. R. Lethaby at the Royal College of Art, London; he won the Soane scholarship in 1906, and went to Greece from 1906 to 1911, where he was based at the British School in Athens.[7] During these years, as a result of his commitment to recording Byzantine monuments, he published a major book on the Church of St Eirene at Constantinople (the sister Church of St Sophia), and recorded other sites, notably the church (then still in use as a mosque) of St Demetrios at Thessaloniki, which was, by happenstance, burnt down about ten years later, in 1917. His precise and elegant drawings and watercolours of this church, done to scale and including *squeezes* of its wall mosaics, are the best remaining evidence of its fabric, and demonstrate the meticulous care with which he worked in the field.[8] He made these *squeezes* by pressing moistened paper onto the mosaic surface and pulling it away when dry, then painting each impression of the tesserae with its colour, so giving an exact record of the now lost mosaic. He also assisted in excavations in Greece and in Sudan, where he spent the season of 1910 at Meroë. But his life changed completely in 1912 when he joined the team of Edwin Lutyens and Herbert Baker in helping to design and build the new capital complex of New Delhi (to replace Calcutta). His name is still today recorded on the plaques in the parliamentary and other buildings. When the project reached its completion in 1929, George chose to stay and work in private practice in Delhi (building the campus of St Stephen's College), and to concern himself with the training of students (for example at the Delhi Polytechnic

[6] The letter addressed to Mrs Shearer is in the RIBA Archive, now kept at the V&A in London, ref GeW/1/9. It commends the work of Choisy, while deeply criticizing other French, German, and Italian approaches to the history of architecture. It also condemns Byzantine building as lacking finesse—'clumsy and bungling beyond comparison'.
[7] For studies on the BSA at this period see Michael Llewellyn-Smith, Paschalis M. Kitromilides, and Eleni Kalligas, eds., *Scholars, travels, archives: Greek history and culture through the British School at Athens* (Athens, 2009). For the archive of materials, see Amalia G. Kakissis, 'The Byzantine Research Fund Archive: encounters of Arts and Crafts architects in Byzantium', pp. 125–44; Eugenia Drakopoulou, 'British School at Athens research on Byzantine Attica', pp. 145–51; and also the web pages at <www.bsa.ac.uk>.
[8] His measurements of the Church of St Demetrios were done in Apr. and May 1907, and his drawings of the mosaics were done from 27 July to 16 Nov. 1909. All are now essential materials for the study of the church and especially for its mosaics, due to severe damage to its structure by a fire in 1917 (the present church is a brutal reconstruction); see R. S. Cormack, 'The mosaic decoration of St Demetrios in Thessaloniki: a re-examination in the light of the drawings of W. S. George', *Papers of the British School at Athens*, 64 (1969), pp. 17–52. Still important is his monograph: W. S. George, *The Church of St. Eirene in Constantinople* (London, 1912). For a diary of his work in Greece see his statement of 18 Nov. 1911, now in the RIBA Archive at the V&A Museum in London, ref GeW/1/1.

at the Kashmiri Gate). It is clear from his work and career in India that he adopted many features from local and traditional Indian architecture. Whereas Lutyens was scornful of such past traditions as the seventeenth-century Mughal architecture of the Taj Mahal (1632–53), the inclusion in the architecture of New Delhi of domes that repeat its profile suggests that such participants in the programme as George did manage to incorporate local traditions in the otherwise Europeanized designs. The Taj Mahal was in poor condition by the nineteenth century, and was restored through the interest of the viceroys, particularly Lord Curzon, who around 1905 laid down the present setting with marble benches, all in the style of the lawns of London.[9] George came to India with a similar sympathy for the traditions of India, albeit, like the viceroys, with a knowledge of the attractive features of his homeland. Perhaps the idea of representing stone ornamental Indian elephants, which recurs several times in the architecture of the Parliament Building at New Delhi, was in part traditional, but in part an example of the eclecticism of George himself, who would probably have seen and noted the identical motif of African elephants in the Great Enclosure at Musawwarat in Sudan, not far from Meroë (Figures 4.2 and 4.3).

Figure 4.2:   Parliament building, New Delhi.

[9] See Giles Tillotson, *Taj Mahal* (London, 2008).

Figure 4.3:   Great Enclosure at Musawwarat, Sudan.

The relevance of W. S. George as a case study in this chapter is to contrast the progress of his career with that of Robert Weir Schultz, but it needs to be noted that George was not the only architect of the group who worked at the British School in Athens and immersed himself fully in the recording of the monuments of Greece, but who was later, to all superficial appearances, to eliminate the experience from his later activities. The case of Ramsay Traquair (1874–1952) is equally paradigmatic. He worked energetically at the British School at Athens from 1905 to 1909 but was then appointed to the chair of architecture at McGill University in Montreal in 1913; he remained there till his retirement in 1939 and lived in Canada for the rest of his life. The question of the influence of Greece—or rather the lack of it—on the career of Traquair was documented in the course of an archival interview about his life. The inter-viewee was his colleague, Emeritus Professor Norbert Schoenauer (1923–2001), the interviewer was Daniella Rohan, and the discussion took place in Montreal on 15 August 1997.[10] The relevant passage is:

> *Can you comment on Traquair's early studies concerning Byzantine, Greek, and Roman religious architecture, and how they influenced his first commissions?* 'I really doubt whether his Byzantine church studies influenced his architectural

[10] See <http://cac.mcgill.ca/traquair/interviewnorbert/php>.

work later on. Academically, it was very, very important. After all, the first articles that he published were on Greece and on Constantinople, but I think the influence as such, of Byzantine architecture, was not as important as his contact with the Arts and Crafts movement in Edinburgh.'

This interview implies the separation and divergence of the Arts and Crafts movement and the architectural tradition of Byzantium. But, through the case of Weir Schultz, who integrated his knowledge of the Arts and Crafts movement and of Byzantium under the reasoning of W. R. Lethaby, a much more complicated picture emerges.

Robert Weir Schultz (1860–1951) was, throughout his life, a doctrinaire Arts and Crafts architect, whose acknowledged masterpiece, the Anglican All Saints' Cathedral at Khartoum, built largely between 1906 and 1913, is the subject of this chapter.[11] My argument is that the building and its special features are unintelligible without first exploring his relationship with Greece, and that its concept is underpinned by the aesthetic principles of Byzantine builders without too obviously imitating their forms.

Robert Weir Schultz was based at the British School at Athens from 1888 to November 1890, recording classical and Byzantine monuments. He worked jointly during this period with Sidney Barnsley (1865–1926), who later worked as architect and furniture maker in the Arts and Crafts tradition.

Schultz only went to Greece because in 1887 he won the Royal Academy Gold Medal and Travelling Studentship—the subject of the competition was to design 'A Railway Terminus'. It was Lethaby who gave him the advice to use the money for travel in Greece and the Near East, and the consequence was that he found a mission in recording the decaying relics of Byzantium. An interest in the Greek middle ages was a new development in Athens at the time. The Director of the British School, Ernest Gardner, wrote on this subject in his annual report in 1889:[12]

> The time is almost past when Byzantine churches could be pulled to pieces, without a protest, on the chance of finding an inscription in their ruins ...
> Byzantium is practically a new branch of Archaeology in Athens, so far as recognition by the government and foreign schools is concerned.

Schultz was fascinated by Byzantine Greece, but he also appreciated classical buildings when he recognized their connections with Arts and Crafts aesthetic. His thinking emerges in an article he published in the *Journal of Hellenic*

[11] Schultz has been the subject of some excellent publications, notably those by David Ottewill, 'Robert Weir Schultz (1860–1951): an Arts and Crafts architect', *Architectural History*, 22 (1979), pp. 88–115, 161–72; and Gavin Stamp, *Robert Weir Schultz, architect, and his work for the marquesses of Bute: an essay* (Mount Stuart, 1981). He was born in Scotland, but, in Dec. 1914 (anticipating British anti-German hostility to his surname), he changed his name from Robert Weir Schultz to Robert Weir Schultz Weir.

[12] *Journal of Hellenic Studies*, 10 (1889), pp. 254 and 277.

Studies in 1891 on the north door of the Erechtheum, which ends with the words, 'I venture to say in conclusion that, altered and transformed as I have endeavoured to prove it has been, the north doorway of the Erechtheum as it stands to-day is still the finest and most beautiful example of a doorway that has been handed down to us from classical times.'[13] However, his time was predominantly spent recording Byzantine pieces, as can be seen in a photograph of him (seated) and Barnsley (standing), recording Byzantine sculpture in Athens (Figure 4.4).

Schultz spent substantial periods in Greece in 1888, 1889, and 1890. In 1891 he set up a practice on his own in London and, from that time on, his work on Byzantium was restricted to working on his drawings and photographs, and on the important publication with Sidney Barnsley, *The monastery of St Luke of Stiris in Phokis, and the dependent monastery of Saint Nicolas in the Fields, near Skripou in Boeotia* (London, 1901). He was instrumental in collecting and collating the drawings of the Arts and Crafts architects who worked in Greece, under the auspices of the Byzantine Research and Publication Fund (set up in 1908), and was (as noted in the catalogue) a member of the exhibitions committee that organized the show, 'British Archaeological Discoveries in Greece and Crete 1886–1936' at the Royal Academy of Arts in London in 1936. The materials produced by George, Schultz, and the other architects who worked at the school are now collected in the archive at Athens.[14] Among many Byzantine monuments that they visited, planned, photographed, and studied, Schultz and Barnsley made valuable records of St Demetrios at Thessaloniki (these, made on their visit about twenty years before the work of W. S. George, form a valuable supplementary dossier to his), and the monasteries of Hosios Lukas and Daphni.[15] Their drawings were made with great care and precision, and their black-and-white plate photography shows intense expertise in controlling the lighting—their draughtsmanship and photography sometimes make a poignant contrast with current, often more hurried, digital recording (Figure 4.5). This painstaking work, it is argued in this chapter, was a seminal influence on their subsequent methods of designing and building (and forms the background for some of Schultz's later resistance to the mechanical advances of the twentieth century).

After their return to England, Barnsley and Schultz enjoyed separate careers, but they remained in touch. Sidney Barnsley was immediately commissioned to build the Church of Holy Wisdom at Lower Kingswood, Surrey; begun in 1891, its simple neo-Byzantine form (it has some connections with

---

[13] R. W. Schultz and E. A. Gardner, 'The north doorway of the Erechtheum', *Journal of Hellenic Studies*, 12 (1891), pp. 1–16.
[14] See <www.bsa.ac.uk>, Byzantine Research Fund.
[15] The crucial relevance of their work for modern study is explored by Robin Cormack, 'Rediscovering the Christ Pantocrator at Daphni', *Journal of the Warburg and Courtauld Institutes*, 71 (2008), pp. 55–74.

Figure 4.4:   Recording Byzantine sculpture in Athens, 1890.

St Eirene in Constantinople) was rapidly finished and it was dedicated in 1892.[16] Barnsley soon moved to the Cotswolds and, in partnership with his brother, Ernest Barnsley, and Ernest Gimson, specialized in the design and production of Arts and Crafts furniture.[17]

---

[16] J. B. Bullen, *Byzantium rediscovered* (London, 2003), pp. 166–8.
[17] See Mary Greensted, *Gimson and the Barnsleys: 'wonderful furniture of a commonplace kind'* (London, 1980).

Figure 4.5: The interior of the monastery of Hosios Lukas at Stiris, Greece, looking west (between 1888 and 1890) (British School at Athens Archive: BRF-02.01.04.055).

It was in 1906 that Schultz was commissioned to prepare plans for a new Anglican cathedral in Khartoum.[18] The circumstances of this commission arose in the period after the death of General Charles George Gordon, governor-general of Sudan, in 1885, during the Mahdist revolt. A new Anglo-Egyptian

---

[18] The account of David Ottewill, 'Robert Weir Schultz (1860–1951)', pp. 88–115, esp. pp. 104–8, is an excellent narrative and analysis of the work at Khartoum (among other commissions) with

condominium was declared by Horatio Herbert Kitchener on 4 September 1898 (the state lasted till 1956). Lord Kitchener of Khartoum immediately built a new British colonial centre along the banks of the Nile, but was faced with the fact that the only building traditions were, as at Omdurman, mud brick structures, which looked far from imposing. To begin with, Kitchener wanted an impressive palace on the site of Gordon's final residence. He commissioned George Gorringe, an officer in the Royal Engineers, to undertake the work. Gorringe started by laying out the road system in 1899, and then we learn from his notes that: 'I cleared the site and then wrote to England for books on Italian and other architecture. These arrived in due course and with the help of plans, elevations and architectural details which they contained I designed the first and second floors, the staircases and verandas of the new palace, everything being submitted to and approved by Lord Kitchener. The designs for the original Government Offices were also prepared by me. As regards the portion of the Palace facing the river, the ground plan and the shape of the windows on the ground floor differed little from those of Gordon's Palace.'[19] The outcome was the largest building in Khartoum at the time—today the presidential palace of Omar al-Bashir. A critic described this building as 'a wedding-cake of a building in a pastiche Venetian style, no more familiar on the banks of the blue Nile than St Mark's would have been'.[20]

In contrast with the palace, the All Saints' Cathedral is a much more provocative and creative building. When the design was exhibited at the Royal Academy in 1909 (Figure 4.6), a reviewer in *The Builder's Journal* (8 May 1909) wrote—'A very curious piece of architecture, the style of which we presume is suggested by local associations. It is a long, low, solid building with transepts ... We cannot call it beautiful but it is an original and interesting one, like nothing else one has seen in the way of a church.'[21] A later comment took the view that: 'Khartoum Cathedral is an interesting piece of work, but we cannot describe it as other than an eccentric one, even for Mr R. Weir Schultz; possibly experiments such as this help to keep the art of architecture alive.'[22] *The Builder's Journal* wrote 'it has no reminiscence of any particular style'. Such comments underestimate the quality of the building and the commitment of the architect to design and achieve a building that established a new image of Christianity in an African context. The aim of the analysis here

---

the necessary documentation, though all the plans and specifications once kept at Khartoum have been lost.

[19] Qu. by M. W. Daly, *Empire on the Nile*, p. 26.

[20] M. W. Daly and Jane R. Hogan, *Images of empire: photographic sources for the British in the Sudan* (Leiden, 2005), p. 232.

[21] *The Builder's Journal*, 8 May 1909, p. 546.

[22] Qu. in Ottewill, 'Robert Weir Schultz (1860–1951)', p. 108.

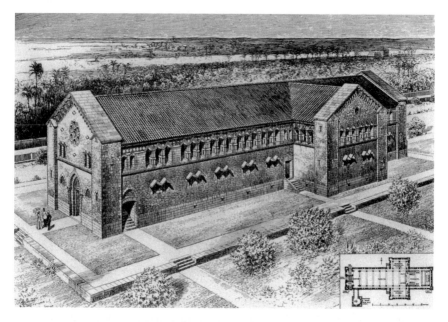

Figure 4.6: All Saints' Cathedral, Khartoum, as planned by Robert Weir Schultz in 1909.

is to show how the combination of Arts and Crafts thinking and Schultz's practical and conceptual knowledge of Byzantium led him to the formation of a building that can certainly be seen as a sort of hybrid in architectural terms, with plundered ideas from many sources, but which succeeds in creating a highly effective sacred structure for its special location and circumstances.

A site for the church was designated close to the palace where Governor-General Charles George Gordon was killed in 1885; the foundation stone was laid in 1904 by Princess Henry of Battenberg (Queen Victoria's daughter). Schultz gained the commission in February 1906, and by November his designs had been accepted (originally the church was intended for a congregation of three hundred but this was increased to six hundred). Schultz collected information about the soil conditions, local materials, and local customs, but he only visited the site twice, first in January 1907, when he stopped off at, studied, and sketched museums and buildings in Cairo and elsewhere in Egypt on the way south, and secondly for the consecration in 1912—the service was on 26 January, chosen as an anniversary of Gordon's death, though the church roof was still not, at the time, completed.

Schultz was able, on his journey out to Khartoum, to examine and draw the Coptic Christian and Islamic heritage of Cairo and other sites, but the early Christian architecture and decoration of medieval Nubia, which was only effectively discovered by the excavations at Faras and Dongola as part of the UNESCO rescue mission of the 1960s, before the building of the Aswan High Dam, was a closed book to him at that time.[23] For Schultz, the heritage of Christianity in the region would have been the non-Orthodox Coptic church rather than the Nubian church. In any case the most predictable form for such an Anglican church to take at this time was surely Victorian Gothic (as in the case of St Paul's Anglican church at Athens of 1843), and Schultz might well have been tempted to take as his model Lethaby's Arts and Crafts version of Gothic in his Church of All Saints at Brockhampton (between Hereford and Ross-on-Wye) of 1900–01. But Schultz produced something quite unexpected, less so in the plan but more in its articulation and details. Like Brockhampton, it was a transept basilica. His concept reflects his careful questioning about the site and the local factors, and takes the answers into account: the proximity of the Nile signalled the danger of regular flooding, so he planned deep foundations and a raised platform. As for the side doors, their function was to give extra ways of access during the frequent sandstorms of northern Sudan, which came from either the north or the south.[24] Yet his solution more significantly mirrors the design of the Byzantine church that he had so carefully recorded in his time in Greece: the model is the sixth-century Church of St Demetrios at Thessaloniki (Figure 4.7). This evocation of an early Christian church in Greece gives the clue to the intellectual concept of Khartoum Cathedral. The Anglican community at Khartoum is visually

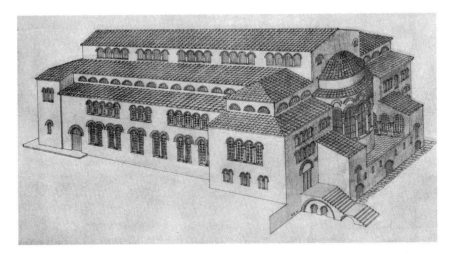

Figure 4.7: The Church of St Demetrios, Thessaloniki, as reconstructed from the drawings of R. W. Schultz and W. S. George (British School at Athens Archive).

[23] W. Y. Adams, *Nubia: corridor to Africa* (London, 1977).
[24] Robert W. S. Weir (as signed) gives his own account of the building history in *The Builder's Journal*, 19 May 1916, pp. 371–3.

transported not to the medieval Gothic past of England, but to the world of primitive Christianity. The church, through its architecture, celebrates the early and universal Christian church.

This interpretation of the design can be enhanced by considering further aspects of the architecture, the decorative details, and their sources. Schultz, in his 1916 description of the church, explains how he handled the local conditions of materials and workers. At the same time, the Arts and Crafts nature of the furniture and fittings takes us back to a period of individual craftsmanship and truth to materials. In order to investigate the original interior of the church, some further information is necessary about its development.

The building today is no longer in use as a church. The progress of its construction was slow, as the funding came predominantly from subscriptions and donations. In fact, the bell tower and its integral baptistery on the south side was designed in 1913 but only built and completed in 1931. After an attempted coup in Khartoum against the president in July 1971, the church was closed down and all public access to it was forbidden, due to its proximity to the palace. The tower was demolished, leaving only the stone font incongruously in place (Figure 4.8). Happily, however, the building is now regularly open to the public, and is well maintained, through its secular use as the Museum of Sudanese History. A memorial plaque remains at the west end:

Figure 4.8:   All Saints' Cathedral, south façade.

'In memory of Robert Weir Schultz Weir Architect of this Cathedral died 29th April 1951 aged 90 years.' Nevertheless, many of the original portable liturgical fittings and fixtures are absent. They have been removed. It transpires, however, that they are not lost. They have been transferred to a new Anglican All Saints' Cathedral in a less central part of Khartoum. This new building, with a brutal concrete shell construction, would no doubt have been architectural anathema to Schultz (Figure 4.9). But it has at least preserved and continues to use his furniture, and its façade takes over the triangular gables of the first cathedral. Its foundation stone was laid on 27 May 1979. The furniture from the previous cathedral was installed in the chancel area (Figure 4.10) and elsewhere (such as the small portable font near the west door).

In building the cathedral Schultz was highly sensitive to the climate and position in the design, but he records in his 1916 publication how he also took into account the local factors of materials and labour. Timber was a commodity in short supply, and the best source of masonry was the quarry of local sandstone at Gebel Auli, a hill about twenty miles up the White Nile. The only skilled labour in Khartoum was Italian and Greek (Figure 4.11), and both male and female unskilled Sudanese workers handled the heavy work (Figures 4.12 and 4.13). Hence the highly conscious choice of simplicity

Figure 4.9: West façade of the new Anglican All Saints' Cathedral, Khartoum, 1979.

Figure 4.10:   Chancel of the new Anglican All Saints' Cathedral, Khartoum, January 2009.

for the structure and for the articulation of the features, shown most conspicuously in the plain triangular gables for the windows. The rubble walls are
massively thick and in the tropical sunlight the windows are small, deep, and
dark-glazed, all in the attempt to achieve a cool interior. The double roof uses
precast concrete. The window frames are made of steel and were manufactured in London. The organ was manufactured by Walker of London. The
stained glass was made by Miss Mabel Esplin (1874–1921) of Hampstead.[25]
The doors and chancel screen are teak, and the other furniture is made of
unpolished Cuban mahogany. The whole operation on site was managed by a
master mason, John Latimer from Dumfries, who went out in December 1906
(he was assisted by Captain Done RE, director of military works in the Sudan,
though this was apparently not an easy partnership).

   While it is appropriate to emphasize the attention given to the site and
local circumstances, at the same time Schultz made a series of intellectual
choices that reveal his complex use of the past in the conception of the church.

[25] An exhibition and catalogue at the William Morris Gallery, London, in 1985–6, *Women stained
glass artists of the Arts and Crafts movement*, included the drawings by Mabel Esplin and Joan
Fulleylove for Khartoum Cathedral.

Figure 4.11: Construction of the nave windows, seen from interior, with skilled workers, lantern slide (RIBA Library Drawings and Archives Collections: LAN 449).

Figure 4.12: Construction of chancel windows with local Sudanese workers carrying formed stonework up a ramp, lantern slide (RIBA Library Drawings and Archives Collections: LAN 447).

Cumulatively, they contributed towards the genesis of a colonial monument of its time and period.

A first example of his adaptation to circumstances in a deliberate way is his handling of the local materials. The sandstone was of two colours, yellow

Figure 4.13: Transport of masonry with local Sudanese worker, lantern slide (RIBA Library Drawings and Archives Collections: LAN 446).

and pale red, and the blocks are laid in alternating patterns; these contrasts were used to great effect in the ribs of the arches inside the church. Colour is used in the same way in the arches of the Church of St Demetrios at Thessaloniki and also in the Islamic monuments of Cairo. The thick walls have a plain dressing on the interior side, but on the exterior the stone is laid as rubble, yet in a way that conspicuously evokes the Cyclopean walls of Mycenaean sites in Greece (Figure 4.14). The patterned piercing of the windows reflect Byzantine designs, but as mediated by the Coptic and Egyptian Arabic architecture of Cairo. The roof is covered with red Roman tiles, like the Byzantine churches of Greece. However, the triangular window gables would seem to derive from the Anglo-Saxon churches of England, though they can be found also in Greece and Egypt. The monogram over the west door is one regularly found in Byzantine churches: 'Jesus Christ Conquers' (*Iesos Christos Nika*). The interior vaults are not pointed Gothic vaults but made in the Byzantine scheme described by Choisy in his book of 1883, and observed in Greece by Schultz. The method economizes on the use of wood by building without elaborate centring. The great west window—from the interior—gives the impression of an English rose window (Figure 4.15). The stone openwork design is an extraordinary combination of Gothic tracery and Byzantine or Coptic forms. The interlocking ribs and inverted arches of

Figure 4.14:   West façade of All Saints' Cathedral, Khartoum.

Robin Cormack

Figure 4.15: Interior of All Saints' Cathedral, Khartoum, towards the west.

the great west archway (above the Latin dedication of the church to All Saints) are (at least in concept) reminiscent of more luxuriant English models, such as Wells Cathedral. For Ottewill 'it is as though Coptic and Gothic forms intersect'.[26] The memorial chapel to Gordon is spacious and light. In the tradition of classical monuments in Greece and Italy, the dedication is in large bronze capital letters. Some letters have been lost but the dedication can still be read (and was recorded by Schultz in 1916):

> PRAISE GOD FOR
> CHARLES GEORGE GORDON
> SERVANT OF JESUS CHRIST
> WHOSE LABOUR WAS NOT IN VAIN.
> IN THE LORD.

By chance, today the museum holds Gordon's own upright piano, next to the ornate Arts and Crafts organ, and inside a simple high wooden screen with square and diagonal frames, which is perhaps a genuflection to Arabic woodwork in Egypt. The stone decoration of the chancel is in low relief, with reflections of the eleventh-century style and motifs of the architectural decoration

---

[26] Ottewill, 'Robert Weir Schultz (1860–1951)', p. 107.

of Hosios Lukas. The nave of the church in 1912 had moveable chairs and not pews, and in this respect is like a Byzantine church. A bank of chairs in the chancel for the clergy were made partly of stone, partly of wood.

The photographic record of the opening on 26 January 1912 records the state of the church outside (Figure 4.16) and inside (Figure 4.17). The west front and roof were unfinished, and much of the interior furniture had yet to be made. The governor-general, Sir Reginald Wingate, had been one of the prime movers for the necessity of a conspicuous Anglican Christian emblem in Khartoum, and ensured that the consecration was a major event. The proceedings are described in a contemporary account:

> Just before 9-30 we heard the National Anthem being played outside, and the Governor-General entered and walked up the central aisle to his special seat in the chancel, being preceded thither by the two churchwardens, Sun and Fleming. These happened to be judges, and as judges they were wearing their levee uniform, which consists of knee-breeches, silk stockings, lace ruff and cut-away coat, with a legal gown overall. These and other uniforms lent a certain dramatic or even theatrical aspect to the scene ... The ceremony was impressive and went without a hitch, having been carefully rehearsed beforehand.[27]

Inside, the bishop of London delivered the sermon, invoking the memory of Gordon and his service. *The Times* weekly edition of 2 February 1912 wrote

Figure 4.16: The unfinished west façade of All Saints' Cathedral at the consecration in 1912, with the entry of the governor-general (RIBA Library Drawings and Archives Collections: Album: A 310/11).

---

[27] Diary of H. C. Bowman, 1 Feb. 1912 (Middle East Centre, St Antony's College, Oxford); qu. by M. W. Daly, *Empire on the Nile*, pp. 98–9.

Figure 4.17:   The interior of All Saints' Cathedral during the consecration in 1912, looking east (RIBA Library Drawings and Archives Collections: Album: A310/29).

that 'it was of Gordon chiefly that men were thinking ... of him men will always think when they see the Cathedral at Khartoum'.[28] The instant reaction of *The Illustrated London News* was that the church was 'in the Byzantine and also the Gothic manner', while the *Church Times* wrote that it was 'a more than usually beautiful building'.[29]

Reconsidering the church not so much as a memorial to Gordon, but as visual evidence of the British attempt to make a symbolic spiritual impact in the desert environment of Sudan, what at first sight might seem to be a medley of influences and sources is on analysis more profound. A piece-by-piece examination gradually reveals a consistent programme of the re-creation of the forms and methods of church design and building from the early period of Christianity. What was also quite distinctive in the cathedral was the homogeneity and elegance of the furnishing and fittings in wood. Some of these (such as the organ facing, the simple rood screen, and doors) remain in situ. But to understand the full picture means investigating the pieces in the new cathedral.

[28] Quoted by Daly, *Empire on the Nile*, p. 99.
[29] *Church Times*, 27 Jan. 1912, p. 115.

Schultz had insisted, on accepting the commission, that he was to design all the furniture and all other fixtures and fittings.[30] He decided it was out of the question for this furniture to be made in Sudan and he commissioned the carpentry from Ernest Gimson and the Barnsleys at Sapperton in the Cotswolds, choosing the two woods that he thought would survive best in the dry heat of Khartoum. Everything was made in England and then shipped out. The west doors were made by Sidney Barnsley. In designing the furniture to fit the simple forms and designs of the architecture, he succeeded in producing a remarkable synergy of the Arts and Crafts movement and Byzantium. A comparison of the forms of the chairs and desks and the use of a domical canopy (Figure 4.10), along with his photographs of the monastery of Hosios Lukas in the late nineteenth century (Figure. 4.5), and with his drawings of the furniture, which in his time were in the eleventh-century Byzantine Church of St Theodore at Athens (Figure 4.18), reveals the connections with Greek Orthodoxy.

An idea of how the designer Schulz and the craftsman Gimson worked together and stimulated each other in reaching the final appearance of this furniture is best illustrated in an exchange of letters about the priest's desk for the memorial chapel of General Gordon (Figure 4.19). When Ernest Gimson received the drawings (which are dated 1913), he objected to the simplicity of the woodwork and wrote down his reactions and solution (28 October 1913): 'Don't you want some little tops to the uprights? It hardly looks constructional to leave so little wood (and end grain too) above the tenons of the rails.'[31] Schultz accepted this refinement, both on this piece and on the rest of the furniture. It is these 'little tops' that have become one of the defining hallmarks of this set of carpentry for the cathedral. And it is this feature that confirms the identification of the Arts and Crafts furniture in the new Cathedral of Khartoum as the original set from the previous cathedral (Figure 4.20).

The argument of this chapter has been that the Anglican All Saints' Cathedral at Khartoum is only to be understood through considering the career of the particular architect who is identified with its conception. Schultz, through this prominent building close to the Nile, had a formidable and distinctive role in the development of Khartoum. The cathedral cannot be treated as simply an eccentric document of its period. It is of exceptional importance in illuminating the colonial mentality. Without looking at the special experience of Robert Weir Schultz and of the other architects who explored the medieval monuments of Greece at the beginning of their careers, the Anglican cathedral at Khartoum would be an enigma. But through comparisons with the monuments and philosophy that inspired its features, it becomes possible to unravel its meanings.

---

[30] Ottewill, 'Robert Weir Schultz (1860–1951)', p. 106.
[31] Documented by Ottewill, 'Robert Weir Schultz (1860–1951)', pp. 106–7 and n. 119.

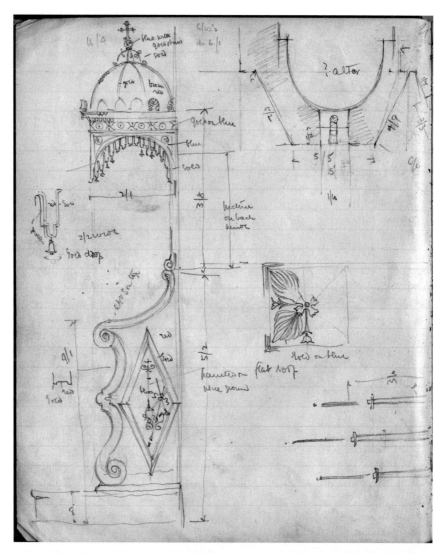

Figure 4.18: Church furniture in St Theodore, Athens, recorded by Schultz (British School at Athens Archive: R. W. Schultz, notebook 5, p. 5).

What underpins this philosophy is the influential teaching of Lethaby. This influence emerges very clearly in the writings and lectures of Schultz throughout the course of his life. Already, in 1897, he wrote a reflective article on the ways in which Byzantine art and architecture were relevant to modern architecture:[32] 'the main lessons to be learned from the Byzantines are on the

[32] Schultz, *Architectural Review*, 1 (1897), pp. 192–9 and 248–55; see also Ottewill, 'Robert Weir Schultz (1860–1951)', p. 91.

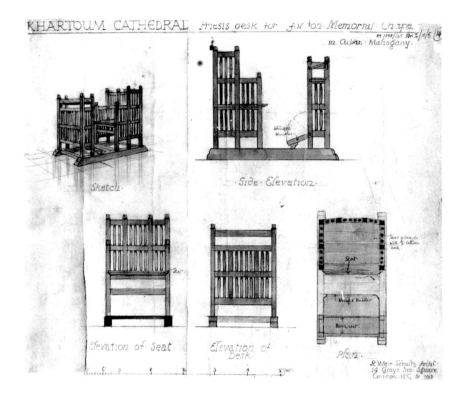

Figure 4.19: Design by R. W. Schultz for a priest's desk in the memorial chapel for General Gordon (RIBA Library Drawings and Archives Collections: PA 1093/5 (14)).

structural side, their straightforward building methods, their grappling with great problems of construction, their legitimate and economic use of materials both in a structural and decorative sense'. The point is made clear in this same article that what Schultz had taken from the study of Byzantine architecture was to emulate their methods, not their forms. If these principles are borne in mind in front of the cathedral at Khartoum, no observer would interpret it as a neo-Byzantine church (though Schultz's contributions to St Andrew's Chapel (1912–16) in Bentley's Westminster Cathedral at London shows his knowledge of Byzantium more directly). Yet it is implicitly 'Byzantine' in its ground plan, some of its forms, and in its method of construction.

The plaque that remains in the church in memory of Schultz is an essential pointer to the character of the architect and of the church itself. In the years from 1888 to 1890 Schultz was immersed in the recording of Greek monuments. He has left a photographic record of himself in these years: on one occasion he is seen studying Byzantine sculpture (Figure 4.4) but in another he is seen going native, dressed as a Greek monk with beads and

Figure 4.20:   Priest's desk in the new All Saints' Cathedral, Khartoum.

without shoes, a clear indication of his absorption with the image of medieval Greece (Figure 4.21). Just as Schultz immersed himself in Byzantine Greece and its values, so his cathedral in Khartoum can be read as a progressive adaptation of traditional architectural values in the creation of a modern building. Schultz was no mere reactionary, though his writings did not show much enthusiasm for the changing methods of educating architects in his life-time. This church does not export British norms of design to the empire, nor is it in any local Sudan tradition, though its features respond to Sudanese climate and its structure consists, in the main, of local materials. The pre-dominant details refer to the Christian architecture and decorations of Greece, but they are transformed into something far beyond their Byzantine origins, and with the Cyclopean walls the church declares its connections with ancient Greece. Its congregation of six hundred Anglicans would have found enough familiar features to remind them of faraway English Gothic but at the same time without forgetting that they were nearer to the sources of Christianity in Khartoum. This primitive Christian inheritance was underlined by the refer-ences in the architectural forms to early Anglo-Saxon church architecture and its contemporary expression in Coptic Egypt, later to evolve into the Arabic forms of medieval and modern Cairo.

Figure 4.21: Robert Weir Schultz as a monk, Art Workers Guild Album, *c.*1890.

The cathedral at Khartoum is a provocative case study for any debate on colonialism and hybridity. The role of the architect Robert Weir Schultz can be seen in two separate, but interlocking, stages. In his period of work in Greece he was committed to the recording of ancient and Byzantine remains, and this work was done with great accuracy so that his drawings, plans, notes, and photographs in the archive at the British School at Athens remain a fruitful resource for researchers into the antiquities of Greece, often giving vital evidence about subsequently lost monuments. The next stage of his activity as a distinctively committed Arts and Crafts architect developed in subtle ways out of his experience in Greece, and offers a quite different perspective for study. It is his commission in Sudan, which demonstrates how a significant merging of these two superficially disparate elements was possible. As a consequence of his various decisions in designing and building the cathedral, which can be precisely documented, the work of Schultz in this case offers an instructive example of cultural syncretism.

Clearly, such a building had never been seen in Sudan before. But, equally clearly, it cannot be matched in England either. The building materials were local, yet the exterior appearance of the building owes little to Sudanese heritage and more to a complex amalgam of evocative sources from several countries, several dating from the early Christian period. The fittings were made in England and imported wholesale; they reflect contemporary Arts and Crafts taste, yet their appearance owes as much to Greece as to Britain. In one sense the outcome of all these circumstances is a monument that appears to belong nowhere. This investigation has argued that, on the contrary, it was particularly eloquent as the first Anglican cathedral in an area of the world where Christianity started. In one sense it can be regarded as a 'Sudanese' monument, but only in a conceptual sense. It has been possible to identify some of the specific connections between the monument and the British, Greek, and Egyptian forms and ideas that it has adopted. However, these visual connections mask the underlying assumptions that influenced the creative choices of the architect, consciously or unconsciously. What has been emphasized so far are its religious antecedents. But the cultures from which the various features were chosen had other associations. Byzantium, as the successor to the Roman empire in the east, had a pedigree as a long-lasting and successful regime because of the decision of Constantine the Great to embrace Christianity. To see the church as Byzantine in form is to evoke successful empire, to see the masonry as Greek is to evoke the cultural origins of Europe, and to see the Coptic elements is to evoke the power and antiquity of Egypt. In this respect, the English Arts and Crafts elements of the church act in their turn to coordinate all these diverse sources into an integrated symbol, which can be read as an affirmation of the British imperial achievement in the unification of the past and present.

Part III

The Biblical World

If the classical world provided one of the crucial models for British imperial expansion, the biblical world provided one of its crucial motors. Much attention has rightly been paid to the entangling of Christianity and commerce in what Krishan Kumar has called the 'missionary nationalism' of the British: the impulse to spread British values abroad that made the British imperial enterprise so forceful and ambitious. Just as the governing classes held the classics to be part of their own patrimony, and thus the classical world in some metaphorical sense at least part of their own territory, so they held the Bible even more firmly to be part of their own patrimony, and the Holy Land their land.

However, just as we have seen in the British imperial encounter with the classical world, the imperial encounter with the actual land of the Bible generated all kinds of strange ambivalences. Again hubris was one response—the modern empire could do the work of ancient empires, but better, and more durably, especially as the British saw themselves in the Holy Land as the greatly superior successors to a more recent empire in decline, the Ottoman. But another response, again, was reverence. There was an even greater tradition of longing for the places of the Holy Land than there had been for the monuments of antiquity, and a tradition too, at least since the Crusades, of considering Western Christianity as the natural custodian of those places. While this attitude could entail disdain for competing heritages—pharaonic or Islamic—and it could impose a ludicrously Western Christian idealization upon Eastern Christian and Jewish sites, it could also engender a positively Ruskinian tenderness for local particularity and in-situ preservation that tempered the rage for possession. And that tenderness could, in turn, be exploited—at the end of our period—by Arab and other nationalists, arguing that, in fact, the Holy Land was their land after all.

Part III

The Biblical World

5

Unholy Water:
Archaeology, the Bible, and the
First Aswan Dam

DAVID GANGE

THE FIRST ASWAN DAM was the largest and most controversial civil enterprise of the early years of the British mandate in Egypt. Indeed, after the initial military intervention in 1882, General Gordon's foolhardy expedition to hold Khartoum was the only Egyptian affair to surpass the dam in terms of British press coverage. While endowing Egypt with a constant supply of water from the Nile and the increased agricultural potential this implied, the first two stages of the dam (1902 and 1912) destroyed or endangered hundreds of monuments and eradicated many of the age-old rhythms of the Egyptian year.

This colossal project took thirty years to plan, build, and undergo its first round of corrections, between 1882 and the early 1910s. Because of this the dam was completed in a substantially different political and cultural environment from that in which it had been conceived. International relations, British imperial attitudes, Egyptian involvement in the politics of empire, and archaeological practice in Egypt had all changed dramatically. Interpretations of the relationship between past and present had altered and with them the priorities of preservation: new answers had been found to several old questions. Attitudes changed, for instance, to what kinds of material artefacts were worth preserving from the onrush of the new reservoir; to the identities of those who were qualified and politically appropriate custodians of this material heritage; to the resources and techniques that they should seek to deploy.

The extended, ideologically charged debates over this dam are revealing with regard to several issues in political, imperial, and cultural history; they show British administrators at their most able—and determined—to act without cooperation from their French and Egyptian counterparts (French and Egyptian control of the departments responsible for roads and public buildings, for instance, would have made the kinds of activity that surrounded the dam impossible). Within British and Anglo-Egyptian society, this was one of

Proceedings of the British Academy, **187**, 93–114. © The British Academy 2013.

the few endeavours that pushed the interests of those who studied early Egypt—geologists, archaeologists, anthropologists, Egyptologists, ancient historians, and (equally importantly) theologians—into unavoidable contact with the designs of administrators, politicians, engineers, and lawyers. It was one of the few events in which nineteenth-century Egyptology was made 'imperial' in that term's most domineering sense. If orientalism on the Saidian model is a helpful way of interpreting this period's readings of the Egyptian past, then it will be here that it might operate most successfully, since this reservoir forced British Egyptologists as well as engineers to act on explicit value judgements made over Egypt's past and present.

Other important strands of this story will be the developments that place the period between 1880 and 1910 among the most dramatic in the history of Egyptology. The first histories of Egypt to make extensive use of hieroglyphs were only just beginning to enter circulation in the early 1880s.[1] Only very gradually over the following decades did some of these handbooks become the first to relegate classical and biblical sources (and often their associated teleologies) to subsidiary roles. By the early 1880s the last generation to be sceptical about the usefulness and scope of hieroglyphs had finally left the field. In association with this, an extraordinary range of new Egyptological techniques and approaches were being developed, including those associated with Flinders Petrie and, a little later, George Reisner. Until this point one of the principal reasons for the disregard of small artefacts by Egyptologists was that they could only be placed in chronological order on the basis of relative sophistication. Since assumptions of Egyptian decline from sophisticated biblical beginnings had great scholarly support, many argued that the most highly developed items must come from the most remote periods of the civilization. The result was that some scholars dated Egyptian artefacts in a sequence that was almost the exact reverse of that favoured by others. Artefacts, many mid-century scholars argued, were more or less useless historical witnesses unless they bore datable inscriptions. Until a trajectory of Egyptian history could be substantively agreed on, as began to happen in the late 1890s, few conclusions could be drawn from this kind of evidence.

Agreement on such a historical trajectory was only possible once Egyptian prehistory had finally been widely accepted, and techniques developed for its study: recognition of this was the single essential key to rapid development in Egyptological science. The area flooded by the Aswan Dam was among the most fruitful potential sites for the study of this new aspect of archaeology in

[1] An extreme illustration of this would be comparison of Petrie's *History of ancient Egypt*, published in four volumes during the 1880s, with George Rawlinson's 1870s two-volume *History of ancient Egypt*: in terms of linguistic content most of Rawlinson's work could have been written in the 1830s, while Petrie's is easily datable as a product of the fin de siècle.

Egypt. When water actually deluged a large swathe of Upper Egypt in 1902, the remains that many experts most lamented the loss of were types of early evidence that had been utterly unimagined by the original exponents of the plan less than two decades earlier. When plans for the dam's expansion were drawn up, a diverse array of scholars was driven by this regret to produce a large-scale salvage operation for early human remains under the auspice of the first Archaeological Survey of Nubia. In fact, the accelerated archaeological endeavour of the years running up to the second Nubian deluge would be instrumental in developing understandings of Egyptian and Nubian prehistory: they would bring anthropologists, including Grafton Elliot Smith, into the field alongside a sophisticated new breed of Egyptologists headed by Reisner. This would amount to a significant expansion of the expertise, approaches, and ideological range of those active in interpreting the deep Egyptian past.[2] By this point British and American Egyptology was approaching a state in which it could, for the first time, be called a 'discipline'; it now had a university presence and, thanks to Petrie, the beginnings of a pedagogic system. It was no longer the loose alliance it had been in the 1870s, between a few scholars with very different interests whose expertise in ancient languages was largely confined to Greek and Hebrew.

However, it should not be assumed that this series of expansive disciplinary developments amounted to the eradication of ideological domination over either Egyptology or the Aswan Dam project. In fact, from 1880 until well after the turn of the century it was these ideologies that most inextricably entwined archaeology and engineering: teleological schemes were universal, their primary purpose being to draw public support to expensive preservation or engineering concerns. The divergent ways in which these teleologies were conceived reveals much about the different preservation priorities of the various interest groups involved, and shows both where preservation united scholars and administrators, and where it caused friction amongst them. There was rarely any simple choice between 'progress' and 'preservation' here: except for one or two extreme cases no actors in this process were willing to say that the reputation of British rule in Egypt rested exclusively on either the infrastructural development that could revitalize the economy or the paternalist custodianship of Egyptian history.

In the usual style of the British empire, engineers and administrators gave the Aswan Dam a grand historical pedigree, and fitted it into a narrative of history that began in the Old Testament. Joseph, it was argued, had been the first incomer to Egypt to use hydraulic expertise to revolutionize the nation's

---

[2] The output of this unprecedentedly large project began with H. G. Lyons, G. E. Smith, and F. W. Jones, *The archaeological survey of Nubia, report for 1907–8*, ed. G. A. Reisner (2 vols., Cairo, 1910); post-1909–10 volumes ed. C. M. Firth.

agriculture. Some even argued that the pyramids had been built by Joseph to store water in times of drought, and had been set in verdant gardens watered by sophisticated irrigation technologies.[3] British engineers were lionized as latter-day echoes of Joseph and should, administrators such as the American lawyer Francis Cope Whitehouse argued, attempt to re-create aspects of the system that he, with divine guidance, had developed. Even after the turn of the century many, including Sir William Willcocks, who had been among the leading civil engineers on the dam and one of the most influential players in the project, looked at the modern Bible lands and asked where their ancient prosperity had gone.[4] Where was the glorious city of Ur, home of Abraham? The answer he gave was that the rivers on which these cities' trade throve had changed their levels or courses, forcing catastrophic decline. The damming of the Nile, or alternatively the exact re-creation of 'Joseph's' waterworks further north, was therefore seen as the first step in a much more expansive project that would include restoring the Tigris and Euphrates to their biblical trajectories, then overseeing the construction of a glorious new Ur that would be both a European pleasure resort and the focal point of revitalized trade in the regions damaged by the messy retreat of the Ottoman empire.[5] It is quite astonishing that these figures dreamt up these wild schemes at the same time as they ridiculed the regime that had governed Egypt under Ismail in the 1860s and '70s for its naive willingness to spend extravagantly on speculative schemes.

It is important that the widespread biblical mania over this project is not seen as a mere justification for a scheme that saw the British empire at its most brashly interventionist, but is recognized as crucial to what this event, and indeed that empire, was. It was reality not smokescreen, and an underlying assumption, not a superficial explanatory gloss. In a nation and empire increasingly diverse and increasingly divided, biblical themes were a powerful common resource of Protestant culture, uniting millions across the globe in the same intellectual and demonstrative traditions. Historical interest in Egypt was rarely a simple product of empire, but more often a product of religion, which empire began to amplify and embellish with new providential twists.

---

[3] Francis Cope Whitehouse, 'The Raian Moeris; or storage reservoir of Middle Egypt', *Proceedings of the Royal Geographical Society*, 9 (1887), pp. 608–13; see also Margaret S. Drower, *Flinders Petrie: a life in archaeology* (London, 1985), p. 60.
[4] W. Willcocks, *The restoration of the ancient irrigation works on the Tigris, or the re-creation of Chaldea* (London, 1903).
[5] The most explicit expositions of this theme were penned in the 1910s, at which point diffusionist ideas regarding the migrations of racial groups—many of which harked back to the dispersion of the sons of Noah in Genesis 10—were gaining influence within archaeology and ancient history-writing.

The figures who will be explored in this chapter even attempted, heavy-handedly, to universalize the Bible's earliest books by making them into a resource shared with the Egyptian people. It was emphasized repeatedly that the engineering works of Joseph could be identified through the preservation of their names in Arabic tradition. Using the local knowledge of villagers in Middle and Lower Egypt was seen as the key to drawing on the inspired knowledge of this Islamic prophet and Christian patriarch. So *The Illustrated London News* presents explorers and engineers soaking up information, as their Egyptian guides gesticulate at each sacred puddle, rivulet, or landmark.[6] This was hardly the 'peasant studies' agenda of the 1930s, explored by Timothy Mitchell, but, in constructing the idea of a powerful *fellah* folk memory, it did undercut other tropes of this period that denied the 'authenticity' and historical pedigree of the Egyptian people.[7]

One of the most significant constants that shaped these providential schemes was the idea of long decline stretching across the pre-classical world. Human prehistory in Europe had been widely recognized by the early 1860s, and this caused an enormous increase in the use of Egypt's distinctly different historical trajectory as evidence against the linear rise of civilization from barbarism. In the 1880s Egypt was regarded in some circles as one of the only plausible sources of evidence against Palaeolithic man and, as anthropologists and palaeontologists such as Richard Owen complained, it was widely employed in this context.[8] But the recognition of Egyptian prehistory in the late 1890s substantially reduced the scope for some forms of providential reading of the civilization. Gradually, the historical framework in which projects like the Aswan Dam were conceived shifted from models featuring patriarchs such as Joseph towards schemes of anthropological diffusion, and also towards intensified competition with France, enflamed by Pierre Loti's vitriolic prose poem *La Mort de Philae*. Right at the end of the period covered in this chapter, the rhetoric used by Egyptologists, historical scholars, and administrators begins to shift from preservation or restoration of 'our biblical heritage' to preservation of the evidence necessary to reconstruct the racial history of mankind. Where, in 1882, providential, romantic, and anthropological concerns had all centred on temples like Philae, and employed much the same rhetoric, a great deal of attention was now focused on the vast numbers of human remains lying buried in the ancient cemeteries of Nubia, and used entirely different language. Diffusionism and eugenic readings of the

---

[6] See also Cope Whitehouse, 'Projected restoration of the Raian Moeris and the province, lake and canals ascribed to the patriarch Joseph', *Proceedings of the Royal Geographical Society*, 11 (1885), pp. 756–8.

[7] Timothy Mitchell, *Rule of experts* (Berkeley, CA, 2002), pp. 123–52.

[8] Owen's comments are recorded in Edward William Lane, *The genesis of earth and of man* (2nd edn., London, 1860), editor's preface to second edition, p. v.

'revolutions of civilization' both gathered momentum. But feelings of biblical destiny didn't disappear; they coalesced into increasingly racialized
schemes of the kind that would culminate in the Balfour Declaration of 1917.

The starting point for this chapter is a meeting at The Avenue, 76 Fulham
Rd, London: the home of the artist Edward Poynter. On 4 August 1888 many
of the dramatis personae of this chapter were gathered there at Poynter's
request. The Egyptological community was represented by Flinders Petrie
and Wallis Budge; the colonial administration furnished Colonel Ardagh, Sir
Colin Campbell, and General Donnelly; the artistic establishment supplied
Sir Frederick Burton, Henry Wallis, Lawrence Alma-Tadema, Frank Dillon,
Thomas Armstrong, and Poynter himself; Cecil Torr, folklorist and historian
of early Greece, was also present.[9] The occasion was the inaugural meeting of
the Society for the Preservation of the Monuments of Ancient Egypt
(SPMAE), and its start was not auspicious.[10]

In the face of the threat posed to Egyptian monuments by ambitions to
overhaul Egyptian agriculture and commerce, Wallis and Poynter had spent
the summer of 1888 mobilizing all their connections in politics, archaeology,
engineering, architecture, and the arts. They aimed to establish a body that
could deal with the immediate threat of reservoir-building, but that would
outlive this campaign to promote the cause of ancient Egypt's crumbling
monuments more generally. The aim was to raise funds from the British public, which would then be channelled via the Egyptian government to those
who could carry out preservation work on temple structures and tombs. 'If,'
the Society warned a patriotic public, 'when the last British Regiment has
quitted the Port of Alexandria it is found that the temples and tombs, which
hold the records of long succeeding dynasties, have become through our
neglect little more than heaps of shapeless ruins, there can be no question
respecting what will then be the righteous judgement of indignant Europe.'[11]
This body was initially envisaged as a fundraising adjunct to the Egypt
Exploration Fund (EEF), Britain's major organization for archaeology in

---

[9] London, Egypt Exploration Society (EES) Archive, Box VIII item 1, 'Revised circular:
statements, prospects of the committee', 8 Aug. 1888; this cast list was soon augmented into a
working committee by the addition of artists Frederick Leighton and W. J. Loftie, and historical
scholars Austen Henry Layard, Edward Maunde Thompson, Peter le Page Renouf, and Reginald
Stuart Poole. Amelia Edwards, Archibald Henry Sayce, John William Waterhouse, G. F. Watts,
and William Holman Hunt were successfully brought on board as members. Attempts to secure
the support of John Ruskin, a member of the EEF, were not successful.
[10] All the archival material relating to this organization is housed within the archive of the Egypt
Exploration Society, where it was deposited after the SPMAE's demise. Other than this, sparse
material on the organization can be found through archival material relating to Poynter and to
Robert Cecil (Lord Salisbury) who provided the Society's principal political link.
[11] EES, 'Revised circular', VIII.1.

Egypt, which was well represented among those invited on to the new Society's committee.

However, by the time the Society's inaugural meeting took place Wallis and Poynter had each developed very different ideas about what preservation was and how it might be achieved. Wallis, enamoured by the unprecedented popularity of contemporary Egyptology, felt archaeologists like Petrie to be the new Society's most important constituency. He hoped that the British Museum might gain artefacts in return for the Society's munificence. Poynter had begun to worry that it was archaeologists from whom the temples of Egypt needed protection. Realizing the influence of Egyptologists among the proposed committee of the Society, Poynter covertly invited an American lawyer who shared his suspicion of archaeologists: Francis Cope Whitehouse. Cope Whitehouse had, in fact, spent much of the previous five years collating a study of the engineering knowledge of the ancient Egyptians: those five years had seen his once amicable relationship with Egyptologists substantially sour.

Poynter's attempt to gain Cope Whitehouse as an ally roused greater irritation from Wallis than Poynter had foreseen; as the meeting opened, a minor diplomatic incident took place, in which Wallis forcibly prevented Cope Whitehouse's entry. After a brief scuffle, the American skulked off into the London night, protesting that he had never witnessed such 'disregard of the normal social laws'.[12] The fallout, in correspondence between several of the actors, continued for several days.[13] During this process Cope Whitehouse recorded his opinion of those present:

> I am heartily with your *words*, but how about the *deeds* of some of your number. The appeal to *protect* ancient monuments scarcely comes with a good grace from those who are asking money to *rob* the valuable stones of Bubastis, and appealing on the grounds that their excavations have been so conducted as to threaten with destruction monuments which have survived the ages since the Exodus ... Schweinfurth told me that Virchow had said to him that the horrors of Königgratz had not prepared him for the revolting sight of Petrie's mangled remains of Hawara.[14]

Poynter's Society, Cope Whitehouse feared, would become a cloak to hide Petrie's nefarious dealings: 'When the wolves propose to preserve the sheep it is the duty of anyone who knows what is under the sheep's clothing to call

---

[12] Cope Whitehouse to Poynter, 5 Aug. 1888, EES, VIII.a.7.

[13] Cope Whitehouse to Poynter, EES VIIIa.7 offers one of several descriptions of the event, revealing that Wallis had already instructed Poynter's attendants to refuse Cope Whitehouse entry to the building, despite his military escort—Sir Charles Cookson and Commander Chadwick, 'Naval attaché to the US legation'.

[14] EES, VIIIa.3, Cope Whitehouse to Poynter, 27 Sept. 1888; see also Petrie's reply, more weary than outraged, 29 VIIIa.4, Sept. 1888; and further correspondence between Cope Whitehouse, Wallis, and Poynter, VIIIa.5, 4 Oct. 1888,; 5 Oct. 1888, VIIIa.7; VIIIa.8, 8 Oct. 1888.

public attention to it'; 'it is the duty of the SPMAE to take action against the EEF and Petrie'.[15] The in situ reconstruction of Pompeii, he argued, must be the model for all archaeology.[16] This was especially important in Egypt where 'a spree of temples will be discovered, rising from their remains' to be carefully preserved as living architecture, not the EEF's 'revolting exhibitions' that contravene 'artistic as well as moral law'.[17]

Despite Cope Whitehouse's swift ejection from the meeting, the sentiments Poynter enlisted him to express did hit home, and helped to sever any incipient ties between the archaeologists of the EEF and the SPMAE. As the collector and banker Sir Robert Hamilton-Lang wrote to Poynter:

> I see now that that idea [of a combined organization] is impracticable. The Egypt Exploration Fund aims at acquiring antiquities, whereas your society aims at the preservation of what is already known in the interest of historical and archaeological science. My sympathies all go with your society. Yours is not the lure of possessing, but that of preserving and knowing thoroughly the hidden wealth ... which the monuments of ancient Egypt represent. It recognizes that the Egyptian fellaheen are not in a position to pay for the care which these monuments of the past deserve, for the funds of the Egyptian treasury represent simply what are extorted from a very poor people.[18]

This suspicion of leading Egyptologists comes as something of a surprise, since the history of Egyptology generally elevates Petrie and the EEF to the status of preservation trailblazers. It is worth noting that amidst Petrie's famous public ridicule of the techniques of his contemporaries, such as Edouard Naville, he was subjected to similar, equally vitriolic, criticism. The EEF had been founded by Amelia Edwards, whose fame derived, in part, from her Egyptian travelogue—*A thousand miles up the Nile*—which has been presented as one of the nineteenth century's great statements of preservationist concerns. Her early rhetoric posited the EEF as a preservation organization, and she is often associated with heritage pioneers such as Octavia Hill. But, in 1882, when Edwards put her ideas into practice, her attitude was much less straightforward. It wasn't so much politics or other practical concerns that complicated her approach, but Egypt's most universal and enduring popular association: religion.

The difficult relationship between preservation and religion, in which the latter almost always prevailed, was immediately evident in the EEF's first excavation. This was an attempt to rediscover the route of the Exodus, and soon seemed to have uncovered a fortified settlement built by enslaved Hebrews in

[15] VIIIa.8, Cope Whitehouse to Poynter, 8 Oct. 1888.
[16] VIIIa.5, Cope Whitehouse to Poynter, 4 Oct. 1888.
[17] Ibid.
[18] VIIIa.38, Robert Hamilton-Lang to Poynter, undated.

Egypt: Pithom.[19] Edwards's response was to demand that five hundred of the Hebrew bricks from these emotive walls be removed and shipped to England. These would be biblical relics to keep her subscribers sweet, but also biblical evidence to promote what had quickly become the EEF's most visible purpose: a missionary endeavour to bolster the British people's faith in the Old Testament. EEF-sponsored lectures were given across Britain, celebrating the bricks of Pithom as restoring the disputed historical status of the Bible. The site itself was treated as a scene to be recorded but dismantled and dispersed: pure plunder. The uniquely frenetic biblical activity of archaeology in the 1870s and '80s easily swamped preservationist concerns.

These are the kind of endeavours that defined Poynter and Cope Whitehouse's expectations of Egyptology. Poynter, who—like Ali Pasha Mubarak and many contemporary archaeologists—was an engineer by training, repeatedly and explicitly stated that Egyptologists who were not trained engineers or architects could not hope to know how to maintain rather than impair the Egyptian monuments: 'Not Egyptologists, but engineers are needed. The dignitaries who held the care of the Temples in Pharaonic times were really trained architects, and it is only those who have had this scientific education who can fairly be required to perform the same duties at the present day.'[20] He saw his role as collecting funds that would neutralize the corrosive effects of the knowledge-gathering of Egyptologists by providing doors to tombs, bolstering pylons, and building brick structures to house the most delicate temples.[21] Cope Whitehouse, on the other hand, demanded that the work of current Egyptologists be ended altogether. He did everything in his power to undermine them intellectually and morally. These ideas were fought out through the single most complex preservation issue in fin de siècle Egypt, the question of irrigation and reservoir construction. This took place on a world stage, drawing in Americans such as Cope Whitehouse, because of the project's utterly groundbreaking nature and scale: it was here that a precedent for heritage-defying reservoirs from the Hindiya and Tryweryn to Ilisu was set.

II

The framework in which the Western powers operated in Egypt between 1882 and 1912 was defined by a status that was liminal in several ways: the conception of this region was much more tortuous than a simple East/West binary.

---

[19] E. Naville, *The store city of Pithom and the route of the Exodus* (London, 1883).
[20] 'Revised circular', EES, VIII.8.1888.
[21] See EES, VIIIe-Misc, 'Revised circular', F. Grenfell to Poynter, 23 Jan. 1889; EES VIIIa.13, 'Summary of Grand Bey's report'.

Some ambiguities were primarily conceptual. Ancient Egypt was venerated as a Bible land, but scorned as a biblical enemy; this Muslim state had once been a crucible of early Christianity; Arabic culture occupied the same sites as a prestige capital of Hellenistic learning. But other ambiguities had more immediate practical implications. Egypt was one of the great Mediterranean civilizations, yet it was not seen as part of the world in which European conventions of conduct were required: hence, when Napoleonic plunder was returned to Greece and Italy after 1815, it was not seen as a conscientious necessity to repatriate Egyptian antiquities. Egypt was a zone of imperial influence, but not part of the empire, therefore debates on its heritage were even more disorganized, piecemeal, and politically tortuous than those of Cunningham, Beglar, Cole, and Fergusson in India.[22] The closest precedent for this 'protectorate' status—the Ionian islands in the late 1850s, an affair that was also administered by Gladstone in a haze of historical fantasy—did not promise useful or desirable guidance.

The division of power within Egypt provided further delineation of the framework of intervention. It was because of the contingencies of this division that irrigation, from 1882 to the First World War, played so dominating a role in British conceptions of Egyptian politics and preservation. The British reorganization of the Egyptian administration after 1882 was, because of lack of funds and bureaucratic capacity, piecemeal and incoherent: as Robert Tignor has shown, elements of the British Indian administration were grafted onto existing Ottoman, French, and Egyptian institutions.[23] The structure of the Egyptian Public Works Department meant that where French interests retained a foothold in the body responsible for buildings and roads, the other major department—water supply and irrigation—was headed by one British and one Egyptian official.[24] Water offered the possibility of influence that was less inhibited by competition from other European powers than any other area of Egyptian development. It also offered the most likely source of remuneration that could help service the vast Egyptian debt. Sir Colin Scott

[22] The comparison with India was frequently made; sometimes it was used to demonstrate the limits on action in this contested protectorate, sometimes to present Egypt as a second chance: 'The reservoir question is now to be spread over a longer period of time and not rushed and I have every hope that the new dynasty will not rush matters so fast as the first dynasty of Anglo-Hindoos did'; EES, VIIId.5, J. C. Ross to Poynter, 29 Aug. 1892.

[23] For Robert Tignor's earliest but now dated statement of this case see 'The Indianization of the Egyptian administration under British rule', *American Historical Review*, 68 (1963), pp. 636–61; for a much more up-to-date (and politically sensitive) version see Tignor's magisterial *Egypt* (Princeton, NJ, 2010); it is worth noting that several of the British administrators in Egypt, including William Willcocks, had never even visited Britain, having been born and trained in British India before being posted to Egypt.

[24] This situation is outlined in detail in Evelyn Baring to Poynter, 7 Mar. 1891, EES, VIII.c.3; education and public health were unlikely to offer returns that could help service the massive Egyptian debt, so were given a consistently low priority by the British administration.

Moncrieff celebrated this potential for practical action in a paean to the British inspector-general of irrigation, Major Robert Hanbury Brown. He mocked French impracticality (blamed for the cracked and virtually unusable 1863 barrage built in the Nile Delta) and 'Mameluk misrule', before concluding that 'it has fallen to the honourable lot of a small band of English engineers, most of them trained in India, to effect a revolution in the irrigation system of Old Egypt'.[25]

By this point, the Nile was also written firmly into British self-conception. Its outflow, the Mediterranean, was conceived as a pleasure ground for British steamers; its twin sources had been anglicized as Victoria and Albert Nyanza; the whole length of the river was accessible to British vessels; figures as iconic as the Prince of Wales and General Gordon had made widely publicized journeys. The battle of the Nile remained only a little less richly evocative of British naval prowess than Trafalgar.[26] But, equally importantly, Egypt was the scene in which Israelite history began, the point at which the Hebrews became a nation—given a biblical rather than classical rendering, the progress of modern civilization that was assumed to culminate in Britain began by the Nile.

All these aqueous allusions fed into the preservation debates of the 1880s and '90s. The SPMAE made evocative use of water in both its most high-profile campaigns: the pumping of the Nile through Karnak as a means of desalination; the attempt to forestall the building of the Aswan Dam. But Cope Whitehouse went much further: he was a man obsessed with rivers and irrigation. He was one of the figures who suggested that the pyramids may have been intended to store water to feed the luscious groves of a lost oasis at now-desolate Memphis. He closely identified water with civilization and suggested that water supply was the single factor that most profoundly dictated the shapes of human habitation. He argued that the forms society takes are primarily dependent on the ways in which it receives and then controls its water: even small changes in water supply could be deadly and apocalyptic or could turn a poverty-stricken backwater into an economic powerhouse within the space of two generations.

Cope Whitehouse led a widely publicized campaign to avert the need for a dam at Aswan.[27] His alternative was the re-creation of an ancient reservoir

---

[25] R. H. Brown, *The Fayum and Lake Moeris* (London, 1892), preface by C. Scott Moncrieff.

[26] The event had been subjected to a host of poetic, dramatic, and pictorial celebrations: 'Nelson's triumph: or Buonaparte in the dumps' at the Astley; 'The mouth of the Nile', a play by Thomas Dibdin; a host of other plays and pantomimes including a 'Harlequin in Egypt'; verses by William Sotheby, Joseph Brereton, William McGonagall, and Cornelia Knight; even James Gillray sometimes undercut satirical expectations: the Nelson of Humphrey's 'The extirpation of the plagues of Egypt', for instance, was a victorious conflation of Moses and Hercules.

[27] This campaign included dozens of articles and lectures. Many of these will be referenced below, three sources of alternative perspectives are Cope Whitehouse, 'Moeris: the great reservoir of

several hundred miles further north. This was modelled on Lake Moeris, which was mentioned, and accorded vast proportions, by Herodotus. Cope Whitehouse assumed this to be a colossal construction project that had been carried out by the biblical Joseph centuries before Herodotus' tour. By rebuilding this venerable lake, 'mystic Lake Moeris' as Moncrieff styled it, Egypt's irrigation needs could be met without any destruction of ancient monuments.[28] This would be restoration on a vast geographical scale, far more expansive and profound than any 'cosmetics' applied to the façades of European churches.

Cope Whitehouse was developing these themes in the early 1880s, although at that point he had not yet developed his acute antipathy to Egyptologists. When the scuffle at Poynter's home occurred in 1888, Petrie was among those most adamant that Cope Whitehouse must not be given a hearing; but earlier, in 1883, the two had travelled extensively together in Egypt.[29] They had shared a friendly but already slightly irritable relationship, each being sceptical of the other's grand providential readings of the Great Pyramid. Cope Whitehouse, 'a tall, good-looking man of forty; of independent means' was already so enthused by his fascination with Egyptian hydraulics that Petrie called him 'my American wild goose' and wrote: 'When "my theory" does not come in (as it does like King Charles' head) he is—barring his habit of talking torrentially—a pleasant and gentlemanly American.'[30] The British press preferred the nickname 'Copious', coined for Cope Whitehouse's prolixity whenever he gained a platform for theories on the ancient management of water.

This obsession with the restitution of biblical engineering was not a phenomenon confined to Cope Whitehouse, however. There was a whole flock of 'wild geese', many of whom occupied lofty positions in the British administration of Egypt. A series of works by Sir William Willcocks expressed this idea, beginning with *Irrigation in Egypt* (1889), followed by *The Assuān Reservoir and Lake Moeris* (1904), then—and most dramatically—*The Restoration of the ancient irrigation works on the Tigris, or, the Re-creation of Chaldea*, published posthumously in 1911; Willcocks was an administrator of sufficient local repute to have a Cairo street and sporting club named in his honour.[31] His latter work argued that now the British had developed the

---

Middle Egypt. With the topography and construction of the pyramids', *United States Naval Institute Proceedings*, 11 (1885), pp. 325–30; Georg August Schweinfurth, 'Lake Moeris: justification of Herodotus by the recent researches of Mr Cope Whitehouse', *Bulletin of the Khedivial Geographical Society*, 22 (1883), pp. 1–8.

[28] Brown, *The Fayum and Lake Moeris*.

[29] Cope Whitehouse, 'Lake Moeris and recent explorations in the desert near the Fayoum', *Proceedings of the Society of Biblical Archaeology*, 4 (1881), pp. 124–35; Drower, *Flinders Petrie*, pp. 60–2.

[30] Drower, *Flinders Petrie*, p. 60.

[31] 'Rue Willcocks' Gezireh, is now Taha Hussein Street, Zamalek; Willcocks' 'Villa Oleander' is no. 20, now the César Levy Building.

Egyptian economy by imitating Joseph, they should rebuild the reservoirs of ancient Assyria and spread prosperity to the point of creating another Egypt. The Hindiya Barrage, opened in 1914, was conceived as a first step towards this goal.

Like many other British officials in Egypt, Willcocks saw ancient monuments as throwing down a gauntlet to the modern engineer.[32] If the British government could match the ancients then supplies of cotton, tax revenues, and a healthy productive population could be guaranteed. Egyptian civilization was thought to have begun with the colossal effort of redirecting the Nile at Memphis, and another outmuscling of the river seemed like a fitting way to begin a new era for the country. The Nile valley would, in the words of one engineer (and former consul-general in Egypt), once again be 'the theatre of a gigantic engineering exploit, audacious perhaps, but certain of success and ministering to man's necessities'.[33] Outlay on the project was predicted to be 'some of the best money Egypt had spent' since the building of Lake Moeris 'four-thousand years ago'.[34] The biblical Joseph who saved Egypt from famine was *the* ancient model. This is a powerful reminder that the people who seemed to be showing least concern for the destruction of monuments were far from insensible to the claims of this ancient civilization. Destroying ancient temples by flooding Upper Egypt was an act of historical restoration. Even the schemes that seemed to minister most powerfully to Egypt's present needs were referred back to the desires of the pharaoh Amenhemat. This strange mixture of the industrial and biblical, the ancient and progressive, is evoked in the many rhetorical affinities drawn by Willcocks and Cope Whitehouse. The latter, for instance, liked to describe Lake Moeris and the Raian Delta as 'the Yorkshire of the Pre-Christian world' in order to emphasize both venerable tradition and vast productive capacity.[35] It is this kind of rhetoric that demonstrates just how false is the idea of any straightforward choice between industrial progress and historical preservation.

By the time of the establishment of the SPMAE, irrigation schemes had entered the first stages of development. The greatest potential loss in the cause of progress was seen to be Philae, the pearl of the Nile. This site was well known in Britain and was already associated with Poynter. His breakthrough into the art establishment had been a huge canvas entitled *Israel in Egypt*,

---

[32] This theme, comparing the Great Pyramid with projects like modern Nile bridges, can be found scattered throughout the 1874 edition of Samuel Smiles's *Lives of the engineers* (5 vols., 1874); see, for instance, vol. V, pp. 249–50.

[33] Frederic Courtland Penfield, 'Harnessing the Nile', *Century Magazine*, 57 (1899), pp. 483–91, at p. 483.

[34] Ibid.

[35] Cope Whitehouse, 'Lake Moeris, from recent explorations in the Moeris Basin and the Wadi Fadhi', *Journal of the American Geographical Society of New York*, 14 (1882), pp. 85–108, at p. 89.

based on the biblical description of the construction of Pithom by Israelite slave labour. Poynter had combined several sites to construct the background for his procession of Hebrew slaves, and had made a feature of Philae despite its location at the opposite end of Egypt and its construction over a millennium later. Because cities like Memphis and Pithom were now mere scenes of desolation, Poynter allowed Philae's impressive architecture to stand in for the lost remains of the Bible's major sites. Twenty years on, Poynter, who was soon to receive the twin honours of director of the National Gallery and president of the Royal Academy, in London was a powerful voice in Philae's cause who could gain the ear of politicians and administrators alike.

The governments involved—British and Egyptian—did give some consideration to the endangerment of Philae. By 1888 and the foundation of the SPMAE, the Egyptian government had charged Willcocks, in the newly created position of 'Director General of Reservoirs', with weighing up possibilities. They had despatched Cope Whitehouse to his Egyptian Yorkshire to measure and cost his biblical proposals. Alternatives to the Aswan Dam were, at least superficially, being considered, and this assessment was carried out with dialogue between many different interest groups.

The Lake Moeris project was a far more demanding and costly task than even a dam at Aswan would be, and Cope Whitehouse, fanatical in his cause, was faced with the gruelling task of raising enthusiasm for the huge expenditure. He exploited the memory of General Gordon by arguing that a revived Mahdist movement might aim to direct acts of terrorism towards a Nubian dam, 'destroying all the monuments of Egypt except the pyramid and the sphinx': a northern Moeris reservoir, insulated against unrest in the Sudan, would be less susceptible.[36] But his primary publicity tactic involved lashing out at Egyptologists and attempting to reshape accepted topographies of biblical Egypt. He began by trading off the celebrity of the EEF's Pithom excavations. He argued that their identification of the Land of Goshen in the Eastern Delta was mistaken: the Raian Basin was the real site, and Pithom had in fact stood by the side of Lake Moeris. Under titles like 'The Projected Restoration of the Reian Moeris and the Province, Lake, and Canals of the Patriarch Joseph', he spoke to the British Association, the Royal Geographical Society, the American Archaeological Association, and even the Chamber of Commerce.[37]

In these presentations he argued that Egyptian ownership of Egyptian monuments was fundamental to the country's economic and cultural development. Britain and America must:

[36] Undated document, EES, VIII.d.15.
[37] One of the most substantial arenas devoted to the scheme was an 1887 meeting of the Royal Geographical Society in Manchester, at which a collection of papers on Cope Whitehouse's schemes were delivered. Reports by Colonel Ardagh and Major Conyers Surtees were published in *Proceedings of the Royal Geographical Society*, 9 (1887).

use their moral influence to secure to Egypt the undisturbed possession of the treasures accumulated in the past, as well as to aid its industrious peasants to obtain such further benefits from the Nile as will put the government once more in a position to devote its surplus earnings to the advancement of art and science within its borders and extend humanizing influences through Central Africa.[38]

The Aswan Dam would destroy the Egyptian cultural legacy while it created an economic one; it severed future and past. Doing nothing caused a similar rupture by privileging past over future. Cope Whitehouse pressed home his conclusion: only the Lake Moeris project maintained a continuum by treating past and future with equal respect. Moeris, he asserted, was the name of the pharaoh who invested Joseph with high office; Egypt's ancient prosperity was based on aid for this native king brought by a benevolent, technologically advanced outsider. Here was a model for the new golden age.

By now Cope Whitehouse was naturally anathema to Egyptologists, but he had better political connections than them. His scheme was discussed repeatedly in parliament, where several MPs forcefully pressed the project. But Sir James Fergusson, undersecretary of state for foreign affairs, vacillated, before eventually declaring the scheme too costly.[39] Cope Whitehouse was given considerable backing in the American press, who mocked 'the unexplained opposition of the English officials ... to the advice of their own expert'.[40] Cope Whitehouse had managed to inspire an astonishing amount of enthusiasm for this utterly impracticable scheme.

The reactions of archaeologists and the preservation societies to the Aswan Dam proposals were much less sensational. Even the artists and architects of the SPMAE created limited publicity relative to Cope Whitehouse's sensationalism: their approach was to lobby politicians such as Robert Cecil (Lord Salisbury, at this point secretary of state for foreign affairs) and Evelyn Baring (Lord Cromer, consul-general of Egypt) with a lengthy list of signatures.[41] Correspondence with Cecil was frequent and detailed: the dam must go ahead, the Society argued, but could it not be placed so as to avoid flooding Philae? A little of their time was even spent trying—in true Ruskinian fashion—to make sure that any dam that was built wasn't decorated with

---

[38] Cope Whitehouse, 'The Raiyan Moeris', *Journal of the American Geographical Society of New York*, 21 (1889), p. 536.

[39] 'Egypt—The Storage of the Nile Waters—The Raian Basin', Parl. Debs. (series 3) vol. 329, cols. 1216–7 (2 Aug. 1888).

[40] 'Raiyan Canal', *Bulletin of the American Geographical Society*, 40 (1908), at p. 90, quoting 'a Senate document (No.104 January 1906)'.

[41] These petitions (EES, VIIIb, VIIIc) were couched primarily in aesthetic terms: 'considered from an artistic point of view, these sculptured stones are abounding in the highest qualities of conception and execution'.

functionless Egyptian columns that had no place in modern architecture.[42] If the SPMAE's protests were less dramatic than might be expected, the EEF's protests were astonishingly subdued: progress, they argued, must come first. Amelia Edwards, who had died before this debate reached its conclusion, was the only leading member of the Egypt Exploration Fund to voice her opposition in strong terms. The Fund had an engineer as its president, and British Egyptologists themselves, including Petrie, had spent so much of the last decade attempting to define themselves as practical men of science, rather than aesthetes, linguists, or classicists, that they were much more inclined to see the perspective of the dam builders than to commit themselves to the aesthetic terms on which artists such as Poynter and Dillon expressed the SPMAE's opposition.

Most confusingly of all, the most vehement protests against the historical consequences of the dam came from the man who designed it. Willcocks spoke of devastation at Philae as tearing a leaf from the book of history, destroying more in one act than could be done in any other nation of the world. Within the British political, engineering, and archaeological communities recognition of the need for a reservoir was unanimous. Horror at its archaeological consequences was widespread, and real alternatives were scarce. Few, except Cope Whitehouse, held convictions that weren't pitted with regret and equivocation.

These equivocations in the planning of the dam have been consistently ignored or misconstrued. Indeed, the most recent (though flawed) study of the affair comes in an otherwise excellent volume on British engineers in Africa by Casper Andersen.[43] Andersen presents those who oppose the dam as 'Egyptologists', pitted against the engineers who supported it. Yet his chapter does not quote, nor even name, a single Egyptologist. The figures he designates Egyptologists include Edwards but also Poynter and Dillon. Tensions between Edwards and the EEF's engineer-president John Fowler are noted, although the fact that the EEF's excavators and surveyors were as likely to side with the engineer as with Edwards are not. What is also neglected is the fact that artistic opposition to the dam was deeply at odds with the concerns of Egyptologists: with the single exception of Wallis, artists were critiquing rather than supporting the agenda of the excavators. Andersen's chapter thus has a tendency to simplify a very messy range of equivocal opinions into a pair of predictable and mutually opposed united fronts.

Just as perverse as the equivocations of all parties during the 1890s is the fact that it was after the dam was opened (in 1902) that this debate really

[42] Another miscellaneous SPMAE document of 1894, EES, VIII.d.21, asks, 'what in the name of heaven is the sense of building Egyptian pylons in the present day?'
[43] Casper Andersen, *British Engineers and Africa, 1875–1914* (London, 2011), pp. 137–59.

heated up. After much stalling, the plan that went ahead was a compromise that suited no one—Philae was only subjected to limited flooding (up to five months a year)—but the capacity of the Aswan Reservoir was far smaller than was needed. Lake Moeris *had* been dismissed as too costly, but widespread dissatisfaction forced it straight back onto the agenda. The government proposed that the dam be extended, but this was a risky project that would lead to even more extensive destruction. So Willcocks, again charged with analysing and costing the scheme, proposed that this compromised Aswan Dam be combined with Cope Whitehouse's original Raian Basin proposal.[44] The cheap option had failed, and an initial outlay of a few million pounds extra would, he extravagantly claimed, be insignificant next to potential rewards of £200 million over the next twenty years.

It was now that Willcocks began to pursue his most elaborate biblical ideas. *He* was now Joseph wandering through Goshen. There was no more perfect project than a reconstructed Lake Moeris, he argued, because it restored biblical conditions: 'To the imagination it affords one of the most fascinating views which the mind of man can conceive.'[45] He added—almost as an afterthought—'Viewed from its humanitarian side it is equally attractive.'[46] Willcocks championed the scheme by publishing widely; works included his volume on the restoration of the Tigris and the homeland of Abraham.

His theories were based on an idea that had regained widespread popularity thanks, in part, to 1870s and '80s archaeology: that there had been an archaeologically verifiable golden age of biblically ordered civilization covering the whole of the Near East in deep antiquity. Willcocks claimed that, with a little creative engineering, this golden age would be resurrected by 1950. In his most staggeringly strange statement of this case, he described the only immediately visible differences between Egypt in its ancient majesty and its coming glory: these were 'a statue of Cecil Rhodes on the Equator, and one of Mr Cope Whitehouse on the cliffs' overlooking Lake Moeris.[47] Unlike the Aswan Reservoir, Lake Moeris wouldn't be just an engineering marvel, but one of the great pleasure resorts of Europe. The man who had engineered the Aswan Dam here pointed to the British, French, and Egyptian press's scandalous images of a submerged Philae, and asked the public whether they really wanted this all year round.

At the same time, the case against proposed extensions received emotional weight from Pierre Loti in a 150-page literary condemnation of British actions, *La Mort de Philae*, which was quickly translated into English. He depicted

---

[44] These views, set out in many of Willcocks's lectures after the turn of the century, are reported in several media including 'Raiyan Canal', *Bulletin of the American Geographical Society*, p. 90.
[45] Ibid.
[46] Ibid.
[47] Ibid.

himself inside the flooded Temple of Isis by moonlight, hearing the 'mournful booming' of 'things that topple' as the goddess regards her disgrace and quails before the commercial taint that poisons her inner sanctum.[48]

British Egyptologists were challenged to defend their conduct. It was suggested that personal enmity to Cope Whitehouse, and entanglement in the imperial regime, had led them to neglect their duty to history: they had voiced their opposition all too quietly and politely. Petrie now began to direct similar fury at his colleagues for their weak resistance. But his proposal of moving the temple block by block or raising it wholesale (suggestions similar to those posited by Sir Benjamin Baker, architect of the Manchester Canal, and which eventually happened in the 1960s) had been dismissed with remarkably little consideration:

> On the proposals to demolish the temple and to rebuild it elsewhere, or to hoist it beyond reach of an artificial inundation, it is hardly necessary to speak. Their originators have perhaps ere this perceived that such ideas are based upon a complete misunderstanding.[49]

The press similarly opined that 'the proposal to move Philae stone by stone was too fantastic even for the pen of a Jules Verne'.[50] Arthur Weigall responded on behalf of the EEF, but maintained the detachment they had initiated. He argued that 'the temporary and apparently harmless inundation of the ruins for five months each year is well worth the several millions of precious government money' that would have been expended on any other suitable irrigation project. The colour of Philae's reliefs *would* be lost, he conceded. But in an extraordinary turn of phrase for a twentieth-century archaeologist, he claimed that 'artistically [the loss] will not be much felt'.[51] He continued, 'Sentimentally of course, one deeply regrets the flooding of the temple'; but he insisted that those who placed sentiment above practical considerations were the intellectual equivalent of the drunks on the Old Kent Road each Saturday night, 'whose legs had lost their cunning'.[52] This was a view shaped by the tensions of the 1880s and '90s, as a result of which Egyptologists had worked hard to distance themselves from the aesthetic concerns of classical archaeology and to reorient conceptions of what archaeological disciplines involved, from association with 'the fine arts' and 'critical study of languages' towards chemistry, physics, mathematics, and engineering.[53]

---

[48] P. Loti, *Egypt (La Mort de Philae)*, trans. W. P. Baines (London, 1909), p. 149.

[49] [Anon], *Reservoirs in the valley of the Nile* (London, 1894), pp. 6–7.

[50] Penfield, 'Harnessing the Nile', p. 483.

[51] A. Weigall, *The treasury of ancient Egypt* (Chicago, 1910), p. 271.

[52] Ibid., p. 276.

[53] The introduction and first chapter of Petrie's *Methods and aims in archaeology* (London, 1904) reflect this tension, but it can be seen even more clearly in the classical establishment's hostile reception of Petrie's work in the 1880s, e.g. W. M. F. Petrie, 'Naukratis', *Athenaeum*, 3076 (1886), p. 471.

After 1910 Petrie took a hard line against present-focused attitudes that, to him, invalidated the whole Egyptological endeavour. He increasingly voiced opinions that placed the past on a stronger footing than the present. 'I am sometimes asked,' he informed a Manchester audience:

> what is the good of [Egyptian Monuments], and my reply is that the good of them is to enable us to realize how man has existed, how he has lived and developed, and to carry forward the great mass of knowledge which is the justification of man. What rather is the good of life without these outlooks? It would be better to wipe out three-quarters of the population of the world than to destroy the storehouses of human knowledge and ideas, for the population would be replaced in a century, but it would take a hundred thousand years to renew the accumulations of the human mind.[54]

Petrie was now taking a much more hard line, not to mention impassioned, stance on destruction than he had a decade earlier, when he usually voiced sentiments along these lines in religious, rather than civilizational, language. But even here, when giving the past so astonishing a pre-eminence over the present, Petrie is speaking to the Trustees of the Manchester Museum, exhorting them to acquire all the Egyptian antiquities they can lay their hands on; there is no echo here of the aesthetic concerns of John Ruskin and the Society for the Preservation of Ancient Buildings, nor of the interests of Dillon and Poynter. Notice also how, like Weigall, Petrie is absolutely insistent on evading any kind of rhetoric that might be associated with either 'sentiment' or the aesthetic (terms more or less synonymous in Petrie's vocabulary).

This shift in Petrie's outlook is entirely compatible with developments in the views of European Egyptologists. As the extension of the Aswan Dam became a certainty, and as the Lake Moeris project was once again judged to be a costly romantic fantasy, the serious archaeological steps that had been absent from the first stages of the process did take place. In December 1904 Gaston Maspero, Director-General of the Antiquities Department of Egypt, embarked on a seven-week tour of Nubia and compared the current state of the monuments with sketches made over the previous two centuries. The monuments, he argued, had been seriously damaged and the time for urgent action had come. Within two years, the Archaeological Survey of Nubia had been founded: its nature and scale are striking measures of the transformation of the archaeological world that had occurred within one decade. Significantly, the Archaeological Survey's emphasis was on the beginnings of Nubian history. The Egyptologists involved included experts on the earliest dynasties such as George Reisner, and scholars of prehistory and anthropology such as

---

[54] W. M. F. Petrie, 'The Manchester Museum: opening of the Jesse Haworth building', *Museums Journal*, 12 (1912), pp. 172–7.

Grafton Elliot Smith. As the Survey got under way, Reisner's earlier prehistoric work at Naga-ed-Deir was being published. His approach substantially extended the archaeological developments that the EEF and Petrie had, with partial success, attempted to instantiate in the 1880s and '90s: it emphatically denied the quest to stock museums and affirmed the need to record all archaeological activity in painstaking detail.[55] The Survey's first publication established its priorities:

> intimate acquaintance with early Egyptian art and civilization was especially valuable in the study of this region, for it ... provide[d] a firm basis for anthropological studies; for a thorough study of such a region involved not only the collection of objects and reconstruction of the culture of the people who had once inhabited the valley, but also the determination of their race and ethnological affinities.[56]

The focus was no longer on Philae, but on revealing what 'the large number of ancient sites which are not known, but which very certainly exist' might reveal of the migrations and interactions of early man.[57] The vast majority of this huge salvage operation took place in the cemeteries rather than temples of Egypt, sometimes on extremely ancient material dating back to *c*.3500 BC. Separate historical eras, millennia apart, were soon established and the Survey's three main focal points were designated A, C, and X Group. The histories of these groups were interpreted in terms of racial migrations, invasions, 'blending', and 'grafting': 'the X-group people' for instance 'were strongly Negroid aliens who had suddenly made their way north into Nubia'.[58] In keeping with many archaeological works of the subsequent two decades— V. Gordon Childe's *The dawn of European civilization* and Petrie's *The revolutions of civilization* for instance—the emphases here were on establishing the regional distribution and physical characteristics of various prehistoric ethnic groups.[59] The assumptions that diffusion emanated from a common source and took place alongside gradual racial differentiation was maintained by Elliot Smith throughout all the works that used his Nubian research; it was one of many schemes in early twentieth-century Egypt that still owed its framework to biblical histories of Noah and his sons. The migrations of Genesis 10 remained the paradigm behind many expressions of these new

---

[55] M. A. Hoffmann, *Egypt before the pharaohs* (London, 1980), pp. 252–3.

[56] H. G. Lyons, preface to Lyons, Smith, and Jones, *The archaeological survey of Nubia*.

[57] A. Weigall, *A report on the antiquities of Lower Nubia* (Cairo, 1907).

[58] G. Elliot Smith, *Archaeological Survey of Nubia, Bulletin 5* (1910), p. 12.

[59] W. M. F. Petrie, *The revolutions of civilisation* (1911); V. G. Childe, *The origins of European civilisation* (London, 1925); as with every other ideological movement that shaped archaeology, these themes were not confined to archaeological discourse: the contemporary civilizational schemes of H. G. Wells and even W. B. Yeats, for instance, employ comparable models.

preoccupations, which treated material that had been beyond the possibilities of conception at the time of the Aswan Dam's design.

III

The heady ideological dreams of almost all the players involved in the construction of this dam had the kind of biblical resonance that guaranteed extensive interest in turn-of-the-century Britain. They made the dam—despite all the destruction it involved—an act of historical restitution. So this project was variously construed as Britain's major bequest to the seamlessly continuous narrative of Egyptian history, and as a vicious legacy of the destruction of irreplaceable archives of human history. Strikingly, until after the construction of the first dam, Egyptologists themselves, almost all self-consciously, subscribed to the former view, and those who gave historical preservation an importance that rivalled present expediency were almost all engineers, lawyers, politicians, or literary and artistic authorities. These figures wrote with despair of the lack of support they received from the scholars they regarded as the chief custodians of Egypt's ancient culture. As we have seen, the tensions this raised resulted, at least once, in violent confrontation; and productive friendships could turn to bitter enmities by the positions taken on this volatile expression of Britain's responsibility to both past and present. The feature that differentiated these events from preservation debates in India or elsewhere in the empire was the profound sense of homecoming that nineteenth-century activity in Egypt involved. Egypt was not the exotic East, but a familiar biblical inheritance: Joseph could be variously Hebrew and Egyptian but also a revered model of inventive Englishness.

The recognition of Egyptian prehistory at the turn of the century changed the nature of this debate dramatically and irrevocably. Maspero's 1904–05 tour coincided with the beginning of international cooperation in exploring regions of Egyptian and Nubian history in which race, not the deeds of the patriarchs, was the dominant concern; anatomical, not architectural, remains were the dominant resource; knowledge, not monuments, was the primary target of preservation concerns. International and interdisciplinary cooperation, as well as the impact of prehistory, created a situation in which some of the idiosyncrasies of 1890s British approaches were lessened. Many who had once been committed to explicitly biblical schemes, Petrie for instance, turned to constructions of the past in which remnants of biblical assumptions simmered beneath conceptions of cycles of civilization and waves of racial migration. Egypt had finally, briefly, become the realm of exotic ethnic interactions, shorn of its traditional familiarity. The first Aswan Dam didn't just coincide with these changes: it helped drive and galvanize them. It caused engineers such as Willcocks and politicians like Cecil to think archaeologically and historically, and forced archaeologists like Reisner to develop methods of permanently and completely recording evidence of human habitation, to see their work in relation to present expediency, and to disregard conclusively the interests of national museums. The convolutions along the way demonstrate just how much politics was still viewed historically—the present entangled in vast teleologies—and just how much the pressures to view archaeology as a science more than a humanities discipline led to the devaluing of anything that might be considered 'sentimental' or 'aesthetic', including, in this case, the preservation of monuments.

6

The Cotswolds in Jerusalem:
Restoration and Empire*

SIMON GOLDHILL

THERE IS NO CITY in the world that has been fought over as continuously and as
heatedly as Jerusalem, thanks to an unholy combination of religious, political,
and nationalist passions. In the most direct terms of imperialist activity, there
have been at least 118 recorded military campaigns against Jerusalem, and it
has been captured or recaptured by force forty-four times over the centuries.[1]
For the earliest accounts of the sacking of Jerusalem—the Babylonians,
Assyrians, Romans—plunder plays an essential role: the treasury of the Temple
was an evident lure, and most wars in antiquity were understood to be undertaken for the accumulation of movable property, just as empire was expressed
by the ability to exact tribute or tax. The Arch of Titus, with its celebrated
images of the triumphal procession through Rome of the ritual objects captured from the Temple of Jerusalem, is just one vivid icon of how looted
objects from one culture become the paraded signs of might at the centre of
the victorious empire's capital—eventually to play an uncomfortable role in
contemporary art history and the contested national politics of collecting.[2]

From Constantine onwards, however, and especially through the
Crusades—despite numerous examples of vile murder and rampant looting
and destruction—the rhetoric of these holy wars has been constructed around
models of reconstruction and restoration rather than the blunt desire for

*Thanks to the editors, Peter Mandler and Astrid Swenson, for helpful comments on the chapter
and in the course of our work together in the Cambridge Victorian Studies Group. Versions of
this work were delivered first at the 'Plunder and Preservation' conference in Cambridge; then as
the Schaffner Lecture, in my role as the Schaffner Professor in British Studies at Chicago, and
finally as the Maccabaean Lecture at King's College, London. Thanks to the audiences in each
place for questions that helped me make my arguments more precise.
[1] E. Cline, *Jerusalem besieged: from ancient Canaan to modern Israel* (Ann Arbor, MI, 2004); for
more recent campaigns see, e.g. B. Morris, *1948: the first Arab–Israeli war* (New Haven, CT,
2008); M. Oren, *Six days of war: June 1967 and the making of the modern Middle East* (Oxford,
2002).
[2] See most recently, with further bibliography, J. Cuno, *Who owns antiquity? Museums and the
battle over our ancient heritage* (Princeton, NJ, 2008).

plunder.[3] Western maps placed Jerusalem as the centre of the world, and
Christian thought made the earthly Jerusalem a mirror of the heavenly city.[4]
Fighting for Jerusalem was a struggle to make the Christian empire integral—
to inhabit its centre, to make the world properly *Christiandom*. To plunder
Jerusalem became an inexpressible aim, and has remained so. From the time
of Constantine, the *preservation* of the holy sites has been a battle cry of
Christians, taken up and echoed by Muslims, and, more recently, by Jews,
whose religious language of exile, loss, and rebuilding runs throughout these
centuries' clashes. The rhetoric of the crusades has had a long afterlife: its
legacy of violent possessiveness runs through the politics of the Holy City,
even, and especially, in arguments over preservation. But by the same token,
Jerusalem can never be simply the object of imperial expansion, just another
province (even when it actually was a provincial backwater, a site of exile, as
it seems to have been for centuries of Muslim sovereignty[5]). Capturing
Jerusalem by force has repeatedly been expressed not as a gesture of imperialism, but as an act of restoration and preservation of an already imagined
centre of empire—imagined as lost, forgotten, sullied by earthliness, and
reclaimed for an ideal model of rebuilding.

This paradoxical ideal of destructive rebuilding—restoration *as* preservation—which is often dependent on an archaeological dynamic of excavation
to recover the authentic, goes back a very long way in the history of Jerusalem.
In the first century BCE, Zerubbabel's Temple had stood for nearly five hundred years.[6] The first Temple of Solomon had been destroyed and looted by
Nebuchadnezzar in 587 BCE, and, from the start, Zerubbabel's rebuilding
some seventy years later was marked as falling short of the ideal. As the pro-

---

[3] See, most recently, J. Riley-Smith, *The crusades, Christianity and Islam* (New York, 2008) and
J. Riley-Smith, *The Oxford history of the crusades* (Oxford, 1999); also, from a Muslim perspective,
C. Hillenbrand, *Crusades: Islamic perspectives* (New York, 1999), and M. Cameron Lyons and
D. Jackson, *Saladin: the politics of the holy war* (Cambridge, 1982). K. Armstrong, *Holy war: the
crusades and their impact on today's world* (London, 1988) has been influential.

[4] See B. Kühnel, 'Geography and geometry of Jerusalem' in N. Rosovsky, ed., *City of the great
king: Jerusalem from David to the present* (Cambridge, MA, 1996), pp. 288–332; M. Levy-Rubin
and R. Rubin, 'The image of the Holy City in maps and mapping', in Rosovsky, ed., *City of the
great king*, pp. 352–79; and, for a more general view, J. Black, *Maps and politics* (London, 1997).

[5] See the still useful G. Le Strange, *Palestine under the Moslems, 650–1500* (Beirut, 1965); A. Cohen,
Economic life in Ottoman Jerusalem (Cambridge, 1989); and G. Gilbar, ed., *Ottoman Palestine
1800–1914* (Leiden, 1990). The essential guide to the fabric of the city is Y. Natseh's *Ottoman
Jerusalem: the living city 1517–1917*, ed. S. Auld and R. Hillenbrand (London, 2000) (and I thank
Yusuf Natseh for guiding me round Ottoman Jerusalem). See also for Western views, F. Peters,
*Jerusalem: the Holy City in the eyes of chroniclers, visitors, pilgrims and prophets from the days of
Abraham to the beginnings of modern times* (Princeton, NJ, 1985); N. Chareyron, *Pilgrims to
Jerusalem in the middle ages*, trans. W. D. Wilson (New York, 2005); most recently, S. Yeager
Jerusalem in medieval narrative (Cambridge, 2008).

[6] For the details of the following paragraph see S. Goldhill, *The Temple of Jerusalem* (London,
2004) and S. Goldhill, *Jerusalem, city of longing* (Cambridge, MA, 2008) pp. 45–92.

phet Haggai lamented, 'How does it look to you now? It must look like nothing to you!' What's more, the prophet Ezekiel had portrayed an ideal,
spiritualized Temple —any rebuilding could be nothing but a material and
insufficient imitation. So when Herod came to construct his magnificent
Temple in the first century BCE, he first had to destroy the ancient Temple of
Zerubbabel, and then to redesign the whole landscape of the city by building
the huge platform of the Temple Mount, which still stands. He did this in the
name of 'restoring this first archetype of piety to its former stature'. That is,
the Temple of Zerubbabel did not match the dimensions or glory of Solomon's
first temple, and had to be removed—'restored'—in order for Herod's glorious
new building to fulfil its blueprint as ancient archetype.

Constantine, in the fourth century CE, directed Makarios, bishop of
Jerusalem, to destroy the 200-year-old Roman Temple of Venus, and dig up
the forum in what was then called Aelia Capitolina, because under it they
would find the cave in which Jesus was buried. They duly did—and when
Constantine's mother, Helena, visited the city, she found also the three crosses
of the Crucifixion in a nearby ditch, miraculously undamaged. The Church of
the Holy Sepulchre was built over the site. In the early ninth century, the dome
of the rotunda of this church was replaced by an open cone, a form it retained
until the nineteenth century. But in 1009, the church was wholly destroyed by
Caliph al-Hakim ('the mad'), so that only part of the walls of the rotunda and
part of the tomb survived. It was rebuilt, slowly, over the subsequent years. In
the twelfth century, the site was redesigned by the Crusaders who gave the
church the different footprint and the façade it now has—though the whole
church was badly damaged by fire in 1808, when the cone was replaced by a
huge dome again. (Re)covering and uncovering the tomb in the name of
revealing—and revering—the true site of the crucifixion and burial of Jesus is
a centuries-long process that has not yet finished.[7]

The Muslim building of the Dome of the Rock and the Al-Aqsa Mosque
on Herod's Temple Mount (*har habayit* in Hebrew, *Haram al-Sharif* in Arabic)
also has a foundational story of uncovering and restoration. When Omar first
captured Jerusalem in the Muslim imperial expansion, he asked the Christian
bishop, Sophronios, to show him where King David had prayed. The site had
long been used as a rubbish dump by the Christians, happy to make a vivid
icon of the failure of Judaism by leaving its holiest site an ostentatious ruin.
Omar, outraged at the disrepair, forced Sophronios to help clear the rubbish

[7] For further details see Goldhill, *Jerusalem, city of longing*, pp. 1–45. For the ongoing process, see
the optimistic R. Cohen, *Saving the Holy Sepulchre: how rival Christians came together to rescue
their holiest shrine* (Oxford, 2008) and, from a less scholarly perspective, V. Clark, *Holy Fire: the
battle for Christ's tomb* (San Francisco, CA, 2005). For general background see W. Zander, *Israel
and the holy places of Christendom* (London, 1971); and on the architectural history, M. Biddle,
ed., *The Church of the Holy Sepulchre* (New York, 2000).

away with his own hands, before establishing the prime religious institutions of the Haram. Again, the logic of excavation, the destruction of the current surface, to uncover the site of holiness, to build memorials there, and to (re)tell the stories of such a process as part of the veneration of the site, are integral to the construction and comprehension of a religious site in Jerusalem.

For the specific history of Jerusalem, then, the terms plunder and preservation cannot adequately capture the play of rhetoric and practice. Plunder has little purchase in the rhetoric of any group, despite repeated acts of aggressive capture and the recovery of objects of religious significance. Imperial ambition for the Holy Land is repeatedly structured through a religiously inflected language of reintegrating a world map by recovering its rightful centre (rather than the standard imperial rhetoric of expanding the boundaries of empire or exporting civilization or even commercial benefit). Preservation of the holy sites is often a banner for violent possessiveness in political and religious conflict, and has repeatedly taken the form of drastic reconstruction. Each of the major religions tells aetiological tales of their religious sites, which depend on the archaeological dynamic of destroying the accretions of more recent societies to discover the authentic past: destructive rebuilding as religious expression. Jerusalem is thus a perfect space for considering what is at stake in the claims and the practice of restoration and preservation.

My test case for exploring the specific dynamics of preservation in Jerusalem is the extraordinary story of how a middle-aged English civil servant changed the face of the Holy City at the beginning of the twentieth century—within a precise context of the British empire's engagement with the Middle East—by enacting his deeply held aesthetic ideals, forged in the later years of the nineteenth century in London and the Cotswolds. The story will indicate an important lesson about the time lag between the development of aesthetic credos and the enactment of policy. But it will also set up strong and, I hope, productive echoes with the other chapters of this book, in its detailed analysis of how British imperial policy functioned—as we explore its roots in particular social and intellectual groups—and in its strongly articulated relation to a much wider history, which the chapter began by sketching, and the ideological commitments that run through the understanding of such a history. It will provide a particularly telling example of how cultural contact with another society is enacted through some very home-grown cultural anxieties.

Before we meet the hero of my story, I want to outline some particular lineaments of nineteenth-century imperial ambition in Palestine, which provide a crucial background for British policy under the early Mandate.[8] The

---

[8] A vast bibliography could be given here: see by way of introduction (each with further bibliographies): E. Bar-Yosef, *The Holy Land in English culture 1799–1917* (Oxford, 1998); Y. Ben-Arieh, *The rediscovery of the Holy Land in the nineteenth century* (Jerusalem, 1979); Y. Ben-Arieh

slow collapse of the Ottoman empire during the nineteenth century, together with the invention of the steamboat, opened the Middle East to an explosion of tourism and archaeology, twin harbingers of the political imperialism which changed the map of the region.[9] More descriptions of journeying in the Holy Land were published in Europe in the first three-quarters of the nineteenth century than in the previous 1,500 years put together: more than 2,000 books and essays in 75 years.[10] The image of Jerusalem was being reforged by the widely circulated prose and photography of Western, gazing, reflecting visitors, who mediated the long history of imagining the Holy Land by a new claim on reality—having been there and seen it as it is.[11] So too, archaeological and cartographical exploration constructed a new image of the (real) East through Western paradigms. There can be no doubt about the connection of imperialism and science here. At the foundation of the Palestine Exploration Fund in London, the archbishop of York ringingly declared (to applause) that we are interested in Palestine because 'Palestine is ours'.[12] That is, the Christian history of the Holy Land linked Anglican Britain to Palestine, inevitably, rightfully, spiritually as well as politically. Captain Warren, a Boy's Own hero of Jerusalem exploration, concluded his best-selling book on biblical archaeology as follows: 'Will not those who love Palestine, love freedom, justice, the Bible, learn to look upon the country as one which may shortly be in the market? Will they not look about and make preparations and discuss the question?'[13] The idea of a country being 'in the market' is a strikingly direct expression of the economic roots of the British imperial project. The ideological buttresses of the project are no less directly expressed: the Bible, justice, and freedom. When the First World War made Palestine strategically crucial, because of its control of the supply routes to India, political pragmatism drew on both the shifting image of the Middle East, and on the deeply felt religious and ideological commitment to Palestine as the homeland of Christianity, to found and support its realpolitik. It is from within this milieu

and M. Davis, eds., *Jerusalem in the minds of the Western world 1800–1948* (Westport, CT, and London, 1997); H. Hyamson, *British projects for the restoration of the Jew* (Leeds, 1971); the still valuable A. Tibawi, *British interests in Palestine 1800–1901* (Oxford, 1961).

[9] See S. Goldhill 'The discovery of Victorian Jerusalem', in D. Gange and M. Ledger-Lomas, eds., *Biblical cities* (Cambridge, forthcoming). See also N. Silberman, *Digging for God and country: exploration, archaeology and the secret struggle for the Holy Land* (London, 1982); J. Buzard, *The beaten track: European tourism, literature and the ways to 'culture', 1800–1918* (Oxford, 1993).

[10] See Y. Ben-Arieh, 'Jerusalem travel literature as historical source and cultural phenomenon', in Ben-Arieh and Davis, eds., *Jerusalem in the minds*, pp. 25–46.; R. Röhricht, *Bibliotheca geographica Palaestinae: chronologisches Verzeichnis der von 333 bis 1878 verfassten Literatur über das Heilige Land* (London, 1989).

[11] Discussion and bibliography in Goldhill, 'The discovery of Victorian Jerusalem'.

[12] *Palestine Exploration Fund Quarterly* (1875), p. 115.

[13] C. Warren, *Underground Jerusalem* (London, 1876) p. 559; cf. pp. 363, 458–9.

that the political movement of Restorationism, the desire to return the Jews to Palestine, arose in the 1840s in particular; by the end of the nineteenth century it had become prominent in Zionist ambition among Christians and, latterly, Jews, in Britain.[14]

From the end of the Crimean War, when restrictions on foreigners owning land in Jerusalem began to relax, following the Ottoman government's recognition of European help in the fight against the Russians, the major European powers each began building in Jerusalem as a form of nationalist expression.[15] The collapse of the Anglo-Prussian Jerusalem bishopric led to the foundation of St George's Cathedral by the British in the style of a home counties' church with an Oxford college attached, while Kaiser Wilhelm inaugurated the austere Lutheran Church of the Redeemer (along with Dormition Abbey and Augusta Victoria, built with expensively imported German materials to a German design). The Italians built their hospital as a replica of the Palazzo Vecchio in Florence; the French built their neo-classical Notre Dame pilgrim hospice with a huge statue of the Virgin Mary on its roof copied from Our Lady of Salvation in Paris. The Austrian hospice, a building that would not be out of place in the Tyrol, served strudel and coffee in the Old City. The Russian Compound, with its Slavonic crosses, onion-domed cathedral, and pilgrim hostels was almost a walled town of its own, opposite the New Gate. The exotic, Eastern city of alleys and dirt, described in those thousands of travel reports, was being redesigned, as the European powers each constructed a major building project in their own image as a centre for their own presence in the city—and nervously, competitively, watched each other for signs of overstepping the balance of imperial interest in what all determined was a city soon to be fully 'in the market'.

The long history of imagining Jerusalem, now mediated by new British, Christian imperial concern for the Holy Land, coupled with twenty-five years of nationalist, competitive building in Jerusalem itself, provides the broad frame for the Mandate's policies on preserving the fabric of the city of Jerusalem. But the specific line this policy took, turns out to depend on the hero of my story, Charles Ashbee, the son of Henry Ashbee, the famous bibliographer of pornography, associate of Burton, Swinburne, and others, who published under the pseudonym of Pisanus Fraxi, and may, according to Ian Gibson, be 'Walter', the author of the pornographic classic *My secret*

---

[14] See Hyamson, *British projects*; and especially Bar-Yosef, *Holy Land*; and, most recently, S. Brown, *Providence and empire: religion, politics and society in the United Kingdom 1815–1914* (Harlow, 2008).

[15] See Y. Ben-Arieh, *Jerusalem in the 19th century: the Old City* (New York, 1984); Y. Ben-Arieh, *Jerusalem in the 19th century: emergence of the new city* (Jerusalem and New York, 1986); D. Kroyanker, *Adrikhalut bi-Yerushalayim* [in Hebrew] (6 vols., Jerusalem, 1985–93); Goldhill, *Jerusalem, city of longing*, pp. 227–77.

life.[16] Charles Ashbee (always known in his intimate circle as CRA or Charlie) is best known for his role in the Arts and Crafts movement in England. In 1888 he had founded the Guild of Handicrafts with £50 and four associates. Inspired by John Ruskin and William Morris, this little workshop in the East End of London grew through the 1890s to take up a central place in the Arts and Crafts movement. By 1902 it had outgrown its premises and its earlier ambitions so much that Ashbee was able to move the whole operation to the Cotswolds, to the village of Chipping Camden, where his picnics, naked bathing, amateur dramatics, and cycling trips around the countryside became a mildly shocking feature of the Cotswolds' scene, and a fashionable site to visit.[17] It was in the 1890s too that Ashbee started going to America to lecture and to spread the word of his particular brand of Romantic Socialism, Garden City architectural principles, and Arts and Crafts commitment to designed objects and local materials.[18] He became a particular friend of Frank Lloyd Wright, and developed a special love for the Chicago waterfront. After his lecture in Chicago on the awfulness of the modern city had horrified his audience, who felt their city had been grievously insulted—it prompted a storm in the local press—he went on to describe Chicago's integration of architecture and nature in glowing terms, with praise for its 'creativeness ... buoyancy [and] exhilaration', and said that nothing had moved him as much, except—a typical local touch, this—standing on the back bridge of King's College, Cambridge.[19]

The juxtaposition of King's College and Chicago captures something of Ashbee's particular blend of modernism and deep-rootedness in an English tradition. This also helps explain his passion for the preservation of old buildings—as a modernist concern—or, to be more accurate, his love of eighteenth-century buildings and medieval structures. He himself summed up his view on the value of the past: 'It was war with commercial vandalism that made men

---

[16] On the life of Ashbee see A. Crawford, *C. R. Ashbee: architect, designer and romantic socialist* (New Haven, CT, 1985), and F. Ashbee, *Janet Ashbee: love, marriage and the Arts and Crafts movement* (Syracuse, NY, 2002); on Henry Ashbee, see S. Marcus, *The other Victorians: a study of sexuality and pornography in mid-nineteenth-century England* (New York, 1964), especially pp. 34–76; I. Gibson, *The erotomaniac: the secret life of Henry Spencer Ashbee* (London, 2001). 'Pisanus Fraxi' is an anagram of 'fraxinus' and 'apis', pseudonyms under which Ashbee *père* published learned notes, and which in Latin mean 'Ash' and 'Bee'.

[17] See F. MacCarthy, *The simple life: C. R. Ashbee in the Cotswolds* (London, 1981). Janet Ashbee describes in mocking terms a tea party with Lady Elcho, Mrs Patrick Campbell, the Mitford daughters of Lord Redesdale, and Sidney and Beatrice Webb (MacCarthy, *Simple life*, pp. 80–2), as well as the visit of the just retired prime minister, Balfour (p. 143).

[18] See C. R. Ashbee, *American sheaves and English seed corn: being a series of addresses mainly delivered in the United States* (London and New York, 1901): he went to the USA as a representative of the newly formed National Trust.

[19] See Ashbee, *American sheaves*, pp. 90–109, qu. at 108–9; the story of the row, with the cartoons from the press, is told in Crawford, *C. R. Ashbee*, pp. 96–8.

turn to the past as a citadel that had to be defended: the Historic conscience came with the aesthetic rebellion against commercialism.'[20] Hence, 'much of my own professional work has been the preservation and protection of beauty'.[21] But Ashbee was also conscious of how carefully a veneration of the past needs to be policed: 'This preservation of the past had its evil side, Veneration begat idolatry ... The movement ended in an orgy of bric-a-brac in which the prices were kept up by American buyers and manipulated by gangs of Jews.'[22] And this touch of racial thinking is followed through elsewhere in his writing: buildings such as Shakespeare's house at Stratford-upon-Avon 'have in them a quality of their own that will not die, unless through negligence, the blindness, the death of the race itself. Beauty, in that it is an attribute of Divinity, has in it a race consciousness.'[23] Ashbee was also a friend of Lord Redesdale, father of the Mitford girls, and translator of Chamberlain's *Foundations of the 19th century*, a fundamental text of German racism and anti-Semitism.[24] Since we will end with Ashbee in Jerusalem, it is worth noting that he was, surprisingly and without public acknowledgement, technically Jewish: his mother was a German Jew from Hamburg. In his reminiscences, however, he always distances himself from Jews, portraying them as 'other' to himself, and, indeed, is scathing about the potential of Zionism and about the Jews he encountered in Jerusalem.[25]

Ashbee's campaigns and writings led not just to a new public interest in what would come to be called architectural heritage, but also to the establishment of the Survey of London, the publication that still thrives as the official history of London, and is still used for the listing of buildings in London— probably Ashbee's greatest contribution to the cityscape of London.[26] His campaign to preserve Trinity Hospital in the East End of London is still recognized with a plaque on the wall of the building.[27] He was also a strong and active supporter of the Garden City movement. He designed a whole town for King's College, Cambridge, to build in Ruislip—the full-scale design is still in the College library, kept rather ignominiously behind a filing cabinet; the

[20] C. R. Ashbee, *Where the great city stands: a study of the new civics* (London, 1917), p. 22.

[21] Ibid., p. 26.

[22] Ibid., pp. 24–5.

[23] Ibid., p. 25.

[24] See G. Field, *Evangelist of race: the Germanic vision of Houston Stewart Chamberlain* (New York, 1981).

[25] C. R. Ashbee, *A Palestine notebook, 1918–1923* (London, 1923), especially pp. 105–15 on Zionism.

[26] See C. R. Ashbee, *The Survey of London: being the first volume of the register of the committee for the survey of the monuments of Greater London containing the parish of Bromley-by-Bow* (London, 1900).

[27] See C. R. Ashbee, *The Trinity Hospital in Mile End: an object lesson in national history* (London, 1896) for details of the campaign.

town was never built[28]—and he also published increasingly polemical but still interesting treatises on how the material conditions of the city could be improved—in which, with great prescience, he called the automobile 'the enemy of architecture'.[29] In the 1890s, Ashbee became a public figure—a quirky icon for the possibility of standing out against the unthinking march of industrial progress in the name of craftsmanship, city planning, and a turn back towards the traditional values of medieval artistic production.[30] He ascribed his inspiration 'to the founder of Christianity, to the Athenian citizen, to the medieval state builders, to the modern exponent of socialist economics'—a classic 1890s combination!—and aimed to reconstruct citizenship and production 'in conformity with the ways and methods of the medieval Guild'.[31] His art, his campaigning, and his lifestyle, set him at the centre of the self-conscious sense of modern progress through a love of the past that is so typical of the 1890s. 'Aesthetics and History' could, he argued, save us from 'the sordid materialism' of modern life'.[32] It is as such a figure that Ashbee has entered the history of the Arts and Crafts movement.[33]

Ashbee married in 1898 (his father, from whom CRA was completely estranged, did not attend the wedding),[34] though he was gay. He was great friends, as a student at King's, with Edward Carpenter, the art critic and sexual guru, and with the essayist, Sinologist, and fellow of King's, Goldsworthy Lowes Dickinson, both of whom led him to recognize his own sexuality. (Lowes Dickinson remained Ashbee's closest and most trusted friend over many years.) In 1897, the 35-year-old artist met the 17-year-old Janet Forbes, and proposed soon afterwards. He wrote to her with a surprising candour: 'Comradeship to me so far—an intensely close and all absorbing personal attachment, "love" if you prefer the word—for my men and boy friends, has been the one guiding principle in life'; 'There may be many comrade friends but only one comrade wife'; 'These things,' he concluded, 'are hard to write about.'[35] He hoped that the 17-year-old girl would understand. It is not clear she understood at all.

[28] See Ashbee, *Where the great city*, plate 55.

[29] Ashbee, *Where the great city*, is the fullest statement of this principle.

[30] See C. R. Ashbee, *Transactions of the Guild and School of Handicraft* (London, 1890) and idem, *Chapters in workshop re-construction and citizenship* (London, 1894).

[31] Ashbee, *Chapters*, pp. 12, 125.

[32] Ashbee, *American sheaves*, p. 95.

[33] Crawford, *C. R. Ashbee*, is best; see also MacCarthy, *Simple life*, for the Cotswold years.

[34] The estrangement is unexplained, but possibly associated with the divorce of Henry Ashbee: his wife and unmarried daughters moved in with his son. The estrangement was total and lasted until death. Henry Ashbee's will, with scandalous malice, left money to his daughters only if they could prove to trustees that they could not earn a living and if they were not living with Charles. The press were horrified and fascinated. See Gibson, *Erotomaniac*, pp. 150–1.

[35] Letter, 2 Sept. 1897, cited in Ashbee, *Janet Ashbee*, p. 25, and, more fully, in Crawford, *C. R. Ashbee*, p. 75.

But they did get married ... On the wedding night, he kissed her fondly and went off to write a letter to his mother about how he would always love *her* more than any other person alive.[36] After three years of unconsummated marriage, Janet fell in love with another man, Gerald Bishop, who was also married, and who reciprocated her feelings. But duty and morality prevailed, and this relationship was also unconsummated. After six years, Janet, not unsurprisingly, had a mental breakdown, to which Charles responded with heartening sympathy, and they had four daughters in rapid succession. The letters and diaries of this marriage give a fascinating insight into the daily workings of a relationship caught between the strictures of public morality and the gradual development of a personal honesty deeply at odds with that morality. He describes to her picking up a guardsman on the Strand and taking him off on a walking holiday in France; she replies that she cannot deny shedding a tear over his letter, but adds that since he had been so good to her over her difficulties previously, she gave his holiday romance her blessing. This is not exactly a traditional Victorian marriage.[37]

By 1916, however, things had taken a turn for the worse in Ashbee's career. Many of the guild workers were killed in the Great War; fashion and austerity greatly reduced demand for the work anyway. Ashbee, now in his fifties, was too old to fight. He applied for the rather dispiriting job as a lecturer in the Egyptian Ministry of Public Instruction in Cairo, and duly set off for Egypt.[38] (It is not clear there were any other applicants.) It was from Egypt in 1919 that he was summoned to Palestine by Ronald Storrs. This too is an extraordinary story. Ronald Storrs was the first military commander of Jerusalem under the Mandate. Storrs had heard Ashbee give a school talk at his high school, Charterhouse, when Storrs had been a boy—and remembered it as the only interesting 'entertainment' talk he had heard at school. So he summarily invited Ashbee to become the first civic adviser—town planner—of Jerusalem: this is really the old boy network at work.[39] So in 1919, in late middle age, Ashbee took over in Jerusalem.

He was faced by an Ottoman town where a significant majority of the population were poor Jews, and where the starvation and economic deprivation of the war had been particularly intense. Although the town had now

---

[36] See Ashbee, *Janet Ashbee*, p. 34.

[37] See ibid., pp. 133–6.

[38] Volume five of Ashbee's unpublished memoirs, 'Fantasia in Egypt', records his experiences and reactions, which he sums up as 'a sense of impotent rage and humiliation', a 'sourness' (p. 10), and (p. 110) as the 'fantastic irrelevance' of his work there. He submitted a report to Lord Milner's commission, parts of which are included in an appendix to the same volume. He was involved with education, and maintained an interest in preservation, but had little outlet for his broader architectural interests.

[39] R. Storrs, *Orientation* (London, 1939), p. 323.

begun to spread beyond its sixteenth-century walls, it still had no reliable water supply and barely a single paved road (but no cars either). Its regular tourist trade had collapsed with the war and with the Russian Revolution; it had little industry, and no natural resources. Many buildings, including those of most religious significance, combined intense politicized feeling with years of neglect.[40] Ashbee worked closely with Storrs; they had the authority to pass the legislation they needed, and to enact it successfully. As Ashbee wrote in his first report to the War Office: 'Jerusalem is unique, a "city of the mind", and in it anything is possible.'[41] The results of his ambition are remarkable.

Ashbee's first report, prepared for Storrs and the War Office, was a review of 'Arts and Crafts in Jerusalem.' This might not seem an obvious starting point for town planning in war-torn Jerusalem—but it reveals Ashbee's particular intellectual formation all too clearly. Ashbee travelled the city, cataloguing and exploring its workshops, and collecting postcards and photographs of 'native craftsmen at work', a genre of image popular in the nineteenth century (and easily seen as part of the imperializing gaze). This led him to suggest some quite bizarre remedies for the city, such as revitalizing the industry in indigo dyeing, although there were only two elderly indigo dyers in the city. But it also led to some far-reaching projects, as we will see, including the repair of the Suk, the covered market of the Old City.

It is fascinating—and, within the frame of contemporary dissension over the architectural fabric of Jerusalem, extraordinary—that there appears to have been minimal local resistance to his plans. Jerusalem had suffered very badly indeed during the last years of the war from famine, disease, and the freezing weather as much as from violence—and restoration was desperately needed.[42] There was already considerable antagonism between the various parties in the Holy City, but, although Ashbee was involved in the argument over the Western Wall (the significance of which he rather airily dismisses[43]), his own policies appear cannily to have largely avoided specific religious and political problems. The deputy mayor, a Syrian Greek, said to him, 'You English are doing so much here, planning such a wonderful city, showing us the way to so many new and strange things, that I suppose in twenty years'

---

[40] General account in Y. Ben-Arieh, *Old City*; Y. Ben-Arieh, *New City*; see also E. Jaffe, *Yemin Moshe: the story of a Jerusalem neighbourhood* (London, 1988); R. Kark, *Jerusalem neighbourhoods: planning and by-laws (1855–1930)* (Jerusalem, 1991); E. Zoin-Goshen, *Beyond the wall: chapters in urban Jerusalem* (Jerusalem, 2006). David Woodward, *Hell in the Holy Land: World War I in the Middle East* (Lexington, 2006) is useful on the military background.

[41] This first report is unpublished, and Ashbee's copy is now in the Ashbee papers in the library of King's College, Cambridge. He used the same language in C. R. Ashbee, *A Palestine notebook*, pp. 3, 18.

[42] See G. Biger, *An empire in the Holy Land: the historical geography of the British administration in Palestine, 1917–1929* (Jerusalem, 1994).

[43] Ashbee, *Notebook*, pp. 146–8.

time we shall want to be turning you out.'[44] The deputy mayor's anticipated timing was only a little awry, and Ashbee may have missed any bite or irony behind his comments; indeed, Ashbee responded: 'that's the right spirit. It isn't "nationalism", or the "empire" that counts, but the idea, the fact of devotion and beauty'—as if politics or commitments (in either direction) could and should be simply subordinated to Arts and Crafts principles.[45] But Ashbee's stay in Jerusalem was also a remarkable window of opportunity between the difficulties of the First World War and the imminent Arab nationalist riots and, later, more violent Arab/Jewish conflict—a moment when the combination of the firmness of British rule, a genuine and recognized need for the reconstruction of the civic infrastructure, and the lack of resistance in such cultural matters, made his work possible.[46] He had broad support in Britain in high places—he describes his meetings with Curzon at the Foreign Office, with the American ambassador, with 'Zionist friends', with the archbishop of Canterbury, and with Lord Milner, who told him to go to the prime minister because 'he will help you, he believes in Jerusalem'.[47] He also published a report of his work in *The Times* of 5 February 1919. *The Times*' staff added its heading to his report, 'the Napoleonic Vision', which captures something of what Ashbee calls the 'effervescent optimism' of this period.[48] Although he continued to bemoan the fact that 'our politicians thwart our administrators',[49] in Jerusalem the feisty administrator could, for once, temporarily transcend such political barriers. Ashbee made the most of this opportunity.

Ashbee and Storrs put in place four particularly important strategic policies in response to their initial survey of the city. First, a law was passed that forbade all building material except Jerusalem stone—and they explicitly banned corrugated iron. (We do not need Wolverhampton in Jerusalem, as Ashbee put it.) It is still the law that all buildings in Jerusalem must be at least faced with Jerusalem stone—although most people today seem to believe it is an Israeli regulation. The motivations behind this law are typical of the Arts and Crafts movement, and of Ashbee's own writing on the built environment: the requirement to use local materials, traditional materials, and a resistance to modern mass-produced industrial products. As we will see, this desire to recover traditional materials also led to some more paradoxical decisions. The

---

[44] Ashbee, *Notebook*, p. 167.
[45] Ibid.
[46] See Biger, *An empire in the Holy Land*, for the broader context of the reconstruction of Palestine.
[47] Ashbee, *Notebook*, pp. 61–77. By 1922, however, plans under the name of the high commissioner, Herbert Samuel, for the development of Palestinian arts and crafts, inaugurated by an exhibition, were shelved by order of the Colonial Office.
[48] Ashbee, *Notebook*, pp. 78–9.
[49] Ibid., p. 81.

result of this first piece of legislation, however, is a remarkable uniformity of texture and colour in the stone of the city, especially around the Old City, as an expression of historical continuity in architectural materiality.

Second, with equal imaginative scope, and ability to enact a policy, Ashbee changed the whole vista of the city. He declared that the walls, built by Suleiman the Magnificent in the sixteenth century, were the best example of a complete medieval enceinte in Europe, or at least would be when restored.[50] For Ashbee, as for the Pre-Raphaelites, the word medieval was the lure of lures. And, it is worth noting, the sixteenth century could count here as the medieval. The Town Planning Report that Ashbee prepared for the War Office stated as Principle Number One for work in Jerusalem: 'To ensure proper restoration and preservation ... so that its medieval aspect may be maintained.'[51] It is rare that one can see so directly the artistic and historical principle behind a town-planning scheme. In Jerusalem, there is a constant, often violent, battle over what needs to be preserved, what excavated. In order to excavate, the upper levels are inevitably destroyed. Restoring or preserving a lower level means not preserving or restoring fully an upper level. One of the great battles of contemporary archaeology is thus between the biblical archaeologists, who wish always to reach the older levels, usually with the agenda of proving the biblical accounts authentic, and the Christian archaeologists who have an interest in the Roman empire material, and the Islamists, for whom the medieval Muslim palaces are central: the agendas are transparent.[52] But, for Ashbee, it was his Pre-Raphaelite training that led him to privilege the medieval—with huge consequence.

---

[50] C. R. Ashbee, *Jerusalem 1918–1920, being the records of the Pro-Jerusalem Council during the period of the British military administration* (London, 1921), p. 21. That Europe is the frame is typical of Ashbee's vision. Later architects, notably St Austen Barbe Harrison and Clifford Holliday, strove to integrate Eastern/local elements into their new designs: see R. Fuchs and G. Herbert, 'Representing Mandatory Palestine: Austen St Barbe Harrison and the representational buildings of the British Mandate in Palestine, 1922–37', *Architectural History*, 43 (2000), pp. 281–333, and Cormack in this volume.

[51] Unpublished; also in the Ashbee papers in the library of King's College, Cambridge. Interestingly, an article in the Egyptian newspaper *Sphinx* (15 Feb. 1919), which undoubtedly reflects official policy, is a card-carrying rejection of restoration in Morris's terms: 'There is no question of restoration. The aim of the authorities is rather to discover and to preserve all that remains of the past, and to undo as far as possible, the evil that has been done.' The gap between rhetoric and practice, and the shiftiness of the language of preservation/restoration is strongly marked here.

[52] See N. Silberman, *Digging for God and country*; A. Marcus, *The view from Nebo: how archaeology is re-writing the Bible and reshaping the Middle East* (Boston, MA, New York, and London, 2000); and, with equally transparent agendas, N. Abu El-Haj, *Facts on the ground: archaeological practice and territorial self-fashioning in Israeli society* (Chicago, 2001); S. Ricca, *Reinventing Jerusalem: Israel's reconstruction of the Jewish quarter after 1967* (London, 2007).

Ashbee proceeded, first of all, to make the walls the centre of his development plans. Figure 6.1 is the before and after of Ashbee's imagination.
Above is the photograph of the city walls, in a state of some disrepair.
Below, is his idealized drawing of a medieval town, with its towers rising
above a verdant landscape, cleared of all unsightly impediments. 'Rebuilding
the walls of Jerusalem' was a catchphrase of the British Restorationists who
had worked to bring the Jews back to Palestine since the 1840s, as well as
part of the rhetoric of longing in the Bible. Ashbee harnessed this imagery
to the Arts and Crafts agenda. The trees that frame this picture look like
English oaks (they do not, at any rate, look like the trees of the arid environment of Jerusalem). And it is a striking contrast to the innumerable photographs and even paintings of the Holy Land that the two youths in the
foreground are running playfully across the sward, rather than standing or
squatting in still observation, the standard pose of the shepherd or Bedouin

The Jaffa Gate reconstruction as at present, looking towards the city.   *No. 44.*

*The same, as suggested when the unsightly obstructions that hide the wall
line are cleared away.*   *No. 45.*

Figure 6.1:   C. R. Ashbee's image of a new Jerusalem, from *Jerusalem 1918–1920, being the
records of the Pro-Jerusalem Council during the period of the British military administration*
(London, 1921).

in Western imagery.[53] They look, that is, more like stereotypes of British boys romping.

To keep the walls' medieval aspect, he planned to remove the large, ornate clock tower from Jaffa Gate. Figure 6.2 is a famous picture of Allenby marching into Jerusalem to claim the Holy City for the British. The clock tower, a nineteenth-century Ottoman addition, in rather undistinguished, generic Eastern style, rises above him, registering the time of 7.30. Ashbee, shocked at the aesthetic disaster of this construction (as he saw it), suggested that the tower be taken down immediately (it was placed at ground level, near the post office, as a sop to the residents who complained at the removal, on the grounds they needed it to tell the time).[54] Buildings and other structures had been built right up against the walls or into them at various points in the circuit. Figure 6.3 shows the celebrated Fast Hotel, the most popular residence of European travellers, hard by the Jaffa Gate. There are also stalls and sheds either side of the postern. The hotel, and other such buildings abutting the walls, were also demolished to clear the view of the walls. Jaffa Gate was, and is, the most frequented point of entry for the city, and particularly concerned Ashbee. Figure 6.4 shows, to the left, the Jaffa Gate in its most ruinous state (the picture is actually from 1898, nearly twenty years before the British arrived—the selection of image is clearly designed to maximize the rhetorical force of the juxtaposition of the two images, and the British loved to compare the ruinously arrogant and destructive entrance of Kaiser Wilhelm with the modest, restorative arrival of Allenby). To the right is Ashbee's design for its new development (complete now with fully Oriental extras). Notice he reconstructs a moat (which every decent medieval fortress should have), with bridging arches, which he calls a 'fosse' to give the right touch of the Olden Days. A roadway across this territory was not, in fact, built for many more years, but Ashbee did manage to restore the citadel, the so-called David's Tower, with such civic gardens.

In restoring the walls, he also reconstructed the walkway round the ramparts, the 'spinal cord of the Jerusalem Park system',[55] a task that required some particularly awkward reconstruction and destruction, where buildings had been incorporated into the upper level of the walls. This rampart walkway was designed in order for Western tourists to be able to progress round

[53] See Y. Ben-Arieh, *Painting the Holy Land in the nineteenth century* (Jerusalem, 1997); and for the photography see, e.g., Y. Nir, *The Bible and the image: the history of photography in the Holy Land, 1839–1899* (Pennsylvania, PA, 1985); S. Gibson, *Jerusalem in original photographs, 1850–1920* (London, 2003); and, discussed with further bibliography, Goldhill, 'The discovery of Victorian Jerusalem'.

[54] Ashbee himself was prevented from seeing through this part of his plan though it was completed just after he left the city: see Ashbee, *Notebook*, pp. 181–2.

[55] Ashbee, *Jerusalem, 1918–1920*, p. 21.

Figure 6.2:   General Allenby marches on foot into Jerusalem as its conqueror in 1917.

the city at a higher level and to look out across the new town, playing the role
of a medieval or biblical soldier, to appreciate the medieval enceinte. That is,
there is also a constructed level of display here, of spectacle. Jerusalem has to
be viewed as well as lived in, and treated as an art object. This is a turning

Figure 6.3:   The Fast Hotel, just outside the Jaffa Gate in Jerusalem.

The Jaffa Gate as it was when the "Kaiser's   *No. 40.*   *Suggested reconstruction of the fosse at the*   *No. 41.*
breach" was being made, and before the   *Jaffa Gate.*
building of the Turkish Clock Tower.

Figure 6.4:   The Jaffa Gate in 1898, and in Ashbee's imagination, from *Jerusalem 1918–1920*.

point in Jerusalem becoming a museum or memorial of itself—something
that has become the dominant aesthetic of the Old City, with its constant
work on new reconstructions of an imagined ancient life. Ashbee and Storrs
founded the Pro-Jerusalem Council to oversee all the work of restoration.[56]
They published accounts of their work in two beautifully produced volumes.
On the covers (Figure 6.5)—nicely summing up the work on the walls—is a
calligraphic inscription that reads: 'Walk about Sion and Go Round About
the Towers thereof', and below the central tondo, which combines the Star of
David and the Cross in an abstract design, 'Mark Well Her Bulwarks; Set Up
Her Houses; That Ye May Tell Them That Come After.' The book is a
memorial of the memorializing task of reconstruction, its rebuilding of the
past for posterity. The elegant lettering, so typical of the work of Morris, and
the suitably biblical quotations, display and embody the aesthetics that
underlie the messy business of civic planning.

The removal of buildings next to the walls extended to include not only a
ban on any new building near the newly cleared walls, but also a full town-
planning policy based on Ashbee's passionately held Garden City principles.
Figure 6.6 is one such plan: a neat grid pattern, with hubs of public space,
constructed memorials, and diagonal cross streets. There are linked gardens,
a green belt ('clear belt ... in natural state'), and an image of public life based
on Letchworth or Hampstead Garden Suburb—despite the fact that the
walled city and the style of architecture throughout the region was based on
low-lying houses crammed together around small alleys and courtyards, with
agricultural fields and hills beyond. This plan was never enacted. It is entitled
a plan for 'Restoration and Preservation of the Ancient City'—which perhaps
obscures any tension between the two aims, as well as any precise temporal
reference for the antiquity to be maintained. The different concentric areas
are calibrated with clearly marked boundaries. In the Old City, its 'medieval
aspect' is 'to be preserved', which means 'no new buildings': the Old City is
not to be developed in any way to compromise its perceived medieval form
(but embalmed). The next circle will become the 'clear belt'; then there is a
further area where buildings will only be given permission under 'special conditions' determined by their 'harmony with the general scheme'; finally there
is an outer circle for redevelopment: that is where modernity may be placed.

---

[56] It was explicitly based on the principles of the National Trust, for which Ashbee had lectured
in America (Ashbee, *Notebook*, p. 139). Like so many imperial committees, it invited representatives
of the major concerned parties, while maintaining a majority of the ruling administration.
Included in the thirty-two-strong committee were the mayor of Jerusalem; the presidents of the
Jewish Community, Franciscan Community, and the Dominican Community; the Mufti, the
Greek, and Armenian patriarchs; and the chairman of the Zionist commission, as well as
distinguished academics, Patrick Geddes, Hugues Vincent, and Félix-Marie Abel. This was a
committee of considerable distinction.

Figure 6.5:   The cover of *Jerusalem 1918–1920.*

Here live 'Public Buildings'. Figure 6.7 shows a more extended, proposed green belt marked off in the shaded section, with some new trunk roads schematically indicated, and the university added. If the construction of a new city was beyond the power of Storrs and Ashbee to fulfil, the ability to stop new building in the 'clear belt' was rigidly enforced, and, despite some

Simon Goldhill

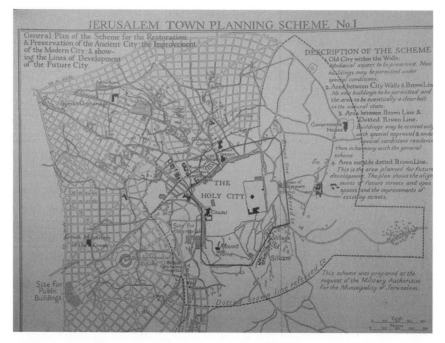

Figure 6.6:   A plan for Jerusalem, drawn up by C. R. Ashbee.

encroachments, is still mainly in operation today. Figure 6.8 is taken from Ashbee's 1917 manifesto, *Where the great city stands*, and is his pen-and-ink drawing of the plan of Letchworth Garden City, halfway between Cambridge and London. It is not simply the case that similar principles motivate both plans: it is also remarkable just how similar the footprint of Jerusalem and Letchworth are made to appear, with their framing of green spaces around urban development around a central cross street. The two plans show with striking clarity how the ground plan of Ashbee's vision was carried from the English Garden City into the Middle East.

The walls of the Old City are one of the most familiar images of Jerusalem. That we can see them the way we can, with such an unimpeded view of their cleared stonework, is the result of the Arts and Crafts aesthetic and the policy of the Garden City movement being brought to Jerusalem in 1919.

Thanks to papers that have only very recently come to light, we can see Ashbee's imaginative thought in process. He travelled the region, collected photographs (his own and those of others), and, in situ or back at his house painted rather beautiful watercolour images of proposed developments, which he put together in juxtaposition in his personal albums. Figure 6.9 is one example of a scheme for a Thomas Cook Hotel on what is now the major thoroughfare, Derech Hevron. The black-and-white photograph is redone in

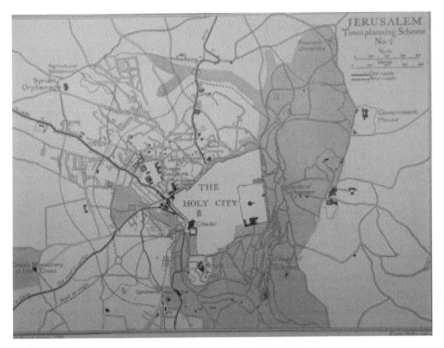

Figure 6.7:   A further plan for Jerusalem, drawn up by C. R. Ashbee.

the pastel colours of the future. The 'real' of the photographic image becomes the imaginative leap of the artist's hand. Yet Ashbee was also in the position to enact at least elements of his vision. In these lovely sketches, we can see in physical form how Ashbee's artistic vision is the grounding of his work as a civic advisor.

The third plank of Ashbee's reforms involved bringing his cherished ideas of the guild to Jerusalem. He had been thinking about this already in Cairo: 'In our view none the less it were better for these lads—the sons of weavers, potters, glass-blowers, cabinet makers—to be practising the crafts they love and studying their much needed service to Western Industrialism than shouting catchword politics in the streets and class rooms', he wrote in a letter to a friend (a remark which reminds us how easily Arts and Crafts became integrated with an imperial policy).[57] His idealism of the male group working together, was also tied up with his own sexual attitudes, inevitably, and he wrote sweetly that he often chose young men to join the guild because of what

---

[57] Vol. five of the unpublished memoirs, 'Fantasia in Egypt', pp. 98–9. He writes also (121): 'The more I think about it the more it seems to me that the Guild—Guild socialism (we haven't got the right name yet) "the Guild Spirit"—is the practical way out of the bureaucratic impasse.' This reflects the more heated remarks in the unedited diaries, e.g. 27 Apr. 1917. He amusingly describes his attempts to get glass-blowing going again in Hebron, in Ashbee, *Notebook*, pp. 153–7.

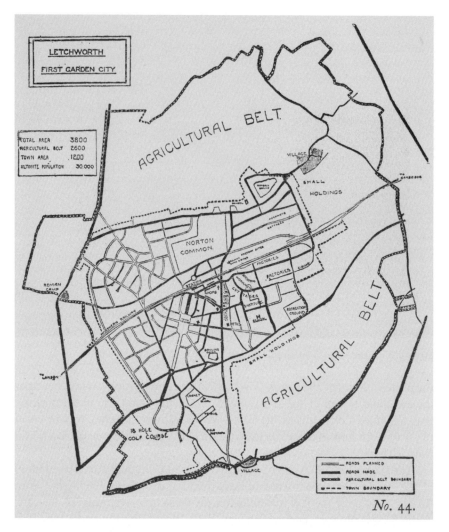

Figure 6.8:   The town plan of the Garden City of Letchworth, taken from Ashbee's *Where the great city stands* (London, 1917).

art could do for them rather than what they could do for art. His interest in guilds and the first report on 'Arts and Crafts' in Jerusalem led directly to the restoration of the Suk, which was falling down both from years of disrepair and from the particularly severe blizzard of 1920, which had an especially deleterious effect on the fabric of the buildings. Ashbee prepared photographs for the Pro-Jerusalem Council, and published a carefully organized before-and-after report. He not only set about repairing the fabric of the Suk, but also established new guilds for Palestinian weavers in particular, institutional-

Figure 6.9: Ashbee's scheme for a Thomas Cook Hotel on what is now Derech Hevron in Jerusalem. King's College Library, Cambridge.

izing his principles of work, once again, albeit now from the position of imperial authority. Figure 6.10 is a wonderful portrait of the ceremony of indenture for new apprentices. The arches of the newly constructed Suk rise cleanly above the ceremony. On the right sit the British matrons in their hats. On the left sit and stand the Arab families. In the middle, standing at the official desk, is Ashbee in military uniform. The ceremony performs the imperial Mandate at all levels: re-educating the natives into their own traditions, now socially restructured with an admixture of the medieval guild; demonstrating and enacting the divide between rulers and ruled through clothing, deportment, and language; developing an economic system that will maintain the wealth of the centre—and doing it all with pomp and circumstance. The Suk is the centre now of Arab Old Jerusalem, visited by thousands of tourists for its exoticism, its old-style Arab market life, and local colour. It is a piquant irony that its material form comes from the link of an 1890s aesthetic policy with a British imperial power structure. What is regarded by so many modern tourists as the most authentic and ancient sign of Eastern exoticism in the Old City is a restoration reliant on the predilections of one British Mandate official.

For the Old City, the Pro-Jerusalem Council established a system of small grants for repairs. This too, however, was tied to a policy of maintaining the

Weaving Apprentices' Ceremony of Indenturing.   *No. 63.*

Figure 6.10:   An indenture ceremony for new apprentices in the Suk in Jerusalem.

traditional fabric of the buildings. They required, for example, that wood windows were replaced or repaired with wood, despite the fact that wood was expensive and difficult to obtain in the environs of the city. The overhanging alley windows also had to be kept in the traditional design. Figure 6.11, from the publication of the Council, shows the paraded fruits of the policy. Metal windows may have been cheaper, longer lasting, and desired by the residents, but the Council, led by Ashbee, took control of the details as much as the broad policy of civic development.

No. 11.

Old wooden window.

No. 12.

On the roof of Sûq el Attarîn.

Figure 6.11:   The restoration details of windows in the Old City of Jerusalem and the damaged suk, from *Jerusalem 1918–1920*.

The fourth strategy I wish to stress is the inverse of the preservation of medieval Jerusalem and the restoration of traditional crafts as the substructure to the medieval city—this shows in the starkest manner how policies of preservation come hand in hand with instituted attitudes of wilful disregard. This fourth policy, it should be clear, was repeatedly enacted in a series of surprising, indeed swingeing decisions, but, unlike the first three policies we have been discussing, it was never explicitly encoded. It is, rather, the flipside of the love of the medieval, prompted as ever by a distaste for modernity—seeing it as no more than a progress towards unthinking materialism and commercial vulgarity. It consists in a stance of sniffy dismissal towards recent, contemporary building where it did not conform to the aesthetic principles of the viewing critics. The test case that displays the policy most strikingly concerns the Russian Compound.

Throughout the nineteenth century, thousands of Russian pilgrims came to Jerusalem for Easter week.[58] Many were very poor, and it took them weeks of arduous travel to reach the city. They came with the aim of receiving sparks of the Holy Fire from the Church of the Holy Sepulchre at the climax of the Easter celebrations. They would catch the sparks in their hats, and would aim to return to Russia and to be buried with their hats. This influx of pilgrims was not just a yearly event but had economic expectations for the residents of the city. In the 1870s, a huge compound was built outside the walls for the pilgrims: a domed cathedral, a hospital, two dormitories for ordinary pilgrims, a fine hostel for noble pilgrims, and a house for the council.[59] This project was completed despite the fact that Russia and Turkey had been at war in the Crimea only a few years before. Indeed, the parade ground on which the Russian Compound began was a gift to the Russian tsar from the Sublime Porte. Both the facts that Jerusalem's military presence lost its parade ground, and that this was a gift from the sultan to his recent enemy in war, are testimony to the intricate and sometimes baffling turns of diplomacy and national interest in this era. The compound was walled, and became its own little Russian town. As New Jerusalem spread, the compound was gradually built around (and what was once a free-standing and distinctive monument to a foreign national presence in the Holy City is now wholly absorbed into the city's landscape). However, in nineteenth-century Jerusalem, the Russian Compound was one of the most distinctive and largest developments outside the city walls.

These fine buildings are all from the decade of Ashbee's youth, and are some of the best examples of nineteenth-century Russian national architecture

---

[58] The most vivid description is S. Graham, *With the Russian pilgrims to Jerusalem* (London, 1913).
[59] See Kroyanker, *Adrikhalut bi-Yerushalayim.*

outside Russia—and therefore of little interest to Ashbee. 'Bastard Moscow', he called it with a sniff. The compound was immediately turned over for civic use. One hostel became a prison, its classical pediments topped now with barbed wire, its courtyard turned over to armoured vehicles and checkpoints (Figure 6.12); the other, with oppressively neat symmetry, became the law court. They have remained dedicated to these functions. The hospital is now the administration for parking offences. The central vista, a ceremonial approach across a rather grand square to the elaborate façade and multiple domes of the cathedral, is now ruined by traffic (Figure 6.13). What could have been a superb Victorian plaza, with elegant buildings around courtyards, has become a sour, overcrowded mishmash of the cheapest redevelopment— which, with an inevitable irony, now also houses the Israeli Authority for the Preservation of Historic Buildings. Ashbee cared to preserve the medieval and what he could call the traditional: he had no eye for 'the Victorian'—near contemporary work—especially when foreign. Decisions about preservation are always also decisions about destruction. Here too the whole shape of the city and how its administration relates to its architecture has been constructed according to a very precise aesthetic agenda, forged in the 1890s and focused on the Arts and Crafts in the Cotswolds.

Figure 6.12:   The transformation of the Victorian Russian Compound into modern administrative buildings.

Figure 6.13: The transformation of the cathedral at the heart of the Victorian Russian Compound by modern development.

Ashbee did not stay long in Jerusalem. He worked there for only four and a half years, before retiring to the house where his wife had been born, near Sevenoaks in Kent. He died as late as 1942, largely a forgotten figure. His last surviving daughter, Felicity, who had travelled with him to Jerusalem, died in 2008. Although Ashbee has been justly reclaimed as a leading light of the

Arts and Crafts movement, and of the historic buildings movement, and even, to a lesser extent, of the Garden City movement, his influence in Jerusalem has been far less appreciated, not least because Ronald Storrs is very chary with any reference to him in his memoirs, even when they starred in a performance of *The Merchant of Venice* (of all plays!) together in that first Christmas in the Holy City. Storrs was 'quite furiously angry' by the publication of Ashbee's warts-and-all memoirs of his Jerusalem stay, and this rage may explain his *damnatio memoriae*.[60] But most importantly, what has been systematically ignored is the influence of Ashbee's intellectual development in the Arts and Crafts and Garden City movements in his activities in Jerusalem. He was responsible for the fabric of the buildings, the design of restorations, and the overall policy of development and preservation for the first years of the Mandate, and much of what he put in place is still determinative of the visual culture of the Holy City. Ashbee brought the Cotswolds to Jerusalem.

It would be hard to imagine a more important symbolic cityscape than Jerusalem, or a place where preservation is more intimately connected with politics, religion, and empire. But here in Jerusalem we have an extraordinary case of the principles of Morris and Ruskin, as taken up and developed by Ashbee, affecting the policies of preservation and planning. The shape, the design, and the use of one of the most important cities in the imagination of the world was fundamentally altered, through 1919 to 1923 (and beyond), according to aesthetic principles laid down in the 1890s. The life of an aesthetic theory is not limited to its immediate years of production or immediate influence but can spread with unpredictable time lags following the unpredictable personal narratives of the artists in question. Ashbee and his theories had their greatest impact when they were no longer fashionable, or even much recognized: but this is when they were most fully enacted. In part, this is because of Ashbee's involvement with the imperial system. The Mandate set out to improve Jerusalem: it brought in a water supply, reliable electricity, trains, tax, justice, and so forth. It saw itself as bringing much needed civilization to the Holy City, and, with the classic cognitive dissonance of empire, the Mandate officials were always baffled and upset by the ungratefulness of the inhabitants who continued to fight for self-determination. Ashbee's cleansing of the city—and the metaphors and realities of cleansing were also central—is an integral part of this imperial project. The aesthetics of the Arts and Crafts movement here becomes fully implicated and intertwined with the structures of imperial authority and power. The surprise of Ashbee's story finally is simply the surprise of seeing how the material life of a Middle Eastern city in the 1920s could be so affected by the emergence of an 1890s

[60] Ashbee, *Notebook*: 'quite furiously angry' is the description of Richmond, Ashbee's friend and replacement (from the Ashbee journals, 24 Jan. 1924).

British Arts and Crafts aesthetic—and all because Ashbee had gone to give a school talk at Charterhouse ...

For Ashbee, the Great War was also a turning point in his ideas of how a city should be preserved: 'The disaster of the Great War has forced upon all men and women the necessity of preserving all that is possible of the beauty and the purpose, in actual form, of the civilizations that have passed before.'[61] He saw the previous thirty years of work as 'shot to pieces by the war'.[62] 'The War has shattered the system', he reflected, but he saw in the idealism and plans of the young as much chaos and despair as hope.[63] Preservation was now not just 'aesthetics and history' aiming for the 'protection of beauty', but the struggle to save civilization itself and create a new civics from the horrifying destruction that mechanization, materialism, and political violence had brought about. Yet it was the very contingency of war that gave Ashbee the opportunity to enact his theories. In a way that was impossible in London or in England, he could enact a full programme of civic and architectural reform in Jerusalem: 'One isn't allowed to do "reconstruction" at home ... one does it here', he reflected, with a sadly triumphant note that he had achieved more in his short stay in Jerusalem than in his previous eighteen years of work in England.[64] 'We have really got great things underway,' he wrote, 'I have started two new industries; restored some old streets; am laying out parks and gardens; saving the walls of al-Quds; have rebuilt Nabi Samuil; started an apprenticeship system among the weavers; am planning new roads, parks, and markets, and making designs for half a dozen important buildings.' There was, as he declared, 'a great idea in it'.[65] The empire was also a place where preservation, reconstruction, a 'new civics' could be tested and embodied without the compromises, negotiations, and vested interests of politics that dominated policy in Britain. The power relations of imperial rule established this civic advisor in an unprecedented position to fulfil the idealist artistic aims by which he had been nourished over so many years—and gave an unexpected and practical sense to the old promise of building a New Jerusalem.

This, then, has turned out finally to be a story about distance. Jerusalem was once an archetypal city of distance, a city from which Jews and Europeans were exiled and to which Mamluk political renegades were exiled. The difficulties of travel and the exigencies of politics made it a city much longed for, and much idealized. Jerusalem became a way of expressing the distance between the ideals of a heavenly city and the mundane corruptions of con-

---

[61] Ashbee, *Jerusalem, 1920–1922*, p. 4.
[62] Ashbee, *Notebook*, p. 77.
[63] Ashbee, *Where the great city*, p. 152; idem, *Notebook*, pp. 164–88.
[64] Ashbee, *Notebook*, p. 31.
[65] Ibid., p. 167.

temporary society. The Victorian age changed the practicalities of this, as in so many other areas. Baedeker in hand, travelling with Thomas Cook by steamship, sending a wire home with news—suddenly the Holy Land of Bible study was a holiday destination, and the disappointments of the smelly, poor, unpaved, unimpressive Eastern city, needed some ... distance: a renegotiation of the image, of the viewer's historic subjectivity, located between the past and the present. Archaeology rediscovered the truth of the biblical past, and reauthorized the city as a *lieu de mémoire*; exploration remapped the city and the countryside as the Holy Land; religious seriousness produced an experience of the past—here was where Jesus had stood—whereby the past's distance collapsed, by historical imagination, into the experience of the present. When the Mandate took over, with its passion for order and practical solutions, Jerusalem offered unique and pressing historical and religious injunctions. If, as the archbishop of York said, 'Palestine is ours', what, then, is the gap between us and them, and how should it be handled? Whose past is this urban landscape? These questions are, of course, still being worked through, but the answer of the first civic advisor who set British policy in the city came from his intellectual formation. He brought his own past with him, that is, his 1890s aesthetics that privileged the medieval on the one hand, and the new Garden City movement on the other: a specific blend of topographical distancing—the Garden City movement is all about creating green distance between urban experiences—and a vision of historical distance, the search for a lost integrated past of labour and architecture in the medieval world. But when I see Ashbee standing between the Arab parents and the British rulers in the Suk, where he hoped to create an integrated community, what one sees most vividly, as so often in the empire, and in Jerusalem above all, is the distance still inscribed between the figures captured in this historical moment.

Part IV

Empires and Civilizations

Outside of the Mediterranean and the Near East, British imperial power did not have to reckon with heritages that were explicitly part of its own heritage. This absence, and British ignorance, facilitated the construction of social–evolutionary schemas—ladders of 'civilization'—which distanced the physical remains of past foreign cultures, consigning them to 'barbarism', or (in some ways less distanced, as more obviously the roots of modernity) the 'primitive'. This was a common intellectual justification for destruction or, to use the contemporary nicety, 'improvement'.

On the other hand, imperial rule in practice found, over time, many reasons to take these vestiges of barbarism more seriously. The construction of the 'ladder of civilization' itself required careful attention to evidences of earlier or more primitive phases. This may have deepened the feeling of distance from the 'native' but it could also foster sentiments of a common humanity, differentiated by time and space, and an interest in the sources and nature of diversity and divergence. Attentiveness to colonized people's histories could itself be a marker of civilization—it seemed not only to demonstrate that the imperialists were better able to measure up and conserve cultural heritages than the colonized, but appeared to soften the whole imperial enterprise by drawing attention to its civilizational rather than its more brutally political or military functions. In many places it proved easier for the state to arrogate preservationist powers to itself in the empire, as part of the civilizing mission, than it did in the metropole, where civilization was supposed to look after itself. Especially towards the end of our period, when several European empires were competing with each other for global prestige, performance of good custodianship or trusteeship could be something to boast about. And, as always, it proved less easy to keep the 'higher' and the 'lower' apart on the ground than it did in the textbooks. Local knowledge about local conditions was always being deployed in the practice of imperial rule, however subtly or subliminally. It often suited imperial rule to wear the garb of local rulers. This, too, provided raw materials for nationalist movements at the end of our period which learned to reclaim that clothing for themselves—even if, in doing so, they often perpetuated the imperial refashioning of indigenous heritage.

7

Appropriation to Supremacy:
Ideas of the 'Native' in the Rise of
British Imperial Heritage

SUJIT SIVASUNDARAM

THERE IS STILL a great deal of uncertainty surrounding the basic terms that should be adopted in explaining cultural contact on the global stage. One difficult issue is how to write of heritages without essentializing them and creating benchmarks of purity and authenticity. The category of the 'native' provides a classic illustration of the point at issue. For the most part post-colonial scholars do not utilize this word, as it is clouded in connotations of racial supremacy. More recently, it has been replaced by a more politically correct word, namely, 'indigenous'. Yet both 'native' and 'indigenous' suffer the same analytical problem: they reify heritages and assume that they can be separated into localized and uncorrupted forms. This chapter is an attempt to study one particular moment in the emergence of the 'native', in the late eighteenth and early nineteenth centuries. The argument is that the idea of the 'native' has roots that stretch in several directions: Pacific islanders, Asians, and Africans played a role in defining territorial identities, bonds of attachment to rulers, and patterns of settlement prior to contact with colonists. But empire, and in particular the British empire, recontextualized mutating senses of the authentic in global maps of heritage, thus minting a new idea of the 'native' out of extant articulations. Throughout this process what appears is not an unproblematic concept of the 'native' or 'indigenous', but how claims of a separate heritage arose in contexts of hybridity and creolization.

Cultural encounters and imperial expansion in this period were different from that of a previous age, because this was a time when the British imperial complex swung east and explored new oceans.[1] The British were seeking to secure their hegemony over other European rivals with regard to empire, and

---

[1] This is not to take on board the now disputed thesis of a 'swing to the east', because the British empire undoubtedly carried on having Atlantic interests. For more on this see P. J. Marshall, *The making and unmaking of empires: Britain, India and America, c. 1750–1783* (Oxford, 2005).

Proceedings of the British Academy, **187**, 149–170. © The British Academy 2013.

their systems of trade were becoming more formal territorial structures of rule. Concomitant with this shift to conquest in Asia and elsewhere, there arose a distinct sense of the British nation and its heritage, and this necessitated an assessment of its placement on the world stage. Theorists of language, migration, ethnology, and other broader facets of culture—encompassing everything from clothes to hair—sought to fit the peoples of the world into boxes, grids, and scales in order to denote progress, civilization, cultural status, scriptural patterns, and racial and national stock. In the midst of these imperial, domestic, and intellectual changes, the British notion of the 'native' shifted between the late eighteenth and mid-nineteenth centuries. Whereas the 'native' first signified the intelligent, noble, and highly skilled craftsman and guide, and the remnant of a glorious past civilization, the term came to stand for the bearer of an inferior civilization, doomed to extinction or never to reach the heights of British achievement. This was a rather dramatic recasting of the idea of the 'native'.

This redefinition is discernible in all three of the contexts of British imperialism discussed below: the South Pacific, Southeast Asia, and southern Africa. One way of understanding the shift from the entanglement of Britons with non-Europeans to a posture of distance is to explain this as an outcome of globalization. Travel and imperialism had a newly expanded reach; this meant that comparisons and placements of cultures and heritages became the norm. At the same time, the historian can make sense of this as a feature of cultural contact. When one heritage is adopted and incorporated within the other, it is redefined in that process, in intellectual and material terms. Once that happens, the history of appropriation is forgotten, allowing a newly resurgent sense of supremacy. The relationship between this shift in the idea of the 'native' and conceptions of race is complex. Some historians have pointed to a turn to stricter forms of race as we proceed through the nineteenth century, and contrasted this ideology of race with the free association and sympathy of the late eighteenth century. However, flaws in this argument have now emerged: race was in use in the earlier period and it could take on a biologized rendition quite early. It is also important not to simplify the late eighteenth-century context of attachment to the non-European world as one devoid of power or notions of superiority. At the same time, old ideas of cultural difference, tied to civilization and climate, carried on reverberating down through the nineteenth century.[2] The shifting sense of the 'native' has thus less to do with race and power, which may have been more consistent aspects of

[2] For a further discussion of the historiography of race and empire in this period, see, Sujit Sivasundaram, 'Race, empire and biology before Darwinism', in Denis Alexander and Ron Numbers, eds., *Biology and ideology: from Descartes to Dawkins* (Chicago, 2010), pp. 114–28.

this story, and more to do with the structures and processes of empire, cultural contact, and globalization.

One reason why it is important to attend to both steps in this story—by starting with British attention to the cultural heritages of the wider world before stressing the harnessing of British culture as an exemplar of a higher goal—is because it takes Asians, Africans, and Pacific islanders seriously. If historians of heritage are concerned with disappearing cultural forms, it is vital that they give agency to the people who practised those renditions of heritage. Each of the cases from the South Pacific, Southeast Asia, and southern Africa brings extant traditions of heritage into the picture, not to urge their purity or lack of contact with a wider world, but to show how, by the late eighteenth century in each of these widely spread areas, the renewal or loss of practices was in motion, somewhat independently of the British empire. In order to trace the changing idea of the 'native', both in a British and non-British context, it is important to clarify how the concept of heritage is utilized in this chapter. A rather wide definition is adopted, which encompasses cultural, intellectual, and environmental knowledge in the contexts of British expansion, passed down over a relatively long period and reframed prior to and in the process of colonialism. In order to guide the argument it may be helpful to class the types of heritage analysed here under three headings, as they appear in the course of the chapter: voyaging, historicizing, and naturalizing.

I

In the Pacific Ocean, exploration or voyaging became the visible face of informal colonization by the end of the eighteenth century. For the British public, the three epic voyages of Captain Cook made the constellation of islands that dotted the South Seas into the definition of the exotic. In the aftermath of his dramatic and violent death, Captain Cook came to epitomize the naval hero: he had dispelled myths of the great southern continent and the North West Passage by accurate surveying, and had scored a remarkable victory against scurvy, by securing the health of his crews. Yet this line of analysis forgets one extraordinary fact about Pacific islanders. They have as much right to be recognized as great explorers.

There is enough evidence to establish how Pacific islanders voyaged across the vast swathes of this oceanic world, prior to European contact. The current consensus is that a corridor of easy voyaging stretched from Southeast Asia to the end of the Solomon Islands. In this circuit, good weather conditions—the winds and currents—facilitated easy navigation. As time passed, islanders sailed even further to the distant reaches of the Pacific, and towards

South America, so progressing from west to east.[3] These journeys were undertaken in single outrigger or large double-hulled canoes, which carried a good amount of water, fermented breadfruit, which could last for about three months, and, at times, plants that could be grown on landing, and even livestock.[4]

The Polynesians, in particular, created a triangle of settlement across the vast Pacific, which had as its points Hawaii, New Zealand, and Latin America. But, from 1500 or earlier, these Polynesian voyages became less frequent, and a series of islands in the triangle of settlement were abandoned. The cause of this change is still debated, but it could be related to changing climactic conditions.[5] The Polynesian system of navigation aided these successful voyages. The islanders relied on star positions at night and the sun at day, the speed of the wind and current, and the swell of the sea caused by different kinds of winds. Because the Europeans cast the Polynesians as the most noble of all Pacific islanders in the period under discussion, the Polynesian system of navigation has been seen until recently as superior to any others in the Pacific. Yet there is some evidence that navigational techniques were shared across the Pacific, and also that there were differences in social and cultural systems within the Polynesian world, which makes an essentialized conception of this triangle of settlement problematic.[6]

The undoing of an overly simplistic and romanticized view of Polynesian navigation should include a deconstruction of how Europeans came to terms with these very voyages and categorized them as exemplars of the 'native'. Europeans were fascinated by the islanders' history of voyaging and settlement. But that interest came to define this heritage as naturalistic, when compared with European skills of navigation. It is striking that the visual archive of British exploration in the Pacific is full of images of local canoes. The canoes that Pacific islanders used to come to the side of Cook's *Endeavour*, on the first voyage, were insignificant in size in comparison with the British vessels, and yet they were the first artefacts made by Pacific islanders that Cook's crew saw. For example, in *A voyage towards the South Pole, and round the world* (1777), two detailed plans of canoes named Amsterdam and Britannia appeared within the text. Rather like plans of European vessels, these denote an attempt to master the scale of canoes by precise measurement (Figure 7.1).

[3] Geoffrey Irwin, *The pre-historic exploration and colonisation of the Pacific* (Cambridge, 1992), pp. 3–7. For Pacific navigation see also D. Lewis, *We, the navigators: the ancient art of landfinding in the Pacific* (Honolulu, 1972).
[4] See for instance, Steven Roger Fischer, *A history of the Pacific islands* (Basingstoke, 2002), p. 33.
[5] Nicholas J. Goetzfridt, 'Navigation in the Pacific', in Helaine Selin, ed., *Encyclopaedia of the history of science, technology and medicine in non-Western cultures* (Amherst, MA, 2008), ii, pp. 1739–43.
[6] Richard Fienberg, 'Navigation in Polynesia', in Selin, ed., *Encyclopaedia*, ii, pp. 1743–6.

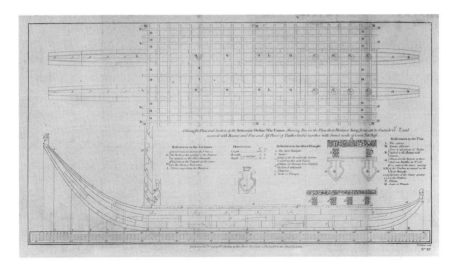

Figure 7.1: 'A Draught Plan and Section of the Britannia Otehite War Canoe', from James Cook, *A voyage towards the South Pole; and round the world* (London, 1777), Plate no. XV. This image shows a detailed plan of one of the war canoes of Tahiti, named Britannia by Cook and his crew. A companion image presented a detailed survey of another canoe named Amsterdam.

Pacific-islander canoes were also made into artefacts of collection and symbols of ornamentation: Herman Spöring, who was in Joseph Banks's party of natural historians and artists, drew a detailed study of the head of a canoe on Cook's first voyage. Another telling set of images was that of the war canoes drawn by William Hodges on the second voyage; the war canoes appear as rather naturalized artefacts in these images (Figure 7.2). But the opposition between the European desire to measure and order, and the Pacific interest in ornamentation and design, must not be exaggerated. Europeans hoped to learn how to make vessels just like those that the Pacific islanders used, while patronizingly praising the craftsmanship of the islanders.

The legacy of this interest was not as much the tropes that were attached to it, but the definition of these canoes as symbols of the 'native'. These studies of canoes fitted into a large enterprise that sought to trace the migration of islanders on a map of race and scripturalism; the 'native' was understood in genealogical terms. Captain Cook famously wrote in Hawaii, the year before he was killed, 'How shall we account for this Nation spreading itself so far over this Vast ocean? We find them from New Zealand to the South, to these islands to the North and from Easter Island to the Hebrides.'[7] Cook's first voyage unravelled the extent to which Pacific peoples spoke related

---

[7] J. C. Beaglehole, *The journals of Captain James Cook on his voyages of discovery*, iii (Cambridge, 1955–67), part 1, p. 279.

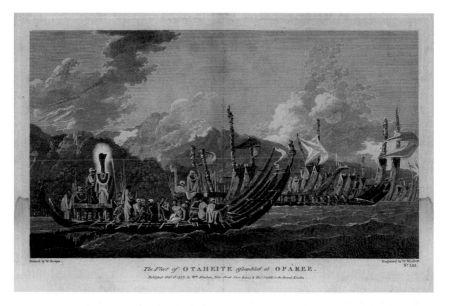

Figure 7.2: 'The fleet of Otaheite assembled at Oparee', from Cook, *A voyage towards the South Pole*, Plate LXI. This image is based on an original drawing by William Hodges, and shows several outrigger canoes out at sea, with Tahitian men on board, including one in the foreground in ceremonial dress.

languages across vast distances. Cook presented his theory of origin in a few lines, according to which he nailed his colours to the idea that islanders travelled from west to east.[8] Tales of the migration of Pacific islanders became entangled in debates about human origins and the question of whether humanity had had one birth or many different births. By 'nation' Cook referred to the Tahitians, whom he took as primary in this process of migration. After Cook came evangelical missionaries, who had been captivated by the accounts of his voyages. In this new age of religion, the question of historic migrations became linked to the biblical narrative. Were Pacific islanders a lost tribe of Israel, the missionaries asked? Ham's curse was critical in the separation of 'nobler' Polynesians from their 'blacker' neighbours to the west, as was the work of missionaries who collected oral histories in an attempt to find vestiges of biblical accounts of creation, the flood, and dispersal.[9]

Yet the making of the 'native' by the insertion of islander heritages into colonial meanings was not predicated simply on the meeting of structures of

[8] Ben Finney, *Voyage of rediscovery: a cultural odyssey through Polynesia* (Berkeley and Los Angeles, CA, 1994), p. 11.
[9] Jane Samson, 'Ethnology and theology: nineteenth-century mission dilemmas' in Brian Stanley, ed., *Christian missions and the Enlightenment* (Grand Rapids, MI, 2001), pp. 99–122.

skill and thought. It was also linked to human stories of collaboration and coercion. This is where it is necessary to go back to Cook's voyages to the Pacific and to meet a highly talented man called Tupaia, who was a high priest, exiled to Tahiti from Raiatea, who came aboard the *Endeavour* on Cook's first voyage. In the words of a recent scholar: 'Tupaia was one of the most intelligent and knowledgeable men in the archipelago—like a natural philosopher.'[10] Cook quickly realized what an asset Tupaia could be to his voyage. For his part, Tupaia was keen to leave Tahiti; his political fortune there was on the wane. In the words of Joseph Banks, who was on board: 'what makes him more than any thing else desireable [sic] is his experience in the navigation of these people and knowledge of the Islands in these seas; he has told us the names of above 70, the most of which he has himself been at'.[11]

Tupaia gave Cook directions for the islands of Huahine and Raiatea. When the ship entered an area of light and variable winds, he prayed: 'O Tane, ara mai matai, ara mai matai!' (O Tane, bring me fair wind!), and cried out when the breeze died down, 'Ua riri au!' (I am angry!).[12] On arrival at Huahine, he stripped down to the waist—and got the ship's surgeon to do the same as a sign of respect to the gods—and mediated in ceremonials that saw the local people give presents in honour of the voyagers' gods.[13] In New Zealand, Tupaia got on very well with the Maori, and when Cook returned again they were distressed to learn of Tupaia's death at Batavia, because some had even named their children after him.[14] So, in the eyes of the islanders, did this voyage become Tupaia's voyage? There is more to support such a line of argument. Tupaia supplied Cook with the information that made possible the drawing of a map of the islands of the Pacific, and this map touched on every significant island group all the way from Fiji in the west to the Marquesas in the east, appearing in concentric circles around his home island of Raiatea:

> Having soon perceived the meaning and use of charts, he gave directions for making one according to his own account, and always pointed to the part of the heavens where each isle is situated; mentioned at the same time that it was either larger or smaller than Taheitee [Tahiti], and likewise whether it was high or low, whether it was peopled or not, adding now and then some curious accounts relative to some of them.[15]

---

[10] Anne Salmond, *The trial of the cannibal dog: Captain Cook in the South Seas* (London, 2003), p. 74.
[11] The *Endeavour* journal of Joseph Banks, 12 July 1769, New South Wales, State Library, CY/3006/352-353.
[12] Salmond, *The trial of the cannibal dog*, p. 96.
[13] Ibid., p. 97.
[14] Ibid., pp. 116–34.
[15] J. R. Forster, *Observations made during a voyage round the world* (London, 1778), p. 511.

While the original has not survived, several versions of this map exist, including one from the Banks papers and another (see Figure 7.3) that was put together later and published by J. R. Foster in 1778.[16] Tupaia may well have known the importance of his expertise, for he conducted himself with pride and a sense of his greatness while aboard. The *Endeavour*'s crew complained that he expected them to pay homage to him, which they found to be beneath their own status.[17] However, the form of the map that was generated from his information is rather curious—it is not a simple token of the indigenous. The version amongst Banks's papers includes the notation that it was 'Drawn by Lieut. James Cook, 1769.' It contains the icon of the ship to denote places visited by Europeans, and is organized around the usual signification of the points of a European compass, even though north and south were confused in the process of drawing up the information provided by Tupaia. At the same time, distances on the map equate with sailing time rather than absolute location. All the islands are named—a practice that was uncommon amongst

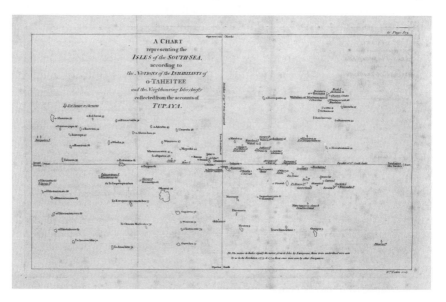

Figure 7.3: 'A Chart representing the Isles of the South Sea according to the notions of the inhabitants of Otahetee and the neighbouring islands chiefly collected from the accounts of Tupaya', from J. R. Forster, *Observations made during a voyage round the world in 1778* (London, 1778), facing p. 513. This should not be read as a replica of the original map drawn by Tupaia, for Forster has imposed a grid, and has attempted to identify the islands in keeping with European knowledge and cartographic tradition.

---

[16] For detailed discussion of the maps: see, Gordon R. Lewthwaite, 'The puzzle of Tupaia's map', *New Zealand Geographer*, 26 (1970), pp. 1–19.
[17] Miles Ogborn, *Global lives: Britain and the world, 1550–1800* (Cambridge, 2008), p. 309.

islanders.[18] This map can then be taken as a hybrid artefact, a middle ground in the process of the creation of the 'native'. It indicates the detachment of islander skills from their historic material forms into new traces on paper, and the errors that are caused in that movement of knowledge into the European corpus.

Tupaia's map is not anomalous—Pacific islanders' charts were used elsewhere and into the early nineteenth century by British explorers. In New Zealand, while Cook was at anchor at Whitianga in 1769, a Maori chief drew an outline of the neighbouring coasts for him.[19] In 1793, the Maori chief Tukitahua drew up a map while in captivity on Norfolk Island, under the charge of Lieutenant-Governor P. G. King. Together with another Maori chief, Tuki—as he was known—he had been taken captive in order to provide knowledge about the techniques utilized to prepare flax, which was deemed critical in supplying the navy with ropes and sails in the South Seas. While at Norfolk Island, Tuki produced a map of New Zealand for the king:

> When they began to understand each other, Toogee [Tuki] was not only very inquisitive respecting England, etc. (the situation of which, as well as that of New Zealand, Norfolk Island, and Port Jackson, he well knew how to find by means of a coloured general chart); but was also very communicative about his own country. Perceiving that he was not thoroughly understood, he delineated a sketch of New Zealand with chalk on the floor of a room set apart for that purpose. From a plan of those islands, a sufficient similitude to the form of the northern island was discovered, to render this attempt an object of curiosity; and Toogee was persuaded to describe his delineation on paper.[20]

For historians of heritage, it may be suggestive to see these maps as islander versions of history. For Tupaia, they are a physical means for recording both his knowledge of the islands, and his visits to them: the map included twelve islands he had visited himself. They fit into a tradition that islanders commonly resorted to, of retelling accounts of contact with other islanders in the past. The difference between Tupaia's and Tuki's status encompasses the ends of collaboration and coercion. These were unusual individuals who made it possible for Europeans to incorporate islander traditions of navigation and to create the 'native'. They belong to the class of iconic islanders that includes Mai, who was celebrated as a noble savage in London.

Captain Cook's voyages quickly became a turning point in British historiography—he epitomized the self-made Enlightenment hero, who rose from humble beginnings and made a place for himself amongst the pantheon

---

[18] This develops the points made by Ogborn, *Global lives*, p. 311.
[19] R. R. D. Milligan, *The map drawn by the chief Tuki-Tahua in 1793* (Mangonui, 1964), p. 1.
[20] Cited in Milligan, *The map drawn by the chief Tuki-Tahua in 1793*, p. 8, from David Collins, *An account of the English colony of New South Wales* (2nd edn, London, 1804), p. 292.

of classical explorers by paying the supreme sacrifice of his life. Yet a case might be made: that this history of heroism was connected and entangled with another kind of heritage—linked with Pacific islanders' long-distance voyages, and the associated skills and historical memories that came with those traditions. Captain Cook's voyages redefined heritage in the Pacific Ocean, and, in particular, consolidated a new sense of the 'native', as separable and at times naturalistic, when placed alongside European naval skills. While islanders already had their ways of defining their networks of settlement and navigation, Cook and his companions allowed those patterns of travel to pass into European knowledge and cartographic understandings of race, migration, and lineage. This new sense of the 'native' was itself based on voluntary collaborations and coercive relations between islanders and Europeans. In this encounter British heritage drew on islander norms, even as the status of the 'native' was recontextualized in the process of its incorporation within colonial traditions.

II

It is time to move elsewhere and to consider another arena where heritages and self-positionings in history met in the context of British expansion. The study of orientalism in the British empire has become something of an industry.[21] By taking the little studied case of Theravada Buddhism it is possible to see how Buddhist religious practices in the cultural realm framed the emergence of British orientalism, and how British history-writing reconceptualized the placement of other traditions of historicism.

One curious fact about the Theravada world of Burma, Siam, and Ceylon, to use period names, is that they all experienced a reformulation of Buddhism by the late eighteenth century, which might be seen as an attempt to purify, indigenize, and, at times, ethnicize religion. In the court of Ava in Burma, Theravada Buddhism reasserted itself as supreme against Mahayana Buddhism and tantric, spiritist, Islamic, and Hindu religious traditions.[22] Monks came under stricter codes of discipline, with respect to the consumption of meat and alcohol. The reformation of Buddhism was tied to the notion of universal kingship or *cakravarti*. The evidence for the king's ability to rule lay in the material world—in the possession of the white elephant, in the building of pagodas and his fantastic court at Ava, and, from 1783, in the newly built

---

[21] For recent histories of orientalism in India, see Michael Dodson, *Orientalism, empire and national culture: India, 1770–1880* (Basingstoke, 2007).
[22] This paragraph draws on Thant Myint-U, *The making of modern Burma* (Cambridge, 2001), pp. 48–59 and pp. 79–82 in particular.

Amarapura. It also lay in his patronage of the Buddhist clergy and their monastic schools, and, importantly for the argument here, in the project of historical narration. In 1829, shortly after the first Anglo-Burmese War, King Bagyidaw kept up a tradition which was at least three hundred years old by assembling learned Brahmins, learned monks, and learned ministers to compile what became the 'Glass Palace Chronicle', which was drawn up after consulting old palm-leaf manuscripts and stone inscriptions. These historians traced the trajectory of the Burmese kingdom in the Irrawaddy valley in order to isolate a true royal line, stamped by the superior solar caste. From this appropriation of the mantle of historical credibility, the Burmese kings of the mid-nineteenth century could also take for themselves the title Myanma, which implied a more ethnic identity. The courtly reformulation of Buddhist traditions in the kingdom of Ava sat alongside a wider movement of social integration; around a common language, Burmese; and around common legal and political institutions.

Next door, the results of Burma's new orthodoxy were clear to see—for in 1767 Burma ransacked the Thai kingdom of Ayudhya, taking tens of thousands of captives as slaves back to Burma.[23] Yet, curiously, this defeat eventually spurred a new resurgence of Thai identity, around a new kingdom based in Bangkok, which successfully withstood attack from Burma in 1785, and launched a counter-invasion in turn; in the wars that followed, Siam was able to hold its own. Like his neighbours, King Rama I of Siam (1789–1809) also sought to restore Buddhism and, in particular, the scholarly status of the monks. His new kingdom at Bangkok was built from thousands of boatloads of bricks transported from the ransacked capital of Ayudhya, which indicates the attempt to resuscitate heritage; the new patriotism was thus built very literally on remembrances of the past. He issued orders to enforce discipline amongst the monks, and appointed groups of monks to inquire into matters of textual interpretation. Perhaps the climax of his patronage of textual exegesis was when he convened a committee of monks in 1788 to revise the entire Pali canon of Buddhist texts. This resulted in 288 manuscripts and a total of 3,568 bundles of written palm leaves. This twinned effort to reform Buddhism, restore past traditions, and construct a secure state was connected to material culture. Rama I's reign saw a fantastic tradition of mural painting, which reveals not a homogenized society but a mix of peoples and traditions. His patronage extended to literature, as this period saw the completion of a full Siamese version of the Indian epic poem *Ramayana*. Rama I's leadership

---

[23] This draws from David K. Wyatt, *Thailand: a short history* (New Haven, CT, and London, 1982), pp. 132–61 and also idem, 'The "Subtle Revolution" of King Rama I of Siam', in David K. Wyatt and Alexander Woodside, eds., *Moral order and the question of change: essays on Southeast Asian thought* (New Haven, CT, 1982), pp. 9–52. See also Klaus Wenk, *The restoration of Thailand under Rama I, 1782–1809* (Tucson, AZ, 1968).

followed the historical precedent of the righteous Buddhist king; his own right to be a king was stabilized by these acts as he cast himself in a lineage of good rule. His historical chroniclers wrote about why Ayudhya had fallen: Ayudhya's king had not been a true Buddhist.

In Ceylon also it is possible to trace similar processes: the kings of the highland kingdom of Kandy sought to restore the status of Buddhist monks by rejuvenating the practice of higher ordination and education for monks. Bands of monks who went as part of missions from one territory to the other connected the island to both Burma and Siam in the early modern period, and palm-leaf texts were exchanged too. One of the island's historical chronicles, which is now the key text of the island's nationalism, The *Mahavamsa*, was consulted in this period in Burma and Siam.[24] Yet to develop the argument that there was a redefinition of the 'native' prior to British expansion it is important to state that this newly resurgent Buddhism set the context for the rise of British orientalism in Ceylon.[25]

From 1796 the British were making inroads into Ceylon: first by taking the coastal territories and then seeking to make the kingdom of Kandy itself a vassal state under the empire. Kandy eventually fell to the British in 1815. Orientalist knowledge was critical to the process of colonization. One of the chief orientalists, John D'Oyly, corresponded on palm leaf with the ministers of the court of the king of Kandy. Yet the format of this early orientalism was moulded by the reformation of Buddhism, which had been undertaken prior to the arrival of the British as invading forces. British orientalists turned their attention to the historical narratives written by the Buddhist clergy, which they procured through channels opened up by the reformation of eighteenth-century Buddhism. Their orientalism arose directly from collaborations with Buddhist priests: these men were descended from the monks who had taken on new prescriptions of ordination and education in the eighteenth century. In the ceremonial sphere, once Kandy fell, the British were anxious to appease what they felt was Buddhist sentiment, and acted as patrons of a festival that marked the sacred kingship of the king, namely the procession of the tooth relic. This cultural patronage fits with the sentiments of the British convention that marked the fall of Kandy, which included this sentence: 'The religion of Boodhoo, professed by the chiefs and inhabitants of these provinces is declared inviolable, and its rights, ministers, and places of worship are to be maintained and protected' (Figure 7.4). In the realm of archaeology and antiquarianism, the colonists paid attention to the very sites that had attracted

[24] Myint-U, *The making of modern Burma*, p. 80.
[25] This is from material that is forthcoming in my book, *Islanded: Britain, Sri Lanka and the bounds of an Indian Ocean colony* (Chicago, forthcoming).

Figure 7.4: 'The King's Palace at Kandy', from William Lyttleton, *A set of views drawn on the spot in the island of Ceylon* (London, 1819), Plate 3. This image shows a ceremonial procession of the Buddha's tooth relic, which appears atop an elephant. The procession is under way in front of the king's palace at the centre of Kandy. In the early nineteenth century, British governors, such as Edward Barnes, served as patrons of this procession, a ritual of Kandyan kingship.

attention on the part of the kings of Kandy.[26] The British governors patronized the same traditions of chronicling that the pre-colonial kings had presided over. Adopting the same idioms, they had palm-leaf texts written in their honour, stretching from the ancient kings to the newly arrived Britons. Instead of verses telling of the merits that accrued from building Buddhist pagodas, these governors were noted to have built roads or introduced new technologies. In one poem, a Sinhala man praised the British governor Edward Barnes as a Buddhist king, for he had rendered the supreme service of building a road to Kandy, and this could now be used by pilgrims journeying to the city's temple: a fitting act of merit for any Buddhist king.[27] This last case indicates how a heritage of historical narration was adopted by the British and recast to encompass a very different context, namely road-building. For

---

[26] Sujit Sivasundaram, 'Buddhist kingship, British archaeology, and historical narratives in Sri Lanka, *c.*1750–1850', *Past & Present*, 197 (2007), pp. 111–42.
[27] See Sivasundaram, *Islanded*, Introduction.

colonists who sought to press the generosity of their benefactions, the ideal of Buddhist kingship was useful for its pliability. This was not then an unconscious entanglement with the resuscitated traditions of eighteenth-century Ceylon, but a conscious attempt to make colonialism politically acceptable.

This case can also be made in Burma—for instance with respect to language—which, as in the Pacific, was another axis for navigating histories and heritages in the context of the advance of the British empire. In Burma the British hoped to master Burmese by attending to Pali, which they saw as the root language, holding the key to Burma's civilization.[28] In attending to Pali they were following the contours of the restitution of learning under the eighteenth-century monarchs of Ava.[29] Unlike in Ceylon, the whole of Burma was not taken by the British until 1886. In this context, missionaries had something of a monopoly on orientalist scholarship. One important figure was Felix Carey, the son of William Carey, the Baptist missionary of Bengal, and the so-called father of the modern missionary movement.[30] Felix, who was trained in Sanskrit, outlined six different ways in which Pali words are adapted into Burmese. When Felix died he left part of the New Testament translated into Burmese, but there was also a Pali grammar, with a Sanskrit translation. Carey sought to fit Burmese, and its historic heritage in Pali, into the history of Sanskrit in neighbouring Bengal.[31] This view was also held among a group of American Protestant missionaries who went to Burma in the early nineteenth century. Note the contention of Francis Mason, who arrived in 1831: 'In Burmah Pali is interwoven with the vernacular, much more than Latin is in English.'[32] The missionaries' view of the historical pedigree of Burmese sat alongside the work of the official British representatives who arrived at the court of Ava. One example is Francis Buchanan, the East India Company's surgeon, who was a member of the first British mission to Ava in 1795, and who returned with a large Burmese herbarium. In an article in the *Asiatick Researches* entitled, 'A comparative vocabulary of some of the languages spoken in the Burma empire' (1799), Buchanan wrote: 'Language, of all adventitious circumstances, is the surest guide in tracing the migrations and connections of nations.'[33] He sketched out the various dialects spoken in

[28] William Pruit, 'The study of Burmese by Westerners with special reference to Burmese Nissayas', *International Journal of Lexicography*, 5 (1992), pp. 278–304.

[29] Myint-U, *The making of modern Burma*, pp. 86, 92, for the court of Ava and the Buddhist clergy's interest in Pali.

[30] Sujit Sivasundaram, '"A Christian Benares": orientalism, science and the Serampore mission of Bengal', *Indian Economic and Social History Review*, 44 (2007), pp. 111–45.

[31] Pruit, 'The study of Burmese by Westerners', pp. 286–90.

[32] Cited in Pruit, 'The study of Burmese by Westerners', p. 293.

[33] Francis Buchanan, 'A comparative vocabulary of some of the languages spoken in the Burma empire', *Asiatick Researches*, 5 (1799), pp. 219–40.

the 'Burman empire', with a view to delineating the thesis that there was one great 'nation' spread across the empire, even if the people were mixed in with a variety of others.

The heritage of the Burmese 'nation' was not only linked to language; Hiram Cox, the rather erratic British agent who was appointed to the court of Ava in the aftermath of the 1795 mission, was particularly interested in architecture and the sciences. He rather boldly set about planning the making of a hot-air balloon in honour of the king, and wrote of the old city of Ava as well as the new capital of Amarapura. In Ava he found a great number of pagodas and religious buildings: 'some finished with domes, some pyramidal, some cones, with a profusion of gilding expended on them', while he complained that the newly built Amarapura was 'evidently the essay of some smatterer of European architecture'.[34]

While Ceylon and Burma eventually fell to the British, Siam never did, nor did it go to war with them. Here diplomacy was the predominant arena for the meeting of heritages. In the missions led by John Crawfurd, later president of the Ethnological Society, and theorist of history, language, and migration, we see the way in which the British had to come to terms with extant heritages, before placing Siam in a map of orientalist scholarship. Crawfurd took pains to note the ceremony that attended his reception by the court of Siam at Bangkok. He wrote: 'This people of half-naked and enslaved barbarians have the hardihood to consider themselves the first nation in the world, and to view the performance of any servile office to a stranger, as an act of degradation.'[35] The attention to the splendours of the court is rather telling; for many of its features arose from the newly resurgent sense of universal kingship. Take, for instance, Crawfurd's comment on white elephants, which locates the reason for the confidence of the Siamese king in a comparison with his predecessors:

> The greatest of the curiosities to which our attention was directed were the white elephants, well known in Europe to be objects of veneration, if not of worship in all the countries where the religion of Buddha prevails. The present king has no less than six of these, a larger number than ever was possessed by any Siamese monarch; and this circumstance is considered peculiarly auspicious to his reign.[36]

Yet Crawfurd's insistence on the specificity of the courtly culture of Siam, when compared with Burma and England, was contradicted by the evidence of the hybridity of traditions evident in this Theravada Buddhist world, even

---

[34] Hiram Cox, *Journal of a residence in the Burmhan empire, and more particularly at the court of Amarapoorah* (London, 1821), pp. 48–9.
[35] John Crawfurd, *Journal of an embassy from the governor-general of India to the courts of Siam and Cochin-China: exhibiting a view of the actual state of those kingdoms*, i (London, 1830), p. 136.
[36] Ibid., p. 148.

with respect to diplomacy. Crawfurd's published narrative of his mission to Siam and Vietnam ends with a rather curious document, which he had acquired from a Mr Gibson, whom he describes as 'so imperfectly educated, that the original was replete with errors in grammar and orthography'. This is Mr Gibson's account of how he had also served a diplomatic mission: not a British mission, but rather one sent by the Burmese king to Vietnam. This mission set off on a European vessel in 1823; Gibson was chosen as he had resided at the court of Ava for many years, and was 'thoroughly versed in Burmese', in addition to 'the Portuguese language, with the Hindostani and Telinga'.[37] The range of Gibson's languages and his service for the Burmese ruler denote the extent of cultural interchange at the end of a narrative devoted to British diplomacy.

Across this world, a case can be made that British understandings of heritage met and arose out of Theravada Buddhist reformulations of history, kingship, and tradition, which were redefining notions of authenticity and heritage. This is seen in relation to the working relationships between Britons and priests, colonial orientalism's views of language, and its reliance and use of courtly and kingly culture. More broadly, it is vital to see that historical narration was renewed with vigour, on the eve of the advent of the British to this world. Yet, in engaging with established traditions of history-writing in Southeast Asia, the British eventually incorporated these senses of the past within their own cultures of history. This meant that the status of 'native' histories was eventually reconceptualized: the architecture, language, and textual work of Buddhist monks and their kingly patrons was classed as 'native' and inferior to the British equivalent; it was seen as superstitious, ornate, and irregular. A good example of this is the *Mahavamsa*, Ceylon's Buddhist historical chronicle. The second British translation, which became the authoritative one, was published by the civil servant George Turnour in 1836. Turnour wrote that it was 'the principal native historical record', thereby making it hegemonic over other narrations; he presented it as the Sinhala historical narrative, thereby tracing the history of the Sinhala nation as separate to that of the Malabars, or Tamils, and accentuating an ethnic story. He defended his focus on 'oriental literature' by comparing the *Mahavamsa* to the mythology of ancient Europe and Asia Minor. He wrote: 'What appears in these histories as fabulous, because literally impossible, is merely the highly figurative language employed which is quite familiar to the Asiatics.'[38] The published version ended with an attempt at an accurate chronology of the monarchs of

---

[37] Ibid., pp. 409–42.
[38] George Turnour, *An epitome of the history of Ceylon* (Ceylon, 1836), p. xii.

Ceylon, and accounts of recent colonial antiquarian discoveries.[39] As the *Mahavamsa* went from palm leaf to printed form its meaning and status was thus altered: it became a commentary on a particular race of people in the universal history that Britons were tracing across their domains. This is not to deny an argument I make elsewhere: that palm-leaf texts and printed texts were entangled within the island of Ceylon; rather, the change of medium is indicative of the transformed context of meaning in global narrations of belonging. Though the British inherited so much from the kingly and priestly culture of the Theravada world, their intervention in it quickly reconstructed and redefined a new sense of the 'native'.

III

In moving to the south, and to the Cape Colony, it is possible to make a similar argument for a different colonial context and another aspect of heritage. Science, and in particular the science of natural history of the late eighteenth and early nineteenth centuries, served as a means of classifying the productions of nature and its inhabitants. While creating an order of cultures and peoples, natural historians relied on the knowledge that they garnered from local peoples, so that the making of the 'native' was channelled through non-European heritages. However, once the 'native' had been forged, it quickly gave way to a new confidence in racial heritage, which was foundational to the type of segregated settlement that arose in southern Africa.

The Cape was arguably a nodal point not just for the British empire, but for other European endeavours of settlement, cultural contact, and imperialism as well, because of its critical position on shipping routes. The Dutch had first sought to found a settlement in southern Africa for strategic reasons, but by the early nineteenth century this had led the way for a more complex enterprise of settlement, farming, and sedentary life amongst those who traced their descent from Dutch forbears. But, in addition to a Dutch connection, the tip of Africa had French settlers, of Huguenot or Protestant origin, and some German and Scandinavian migrants. The Dutch East India Company also imported a good number of slaves from the Indian Ocean world, from Madagascar and Indonesia in particular. The consolidation of British imperialism, with the seizure of the Cape Colony first, in 1795, and the arrival of a greater number of British settlers around 1820, therefore counted as yet another addition to the very multi-ethnic composition of this territory. British

---

[39] Turnour, *An epitome*, pp. ii and xxv, Appendix, pp. 12ff. See also John Rogers, 'Early British rule and social classification in Lanka', *Modern Asian Studies*, 38 (2004), pp. 625–47.

settlers sought to distinguish themselves from other Europeans, and saw
themselves as more liberal as they championed the abolition of slavery.
British interest in the natural heritage of southern Africa arose within this
contested political landscape. Natural history was, at times, a cosmopolitan
enterprise shared amongst all Europeans, but British natural historians
sought to engage the indigenous Khoisan peoples in quite distinct ways when
compared with other Europeans, and this difference arose in part from their
general commitment to liberalism.

Leaving to one side the diversity of Europeans in southern Africa, it is
important to attend to the natural knowledge and heritage of the long-
established inhabitants of this territory, namely the Khoikhoi and San people,
who were seen by the colonizers as pastoralists and hunters in turn. Their
natural knowledge was formed in the context of an extraordinarily rich environment, which is now denoted as unusual for its species diversity and high
degree of endemicity.[40] The San people in the Kalahari desert required an
understanding of their environment for survival: they developed very strong
skills of visual discrimination and memory, as well as tracking.[41] They were
able to predict the occurrence of droughts or wet periods according to the
behaviour of insects or the growth of particular plants.[42] Their botanical
knowledge was linked to a well-developed system of naming plants and
animals. This knowledge formed part of an oral tradition; the San in the
Kalahari learnt their natural knowledge from an elder, and would then have
sought to add to that store of information through personal observation.
Today, Khoisan scientific knowledge is heavily politicized in relation to
debates around intellectual property and indigenous knowledge claims. One
publicized case is the San use of *Hoodia* species as stimulants and appetite
suppressants whilst hunting. This has now been recognized by a Memorandum
of Understanding with the San, which arose after two South African scientists
sought to patent extracts from the plant as an appetite suppressant. Yet such
plunders of knowledge are not new.[43]

British natural historical work coming out of the Cape arose out of traditions of local knowledge. In the words of one recent historian: 'Up to the
early decades of the nineteenth century, a chain of interlinked knowledge

---

[40] See for instance G. Scott and M. L. Hewett, 'Pioneers in ethnopharmacology: the Dutch East
India Company (VOC) at the Cape from 1650 to 1800', *Journal of Ethnopharmacology*, 115
(2008), pp. 339–60.

[41] Paulus Gerdes, 'Mathematics in Africa south of the Sahara' in Selin, ed., *Encyclopaedia*, ii,
p. 1356.

[42] Hans J. Heinz, 'The bushmen's store of scientific knowledge', in Phillip Tobias, ed., *The Bushmen:
San hunters and herders of southern Africa* (Cape Town and Pretoria, 1978), pp. 148–61.

[43] See Scott and Hewett, 'Pioneers'.

informed ideas about the Cape landscape and natural resources.'[44] This link-age of natural traditions arose partly because of the context of farming and settlement that characterized the Cape; Khoisan served in European farms as herders as well as tillers and reapers, so much so that those within reach of European communities had effectively become a servile class at the bottom of the ladder of slaves. This coercive use of Khoisan provided a context for practical knowledge to pass to Europeans about animal husbandry, hunting practices, means of tracking animals, and information about sources of water and the best land for pasture. But more than this, the style of transhumant life that Khoisan people exhibited came also to be the pattern of some European farmers. The hybridity of practices surrounding the use of the environment is perhaps best exemplified by the extent to which separate languages were intermixed in reference to plant names: Dutch and Khoikhoi words and inter-national botanical names were used interchangeably in the Cape in this period.[45] The curiosity of this historical case, when compared with the Pacific and Southeast Asian examples, is the extent of interchange, which generated a kind of creolization; yet this creolization had as its basis a formal and interventionist settler colonialism predicated on hierarchical power.

The arrival of British naturalists to the Cape and their own reliance on Khoisan natural knowledge is interesting in this context, because the British saw themselves as distinct from the Boers, whom they represented as Europeans gone native. Yet this attitude towards the Boers did not mean that British natural history could operate independently of Khoisan assistance; rather the involvement of Khoisans was acknowledged by early British naturalists in order to authenticate the credibility of their findings, to prove the civiliza-tional capability of the Khoisan, and, in turn, to trumpet the liberal and abo-litionist politics of the British in southern Africa. The discourse of civilization, a critical element of early British imperialism in the creation of a ladder of culture and heritage, arose as a trope that took the side of the Khoisan, while stressing their abilities, in order to forge a different relationship to them than that of the Boers. It did not erase 'the native'; rather it encompassed extant traditions. Perhaps the most eminent botanical collector at the Cape was William Burchell, whose wagon has been described as a 'moving laboratory', and who returned to England with 40,000 botanical specimens, 120 skins of quadrupeds of 95 distinct species and 265 different kinds of insects—a

---

[44] William Beinart, *The rise of conservation in South Africa: settlers, livestock and the environment* (Oxford, 2003), p. 29.

[45] This paragraph, and indeed the entire section, relies on Beinart, *The rise of conservation* and Elizabeth Green Musselman, 'Plant knowledge at the Cape: a study in African and European collaboration', *International Journal of African Historical Studies*, 36 (2003), pp. 367–92.

significant contribution to the making of modern science. In exemplifying the tradition of liberal conceptions of the 'native', Burchell wrote:

> In every circumstance connected with the *track of animals*, and consequently of waggons, the *Hottentots and Bushmen*, as well as all the tribes of the Interior, are admirably quick and discerning. Their experience enables them to distinguish almost with certainty the foot-mark of every animal in their country; although many of them so closely resemble each other that few European eyes would see the difference, even if it were pointed out to them. But these natives, whose food and clothing so greatly depend on knowledge of this kind, are most acutely observant of everything relating to it; and the results of their judgement by combining these observations, are often surprising and would lead to a belief that in the powers of reasoning and reflection they are not as low as, in most other matters, they appear to be. And if it can be admitted that this is really the case, it affords in the same individual a striking, and an instructive, example of how much the human intellect may be raised by being duly exerted, and how low it will insensibly sink, if not carefully cultivated and brought to use.[46]

But even as this British tradition is delineated, it quickly dissipates in a broader European intellectual culture. Anders Sparrman is one curious example: he connects Cook's voyages to this Cape context, as he joined Cook's second expedition when it arrived at the Cape. He was a Swede and a pupil of the celebrated natural historian Linnaeus, and was, like the British with whom he kept company, critical of the Boers. He noted in a passage that followed a strident critique of the Dutch, for their lack of interest in 'useful researchers': 'The Peruvian *bark, senega, ophiorbiza, sarsaparilla, quaffia*, with many other useful remedies, calculated for preserving millions of our species, have not we learned them from those we call Savages? and perhaps we might learn still more, if our tyranny had not already, I had almost said, entirely extirpated them, and together with them lost the result of their useful experience.'[47] Despite the self-presentation of these naturalists, it is important to clarify that the Dutch had a well-established tradition of engaging in precisely the same kinds of research as undertaken by Britons and their friends: in the Cape, the work of Carl Peter Thunberg, who was also a Swede and pupil of Linnaeus, was vital. Unlike Sparrman, Thunberg worked for the Dutch East India Company.

This reliance on Khoisan peoples in natural historical explorations encompassed not only the identification of plants and their uses but also the supply of guides and labourers that made it possible for scientific instruments and

---

[46] Cited in Musselman, 'Plant knowledge', p. 381.
[47] Anders Sparrman, *A voyage to the Cape of Good Hope, towards the Antarctic Polar Circle and round the world* (London, 1786), i, p. 144.

travellers to be transported across terrain. For example, John Forbes, who was collecting for the Royal Horticultural Society, made sure to take 'a Native with [him] that could speak a little English in order to obtain the Native names of the Plants both wild and cultivated'.[48] The Scots-born Andrew Smith, who was the first director of the South African Museum, notes that this reliance on guides was essential, because a temporary traveller or resident would never have the same stock of information as a local inhabitant.[49] William Burchell travelled only in the company of the Khoisan, in a journey to the interior from 1811 to 1815. Even as his wagon served as a space for the standardization of information, by recourse to numerous instruments, the zone outside the wagon was an arena of collaboration between Burchell and a team of Khoikhoi men and women, who accompanied him.[50] In Burchell's travels, the route that was taken, what was observed, the uses of plants, and even the gathering of specimens, all emerged out of an exchange between himself and the advice of his guides. The Khoisan tradition of astute observation for survival and husbandry thus fed into not just the context of Boer farming, but into British natural historical explorations.

Yet the making of the 'native' as an astute natural observer, and as a bearer of a vital heritage of information that could benefit British colonialism, inevitably led in time to quite a different conception of Khoisan abilities. The consolidation of British colonialism at the Cape created a new distance between these colonists and the Khoisan. Whereas early travellers had relied on guides and helpers, those that followed came to distance themselves, and, according to one recent commentator, this arose because of the colony's increasing bureaucratization and the establishment of institutions of science, ranging from museums to associations; violent interactions between settlers and Xhosa and Khoisan; and the result of drought and disease.[51] Too much contact with local peoples was seen to lead to degeneration, and indigenous knowledge now appeared superstitious. This new separation also came out of a desire to create a distinctive Cape identity for British settlers, under the umbrella of the British imperial project.[52] Yet these specific historical circumstances in the Cape mirror a broader process in the delineation of the 'native' in these years: exchange and entanglement of traditions of heritage mutated into attitudes of detachment.

[48] Cited in Musselman, 'Plant knowledge', p. 377.
[49] Ibid., p. 378.
[50] Felix Driver, *Geography militant: Cultures of exploration and empire* (Oxford, 2001).
[51] This is the argument of Musselman, 'Plant knowledge', p. 384.
[52] See Beinart, *The rise of conservation*, pp. 47ff.

IV

The British empire of the late eighteenth and early nineteenth centuries might be interpreted as a system of experimentation. Patterns of colonialism evolved steadily from trade to conquest, even as conceptions of heritage were redrafted over and over again. This dynamism should not be simplified by historians into a one-sided story of colonial epistemologies intruding into a silent world, or the timeless patterns of the extra-European world being impacted by the Enlightenment. For British definitions of tradition did not emerge from a tabula rasa: Pacific islanders, Asians, and Africans had defined their senses of culture, even if those patriotic attachments were under new constraints or momentum just prior to contact with the British. These redefinitions of tradition fed into and set the context for British articulations of heritage. There were a series of common interests through which such linkage could occur. Three such avenues are: an enthusiasm for voyaging, a need to stabilize governance by recourse to past tradition, and an attention to nature's productions and their placement in natural schemes. Linkage should not indicate a smooth connection, for British interest in the changing traditions of the extra-European world shifted the form and placement of such heritages. British maps, prints, and collections had universal aspirations, seeking to find a place for the 'native' in comparative and global schemes. This dislocation of tradition led in turn to patterns of detachment, disparagement, and segregation.

This mutating idea of the 'native', articulated by non-Europeans, adopted into British schemes, and then recast into a global process, is an important chapter in the wider history of the making of the 'native'. It is one piece of a longer story, which should include the later episodes of high imperialism and decolonization as well. The idea of the 'native' arose then out of the competing engagement between colonists and colonizers, and out of a shared desire to define tradition and obscure intermixing. Such an argument does not minimize the intrusiveness of colonialism or its violence; it seeks instead to be more precise about the character of colonial categories and place them against extant ideas. At the same time, it stresses how an appropriation of the traditions of the non-European world set the foundation for a culture of supremacy and colonial pride. Collaboration and contestation were not that far apart: one could lead into the other. At the same time, the distinctiveness of British traditions sat alongside rival European colonial programmes. The British sought to distinguish themselves as Christian, liberal, and rational peoples, yet those who studied and made culture for them were a motley band. Just as much as the making of the 'native' as a descriptive term for non-Europeans involved multiple agents, so the nature of British heritage in an imperial context was forged out of a pan-European team of interpreters. Therefore, at the broadest level, this argument points to the complex lineage of ideas of heritage and the way they evolve in relation to political processes and uses.

8

Monument Preservation and the Vexing Question of Religious Structures in Colonial India

INDRA SENGUPTA

THE QUESTION OF RELIGION had always influenced archaeological policy-making and the state-driven practice of preservation of ancient structures in colonial India. This was particularly true after the Revolt of 1857, which was substantially attributed to the injured feelings of the various religious communities in India under the rule of the East India Company. Like policy-making in general after the crown takeover of rule in 1858, the archaeological policy of surveying, classifying, and preserving Indian monuments was careful to adhere to the general policy of religious non-intervention that was adopted by the government of the British Raj in India in the aftermath of the Revolt of 1857. Hence, in official archaeological policy the distinction was made between sites and structures of historical importance, which would be preserved by means of state intervention, and religious structures still in use, where the state would play a marginal, advisory role. In practice, this turned out to be a much more complicated task. This chapter focuses on the most sweeping piece of legislation on the preservation of Indian monuments, the Ancient Monument Preservation Act of 1904. It examines the ways in which the implementation of the law belied the notion of a state-driven system of preservation in colonial India—a manifestation of colonial power—as much of recent scholarship has indicated. It looks at how, in practice, the colonial bureaucracy was forced to engage with the rights of religious communities 'on the ground', which rendered it difficult to maintain the distinction that had been made in law between secular and sacred space. Hence, far from being subjected to the will of an overwhelming colonial state and a Western knowledge system, indigenous religious communities could in fact negotiate their own spaces and assert their own agency within the new legal apparatus. That said, the aim of this chapter is less to contribute to the long-standing debate in studies of colonialism in India on the agency of Indian groups in the face of the power of the colonial state, than to understand the processes of

Proceedings of the British Academy, **187**, 171–185. © The British Academy 2013.

colonialism as uneven trajectories, where the exercise of state power could, in practice, often have unexpected consequences.

The Ancient Monument Preservation Act of 1904 was by no means the first attempt by the colonial government of India to pass legislation on the preservation of historical monuments. Sporadic attempts had been made by the East India Company to conserve historical structures, largely in the heartland of the former Mughal empire in Delhi and Agra, as part of its efforts to legitimize its political presence in India. Following the revolt and the establishment of the Archaeological Survey of India in 1861, however, these attempts gave way to the extensive surveys and documentation of monuments rather than their preservation. At the same time, these efforts went hand in hand with a careless destruction of ancient sites and structures, often to make way for road-building, to use ancient structures as government offices, or for the expansion of cultivation. From the early 1870s onwards, preservation of old structures began to draw the attention of the Archaeological Department again, and orders were issued in 1883 for the preparation of lists of classified monuments in the provinces of British India.[1] However, largely owing to lack of funds, little was done till the turn of the century: as late as in 1902, the total number of ancient buildings under repair numbered less than 150.[2] The real impulse to a frenetic phase of conservation came with the viceroyalty of Curzon and the subsequent passing of the Ancient Monument Preservation Act in 1904. In 1898–99, the total expenditure of the government of India and all provincial governments on archaeology was a total of £7,000 a year; by 1904 this had gone up to £37,000.[3]

The Ancient Monument Preservation Act—henceforth referred to as AMPA—of 1904 was the most comprehensive piece of legislation on the subject in colonial India. It became the basis of subsequent legislation and, as such, has survived till today. Introduced in a climate of intense debate and criticism of the colonial state's apparent apathy to India's ancient monuments, the act was modelled on the Ancient Monument Protection Act of 1882, which was passed for the protection of monuments in Britain and was subsequently adapted in 1892 for Ireland and then amended in Britain in 1900. There were, however, two notable ways in which the Indian Act differed from its British counterpart. The first of these was that the Indian Act was far more sweeping in character and gave the state much more wide-ranging powers to enforce monument preservation. Section 3 of the AMPA, for instance, gave

[1] *Indian archaeological policy, 1915: being a resolution issued by the governor-general in council on the 22nd October 1915* (Calcutta, 1916), p. 10.
[2] Ibid., p. 11.
[3] India Office Records (henceforth IOR), British Library, L/PJ/6/674, File 803, proceedings of the legislative council, Ancient Monuments Preservation Act, Act VII, 1904, President of the council of the governor-general, or Viceroy Curzon, 18 Mar. 1904.

the local government (i.e. the governments of the provinces and presidencies) independent authority to 'declare an ancient monument to be a protected monument within the meaning of this Act'.[4] The government was given the power to acquire the right of purchase or lease or guardianship of a protected monument, albeit in agreement with the owner.[5] Much to the delight of preservationists in Britain (such as the Society for the Protection of Ancient Buildings and the Royal Institute of British Architects) the colonial state in India was willing to adopt a much more interventionist approach to the preservation of monuments than the national government of Britain. The art historian Gerard Baldwin Brown states: 'It is noteworthy that it is fully equipped with clauses, prohibitions, and penal sanctions, of which people in the mother country are so shy.'[6]

The second specific feature of the Indian Act, which distinguished it from its British counterpart, was the special emphasis placed on religious structures. The act made a specific mention of the practice to be followed in the case of religious structures still in use. By and large, structures in use were to be outside the purview of the government. This was in keeping with the provisions of the Religious Endowments Act of 1863, which divested government of the responsibility for managing religious endowments, by setting up local area committees whose task it was to ensure the proper management of temples.[7] Thus, the act tried to ensure the practice of religious neutrality that the colonial government ostensibly came to espouse in the aftermath of the Revolt of 1857. However, if the government happened to gain possession or acquire guardianship of a place of worship, then it was required to properly discharge this role by ensuring that the feelings of religious communities were in no way injured; one example was by regulating the right of entry according to the traditions of the community. At the same time, the Act of 1904 strengthened the interventionist power of the state that had also been conferred on it by the Religious Endowments Act of 1863, which confirmed the right of government to intervene to prevent damage to religious structures. The discussions related to the passing of the bill on the subject in 1903–04 bring this out very clearly. Stating that buildings in private hands were, in general, in a state of decay, the legislative council emphasized in the bill that the protection of such structures was its main objective. It drew on the policy spelled out in section 23 of the Religious Endowments Act of 1863, which 'recognises and saves the right of the Govt "to prevent injury to, and preserve, buildings remarkable for their antiquity and for their historical or architectural value, or required for the

---

[4] AMPA 1904, Section 3.
[5] AMPA 1904, Sections 4–10.
[6] G. Baldwin Brown, *The care of ancient monuments* (Cambridge, 1905; repr. 2010), p. 235.
[7] See Franklin A. Presler, *Religion under bureaucracy: policy and administration for Hindu temples in south India* (1987; repr. Bombay, 1989), pp. 15–27.

convenience of the public"'.[8] It was emphasized that 'it is hoped that the line of action which it is proposed to take may tend rather to the encouragement than to the suppression of private effort'. In keeping with this two-pronged approach of the state, the act provided for agreements for the protection of monuments, which private owners could enter into with the government. However, in the event of refusal, the collector was entitled to acquire it compulsorily; in the case of an endowment, the collector could move the courts to enforce the application of the act. Provision was made for the rights of religious practice, to the extent that in the case of ancient monuments in use for religious purposes the government was to refrain from compulsory acquisition; the government was evidently keen to adhere to this exclusive clause. In a policy statement on archaeology in India in 1915, the governor-general Lord Minto was keen to stress that, by and large, government policy was to avoid interference with the management of buildings used for religious observances. However, in the case of endowments with inadequate means to provide for the upkeep of the buildings, 'Government has frequently rendered financial assistance on condition that the repairs should be carried out on lines approved by the Archaeological Department.'[9]

In practice, however, the coexistence of this policy of non-interference in the management of religious structures still in use and the authority of the government—and not least its financial power—to persuade religious endowments to accept government assistance for structural conservation turned out to be an uneasy one. The state's attempts to keep religious structures out of the purview of the new conservation policy turned out to be much more difficult to implement than the Act of 1904 suggested. The endeavour to keep monumental conservation limited to 'dead' structures became increasingly difficult to maintain, as the new opportunities of getting generous funding for the maintenance of structures still in use began to attract a flood of applications for grants from religious endowments and trusts.[10]

In the implementation of the act, the colonial state did not follow a systematic or consistent policy when sanctioning grants for the maintenance of religious structures in use, or when considering awarding protection to temples or mosques that were in use for religious purposes. In the years after the passing of the AMPA, and especially in the 1910s, the personal interest and consequent intervention on the part of Viceroy Curzon and the director of archaeology, John Marshall, saw increasing attempts to control, regulate, demarcate, and legalize religious monuments in use. This was done, for

---

[8] AMPA, Act VII, 1904, IOR/L/PJ/6/674, File 803, proceedings of the legislative council.
[9] *Indian archaeological policy, 1915*, pp. 20–1.
[10] See, for example, the remarks of T. Bloch, superintendent of the Eastern Circle of the Archaeological Survey in his report of 1905–06. T. Bloch, *Annual report of the Archaeological Survey of India: Eastern Circle, 1905–06.*

example, by fencing or walling off areas, placing noticeboards, and undertaking beautification measures, none of which were uncontroversial. Often the eagerness of the Archaeological Department to act resulted in it failing to follow its own guidelines for determining the ownership of a monument still in use and entering into agreements with the owners before undertaking repairs. In the case of religious monuments in use its actions could often be—or be perceived to be—of an intrusive nature. As a result, potential areas of conflict—and negotiation—began to develop. These centred on certain specific issues, such as the question of ownership of these structures, the question of their use, and, as mentioned earlier, the frequent intervention of the state in the sacred sphere by trying to exercise greater control over maintenance and repair of religious structures.

I

In the eastern Indian state of Orissa, in the city of Bhubaneswar, lie several clusters of temples, one of which is a temple of national importance as a place of pilgrimage.[11] Several of the temples at Bhubaneswar have been in use since late medieval times. With the enactment and subsequent enforcement of the AMPA in 1904, these temples became a significant theatre of conflict between the ambitions of the new archaeological preservation policy and the rights of religious communities to places of worship.[12] This was the case not only because of the sheer number of shrines in the various temple clusters in the city. Many—though not all—of the temples in Bhubaneswar were in use, and the problem was compounded by the fact that temples where worship took place, and those that were not in use, often belonged to the same cluster, that is, they were situated within the same building complex and were often ritually or mythologically related to each other. Thus, it was not easy to determine ownership of any but the most prominent temples. As this section will show, in its eagerness to implement the new act, the Archaeological Survey often rushed in to intervene in the maintenance of temples, without having

[11] Bhubaneswar was made the capital of the state of Orissa in 1948. It was designed as a modern, post-independence city by the German-Jewish architect Otto H. Königsberger in the late 1940s. But prior to this it had predominantly been a temple town and an important cultural and religious centre of Hindus, mostly from eastern India. This led to the sobriquet 'City of a Thousand Temples' that is still used to describe the city in tourist brochures. See, for a history of the transition of Bhubaneswar from temple town to postcolonial city, Ravi Kalia, *Bhubaneswar: from a temple town to a capital city* (Delhi, 1994).

[12] The temples of Orissa had a long and often troubled relationship with the colonial state, which in part went back to the occupation of Orissa by the English East India Company in 1803. See, for this, Yaaminey Mubayi, *Altar of power: the temples and the state in the land of Jagannatha* (Delhi, 2005).

settled the question of ownership. It entered into agreements with the temple trustees and failed adequately to check whether religious sensibilities would be offended by such measures. Protest petitions made by the managing committees of these temples indicate the way in which such actions on the part of the colonial state were seen: on the one hand, as a violation of the rights of sanctity of the communities; on the other, as a carte blanche to temple custodians to act exactly as the state had done, such as by independently initiating works of maintenance without informing, let alone consulting, the government, as the Act of 1904 had clearly prescribed.

Two cases of dispute between temple authorities and the state, both in the years 1910–11 and both related to the Bhubaneswar temple complex, bear this out. The first of these involved the dismantling of a small temple, called the Devi Pad(m)eswari Temple, by the temple committee in late 1910. Asked by the local government to provide an explanation for its actions and to stop further work until the government gave permission to continue, the managing committee formulated its arguments in very precise terms. The committee denied that it was destroying the temple in question, which, it argued, was in a 'neglected and dilapidated' condition, and further claimed that there was nothing in it 'of historical or artistic interest, since it was a massive structure of stone with a stone roof—without any ornamental work thereon'.[13] Further, the committee claimed, the temple had been destroyed only as a last resort: the committee, declared the petition, 'may be taken as quite averse to any demolition. It may be seen that there are several other old and more dilapidated temples standing on without any interference by the Committee.'[14] Thus, all that the temple custodians had done, the committee claimed, was to remove and reuse some of the stones of the demolished temple to repair another one. Finally, the committee called into question what they saw as the government's arbitrary policy of repairing some temples and neglecting others, and asserted that the temple custodians should be allowed some discretion in the matter of undertaking repairs they deemed necessary for the temples.[15]

The second case relates to an incident that took place some months after the one cited above. This time, it was the turn of the temple committee to protest at the demolition of a small temple inside the Ananta Basudeb temple cluster at Bhubaneswar that was being undertaken by the government, in what the committee saw as an arbitrary act. In its petition to the government, the committee now took the regional branch of the Archaeological Survey to task, protesting at the demolition carried out by the government Public Works

[13] National Archives of India - Eastern Regional Centre (Bhubaneswar), Archaeological Survey of India Calcutta Circle (henceforth NAI-ERC, ASI), Calcutta Circle, SL 483, File 26, Babu Priyanath Chatterji, member Bhubaneswar temple committee to the collector of Puri, Cuttack, 20 Nov. 1910.
[14] Ibid.
[15] Ibid.

Department (PWD), without consulting the committee. The committee, the petition claimed, under the Act of 1863, was deemed custodian of all temples and temple property in Bhubaneswar. The committee also argued that the temple 'under demolition' was 'mythologically connected' to one of the main 'living' temples of the complex as part of a triad of shrines: not only would the destruction of the minor temple 'cripple the idea of beauty and congruity', it would also 'wound the religious feelings of the people'.[16]

These two cases bear testimony not only to the often arbitrary action on the part of the colonial state—which, despite the caution advised by the Religious Endowments Act of 1863 as well as the AMPA of 1904, often acted rashly and with little time for the religious sensibilities of the temple users— but equally, and perhaps more significantly, as good examples to show how closely the colonial state was watched and how its own behaviour could be used to attack its own laws. Government officials and those specifically attached to the Archaeological Survey were aware of this, as their letters to the provincial and central governments bear out, and they repeatedly stressed the need for clarity and consistent application of the new laws.

The difficulty of implementing a clear-cut preservation policy along the lines proposed by the Act of 1904, which would sort out the questions of ownership and use, separate the right of worship from the need to preserve old historical structures, and then enforce the new conservation policy, was evident not only in the case of Hindu temples, but other places of worship. Often, the actions of the Archaeological Department could arouse such strong local sentiment that this became a source of concern to the government, as was true of the case of the Jami Masjid in Thatta (Sindh, in modern-day Pakistan). The mosque was built in the reign of the Mughal emperor Shah Jahan in the seventeenth century, and is believed to be one of the finest examples of the rich glazed-tile architecture that was common to the area. In 1913, the mosque was declared a protected monument and in 1914 was deemed to be in need of repairs, funds for which were available only in 1918. According to the reports of the regional Archaeological Survey, the mosque was 'in the possession of a committee of four local Muhammedan gentle-men',[17] who were believed to be incapable of looking after the mosque. In 1919, the superintendent of archaeology for the Western Circle, R. D. Banerji, proposed that the rights of the committee be restricted to religious service and that they 'leave this Department to maintain the monument properly'.[18]

---

[16] NAI-ERC, ASI Calcutta Circle, SL 483, File 26, Babu Priyanath Chatterji, member Bhubaneswar temple committee to the superintendent of the Archaeological Survey, Eastern Circle, Puri, 29 Jan. 1911.

[17] ASI, File No. 314, 1920, R. D. Banerji, superintendent, Western Circle, to the commissioner in Sindh, Poona, 27 Feb. 1919.

[18] Ibid.

The argument that Banerji used to justify this division of authority is illuminating as it is indicative of the fundamental problem that the colonial, state-administered archaeology was confronted with in dealing with religious structures that were now also declared monuments. Banerji claimed that the old Mughal port of Thatta was—by default as it were—the property of the colonial government, as successor to the Mughals and sovereign ruler of India. Following from this claim to ownership of the port, the superintendent declared the mosque, situated in the port area, to be government property as well. However, he generously conceded that local Muslims would not be denied the right to worship in the mosque, declaring, 'this Department has no objection to the use of the Jami Masjid by the Muhammedan community of Thatta'.[19] The consequent resentment felt by the local Muslim community led to the provincial Archaeological Department restricting its activities to the minimum, but the question of who actually owned the mosque remained unresolved. The problem of ownership of and access to religious buildings was particularly acute in the Bombay presidency, where incidents related to these questions repeatedly occurred. In most cases, the issue was about mosques that were originally regarded as government property being taken over by local Muslim communities, who then prevented the PWD from carrying out their repairs. Thus, in these instances, a clarification of the question of ownership seemed to be vital. The central government of India held the view that, once a mosque had been dedicated to public worship, it had become the property of God. Government, as the constituent guardian of the mosque, was responsible for its maintenance, as long as Muslim religious sentiments were not offended and Muslims were allowed to use the mosque for worship. For officials in charge of executing preservation measures, as well as the Department of Archaeology in general, this was an inadequate solution to a complex problem, since they were mindful of the fact that what applied to the Muslims would also have to apply to the Hindus, Buddhists, and Christians. Their central concern remained the exercise of full and total control of the monuments in their charge. Pressure from the various groups of religious communities, however, meant that this control always remained an open question, to be constantly renegotiated.

II

Underlying these conflicts and negotiations was the all-pervasive conviction, repeatedly expressed by the viceroy and the director of archaeology, that a

---

[19] ASI, File No. 314, 1920, R. D. Banerji, superintendent, Western Circle, to the commissioner in Sindh, Poona, 27 Feb. 1919.

centrally driven conservation policy resting on principles of monument preservation that were widely accepted in Britain and Western Europe in the early twentieth century was the only way to save India's monuments from destruction and ruin.[20] The AMPA was introduced in India in a general climate of preservation legislation in Western Europe. The government of India had long been conscious of its shortcomings with regard to the care of India's ancient monuments. Both it and the government of Britain were aware that developments in India were being observed very closely, especially by continental European, French, and German scholars in India. In the prevailing context of the debate on conservation versus restoration in Britain and Europe, in which the centrality of conservation of monuments of historical and artistic importance was emphasized, the same policy was adopted for India.[21] Unlike in Britain, however, and much to the delight of preservationist lobbies in Britain, the colonial state gave itself sweeping legal powers to enforce preservation. When it came to religious structures in use, the colonial state tried to aim for a clear separation of such 'living' monuments from those (secular, government-owned, 'dead' monuments) that would now fall within the purview of the new law. As a significant body of scholarship has shown, the interference of colonial archaeologists in religious structures in India had, throughout the nineteenth century, resulted in conflict and contestation;[22] the belief was strong that the legal apparatus created by the Act of 1904 would provide a clear framework for the management of Indian monuments, without offending religious beliefs. However, the state found itself increasingly

[20] I do not distinguish between preservation practices in Britain and other European nations, since these differences are not the subject of this article. Astrid Swenson's fine study has dealt with the subject in a European transnational context. See Astrid Swenson, 'Conceptualising "Heritage" in 19th and early 20th-century France, Germany and England' (Ph.D. thesis, University of Cambridge, 2007). See also the older study on architectural conservation in Europe by Jukka Jokilehto, *A history of architectural conservation* (1999; repr. Oxford 2009).

[21] The historiography of colonialism often tends to assume that the idea of monuments as relics of history, as objects of the study of the past unconnected to belief or practice, stood for a virtually homogeneous form of hegemonic knowledge brought to the colonies from Europe. Historians of colonialism therefore often overlook the fact that contestations of such a secularizing, historicizing knowledge canon—as, for example, on the question of the restoration of churches—were taking place in the metropolitan culture of Victorian England until well into the middle decades of the nineteenth century. See, for instance, the summary of the debate on restoration, especially church restoration, in the 1913 essay by W. J. Davies, which won the silver medal of the Royal Institute of British Architects. W. J. Davies, 'The preservation of ancient monuments' (MS, 1913, RIBA Archives).

[22] See, for example, Tapati Guha-Thakurta, 'Archaeology and the monument: on two contentious sites of faith and history', in idem, *Monuments, objects, histories, institutions of art in colonial and postcolonial India* (New Delhi, 2004), pp. 268–303; Nayanjot Lahiri, 'Bodh-Gaya: An ancient Buddhist shrine and its modern history (1891–1904)', in Timothy Insoll, ed., *Case studies in archaeology and world religion* (Oxford, 1998), pp. 33–44; also Nayanjot Lahiri, 'Archaeology and identity in colonial India', *Antiquity*, 74 (2000), pp. 687–92.

getting drawn into cases of preservation of temples and mosques in use, and its own attitude was highly ambivalent. While, on the one hand, the aim was religious neutrality and hence keeping away from such cases, it nevertheless began to use the powers of consultation, help, and advice given to it by the Act of 1904 to encroach on what, under the act, was supposed to be the business of the endowments and their managing committees. Underlying this readiness to encroach on the religious sphere was a specific understanding of what its guardianship of India actually meant, or what duties a colonial state, as opposed to a nation state, was 'divinely ordained' to discharge. Guarding India's past, its history, and its heritage certainly belonged to the core public duties of the state. As Curzon famously proclaimed in his manifesto for Indian archaeology in a speech at the Asiatic Society of Bengal in 1900:

> Indeed, a race like our own, who are themselves foreigners, are in a sense better fitted to guard, with a dispassionate and impartial zeal, the relics of different ages, and of sometimes antagonistic beliefs, than might be the descendants of the warring races or the votaries of the rival creeds. To us the relics of Hindu and Mohammedan, of Buddhist, Brahmin, and the Jain are, from the antiquarian, the historical, and the artistic point of view, equally interesting and equally sacred ... Each represents the glories or the faith of a branch of the human family ... Each is a part of the heritage which Providence has committed to the custody of the ruling power.[23]

Living religious practice was firmly excluded from this sphere of public duty. The government's reluctance to spend 'public money' on religious structures still in use rested on a separation of the (private) religious sphere and the public duty of the government to be the guardian of India's past. But when it came to the question of preservation, the government, while intent on being neutral towards religious practice, nevertheless tried to use whatever means it had at its disposal to supervise and control the preservation of religious monuments in use. As such, the rights of archaeology and of monument preservation were given a special position, which was based on the conviction that the methods and approach to preservation that the colonial state had introduced to India were, by far, superior and best suited to preserve India's monumental heritage. At the heart of these methods and approaches was the belief that India's monuments needed to be conserved, not restored, its past historicized, and its relics monumentalized, not modernized.[24] The Bible of preservation

---

[23] Lord Curzon, 'Speech before the Asiatic Society of Bengal, 7 February 1900', in Thomas Raleigh, ed., *Lord Curzon in India, being a selection from his speeches as viceroy and governor-general, 1898–1905* (London, 1906).

[24] A significant exception to this rule related to Mughal monuments. Colonial archaeologists and policy-makers, including Marshall and Curzon, insisted that Mughal structures could be restored without losing their authenticity, since they had been built by craftsmen whose skills had been passed on to their descendants, who continued to practise these skills in the traditional way.

practice in colonial India, John Marshall's *Conservation manual*, defined the task and its accomplishment thus:

> Although there are many ancient buildings whose state of disrepair suggests at first sight a renewal, it should never be forgotten that their *historical value is gone when their authenticity is destroyed*, and that our first duty is not to renew them but to preserve them … Broken or half-decayed original work is of infinitely more value than the smartest and most perfect work.[25]

It is not difficult to see that John Marshall's prescriptive guidelines and his understanding of the task of monument preservation stemmed from the core of the debate on monument preservation that had been going on in Europe since the French Revolution, and which had just about been settled.[26] This was the debate on ruins and the consequent discussions on the repair/conservation versus restoration of monuments, all of which was rooted in a particular understanding of the past and present, and a specific notion of history. In his study *Stranded in the present: modern time and the melancholy of history*, Peter Fritzsche conceptualizes ruins as the site, both physical and imagined, on which, in the post-French Revolution era, both individuals and groups (and later nations) negotiated an essentially new (and modern) relationship with the past. In this sense, ruins serve as both the tangible reminder of the 'pastness' of the past as well as a means of tangible access to the 'half-hidden' pasts invoked by those seeking personal and national–political meanings. As is well known, from such an understanding of ruins emerged the distinction between 'living' and 'dead' structures, between structures that belonged to the present and those that were ancient, historical, which clearly belonged to pre-modern times. Structures from the past—monuments—thus belonged to the realms of history and memory, and as such they were to be musealized. By the 1870s and 1880s, and certainly by the end of the nineteenth century, it was this notion of monuments as remains of history, as objects of study of the past, that came to form the basis of thinking on the built heritage.

A large body of writing on the discipline of history in colonial India has shown that 'modern' notions of time, that is, historical consciousness of a kind of post-Rankean positivist order and a linear notion of time, came to India riding on the back of colonialism. The colonial state saw itself as the guardian of India's past, and for many colonial officials the writing of India's

---

Hence, unlike the building traditions of medieval Europe, the building tradition of the Mughals remained unbroken in India. See extract from Christina Herringham's letter to the committee of the Society for the Protection of Ancient Buildings, in *The Society for the Protection of Ancient Buildings: thirtieth annual report of the committee* (n.p., June 1907), p. 45.

[25] John Marshall, *Conservation manual* (1923, repr. New Delhi, 1990), pp. 9–10 (italics mine).

[26] See also note 20.

history was part of this responsibility.[27] The duty of creating and managing India's monuments was an extension of the same task. Thus, by protecting ancient structures from ruin, by preserving their monumentality, and by maintaining them as records of the past, the colonial government would be discharging its responsibility of educating Indians about their past. A common colonial trope about India's history was the absence of historical consciousness among Indians. Colonial scholars repeatedly pointed out the absence of historical texts in India's literary tradition and, in the early years of Company rule till at least the 1830s, much importance was attached to ancient Indian literary texts as a source of India's history. Following from the lack of historical texts written in the European tradition to shed light on India's past, India's architectural heritage came to be regarded by colonial scholars as the major source of Indian history and as central to the reconstruction of India's past. Scholars of Indian architectural history such as James Fergusson referred to Indian architecture as a 'stone book'.[28] Thus, in the colonial context, the debates on preservation or repair versus the restoration of monuments came to acquire a special and a specific meaning. On the one hand, they were informed by a general colonial understanding of Indian history as a story of degeneration and decline, and of Indians as a people without history; on the other, these discussions were rooted in the self-perception of the colonial state, in its understanding of guardianship and public duties. Included in its public duties was the task of restoring India's history to Indians. Guarding India's ancient built heritage thus became a significant form of legitimation of colonial rule: as the historian Thomas Metcalf has shown, by thus preserving India's 'pastness' the colonial state was in fact creating and ordering difference between Britain and India, and establishing India's eternal 'pastness' as a showcase for a vigorous, modern, industrialized Britain.[29] What followed from this presentist notion of Britain's difference from—and superiority to—India was the idea of Britain's guardianship of India, which the colonial ruling elite, such as Curzon, espoused with passion. In this scheme of things, a progressive modern Britain was best suited to lead India out of its unchanging 'pastness' and into modernity. Hence, India's 'pastness' had to be preserved and musealized for Britain to play its role of both guardian of India's past and India's modernizer.

[27] For comparatively recent analyses of the colonialist historiography of India see, for example, Thomas R. Metcalf, *Ideologies of the Raj* (1995, repr. Cambridge, 2005); Ranajit Guha, *An Indian historiography of India: a nineteenth-century agenda and its implications* (Calcutta, 1988); Nicholas B. Dirks, 'History as a sign of the modern', *Public Culture*, 34 (1995), pp. 44–66.

[28] James Fergusson, cited in John M. MacKenzie, *Orientalism: history, theory and the arts* (Manchester, 1995), p. 95.

[29] Metcalf, *Ideologies of the Raj*, esp. pp. 66–159. See also Saloni Mathur's work on Indian crafts, craftsmen, colonialism, and the cultural economy of Victorian Britain. Saloni Mathur, *India by design: colonial history and cultural display* (Berkeley, CA, 2007), esp. pp. 27–79.

III

But is this really only a story of metropolitan domination of the colony, of the extension of metropolitan debates to the Indian context, and of a hegemonic system of knowledge that left little room for colonial subjects to act? In the past two decades, scholars of India's colonial experience have intensely engaged with these questions, as colonial knowledge and power on the one hand, and the agency of indigenous subjects on the other, have come to dominate the historiography in the field. In the cases of conflict over religious buildings that this chapter has dwelt on, it is evident that the system of knowledge and practice that was introduced by the colonial state was constantly challenged; at the same time, it was adapted and incorporated into the agenda of various indigenous groups. One way of doing this was by taking advantage of the legal apparatus created by the AMPA of 1904, to ask for increasing grants from the state and to formulate arguments that would best serve this purpose. Local communities also had considerable agency and could deal with colonial officials on their own terms. Thus, as I showed earlier, appeals to the state to invest large sums in the maintenance of religious structures were often followed by successful attempts by the custodians of religious structures to exercise exclusive rights to the premises, as often happened in the case of mosques. Final control over these structures, which ultimately became the key issue between the colonial officials and the managing committees of temples and mosques, was negotiated by the custodians of religious structures from a position of relative strength: the tricky question of ownership could be cleverly employed to both get grants from the government for repairs and yet manage the structures themselves. As the case of the Orissan temples shows, the activities of the colonial bureaucracy on the issue of repair and maintenance was subject to critical scrutiny and could often be used by temple custodians as licence to undertake their own programmes of maintenance, without informing, let alone consulting, the state. Temple committees seldom fought shy of asserting their right to engage in architectural repair by accusing the government of inadequate interest or action with regard to dilapidated structures.

The arguments employed by the managing committees of temples and mosques in their petitions, as well as their actions, convincingly indicate that considerable agency lay with these groups when engaging with the efforts of colonial archaeological officials to create historical monuments out of religious structures. The arguments also indicate that, by the early twentieth century, traditional religious groups and communities had not only imbibed the specific ideas of historicism and monumentality introduced to architectural preservation by colonialism, they were also adept at skilfully employing these to avail themselves of the financial aid that the new laws for the preservation of Indian monuments promised. As we have seen in the case of the temples at

Bhubaneswar, arguments of historicism and aestheticism were used both to justify actions taken by the temple committee to demolish structures, and to condemn what the committee felt was indiscriminate and insensitive destruction by the government. Thus, the committee declared its firm commitment to 'improvement' and opposition to demolition, even pointing out, in language that William Morris would have been proud of, that a temple in the controversial temple complex was 'a rare specimen of non-interfered decay'.[30] In its attack on the government's insensitive act of temple demolition, the committee used the criteria of beauty and congruity to argue that demolition should be stopped immediately. Equally, in defending their own actions of removing the stones from a temple that had fallen into disrepair to then be used to repair another one, the temple custodians argued, 'there was *nothing in it of any archaeological or historical interest*, it being a *massive structure* of stone with *a stone roof without any ornamental work thereon*'.[31] Recent research, most notably by Dipesh Chakrabarty, has highlighted the growth in influence that 'scientific' history came to acquire over Indians from the 1880s onwards—to the extent that by the turn of the nineteenth century, the writing of 'scientific' history had moved into the public domain, and become tied up in many different ways with the Indian nation-in-the-making.[32] The categories employed in the petitions indicate the extent to which historical thinking—in the Western European understanding of the term, and, along with it, the philosophy and practice of preservation of monuments from the past—had come to be appropriated by Indians by the early years of the twentieth century.

Yet it is not merely the employment of these categories that provides an indicator of the agency of indigenous groups. It is the clever combination of arguments based on history and aesthetics on the one hand, and religious sentiment and tradition on the other, that stands out. Thus, the temple being destroyed by the government would not only result in an unsightly and asymmetrical structure, it would also destroy the cosmic symmetry and the mythological link between it and its sister temple. The Bhubaneswar temple committee, when defending its own action of using the stones from the temple it had demolished to repair another, claimed that both temples were part of the same complex, situated within the same grounds. The PWD's efforts to do the same were criticized, as the recycled stones were to be used to repair a temple that lay outside the temple complex, thus indicating that there was no spiritual connection between the demolished structure and the one under repair. Thus, the spiritual and spatial connection of the temples was conflated

[30] NAI-ERC, ASI Calcutta Circle, SL 483, File 26, Chatterji to the Collector of Puri, Cuttack, 20 Nov. 1910.
[31] NAI-ERC, ASI Calcutta Circle, SL 483, File 26, Chatterji to the superintendent of the Archaeological Survey, Eastern Circle, Puri, 29 Jan. 1911 (italics mine).
[32] Dipesh Chakrabarty, 'The public life of history: an argument out of India', *Public Culture*, 20 (2008), pp. 143–68.

with their historical or aesthetic relationship. And, in the final account, temple and mosque committees were always aware of the power of the argument that most petitions ended with, and that the government was always vulnerable to: the sentiments of the local religious communities.

IV

In her work on the origins and nineteenth-century history of colonial archaeology in India, Upinder Singh describes the work of conservation undertaken by the colonial state as 'haphazard' and 'ad hoc', characterized by a lack of policy; she also refers to the unevenness of planning, execution, and results of such 'fumbling attempts'.[33] According to her, the organized, centrally planned, and methodically conducted phase of monument preservation began with the era of John Marshall as director-general of Indian archaeology, and Curzon as India's viceroy. This is certainly true, and the passing of the AMPA was proof of this. The act enabled the state to exercise much greater control of the religious sphere when it came to protecting ancient monuments. Nevertheless, colonial monument-making in the context of religious structures remained riddled with ambivalence and a lack of clarity in the implementation of policy, which belied the power of the rhetoric of guardianship that can be found in policy statements and speeches on India's architectural heritage. Colonial archaeologists and administrators were constantly aware of the strength of local religious sentiment in undertaking the preservation of religious structures, as they repeatedly found themselves on the verge of offending local religious feelings. Dependence on local religious community elites thus became vital for the successful implementation of monument preservation policies. This, in turn, enabled local leaders of religious communities to exercise considerable influence on the way in which religious buildings were maintained. By effectively combining historicist arguments of heritage preservation with those of culture and tradition to make successful petitions against state policy, these groups managed to ensure that the making of religious monuments was not left entirely to the officials of the colonial state. As in many other areas of knowledge-related practices in colonial India, here too power did not entirely rest with the colonial state—in its exercise it was much less clear and intentional than the rhetoric of colonialism would have us believe. On an operational level, colonial, state-driven practices of monument-making with regard to religious structures often ended in unplanned and unforeseen ways, as a consequence of the intervention of local indigenous religious communities—who engaged with these practices in a variety of ways.

[33] Upinder Singh, *The discovery of ancient India: early archaeologists and the beginnings of archaeology* (New Delhi, 2004), p. 248.

9

Representing Ancient Egypt at Imperial High Noon (1882–1922): Egyptological Careers and Artistic Allegories of Civilization*

DONALD MALCOLM REID

IN EGYPT, THE YEARS from the British conquest in 1882 to 1922, when Britain unilaterally declared the country's limited independence, constituted the high tide of Western imperial control. This chapter juxtaposes the careers of several Egyptologists with allegorical works of art from this period, as a means of exploring imperial and national claims then being made on the heritage of the pharaohs.

Born around the middle of the nineteenth century, Gaston Maspero (1846–1916), Wallis Budge (1857–1934), and Ahmad Kamal (1851–1923) spent most of their working lives during these forty years of greatest British control over Egypt. Maspero, the French director of the Egyptian Antiquities Service, and his Egyptian subordinate, Kamal, were their countries' foremost Egyptologists in this generation. Among Britons, Flinders Petrie (1853–1942), not Budge, held that distinction. But Budge, keeper of Egyptian and Assyrian antiquities at the British Museum, is highlighted here because his frankness

* This is a revision of a paper read at the conference 'From Plunder to Preservation: Britain and the "Heritage" of Empire, *c.* 1820–1940', King's College, Cambridge University, 21–2 Mar. 2009. I would like to thank Peter Mandler, Astrid Swenson, David Gange, and the Cambridge Victorian Studies Group for organizing the conference and inviting me to participate. This chapter draws on research conducted with support from fellowships of the Fulbright Program (1998–99) and the National Endowment for the Humanities through the American Research Center in Egypt (1999 and 2005). Except as otherwise noted, illustrations are from photographs taken by the author. Some of the material presented here is drawn from Donald Malcolm Reid, *Whose pharaohs? archaeology, museums, and Egyptian national identity from Napoleon to World War I* (Berkeley, CA, 2002). Elliott Colla, *Conflicted antiquities: Egyptology, Egyptomania, Egyptian modernity* (Durham, NC, 2007) has many excellent insights. Maya Jasanoff, *Edge of empire: lives, culture, and conquest in the east, 1750–1850* (New York, 2005) brings British imperialism and antiquities collection in India and Egypt together in a single framework.

about his aggressive methods of collecting is revealing for this book's theme.[1] The careers of two other Egyptologists are also considered: one older and one younger than the Maspero–Kamal–Budge generation. French director of the Egyptian Antiquities Service Auguste Mariette (1821–81) sets the stage, and American James Breasted (1865–1935), whose career did not peak until the interwar era, is considered in connection with one of the works of art.[2]

Three turn-of-the-twentieth-century works of art illustrate competing imperial and national claims, both popular and scholarly, then being made to the legacy of ancient Egypt. These are the façade of the new Egyptian Museum in Cairo (1902), the collar painting in the dome of the Library of Congress in Washington, DC (1896), and a cover illustration of a forgotten Egyptian school magazine (1899). These representations are evaluated against the long-range background of imperial claims conveyed in three early nineteenth-century works of art, which celebrated France's Egyptian expedition of 1798–1801.

Artistic allegories, like cartoons and poems, can sometimes capture elusive ideas and sentiments particularly well. The examples used here drew on various mixes of orientalist, imperialist, nationalist, classicist, and romantic conventions in laying claim to the heritage of Egyptian antiquity. These works are juxtaposed with the careers of contemporary Egyptologists in an attempt to connect scholarly and popular interest in ancient Egypt, illuminate the grand abstractions of the 'isms', and rein in the temptation to over-generalize and assume inevitability in discussing these abstractions.

I

The era of Maspero, Budge, and Kamal drew on legacies of antiquity collection and study from the previous eighty-four years between Napoleon's conquest of Egypt and the British one of 1882. Several overlapping phases, modes, and rationales of collection stand out in this earlier era. The first was antiquities as spoils of war. At the turn of the nineteenth century, Egypt was a key battlefield in a global war between imperial rivals Britain and France. Fading texts painted on the sides of the Rosetta stone in the British Museum read: 'Captured in Egypt by the British Army 1801' and 'Presented by King George III'.[3]

---

[1] For Maspero, Kamal, Budge, and Petrie respectively, see Warren R. Dawson and Eric P. Uphill, *Who was who in Egyptology*, rev. M. L. Brierbrier (3rd edn., London, 1995), pp. 71–2, 224, 278–9, 329–32 (hereafter *WWWE3*).
[2] Mariette and Breasted are treated in *WWWE3*, pp. 62–3, 275–6.
[3] Richard Parkinson, *Cracking codes: the Rosetta stone and decipherment* (Berkeley, CA, 1999), p. 23.

Three early nineteenth-century artistic works forcefully expressed French imperial claims to Egypt that still echoed in Maspero's day. The scholars, artists, and engineers accompanying General Bonaparte's army surveyed the resources—natural and human, ancient and modern—of their intended new colony. Once back home, they compiled the results in the encyclopedic *Description de l'Égypte*. The first volume, dedicated to 'His Majesty the Emperor Napoleon the Great', bears the publication date 1809. The frontispiece depicts the Nile valley from Alexandria to Aswan as a nostalgic treasure house of antiquities, conveniently devoid of any traces of Cairo, Islam, or modern inhabitants (Figure 9.1).[4]

The picture's frame supplies the context: antiquities as spoils of war. At the top, Napoleon is a classical hero, in the mould of Alexander the Great and perhaps Apollo. Preceded by a Roman eagle, he drives his chariot into battle (Figure 9.2), and the Mamluk army goes down before him in oriental confusion. Military standards and the names of battles trail down the sides, and at the bottom of the frame the conquered bring in tribute to Napoleon's crowned imperial monogram. There is no hint of the fact that ten days after Bonaparte's defeat of the Mamluks, Admiral Nelson turned the French expedition into a disaster by destroying its fleet, or that the Rosetta stone shown among the trophies in the foreground rests in the British Museum, not the Louvre.

The second edition of the *Description* (Paris, 1820–30) reframed the publication as a national rather than a Napoleonic project, and dedicated it to restored Bourbon king Louis XVIII. Eschewing the solitary Napoleonic hero, the new frontispiece celebrates instead the French army as a whole as it marches through the haunting ruins.[5] France was no longer formally an empire, but the imperial message comes through unchanged: France claims the fascinating legacy of ancient Egypt as the fruit of military conquest.

A medal struck in 1826 to commemorate the expedition and Louis XVIII's patronage of the *Description* continued the imperial, national, military, classical, romantic, and orientalist themes of the two frontispieces, but also highlighted gender (Figure 9.3). A Gallo-Roman soldier lifts the veil on conquered Egypt, represented as a mysterious, alluring Cleopatra.[6]

---

[4] Frontispiece by Cécile, *Description de l'Égypte*, i: *Antiquités: planches* (Paris, 1809).

[5] The second edition's colour frontispiece is reproduced on the cover of Robert Anderson and Ibrahim Fawzy, eds., *Egypt revealed: scenes from the Description de l'Égypte* (Cairo, 1987). In the present chapter, 'imperialism' refers primarily to European and American formal and informal overseas expansion. In nineteenth-century France, *impérialisme* often referred more narrowly to the regimes and policies of the empire of Napoleon I and the Second Empire of Napoleon III. Although the policies of the Ottoman empire relating to Egypt until 1914 were, by definition, 'imperial', the term 'imperialism' is not applied to them here.

[6] The medal was designed by Barre. See Peter A. Clayton, *The rediscovery of ancient Egypt* (London, 1982), p. 7, and Reid, *Whose pharaohs?*, pp. 142–3.

Figure 9.1: Framing and claiming Egyptian antiquity: Cécile's frontispiece, *Description de l'Égypte*, i: *Antiquités*, 1809.

Figure 9.2: Napoleon defeats the Mamluks, and the Muses return to Egypt: top of frame of the frontispiece to *Description de l'Égypte*, vol. 1.

Figure 9.3: *Victorious Gaul rediscovers Egypt*: medal by Barre, 1826. Courtesy of Peter Clayton.

But Western invasions of Islamic lands—whether in 1798 and 1882 Egypt, or 2002 Afghanistan and 2003 Iraq—were not primarily celebrated as glorious adventures of power and plunder. They were also idealistically framed in compelling dichotomies of civilization over barbarism, enlightenment against obscurantism, liberation versus oppression, tolerance against fanaticism. In the original frontispiece of the *Description*, the classical Muses at the top left of the frame disembark, in a calm, orderly fashion, from the French ship in the hero's wake. The arts and sciences of civilization are returning to Egypt, the land of their legendary birth (Figure 9.2).

Effective as these three allegories inspired by the French expedition are in conveying the intertwining of overseas imperialism and claims on Egyptian antiquity, they reveal little of the individual decisions, interest groups, revolutionary politics, and global war that produced the expedition, or of the degrees of support, opposition, or indifference to it at various levels of French society at the time or over the tumultuous course of nineteenth-century French politics. Neither the conquest of 1798 nor the British one of 1882 were inevitable results of an abstract force called imperialism. Even if studies of how these three artistic statements were received were available, there would still be much they could not tell about the range and depth of French interest, scholarly and popular, in ancient Egypt, the reasons for it, or the political inclinations—imperialist or other—of individuals drawn to the emerging specialty of Egyptology.

Although the second frontispiece and the commemorative medal still unabashedly deployed 'spoils of war' frameworks in the 1820s, Egyptian history was moving on. The rise of Viceroy Muhammad Ali to control of Egypt, from 1805, necessitated a new framework for the acquisition of antiquities. Smuggling aside, major antiquities now left Egypt framed as 'gifts from the ruler', implicitly in return for European diplomatic favours in other fields. Between the 1810s and 1850, the collections of British consul Henry Salt and his French rival Bernardino Drovetti, Jean François Champollion's Franco-Tuscan expedition, and Richard Lepsius's Prussian expedition all left Egypt as gifts from the viceroy. So did the Egyptian state collection, which Said Pasha presented to Archduke Maximilian of Austria–Hungary in 1855. Muhammad Ali and his grandson Khedive Ismail also gave away the mightiest imperial trophies of all: the Egyptian obelisks raised—in imitation of the ancient Romans—in public spaces in Paris, London, and New York between 1836 and 1881.[7]

Whether framed as 'spoils of war' or 'gifts from the ruler', however, the clinching moral justification remained the same in European eyes—enlightened Westerners deserved antiquities because they appreciated, collected,

---

[7] Reid, *Whose pharaohs?*, pp. 37–8, 44–6, 57–8, 100–3.

preserved, studied, and displayed them in public places, museums, and private collections. Egyptians, they claimed, did not. The French captain who transported the obelisk from Luxor to Paris wrote:

> France, snatching an obelisk from the ever heightening mud of the Nile, or the savage ignorance of the Turks ... earns a right to the thanks of the learned of Europe, to whom belong all the monuments of antiquity, because they alone know how to appreciate them. Antiquity is a garden that belongs by natural right to those who cultivate and harvest its fruits.[8]

By the time the last obelisk left Egypt in 1879, bound for New York, it was almost too late. The khedive made good on the gift only by overruling the vigorous objections of Auguste Mariette, the Frenchman in charge of the Egyptian Antiquities Service since 1858. Mariette's appointment had opened a new era in the collection, study, and preservation of Egyptian antiquities. He was proud that although the French had lost the Rosetta stone physically to the British, the intellectual conqueror who deciphered it had been a Frenchman. Champollion's achievement in 1822 not only founded the modern field of Egyptology, but, in Mariette's view, made it pre-eminently a French science.[9]

Politically, Mariette's appointment was one of many signs of a French return to an informal sphere of influence in Egypt in the decades after the humiliating evacuation after the defeat of 1801. By 1858, Napoleon III was pursuing an expansive foreign policy, Ferdinand de Lesseps was driving his audacious Suez Canal project forward, and Egypt's viceroy Said was an eager-to-please francophile. Mariette directed the Antiquities Service until his death in 1881, struggling to suppress unauthorized excavations, control the export of antiquities, and build a great collection in the museum he founded in the Cairo district of Bulaq. The Antiquities Service would remain in French hands for ninety-four years, down to the 1952 revolution—some consolation at least for France's losing the country to Britain in 1882.

Mariette's appointment opened a division in French imperial interests between metropole and colony. From the centre, the Louvre continued to try to acquire the world's finest art and antiquities. But from his informal colonial base in Cairo, Mariette tried to keep masterpieces in Egypt, either on site or in the Bulaq Museum. The most famous Cairo–Paris clash along these lines came when Empress Eugénie suggested that pharaonic jewellery from the Bulaq Museum, which Mariette had lent to the Paris Exposition of 1867, would make a fine gift to herself. Khedive Ismail parried the request with the

[8] Qu. in translation in ibid., p. 1.
[9] Élisabeth David, *Mariette Pacha, 1821–1881* (Paris, 1994) is the standard biography. The best history of French Egyptology is Éric Gady, 'Le pharaon, l'égyptologue et le diplomate: les égyptologues français en Égypte, du voyage du Champollion à la crise de Suez (1826–1956)' (Unpublished doctoral thesis, Université de Paris IV-Sorbonne, 2005).

remark that in matters of antiquities, there was someone at Bulaq more power-ful than he. Mariette stood firm;[10] preservation, he insisted, could now best be pursued in Egypt itself. Despite receiving little diplomatic support from the Quai d'Orsay for most of his career, Mariette fiercely defended the fief that he had carved out on Egyptian soil for himself, for science, and for France.

Midway through Mariette's twenty-three years at the helm of the Antiquities Service, Bismarck shocked the world, by using the Franco-Prussian War to unite Germany. Even though German Egyptological fieldwork between the Prussian expedition of Richard Lepsius in the 1840s and Ludwig Borchardt's excavations, beginning in 1898, was sparse, Mariette worried that the emer-gence of Germany as a political, military, economic, and academic power-house might threaten his, and France's, dominance of Egyptian archaeology. This complicated Mariette's friendship with Heinrich Brugsch, the Prussian Egyptologist who was the director of a short-lived Egyptian school of Egyptology in Cairo from 1869 to 1874. Mariette's refusal to hire the school's graduates doomed the enterprise.[11]

II

Maspero, Budge, and Kamal all grew up during Mariette's twenty-two-year reign over antiquities in Egypt. Maspero, who would inherit Mariette's Egyptological and imperial mantle, started as a double outsider to French society: he was of Italian descent and lacked an acknowledged father. A boarder at the Jesuit Lycée Louis-le-Grande in Paris from the age of 7, Maspero excelled at languages and was captivated early by ancient Egypt. Graduating from the elite École Normale, he began teaching at the new École des Hautes Études at 23, earned his doctorate from the University of Paris, and at 28 took up the chair of Egyptian Philology and Archaeology at the Collège de France. In 1881, the year he turned 35, he founded the École du Caire (later the Institut français d'archéologie oriental du Caire, IFAO) and succeeded the late Mariette as director of Egyptian antiquities.[12]

To France's dismay, Britain conquered Egypt a year later, and in 1883 Sir Evelyn Baring (later Lord Cromer) began his twenty-four-year rule over the still nominally Ottoman province. Baring's misleadingly modest title in this 'thinly veiled protectorate' was 'Agent and Consul-general'. Rudyard Kipling later described Egypt as being:

[10] David, *Mariette*, pp. 181–2.
[11] Gady, 'Le pharaon', pp. 237–8, 243–72; Reid, *Whose pharaohs?*, pp. 113–18.
[12] Élisabeth David, *Gaston Maspero, 1846–1916: le gentleman égyptologue* (Paris, 1999) and Gaston Maspero, *Lettres d'Égypte: correspondance avec Louise Maspero*, ed. Élisabeth David (Paris, 2003).

nominally in charge of a government which is not a government but a discon-
nected satrapy of a half-dead empire, controlled pecksniffingly by a Power
which is not a Power but an Agency, which Agency has been tied up for years,
custom and blackmail into all sorts of intimate relations with six or seven
European Powers ... To fill in the details ... would be as easy as to explain base-
ball to an Englishman or the Eton Wall game to a citizen of the United States.
But it is a fascinating play. There are Frenchmen in it, whose logical mind it
offends, and they revenge themselves by printing the finance reports and the
catalogue of the Bulak Museum in French. There are Germans in it ... (etc.)[13]

Without Maspero's diplomatic skill during two terms of directing the
Antiquities Service (1881–86, 1899–1914), France might well have lost this
cultural enclave to the British or Germans. Maspero encouraged the work of
Britain's Egypt Exploration Fund (EEF, later Egypt Exploration Society,
EES), let British expeditions take generous shares of their finds home, and
brought Britons into his department. The payoff was formally ratified in the
Anglo-French Entente Cordiale of 1904: Britain agreed that the directorship
of the Egyptian Antiquities Service would remain in French hands.

Such were the circumstances under which the French-designed and
French-run Egyptian Museum, built by an Italian construction company, was
inaugurated in Cairo in 1902, at British imperial high noon on the Nile, as an
iconic official monument (Figure 9.4).[14] The massive Qasr al-Nil Palace next
door, which antedated the occupation and now housed troops of the British
garrison, and the 'Residency', which Cromer built several blocks south along
the Nile, were the real seats of power, but a grandiose British imperial architectural statement was out of the question in the veiled protectorate.
Archaeology was not Cromer's priority, and he was willing, within limits, to
let Maspero and the French have their day in the sun by designing the new
museum.[15]

Marcel Dourgnon designed a neo-classical Beaux-Arts edifice with such
Egyptianizing touches as the goddesses at the keystone and in the niches

[13] Rudyard Kipling, *Letters of travel, 1892–1913* (London, 1913) as qu. in Deborah Manley and
Sahar Abdel-Hakim, eds., *Traveling through Egypt from 450 B.C. to the twentieth century* (Cairo,
2004), pp. 14–15.
[14] On the Egyptian Museum façade, see Donald Malcolm Reid, 'French Egyptology and the
architecture of orientalism: deciphering the façade of Cairo's Egyptian Museum', in L. Carl Brown
and Matthew Gordon, eds., *Franco-Arab encounters: studies in memory of David C. Gordon*
(Beirut, 1996), pp. 35–69, and Reid, *Whose pharaohs?*, pp. 3–6, 8. See also Gady, 'Le pharaon',
pp. 619–30. Francesco Tiradritti, 'The Egyptian Museum of Cairo and the Italians', in Maria
Casini, ed., *One hundred years in Egypt: paths of Italian archaeology* (Milan, 2001), p. 227,
mentions the Italian construction firm, Garzzo and Zaffrani. On Maspero's role, see also David,
Maspero, p. 205, and Maspero, *Lettres*, passim.
[15] The Earl of Cromer, *Modern Egypt* (2 vols., London, 1908) provides autobiographical insight.
The standard biography is Roger Owen, *Lord Cromer: Victorian imperialist, Edwardian proconsul*
(Oxford, 2004).

CAIRE
Le Musée

Figure 9.4:   The Egyptian Museum, Cairo, 1902.

flanking the portal (Figure 9.5). Two years after the inauguration of the
museum, a shrine to Mariette—a statue and the sarcophagus containing his
remains—was added in the garden. Dourgnon wanted to inscribe 'Musée des
Antiquités' and his name over the museum's main entry, but this was out of
the question after Britain's defeat of France in an imperial showdown at
Fashoda in the Sudan in 1898. Cromer did not go so far as to substitute
English for French for the portal inscription; he and Maspero, both ardent
classicists, comfortably agreed on imperial Latin, drafted by Oxford Latinists
and 'corrected' by Maspero (Figure 9.6).[16]

The name of the hapless Abbas Hilmi (II) over the portal was an unavoidable concession to the colonized, but few Egyptians other than the khedive
himself—who had studied at the Theresianum Military Academy in Vienna—
could have made out more than his name in the Latin inscription over the
portal. No Egyptian state school then taught the language. Adding the Islamic
date alongside the ad date was barely a concession to local sensibilities, for it
was doubly disguised in the Latin language and Roman numerals: Anno
Hegirae MCCCXVII.

An unusually thorough observer with a feminist agenda could have picked
out the names of Hatshepsut and Cleopatra on the plaques honouring the
otherwise male rulers of Egypt, and no one could miss the cow-horned goddess Hathor on the keystone of the portal arch. The goddesses personifying
Upper and Lower Egypt, and flanking the portal of the imperial monument,

---

[16] Gady, 'Le pharaon', p. 622. To Dourgnon's dismay, his name was only placed over a subsidiary
entry.

Figure 9.5:   Portal of the Egyptian Museum, Cairo.

Figure 9.6:   Imperial Latin: Egyptian Museum, Cairo.

projected a different appeal (Figure 9.7).[17] European association of the orient with seductive women had lost none of its allure since the French commemorative medal of 1826. The 'wet drapery' look of late classical Greek sculpture concealed little more of the figures of these goddesses than the transparent veil of the veiled protectorate concealed who ran the country. The sculptor and the authorities who approved these statues as public art in Cairo—at a time when upper-class Egyptian women still wore all-enveloping cloaks and face veils when they went—out clearly had only Western audiences in mind.

---

[17] Ferdinand Faivre, a Frenchman, was the sculptor. Gady, 'Le pharaon', p. 622.

Figure 9.7: Nekhbet, the vulture goddess personifying Upper Egypt, flanking the portal of the Egyptian Museum, Cairo. Sculptor: Ferdinand Faivre.

Marble plaques in Latin across the façade conveyed in three parts an interpretative history of civilization and enlightenment, which had come into vogue among nineteenth-century Europeans. At the origin of civilization stood the rulers of ancient Egypt (Figure 9.8). The plaques listed first the gods who had mythically ruled on earth, then selected pharaohs from Manetho's thirty dynasties. Greco-Roman rulers from Alexander through the Ptolemies and Romans down to Justinian completed the sequence of rulers over ancient Egypt.

A single plaque headed 'They wrote about Egypt' conveyed the second theme—the Greek-inspired study of Egypt during ancient times (Figure 9.9). Two of these proto-Egyptologists were Greeks (Herodotus and Eratosthenes), and two Hellenized Egyptians (Manetho and Horapollo). Fourteen centuries of implied silence followed, during which no one could read hieroglyphs. By this reading, the dark or middle ages of ignorance about ancient Egypt lasted through the European Renaissance and into the last stage of the European Enlightenment. Then, in 1822, hieroglyphs yielded up their secrets to Champollion. He and twenty other nineteenth-century Europeans, honoured on two marble plaques and four medallions, constitute the façade's third theme—the development of modern Egyptology.

The diplomatic Maspero carefully calibrated the number of each nationality represented among the twenty-one who were honoured. France topped the list with six scholars, an affirmation of Egyptology as a French science and of

Figure 9.8:   The gods and first pharaohs. Plaque, Egyptian Museum, Cairo.

Figure 9.9: Greco-Roman era writers as proto-Egyptologists. Plaque, Egyptian Museum, Cairo.

French dominance in the Antiquities Service. Britain—the occupying power—came close behind with five, then Germany with four Egyptologists. Italy had three, and the Netherlands, Denmark, and Sweden one each.[18] There were no Egyptians or Americans.

Belief in Western conquest of the East, as a necessary prelude to civilizing it, is alive and well even today, but the façade of this monument of 1902 differed from the earlier art associated with the *Description* in avoiding direct reference to either the French or the British military conquest of Egypt. Instead, the European conquest celebrated on the façade was scholarly.

In other contexts, Maspero, cosmopolitan though he was, did not hesitate to express his patriotism freely. A century after Bonaparte, the discovery of a Latin stela on the island of Philae at Aswan gave him a patriotic thrill. It told how Augustus' governor Cornelius had subdued the Nile valley to the Philae frontier at the first cataract. Noting that Cornelius had been born on 'Gallic soil', Maspero was:

> reminded immediately of the other, more recent inscription, which is prominently displayed on the inner jamb of the great gate at Philae. Eighteen centuries after the Gaul Cornelius, other Gauls ... recorded in stone how in the Year VI of the Republic, the 12th of Messidor, a French army, commanded by Bonaparte, disembarked at Alexandria. Twenty days later, the army, having put the Mamluks to flight at the Pyramids, Desaix, commandant of the first division, pursued

---

[18] Note that Thomas Young, often credited by Britons as the co-decipherer of hieroglyphs alongside Champollion, does not figure on the plaques.

them beyond the cataracts ... one must see in the *Voyage* of Denon or in the volumes of the *Description*, how greatly they were nourished by reminders of classical antiquity, and what a thrill they felt to fly their banners over the rocks where the Legions had carried out, in a few weeks, an enterprise which had seemed almost impossible ...[19]

Like the *Description*, the museum façade of 1902 was a secular monument of French enlightenment, and ignored the biblical associations with ancient Egypt, which still loom large for both Christians and Muslims. Moses and Joseph, Mary, and Jesus would have been out of place on the façade. The plaques even pass over the Roman emperor who turned the empire towards Christianity—Constantine—while mentioning Diocletian, who persecuted Christians so fiercely that Copts date their calendar to the year of his accession —284—and call it the year of the martyrs.[20]

David Gange has emphasized the role of conservative Protestantism in the growth of Egyptology in Britain,[21] and a similar case could be made for the strand of Protestantism in the United States that would soon coin the word 'fundamentalist'. American Protestants were eager to enlist Egyptology to 'prove the Bible' in the teeth of higher criticism, Darwinism, and other challenges of sceptical modernism. In this current volume, the paired sections on the classical and biblical worlds of Victorian Britain work well for the history of Egyptology, even though Champollion's decipherment made it possible to bypass both the classics and the Bible and read directly what ancient Egyptians had written.

Of course, the Western association of ancient Egypt with the Bible was not confined to 'Anglo-Saxon' or Protestant lands. In the Louvre in the late 1820s, the decor of one of two rooms in the new Egyptian section, which Champollion arranged, is a case in point, though the decorative scheme was not his choice. Despite his family's Bonapartist past, Champollion had flourished under the Catholic-minded Bourbon restoration. A ceiling showing *Joseph saving Egypt from famine* is balanced with the classical one next door of *Study and the muse of the arts revealing ancient Egypt to Athens*.[22]

[19] Translated from G. Maspero, 'Une inscription trilingue de C. Cornelius', in his *Causeries d'Égypte* (2nd edn., Paris, 1907), pp. 95–101.

[20] Theodosius and Justinian, both Christians, are listed, however.

[21] D. Gange, 'Religion and science in late nineteenth-century British Egyptology', *The Historical Journal*, 14 (2006), pp. 1083–103.

[22] Reid, *Whose pharaohs?*, pp. 27–8, 141–2.

III

Maspero's dual perches atop elite cultural institutions in Paris and Cairo exposed him to a range of perspectives, including some awareness of modern Egyptian aspirations. Budge, however, from his exclusively metropolitan imperial perch at the British Museum, took a narrower view. He saw it as his mission to expand the museum's collections at almost any price, and boasted in his memoirs of running circles around any official in Egypt and Mesopotamia who tried to stand in his way.[23]

Curiously, Budge struggled with the same initial stigma as Maspero—illegitimacy. Budge too seized on relentless scholarship as his path to acceptance and social standing. Like Maspero, he fell in love with the ancient East as a boy, excelled in languages, and was lucky to find powerful patrons early. Budge won the backing not only of Egyptologist Samuel Birch of the British Museum but also of William Gladstone. Gladstone arranged for Budge's elite schooling at Christ's College, Cambridge, then saw that he obtained a post under Birch at the British Museum. Like Maspero, Budge went on to excavate and preside over a great collection of Egyptian antiquities, and publish voluminously for both specialists and general readers. Both men were also patriots in the high imperial age.

Yet the two were very different. Maspero was both a professor and a museum man; Budge never left the service of the British Museum. Maspero had a broad range of knowledge but clearly defined his specialty as Egyptology. Budge spread himself over Assyriology, Egyptology, and other branches of oriental studies, editing texts in cuneiform, hieroglyphs, Coptic, Syriac, and Ethiopic. Maspero's works were authoritative, but Budge worked so hastily and spread himself so thinly that his publications were unreliable.[24]

Budge arrived in Egypt on his first collecting foray for the British Museum in 1886, the year that Eugène Grébaut succeeded his former professor Maspero

---

[23] E. A. W. Budge, *By Nile and Tigris: a narrative of journeys in Egypt and Mesopotamia on behalf of the British Museum between the years 1886 and 1913* (2 vols., London, 1920). See also *WWWE3*, pp. 71–2. Budge's raids on Mesopotamian antiquities are beyond our scope here. Stephanie Moser, *Wondrous curiosities: ancient Egypt at the British Museum* (Chicago, 2006), provides a fine interpretation of collection development through 1880, three years before Budge's appointment.
[24] The website of the British Museum, Department of Ancient Egypt and Sudan, formerly offered a harsh but honest verdict on the institution's long-term devoted official. Presenting a list of recommended books, it anticipates the question: 'Why are there no books by Budge here?' It is because: 'Budge ignored major developments in the fields of transcription, grammar and lexicography, and was neglectful in matters of archaeology and provenance ... Today, University students are strongly advised not to use them [his publications] because of their basic errors of fact and methodology' <www.thebritishmuseum.ac.uk/aes/faqs/budge.html> (accessed 6 January 2006.

as director of the Antiquities Service.[25] Grébaut (in office from 1886 to 1892) cracked down on illicit digging and the antiquities black market—the very things on which much of Budge's collecting depended. Admittedly, Grébaut was no diplomat, and his reliance on heavy-handed legalism and police raids proved to be counterproductive. Budge delighted in outwitting the ineffectual Frenchman. He much preferred the slacker reins of Maspero, and later of Grébaut's successor Jacques de Morgan, but even when they were at the helm, he rarely missed a chance to denigrate the Cairo Museum and the Antiquities Service. This, in effect, dismissed as hopeless French and Egyptian efforts since 1858 to protect, study, and display pharaonic masterpieces in Egypt itself. Behind Budge's attitude stood the familiar assumption that enlightenment and civilization, patriotism and empire, all converged in London at the British Museum—the ideal imperial centre for preserving and appreciating the cultural treasures of the world.

Consul-general Evelyn Baring—he was not yet Lord Cromer—was appalled at Budge's methods of collection. Fearing complaints from other European powers, he bluntly warned Budge in 1886, 'that the occupation of Egypt by the British ought not to be made an excuse for filching antiquities from the country, whether to England or anywhere else'.[26] The two met again some months later, after Budge had already smuggled most of his acquisitions out of the country and was about to follow them. Baring, recounted Budge:

> warmly protested against Egypt being 'stripped' of such a valuable object [a book of waxed wooden tablets inscribed in Greek], and ordered me to abandon the tablets, and to send them back to the man from whom I bought them. In reply I pointed out to him that every Great Power (and many Little Powers) in Europe already had an agent in the country buying for its Central Museum, and that Great Britain had at least an equal right to have an agent collecting antiquities for it. Sir E. Baring's answer took the form of a preemptory order to me to return the waxed tablets to the dealer, and I felt obliged to remind him that I was not a member of his staff, and that I intended to carry out the instructions of the Trustees, and to do my utmost to increase the collections in the British Museum. Here the interview ended abruptly.[27]

Although the British army of occupation would have been unlikely to conduct an archaeological survey in the manner of Napoleon, Budge discovered that many officers were happy to defy both Grébaut and Baring and help him

---

[25] *WWWE3*, pp. 176–7.
[26] Budge, *By Nile and Tigris*, p. 81.
[27] Budge, *By Nile and Tigris*, pp. 116–17.

smuggle out antiquities for the British Museum. No one spoke of 'spoils of war', but the effect was much the same. Some of the officers who assisted were themselves amateurs of archaeology, and all seem to have shared Budge's conviction that such smuggling served patriotism, empire, science, and civilization all at once.

Of the officers who shared Budge's enthusiasm for archaeology, H. H. Kitchener later became the most famous. Budge's first excavation came at the invitation of General Francis Grenfell, commander-in-chief (*Sirdar*) of the Egyptian army and an avid collector. Hiring Budge to 'clear out' Old Kingdom tombs at Aswan, Grenfell put army resources at his disposal and promised to donate his share of any finds to the British Museum. Portable finds in this case turned out to be negligible, but Budge salvaged this Egyptian trip by plunging into the freewheeling world of *fellahin* treasure hunters and shady antiquities dealers. General de Montmorency, commander of the port of Alexandria, cheerfully smuggled out Budge's collection:

> My enjoyment of my visit to Alexandria was marred by the attempts made by the Service of Antiquities to prevent the export of my cases, and the British Consul-General's [Baring's] letters on the subject. But General de Montmorency declined to be moved either by wishes or threats, and one day he and I stood on the quay and watched my twenty-four cases leave the habour under the care of a friendly officer from Aswan.[28]

The trustees of the British Museum gave Budge a ringing endorsement. As recently as 1995, *Who was who in Egyptology* showed no hint of disapproval of Budge's methods of acquisition:

> he had great success in his dealings with the local inhabitants and in overcoming official obstruction, and obtained for the British Museum many thousands of cuneiform tablets and other Assyrian and Babylonian antiquities, as well as Egyptian sculptures, papyri, and other objects.[29]

IV

The United States figured only on the margins of Budge's, Maspero's, and Cromer's imperial views of the Egyptian world. No American names decorated the façade of the Cairo Museum, and, except briefly in the 1870s, when Khedive Ismail recruited Civil War veterans as military advisers, nineteenth-century American diplomacy in Egypt counted for little. But the obelisk that

---

[28] Budge, *By Nile and Tigris*, p. 118. For the rest of the paragraph, see pp. 74–5, 86–94, 102, 110–11, 119.
[29] *WWWE3*, pp. 71–2.

Khedive Ismail presented in return for the advisers was a sensation when it went up in 1881 in Central Park, New York, behind the Metropolitan Museum of Art. Imperial Rome had boasted a dozen such trophy Egyptian obelisks, and when Paris and London each acquired one in the nineteenth century, the emerging transatlantic power had to have one too. Four years later in 1885, the long-interrupted construction of the world's tallest obelisk—the Washington Monument—was finished on the mall in the District of Columbia. Americans were beginning to tour Egypt in large numbers, and several American museums subscribed to Britain's Egypt Exploration Fund as a way of building Egyptian collections.[30]

An allegorical painting (1896) in the dome of the new Library of Congress building, inaugurated in Washington in 1897, staked an American claim to the heritage of ancient Egypt (Figure 9.10).[31] *Evolution of civilization*, as Edwin Howland Blashfield called his mural, prefigured the basic outline of what would later be canonized in American colleges and universities as the Western civilization survey. In Blashfield's Hegelian vision, the allegorical figures of America and Egypt sit side by side (Figure 9.11): ancient Egypt marked the dawn of—and modern America the culmination of—civilization. Reading around the dome, ten other figures traced the progress of civilization onwards and upwards, mostly in a northwesterly direction, from its presumed Egyptian origin. Next came Judea, then Greece, then Rome. Islam and the Middle Ages followed, then Italy, Germany, Spain, England, and France, finally reaching its apotheosis in contemporary America. An auxiliary scheme lauded each region or stage for a contribution—from 'Written Records' for Egypt to 'Science' for contemporary America.[32]

Some of the swaggering industrialists and financial titans of post-Civil War America realized the acclaim they could garner by pouring money into

---

[30] For early American interest in ancient Egypt see the chapters by Bruce G. Trigger and Gerry D. Scott, III, in Nancy Thomas, ed., *The American discovery of ancient Egypt* (Los Angeles, CA, 1996), pp. 21–35, 37–47.

[31] Mina Rieur Weiner, *Edwin Howland Blashfield: master American muralist* (New York, 2009), Leonard N. Amico, *The mural decorations of Edwin Howland Blashfield (1848–1936)* (Williamstown, MA, 1978), and *The works of Edwin Howland Blashfield*, with introduction by Royal Cortissoz (New York, 1937), provide sketches of his life and works and reproductions of his paintings, including *Evolution of civilization*. Blashfield also did the circular painting in the top of the dome: 'Here Human Understanding sits "lifting her veil and looking upward from Finite Intellectual Achievement (typified in the circle of figures in the collar) to that which is beyond".' Amico, *Mural decorations*, p. 16, qu. *Handbook of the new Library of Congress* (Boston, MA, 1901), p. 7.

[32] The sequence of civilizational achievement was: Egypt—Written Records; Judea—Religion; Greece—Philosophy; Rome—Administration; Islam—Physics; Middle Ages—Modern Languages; Italy—Fine Arts; Germany—Art of Printing; Spain—Discovery; England—Literature; France—Emancipation; America—Science.

Figure 9.10:   Edwin Blashfield's *Evolution of civilization*, Library of Congress, 1896. Courtesy of Library of Congress, Prints & Photographs Division, photograph by Carol M. Highsmith, LC-DIG-highsm-02070.

museums, universities, and libraries. In the USA—as in the Europe to which American robber barons, artists, and scholars flocked for cultural and intellectual guidance in the later nineteenth century—imperial Rome increasingly overshadowed the once popular model of the Roman republic.

Blashfield's father had pushed him into engineering studies at MIT, but the young man dropped out and reached Second Empire Paris in time to be dazzled by both the imperial pomp and the classically inspired Beaux-Arts paintings on display at the Exposition Universelle of 1867. The classical and orientalist master painter Jean-Léon Gérôme had himself encouraged Blashfield to come to Paris. The young American trained in the atelier of Léon Bonnat for nearly a decade (1867–70, 1874–80), with an extended visit to Italy to round out his European training. Back home, a major commission

Figure 9.11:   America and Egypt, detail from Edwin Blashfield's *Evolution of civilization*, Library of Congress, 1896. Courtesy of Library of Congress, Prints & Photographs Division, photograph by Carol M. Highsmith, LC-DIG-highsm-02072.

at the World's Columbian Exposition in Chicago in 1893 won him recognition as a leading academic painter of murals. He excelled at the classical allegories that would prove so popular in American public and private buildings over the next two decades.

Blashfield's homage to Egypt in *Evolution of civilization* may have owed something to Gérôme's orientalist works, but it was his marriage to Evangeline Wilbour in 1881 that brought him into direct contact with Egypt. She was the daughter of Charles Wilbour, a wealthy American businessman who had studied Egyptology in Paris, under Maspero, and in Berlin. In the 1880s, Charles Wilbour spent five winter seasons as Maspero's guest on the steamer of the Egyptian Antiquities Service. Wilbour then outfitted a 100-foot *dahabiya* (sailing houseboat) with an Egyptology library and sailed on his own. Although he generously copied hieroglyphic texts for friends, his failure to publish led to his being summed up as 'a spectator rather than a worker in the field' of Egyptology.[33] Around 1890, Wilbour's daughter and her husband Blashfield accompanied him up the Nile on two voyages, one of which lasted five months.[34]

Blashfield belonged to the generation of Maspero, Kamal, and Budge. While he was painting in the dome of the Library of Congress in 1895–96, two younger men who would put American Egyptology on the map were at the

[33] *WWWE3*, pp. 440–1.
[34] E. H. Blashfield and E. W. Blashfield, 'Afloat on the Nile', *Scribner's Magazine*, 10 (1891), pp. 663–81. Edwin did the illustrations and Evangeline the text.

thresholds of their careers. James Breasted (1865–1935) and his rival George Reisner (1867–1942) would reach their peaks in the interwar period.[35]

While aspiring American artists such as Blashfield were making pilgrimages to Paris and Italy, young scholars crossing the Atlantic for graduate studies were more likely to head for Germany. Breasted's Ph.D. in Egyptian philology from Berlin (1894) set him up for a career at the University of Chicago, where he would found the Oriental Institute and turn it into the prime American centre for Egyptology and ancient Near Eastern studies. Reisner, who also studied Egyptology in Berlin in the 1890s, first excavated for the University of California, then switched to Harvard and became long-term director of the Harvard–Boston Museum of Fine Arts expedition to Egypt.

Breasted took popularizing Egyptology as seriously as did Maspero, Budge, and Kamal. With an addition or two, Breasted's high-school textbook *Ancient times*, published in 1916, might have elaborated its sequence directly from the first four figures of Blashfield's painting—Egypt, Judea, Greece, and Rome.[36] *Ancient times* concluded with a mention of Islam and the Middle Ages—Blashfield's fifth and sixth stages—and then let Breasted's friend, medievalist James Harvey Robinson of Columbia University, carry forward the story of civilization in the publisher's 'Outlines of European History' series. Breasted would have applauded Blashfield's selection of 'science' as contemporary America's contribution to civilization, while insisting that his own emerging discipline of Egyptology was thoroughly scientific.

Did Blashfield's painting—and by extension Breasted's textbook and the characteristically American 'Western civ' course—imply an imperial vision? Modern Egyptians might appreciate Blashfield's homage to Egypt as the originator of civilization, and perhaps recall the Arabic proverb 'Egypt is the mother of the world'. But they might also wonder what happened to their country after the Hegelian spirit of civilization had supposedly moved on to Judaea, Greece, and their successors. Western Europeans generally shared a vision of civilizational progress along the lines of Blashfield's first eleven stages, though his progression after the Middle Ages through fifteenth-century Germany (hailed for the 'Art of Printing'), sixteenth-century Spain ('Discovery'), England ('Literature'—the age of Shakespeare), and eighteenth-century France ('Emancipation') was obviously artificial and open to debate. Blashfield's placing of 1890s America at the evolutionary apex of civilization must have puzzled, annoyed, or perhaps amused, Europeans.

---

[35] Jeffrey Abt, *American Egyptologist: the life of James Henry Breasted and the creation of his Oriental Institute* (Chicago, 2011) has superseded the biography by James's son, Charles Breasted, *Pioneer to the past: the story of James Henry Breasted archaeologist* (New York, 1947). On Reisner, see *WWWE3*, pp. 351–2.

[36] Ancient Mesopotamia and Persia were Breasted's main additions to Blashfield's scheme.

Evolution of civilization can be read as a peaceful, generous acknowledgement of America's debt to other lands and ages. Perhaps Blashfield's vision could broaden the horizons of Americans unable to afford cultural pilgrimages to Europe or cruises on the Nile. But the tunnel vision and teleological assumptions of seeing civilization as leaving the Near East and, except for a brief detour through Islam, marching exclusively through European lands to its apotheosis in contemporary America invited many questions. And was 'science' really the salient feature of the cultural American landscape of the 1890s? Such issues would be vigorously debated in the critiques of the Western civilization framework in the American culture wars that grew in the 1960s.

Did aggression perhaps lurk beneath the surface calm of *Evolution of civilization*? The military dress of Blashfield's figures representing Rome and Spain suggested that their empires were built on something more than the benign-sounding 'administration' and 'discovery' respectively attributed to them. Presumably, many of the subjects of Rome and Spain had no wish to be either administered or discovered. When Blashfield painted a ceiling for the mansion of Philadelphia millionaire George W. Childs Drexel two years after his Library of Congress mural, he made a telling substitution. Six allegorical figures now represented Music, Art, Religion, Law, Poetry, and Philosophy, but the two additional figures belong to a different order. Reusing the figure of the Roman army officer at the Library of Congress, Blashfield now listed his attribute not as 'administration' but as 'conquest'. And the eighth figure was 'patriotism'.[37]

Was it a coincidence that Blashfield's Philadelphia painting dates from 1898, the year the Spanish–American War brought conquest and aggressive patriotism to centre stage? Kipling published his poem 'The white man's burden' in 1899, with the subtitle 'The United States and the Philippine islands'. The poem urged Britain's transatlantic offspring to embrace its presumed racial, imperial destiny in this 'savage war of peace'. And Egypt, far from being the light at the beginning of civilization, is in this poem a land of biblical darkness. Kipling warns that taking up 'The white man's burden' was bound to evoke:

The cry of hosts ye humour
(Ah, slowly!) toward the light:—
'Why brought he us from bondage,
Our loved Egyptian night?'

V

[37] Amico, *Mural decorations*, pp. 18–19. Drexel (1869–1944) inherited the fortune that enabled him to commission the painting while still in his twenties, and to retire at 35.

Only in recent years has there been some attempt to write modern Egyptians into the history of Egyptology as more than archaeological labourers, drago-men, tomb guards, shady antiquities dealers, obstructionist bureaucrats, and benighted nationalists. In the same year as Kipling's poem, the front-page illustration of an Arabic school magazine offered a nationalist riposte to assumptions underlying 'The white man's burden', the frontispieces and com-memorative medal of the *Description*, the façade of the Egyptian Museum, and Blashfield's mural. *Al-Samir al-Saghir* (The young companion) shows an Egyptian woman exhorting children to embrace their ancient heritage as rep-resented by the pyramids and sphinx (Figure 9.12). The proud legacy of the pharaohs, it implies, belongs first of all to Egyptians and can inspire national renaissance.[38]

Like the *Description*'s frontispiece ninety years before, *al-Samir*'s allegory links ancient Egypt and modern awakening. This too is a tale of enlighten-ment: the sun, labelled 'The light of knowledge', beams down, and the jour-nal's subtitle reads 'an Egyptian scientific renaissance magazine'. Ignoring the French and the British military conquests, it shows a peaceful Khedive Abbas II—not a conquering Napoleon—presiding over the scene. Enlightenment here is not reintroduced from Europe by classical Muses in the wake of con-quest. Nor does inspiration spring—as in the museum façade—from Greco-Roman writers and nineteenth-century European scholars. The heroes who frame *al-Samir*'s cultural awakening (*nahda*) are four nineteenth-century Egyptian reformers, the scholar-officials Rifaa al-Tahtawi, Mahmud al-Falaki, Ali Mubarak, and Abdallah Fikri.[39]

Maspero's subordinate, Ahmad Kamal, deserves much of the credit for popularizing the conviction behind *al-Samir*'s picture: that modern Egyptians must reclaim their ancient heritage as a vital ingredient for national revival and independence.[40] Kamal had personally benefited directly from the work of two of the four scholarly educators honoured in the frame. Rifaa al-Tahtawi (1801–73), an al-Azhar-educated *shaykh*, had awakened to ancient Egypt while studying in Paris in the late 1820s—the very years when Champollion was elaborating his decipherment, leading an expedition to Egypt, and orga-nizing the Egyptian section in the Louvre. Returning to Cairo, Tahtawi became the director of a bureau for translating European books into Arabic, attempted to found an Antiquities Service and museum, and later wrote the

[38] The cover is reproduced in Bertrand Millet, *Samir, Mickey, Sindbad et les autres: histoire de la presse enfantine en Égypte* (Dossiers du CEDEJ, 1-1987, Cairo, 1987), p. 31, and Reid, *Whose pharaohs?*, p. 8.
[39] Tahtawi's and Mubarak's contributions to Egyptology are discussed in Reid, *Whose pharaohs?*, pp. 52–4, 95–8, 108–12, 116.
[40] On Ahmad Kamal, see Reid, *Whose Pharaohs?*, pp. 186–9, 201–4, 211–12.

Figure 9.12: Reclaiming Egyptian antiquity: cover illustration of Arabic magazine *al-Samir al-Saghir*, 1899, as reproduced in Bertrand Millet, *Samir, Mickey, Sindbad, et les autres: histoire de la presse enfantine en Égypte* (Dossiers du CEDEJ, 1-1987, Cairo, 1987), p. 31. Courtesy of the Centre d'études et de documentation économiques, juridiques et sociales.

first Arabic textbook to draw on the discoveries of European Egyptology since Champollion.

Ali Mubarak, who studied engineering in Cairo and Paris, had a versatile career as minister, educator, city planner, and writer. In 1869 he founded the short-lived Egyptology school, which started Kamal on the road to his profession. But Mariette feared that the school's German director and its graduates might threaten his—and France's—control over antiquities. Mariette's refusal to hire the school's graduates thwarted its purpose, and it closed. Kamal had to fall back on translation posts until finally making it into the Antiquities Service through a back door.

Mariette's successor, Maspero, was more understanding of Kamal's aspirations, but neither of Kamal's attempts to re-establish the school of Egyptology—in the early 1880s and a quarter of a century later—endured in a colonial system in which Europeans predominated in privileged posts. Kamal's publications in French made him the only Egyptian Egyptologist before the 1930s to win a modicum of European recognition. He also worked hard to popularize ancient Egypt among his countrymen by writing in Arabic. Directly or indirectly, *al-Samir al-Saghir*'s illustration was one of the fruits of his patriotic labour.

Al-Samir shows pharaonic antiquities neither as romantic, deserted ruins nor as prizes for a conquering army; instead they are a lesson for Egyptian children. Although the authorities in the frame are all male, an anonymous woman dominates the centre. Neither a languorous Cleopatra seducing a virile Roman soldier nor a wet-draperied goddess, she is a modern mother, or perhaps a teacher, bent on instructing her children.[41]

Like Blashfield, *al-Samir's* illustrator celebrated the achievements of ancient Egypt. But while Blashfield imagined ancient Egypt as the beginning of a line of evolutionary progress outward, onwards, and upwards to apotheosis in the contemporary United States, *al-Samir's* focus never leaves Egypt. Reconnecting modern Egypt directly to its ancient past, it finesses questions about intervening ages and chains of transmission—how did the nineteenth-century scholarly Egyptian educators learn about the pharaohs? To what extent did they draw on the discoveries of Europeans such as Champollion and Mariette, and to what extent on folk traditions and on Arab authors such as those treated in Okasha El-Daly's *Egyptology: the missing millennium: ancient Egypt in medieval Arabic writings*?[42]

Such questions ask too much of *al-Samir's* allegory. It accomplished its purpose, suggesting that Egyptians were not exclusively indebted to Champollion and his European heirs for knowledge of the pharaonic past. Few Westerners, then or now, have heard of Tahtawi, Mubarak, or Kamal, yet they played significant roles in bringing the heritage of the pharaohs to bear on modern times.

VI

Three early nineteenth-century works of art associated with the *Description de l'Égypte* trumpeted the rediscovery of ancient Egypt as the fruit of French military conquest. Seven or eight decades later, three turn-of-the-twentieth-century artistic representations of ancient Egypt's legacy made no reference to the French and British conquests of the country. The Egyptian Museum façade of 1902 and Blashfield's Library of Congress mural honoured European cultural conquest instead, and placed these in a larger Western, rather than an exclusively French, context. The museum façade situated the pharaohs in a complex story of nineteenth-century European scholarly and

---

[41] For Egyptians' representation of their nation as a woman, see Beth Baron, *Egypt as a woman: nationalism, gender, and politics* (Berkeley, CA, 2005).
[42] Okasha El-Daly, *Egyptology: the missing millennium: ancient Egypt in medieval Arabic writings* (London, 2005).

national–imperial politics. A khedive nominally ruled as an Ottoman vassal in an unacknowledged British protectorate with a French-run Antiquities Service. Blashfield acknowledged America's debt to Egypt and other ancient Mediterranean civilizations, Islam, and medieval and modern Europe, then concluded triumphantly with America and its science as the apex of civilization.

This chapter has juxtaposed works of art intended for the general public with the lives, careers, and worldviews of several Egyptologists of the time. For all the specialists' learning and professed dedication to 'science' or objective scholarship, they were people of their times. They were patriots all, and—in the cases of the Westerners—imperial in their attitudes. Although the point has not been developed here, Champollion might have found little to object to in the imperial message of the three artistic works associated with the *Description de l'Égypte*. The façade of the Egyptian Museum spoke for Maspero, who influenced its design, and Blashfield's painting foreshadowed American 'Western civilization' courses, in the development of which Breasted took a leading role. Turning from the visual arts to poetry, 'The white man's burden' may have captured Budge's attitude as well as Kipling's.

Such European (or Western, including the United States) imperial attitudes helped provoke the nationalist riposte on the cover of *al-Samir al-Saghir*. This picture claimed the legacy of ancient Egypt for four social levels of modern Egyptians—the khedive, reformist scholar-officials, the mother or teacher, and the children. Whether or not the work of Ahmad Kamal directly inspired the illustration, it gave a welcome boost to his campaign to persuade Egyptians to embrace their pharaonic heritage as an inspiration for contemporary renaissance.

What of the subsequent legacy of these works of art and the Egyptologists associated with them? In 1922, Britain's unilateral declaration of Egyptian independence and—in archaeology—Howard Carter's discovery of Tutankhamun's tomb rang down the curtain on imperial high noon in Egypt. But the imperial afternoon—the semi-colonial period stretching from 1922 to the final British and French evacuation after the Suez War in 1956—would prove to be long and frustrating for all parties. Eventually, Nasser's revolution won full independence, in archaeology as well as in national politics. The last French director of antiquities departed in 1952 in the wake of his deposed patron, King Farouk.

Maspero and Kamal retired from the Egyptian Antiquities Service in 1914, and Budge from the British Museum a decade later. Interwar leadership in Egyptology passed to a new generation in France, Egypt, and Britain. In America, Breasted and Reisner, being somewhat younger, dominated American Egyptology for most of the interwar period.

Each of the three turn-of-the-twentieth-century artistic works reflected the specificities of its moment of production. With the intensification of Egyptian nationalism by 1922, an Egyptian Museum façade like that of 1902 would have been out of the question. Indeed, in 1926 Egyptian nationalists defeated a proposal James Breasted developed for a magnificent Rockefeller-funded museum in Cairo.[43] It would have substituted American-led Western international control of Egyptian antiquities for that of the French. Nevertheless, the 1902 vision of Egyptology as a Western-dominated field, with modern Egyptians only on the margins, still lives on in some quarters, among both Egyptologists and their Western publics.

The academic, classical allegories at which Blashfield excelled went out of fashion after the First World War, but the assumptions behind his Library of Congress mural have endured. Blashfield's and Breasted's vision of ancient Egypt at the dawn and the United States at the end of an upwards evolution of civilization endures, with minor adaptations, in Western civilization courses still taught today, despite the vigorous challenges that advocates of world history and other perspectives have flung at it since the 1960s.

Finally, *al-Samir al-Saghir*'s illustration and Ahmad Kamal's career are early examples of a campaign to convince modern Egyptians that Egypt's ancient past is too precious to be left to foreigners alone, and must be reclaimed as a proud part of their own national identity. The discovery of Tutankhamun's tomb in 1922 inspired renewed, successful efforts to train Egyptian Egyptologists. On the popular level, 'Tut' elicited not only a worldwide wave of 'Egyptomania', but also a 'pharaonist' tendency in Egypt that has persisted, despite ups and downs, to the present. It expressed itself in realms as diverse as architecture, painting, literature, sculpture, music, cartoons, postage stamps, banknotes, advertisements, and the names of sports teams. Islam, Arabism, or Coptic Christianity mean more to most Egyptians than ancient Egypt, but Egyptians who would completely reject any identification with the pharaohs may not be as numerous as is often assumed.

---

[43] See Jeffrey Abt, 'Toward a historian's laboratory: The Breasted–Rockefeller museum projects in Egypt, Palestine, and America', *Journal of the American Research Center in Egypt*, 33 (1996), pp. 173–94, and idem, 'The Breasted–Rockefeller Egyptian museum project: philanthropy, cultural imperialism and national resistance', *Art History*, 19 (1966), pp. 551–72.

Part V

The New World

At least as early as 1776, the New World offered special challenges to the British empire's idea of heritage. The separation of the American colonies sharply suggested that there was not a single but at least two disparate heritages, even in the Anglo-colonized portions of the New World. The Monroe Doctrine then put the rest of the Americas out of bounds to British imperial domination. Instead Latin America fell prey to neo-colonial exploitation, including by its own Hispanic elites, that enabled the continuing marginalization of indigenous heritages, even at a time when similar indigenous heritages were being haltingly 'discovered' by the British in Asia and Africa.

Over the course of the nineteenth century, with the rise of the United States to global power, Americans developed their own ideas of heritage. At first the British responded badly to these upstart conceptualizations, deemed vulgarly democratic and commercial. They provided many sites of conflict, such as over American literary piracy and the struggle to assert international copyright. Over time, however, they could also create potential spaces for Anglo-American or even international cooperation. American ideas of heritage also expanded the boundaries of what Europeans had hitherto conceived of as worthy of study and preservation. In what Anglo-Americans conceived of as a civilizationally 'empty' land, early ideas about the natural world as a human, or even as a national, heritage could incubate. That point of view could encourage a hypostatization of 'nature' that further marginalized—to the point of extinction—indigenous peoples and their civilizations.

On the other hand, the early professionalization of archaeology and anthropology in the New World developed a contrary valuation of human diversity that found it easier to recognize alien civilizations than was often possible in the Old World. Thus, the New World became a bewildering laboratory of competing visions of heritage, at the same time confirming Old World hierarchies, challenging them, and transcending them.

10

Publication as Preservation at a Remote Maya Site in the Early Twentieth Century*

DONNA YATES

IN THE LATE 1800s interest in the ancient Maya underwent the complicated transition from speculative musings to what modern scholars consider to be systematic archaeological inquiry. During this transformation, Maya archaeology was largely colonized, in a sense, by the American academic empire. Excavation was undertaken to further a structured concept of science and to solidify the idea of archaeology as an institutionalized discipline. The results of archaeological fieldwork on remote sites were not easily independently verified due to the constraints of the forbidding landscape and the vastness of this largely untapped resource. The known character of a particular scholar was considered to be a sufficient recommendation as to the quality of his textual archaeological record. This dependence on text resulted in a number of factual mistakes that have been repeated in publications and museum displays up to the present day. During this period in the development of the discipline, I assert that archaeological publication, not site stabilization, was regarded as a sufficient means by which a remote site could be effectively 'preserved'.

As a case study I will discuss early twentieth-century excavations within an Early Classic Maya mortuary structure at the site of Holmul, Guatemala. In this extreme case, a report started by Raymond Edwin Merwin, the only archaeologist who had worked at this remote Maya city, was 'completed' after his untimely death by another scholar, George C. Vaillant, who had never visited the site. Due to the perceived notability of Merwin's role in driving Maya archaeology into the realm of systematic science, Vaillant felt that the information he published was reliable and, indeed, required, as the

---

*I would like to thank the editors of this volume for bringing this diverse body of work together and providing helpful feedback. I would also like to thank the staff at the Peabody Museum and the Tozzer Library for allowing me to review Merwin and Tozzer's field notebooks.

inaccessible location of Holmul would effectively prevent archaeological work from being conducted there for nearly a century.

I

It is safe to say that antiquarian interest into the ancient Maya was comparatively late to bloom. To an extent, this was the curse (or perhaps gift) of geography. Before the end of the nineteenth century, the Spanish colonies, and then the nascent and unstable states of Central America, were at the edge of the world. Moreover, the massive archaeological sites of the Maya were located in the remote peripheral regions of these already peripheral territories. The relatively or actually remote locations of these sites allowed the scholars of the day to dismiss the lush Conquest-era descriptions of Mesoamerican culture as 'highly embellished', stating that 'if buildings corresponding to such descriptions had ever existed ... it is probable that some remains of them would still be visible'.[1] This complete rejection of the possibility of an advanced monumental culture within the Americas is strongly associated with contemporary ideas of racial hierarchy.

Following independence from Spain, Mesoamerica's hidden archaeological treasures slowly drifted into Western public view. The continued presence of various European officials and increased US economic interest in Central America facilitated the stream of both Maya antiquities and accounts of ruins that trickled out of the region. This so-called 'Age of Amateurs'[2] was dominated by a combination of 'explorers and the armchair speculators'[3] who did not engage in what modern scholars consider to be true archaeological inquiry.

Despite the production of a variety of volumes and reports of variable quality on the subject of Mesoamerican antiquities (e.g. Kingsborough, 1830–49;[4] Dupaix, 1834;[5] Wason, 1831;[6] del Río 1822[7]), the Maya only truly entered the public consciousness with the publication of John Lloyd Stephens's

---

[1] William Robertson, *History of the discovery and settlement of America* (New York, [1792] 1843).

[2] Robert L. Brunhouse, *In search of the Maya: the first archaeologists* (Albuquerque, NM, 1973), p. 195.

[3] Gordon R. Willey and Jeremy A. Sabloff, *A history of American archaeology* (London, 1974), p. 28.

[4] Edward King, Viscount Kingsborough, *Antiquities of Mexico* (9 vols., London, 1830–49).

[5] Guillermo Dupaix, *Antiquités Mexicaines* (Paris, 1834).

[6] Charles William Wason, 'Antiquities of Mexico', *The Monthly Review*, 1 (1831), pp. 235–74.

[7] Antonio del Río, *Description of the ruins of an ancient city discovered near Palenque in the kingdom of Guatemala, in Spanish America* (London, 1822).

much read *Incidents of travel in Central America, Chiapas and Yucatan* (1841) and *Incidents of travel in Yucatan* (1843). Supplemented by the masterful and striking illustrations of Frederick Catherwood, Stephens's lively accounts of jungle-covered ruins captivated readers of the period and have inspired nearly every Maya archaeologist since.

Through Stephens's account one can truly appreciate how remote the major Maya sites were to actions and functions of the mid-1800s. They existed on the very edge of space and time. Recounting his explorations around the Honduran site of Copán, Stephens wrote that

> the ground was entirely new; there were no guide-books or guides; the whole was virgin soil. We could not see ten yards before us, and never knew what we should stumble upon next.[8]

The remains of the then-unnamed ancient Maya were the epitome of the mysterious unknown.

Stephens experienced a Copán that was completely different from the manicured UNESCO World Heritage site now visited by thousands of tourists each year. He literally could not see the massive stone structures that lay just before him. Stephens's Copán existed behind a seemingly impenetrable geographic barrier, the jungle barring both the curious from visiting and the scholarly from studying. Yet it was clear that Copán was interesting and valuable. Thus Stephens, desiring to present these ruins to the public, attempted to buy Copán with the hopes of dismantling the temples, floating the blocks down the river, and transporting the entire site to New York City where it could be reconstructed and enjoyed.[9] This plan was unsuccessful, yet it is clear that Stephens felt it more feasible to transport this monumental site thousands of miles by sea, than for tourists to visit it in situ.

The very jungle that protects Maya sites from the outside world is also the root of a whole host of wild theories that allow the ruins to become unstuck in time. The dark and mysterious forest has the potential to hide even fantastic impossibilities. The jungle-covered ruin may transform, at least in the mind of the public, into a lost city that is still inhabited by an uncontacted civilization. In other words, in the jungle total preservation seems possible. 'Such beliefs die hard,' observed the British seminal late nineteenth-century explorer turned archaeologist Alfred P. Maudslay, 'indeed they lay such hold of the imagination that from time to time enterprising newspapers … favour us with

---

[8] John Lloyd Stephens, *Incidents of travel in Central America, Chiapas, and Yucatan* (New York, 1841), p. 119.
[9] Victor Von Hagen, *Search for the Maya: the story of Stephens and Catherwood* (Farnborough, 1973), p. 150.

reports of Indian cities still inhabited and flourishing, hidden from the gaze of the vulgar by a wall of impenetrable forest.'[10]

Following the publication of Stephens's accounts, speculation about the possibility of thriving monumental Maya cities filled with uncontacted people living 'by the old ways' began to be voiced. The forest that Stephens described was so impenetrable that the existence of a pyramid-filled Maya 'El Dorado' seemed reasonable. This theory so appealed to public consciousness that P. T. Barnum, always one to have his finger firmly upon the pulse of public interest, staged a stunt that involved two children he claimed were from an intact and functioning ancient Maya city. Despite referring to the children as 'Aztecs', those involved in the Barnum hoax called the fictional lost city 'Iximaya' and cited Stephens directly.[11]

Atlantis, lost tribes of Israel, wayward ancient Egyptians, second comings of Christ, space aliens, and so on get tangled up with the Maya behind the veil of the jungle and, in many cases, these questionable claims existed long before archaeologists arrived on the scene. I believe that this concept of geographic impermeability has shaped both the practice of archaeology and conceptions of site preservation in the Maya region.

II

In the final decades of the nineteenth century and into the start of the twentieth (and perhaps, some would argue, up to the present), the Maya region was within the American archaeological empire and European archaeological interest lay elsewhere. This is not to say that absolutely no Europeans participated in early Maya archaeology, yet it is clear that the overwhelming majority of notable early Mayanists were either from the United States or were funded by American institutions. One need only compare the relative size of the British Museum's Latin American gallery (a small room and a staircase landing populated mostly by objects collected by Maudslay) to the expansive halls dedicated to Mesopotamia to determine the focus of British archaeology at that time. The same observation could be made in any major European museum.

Indeed, once the discipline moved out of the era of 'armchair speculators' and 'amateurs' and into Maya archaeology as a science, the notable few non-American early Mayanists were exceptional exceptions. Most of these Europeans were on the cusp of the major institutionalization and disciplinary professionalization effort that characterized Maya archaeology in the very

---

[10] Anne C. Maudslay and Alfred P. Maudslay, *A glimpse at Guatemala, and some notes on the ancient monuments of Central America* (London, 1899; repr. Detroit, 1979), p. 253.
[11] Brunhouse, *In search of the Maya*, p. 109.

early twentieth century. Because of this they fall outside the now traditional divisions between professional archaeologists and non-professional enthusiasts. Alfred P. Maudslay, for example, was a Cambridge-educated 'adventurer diplomat' who, in the 1880s and 1890s, produced both some of the earliest photographic images of remote Maya sites as well as the stunning casts of Maya monuments that are housed at Cambridge, the British Museum, and Harvard. However, Maudslay never considered himself to be an archaeologist, and he was not formally trained as such. Rather, he referred to himself as a visitor and a traveller who had stumbled onto Mesoamerica after extended diplomatic stints and extensive travels elsewhere.[12] His work was spectacular, but it was early and limited.

Teobert Maler, who was active in Mesoamerican archaeology circles from the mid-1870s until his retirement in Yucatán in 1905, was technically an Austrian citizen when he arrived in Mexico to serve as a soldier with Emperor Maximilian. Yet he stayed on in Mexico after the emperor's surrender and obtained Mexican citizenship. Maler was not trained as an archaeologist and had almost no ties to European scholarship or institutions. His work was published primarily through Harvard's Peabody Museum, much of it posthumously, including a large batch in the 1930s. Indeed, the permit from the Guatemalan government that Maler used to conduct research in the Petén from 1901 until 1908 was actually granted to the Peabody, and the renewal of the same permit resulted in the American-led excavations at Holmul,[13] the dig that is at the heart of this discussion.

Even within a younger generation of Maya archaeologists, who began work in the 1920s and 1930s, non-Americans were sparse and nearly always associated with American institutions. For example, the Danish Frans Blom came to Mesoamerica with no European archaeological training, received a degree from Harvard, and eventually headed the Department of Middle American Research at Tulane University in Louisiana.[14] The notable mid-century British archaeologist J. Eric S. Thompson studied anthropology at Cambridge but was forced to teach himself about the Maya, as no one at Cambridge was conducting research in that area. On his own impetus, Thompson wrote to the famous American archaeologist Sylvanus G. Morley to beg him for a job in 1925.[15]

Thus, with a few notable exceptions, the first wave of Maya archaeologists consisted of Americans who were primarily associated with either Harvard, the Archaeological Institute of America, the Carnegie Institution, and so on.

[12] Ian Graham, *Alfred Maudslay and the Maya: a biography* (London, 2002).
[13] See Alfred M. Tozzer, preface in Raymond E. Merwin and George C. Vaillant, *The ruins of Holmul, Guatemala* (Cambridge, MA, 1932).
[14] See Robert L. Brunhouse, *Frans Blom: Maya explorer* (Albuquerque, NM, 1976).
[15] J. Eric S. Thompon, *Maya archaeologist* (Norman, OK, 1963), p. 5.

While individual Europeans did participate in early Maya work, they were not representative of European archaeological traditions.[16] One could say that the USA staked a claim on the Maya and Europe didn't challenge it.

III

The late nineteenth and early twentieth centuries saw the emergence of American archaeology as a largely self-defined venture, the theoretical foundations of which governed for decades exactly how remote Maya sites were approached, excavated, and interpreted. Although the American school of archaeology had roots in European classicism, from the late nineteenth century onwards American archaeology was built on the same theoretical tradition as cultural anthropology. Both the archaeology and cultural anthropology of the Americas were conceived of as seeking the same truths through slightly different methodologies. This difference between the American and European traditions is reflected in how archaeology is classified at an academic level today. In the United States, archaeology is usually housed within a larger anthropology department and is considered one of the four 'sub-fields' of anthropology. In the UK and much of Europe, archaeology exists as a stand-alone department and is conceived of as a distinct discipline.

To begin to understand why this is the case, it is important to note the conceptual difference between the early study of ancient America and the early study of ancient Europe and the Middle East. In a broad sense, the European archaeological tradition is inherently the archaeology of 'the self'. By excavating barrows in England or studying megalithic monuments in Denmark, Europeans were reconstructing what they saw as their own past and often pushing modern ideas of nationality and culture back almost indefinitely. Less direct but perhaps more important was the claiming of the ancient Greeks and Romans as the spiritual progenitors of European culture and society, and the close kinship felt to biblical civilizations. Europe, at least in the popular consciousness, was built upon an intellectual and social framework that was inherited from the classical and Middle Eastern civilizations. Old World archaeology was, then, a practice in constructing and reaffirming European identity and singularity. It was a quest for modernity's roots.

In contrast, the archaeology of the Americas was, by definition, the archaeology of 'the other'. The ancient civilizations of the Americas flourished entirely outside of Europe's perceived cultural evolution. Bluntly, the Greeks, Romans, and biblical cultures were 'us', and the ancient Maya and other American civilizations were 'them'. To its early practitioners, the archae-

---

[16] Willey and Sabloff, *A history of American archaeology*, p. 64.

ology of the Americas was not culturally autobiographical. Instead it was anthropological; American archaeology was clearly focused on understanding civilizations, however ancient, that were non-Western and culturally separate.

It is in this basic difference between Old World and New World archaeology that we see the motivations behind eighteenth- and nineteenth-century assertions of a European presence in the pre-Conquest New World. By ascribing North American earthworks to a white race of 'mound builders', Mesoamerican pyramids to travelling Egyptians, and just about everything to lost tribes of Israel, the ancient cultures of the Americas were Europeanized and recast as the archaeology of the self. Furthermore, living indigenous groups within the Americas were divorced from archaeological remains and dismissed as racially inferior latecomers.

Perhaps one of the most exceptional aspects of Stephens's travel accounts is that he presents a strong argument for the modern Maya to be the descendants of the civilization that built the sites that he recorded. Controversial in its day, the belief that the ancient civilizations of the Americas were untouched by Europe slowly became the dividing line between American archaeological reality and non-professional fantasy by the latter half of the nineteenth century. By that time American academic institutions were teaching archaeology as a component of an anthropology that was intimately linked to Native American ethnography. American archaeology was embraced as, and existed to be, the archaeology of the other.

By the turn of the century academic investigation into the cultures of the Americas had changed radically, having undergone a process of institutionalization. Now that American archaeology was linked with the nascent discipline of anthropology, its practitioners strove to refine both into a discipline for trained specialists, based on a methodology verging on 'science'. Museums and academic departments were founded. Professional societies sprung up and held meetings. Archaeological fieldwork was funded and students were trained.

This institutionalization of Maya archaeology was centred on the cycle of excavation and publication. In academized archaeology, diggers were required to be scholars and their theories required to be tested through regulated and semi-standardized excavation methods. These methods were passed on through on-site training. Students attached themselves to the field projects of trained archaeologists, both to learn proper techniques and to enter into the academic network of researchers who knew each other well and trusted the results of their perceived shared methodology. The very existence of this network allowed archaeologists to style themselves as scientists rather than adventurers or curiosity hunters.

The publication of excavation results continued the process of legitimization by pushing discussion about the Maya into the forum of the academy.

Outside of in-field training, publication became the primary means by which information about Maya sites was transmitted to other scholars and students. To that end, publications and the field notes behind them became the sole record of many remote sites.

IV

At the start of the twentieth century the archaeologists working in the Maya region were not immune to the preservational sensibilities that prevailed throughout the rest of the world. They were very interested in ideas of intact stabilization, and were duly horrified by the compromised nature of many of the sites they encountered. Destruction at the hands of curiosity hunters and the effects of local stone scavenging had been noted and lamented as early as the mid-1800s. By the twentieth century the less remote Maya sites such as Copán, Quiriguá, Uxmal, and Chichén Itzá were undergoing site stabilization and preservation sponsored by both foreign institutions and local governments. Even with improved access, the stabilization of these sites was difficult, largely due to the ever-present jungle. Sylvanus G. Morley recounted that the Archaeological Institute of America's first foray into the study and preservation of the Guatemalan site of Quiriguá in 1910 was almost entirely devoted to the removal of massive trees. These 'forest titans' not only threatened to smash standing monuments, but also 'were actually leaning towards them [the monuments]', meaning that cutting them down would have 'injured the nearby sculptures'.[17] Morley recorded that it was only after the complete deforestation of the Quiriguá region and the reoccupation of the whole valley that the monuments were exposed enough to even reduce moss growth.

The relatively accessible sites at the edge of the Maya region circled a no-man's-land on the preservation map. Alfred Maudslay, writing in 1899, speculated that the rapid growth of vegetation at deep jungle sites would prevent potential visitors from getting a 'satisfactory view'. He recorded that a Mr W. H. Holms of the Field Columbian Museum of Chicago 'who visited the ruins [of Palenque] in 1895, only four years after I had cleared them, wrote to me to say that he had to use a plan and compass and cut his way from building to building, as a dense growth of over twenty feet in height completely obscured them from view'.[18] Thus, in less than four years the jungle could completely reclaim a cleared site, meaning that even the most basic level of physical site preservation, such as preventing 20-foot trees from taking root on temples, would require a year-round presence. Far from even the smallest

[17] Sylvanus G. Morley, *Guide book to the ruins of Quirigua* (Washington, DC, 1935), p. 10.
[18] Maudslay and Maudslay, *A glimpse at Guatemala*, p. 259.

village, as many scholars noted, and far from a stable source of potable water, preservation of these remote jungle sites was simply not feasible at that time. Due to the logistical impossibility of deep jungle in-situ site stabilization, the turn-of-the-century Maya archaeologists felt that by publishing fieldwork reports they were doing everything within their power to preserve a site for the future.

In order to discuss the concept of textual records serving as a sole preservation tool, especially during a time when in-situ preservation elsewhere was at its zenith, it is important to remember how inaccessible many Maya sites truly are. The prevailing idea among the archaeologists of the early twentieth century, an idea that was not entirely incorrect, was that the remoteness of many Maya sites would prevent nearly everyone (researchers and certainly tourists) from ever visiting. Life in the Petén was often absolutely miserable, filled with constant rain, poisonous snakes, tropical diseases, and fearsome loneliness. For example, the archaeologist Edwin M. Shook contracted malaria and slipped into a coma at the deep jungle site of Uaxactún in the 1930s.[19] The idea that these sites were prohibitively inhospitable to more casual visitors came from the archaeologists' own experiences.

Even if an archaeologist wished to stabilize a deep jungle site on anything other than the smallest of scales, there was little practical way to pull this off. Supplies, which were hauled in on mule-back, were restricted to the basic needs of the excavators: food and excavation equipment. Limited time and scant resources were thus used for what the archaeologists considered to be important scientific inquiry into the past. They rarely attempted to physically preserve structures that they felt that no one would ever see. Thus, on-site recording followed by publication was the only preservation tool available to the early archaeologists working at remote Maya sites. Archaeology was (and still is) considered to be a destructive but necessary process, and the proper dissemination of excavation reports is believed to mitigate this destruction. A published archaeological report became the 'site record' and, as such, was the official 'textual copy' of a site for other scholars to use, written in recognition of the impossibility of excavating the same material twice.

This site record became doubly important for very remote sites. The difficult terrain of the Maya region prevented independent verification of even the most basic information presented in archaeological texts, while the seemingly endless supply of newly discovered ruins focused excavation attention away from previously excavated remote sites. The reliability of a particular archaeological publication rested on the perceived believability of the original excavator. This is where the construction of an academic network comes in.

[19] Edwin M. Shook, *Incidents in the life of a Maya archaeologist as told to Winifred Veronda* (San Marino, 1998), p. 40.

People in the same academic network trusted the work of their colleagues, and character was a testament to research skill.

Information about difficult to reach yet important sites was required in order to 'preserve' said site, rendering it usable for academic comparative study in the future. However, if a researcher was unwilling or unable to complete and publish an excavation report, at times it was published for him, having been completed by others. In some cases, these others had not visited the site being discussed and the resulting publications thus are filled with assumptions and errors. But, as the completed publications represented preserved archaeological sites, they were both transmitted and believed.

V

In 1906 Raymond E. Merwin enrolled as a graduate student at Harvard. He had completed a bachelor's degree in 1903 and a master's degree in 1904 at the University of Kansas where he taught sociology and anthropology. From 1906 to 1908 he was a Hemenway Fellow at Harvard, and during this period he conducted archaeological excavations at the Madisonville Cemetery and the Turner Mounds in Ohio, and the Volk site in Delaware. Merwin was appointed Fellow in Central American Research at Harvard in 1908/09, and in 1909/10 he accompanied Alfred M. Tozzer on an exploratory trip to Guatemala and British Honduras. It was on this first trip that Merwin and Tozzer visited, among other sites, the ancient Maya city of Holmul.

Holmul is located on the eastern edge of Guatemala's Petén region, very near to the Belize border but quite far from modern settlement (see Figure 10.1). It is a massive, monumental urban area that seems to have been occupied during the entire span of the Classic Maya period as well as back into the Late Preclassic. Holmul, like most Maya lowland sites, experienced a population peak during the Terminal Classic and then fell into decline and abandonment by around AD 900. Tozzer and Merwin learned about the existence of Holmul from a map produced by Teobert Maler for the Peabody Museum in 1908: 'Maler had evidently heard of these new ruins but he had never seen them.'[20] The two archaeologists spent a few days on site, after which Merwin suggested that he would like to 'make careful investigation of Holmul'.[21] Thus, in the 1910/11 field season, Merwin conducted intensive excavations at Holmul. These excavations have since been lauded as the first 'scientific' archaeological excavations to have been undertaken in the Maya region.

---

[20] Tozzer, preface in Merwin and Vaillant, *The ruins of Holmul*.
[21] Ibid.

Figure 10.1:   Map of Guatemala showing the locations of Holmul and other sites mentioned in the text.

Merwin's field notebooks record that he spent much of the season conducting stratigraphic excavations within a structure that he called Building B of Group II.[22] At first glance, Building B is not the most exciting structure at Holmul: on their initial visit to the site Tozzer and Merwin took only basic measurements of the mound and did not record any notable features.[23]

---

[22] Merwin's field notebooks as well as Tozzer's contemporary field notebooks are housed in the archives of the Peabody Museum under accession numbers 10–63, 11–16, 14–64, and 15–73.

[23] Alfred M. Tozzer, *Field notebook 8, 1909/10, 'Siebal, Holmul'*, Peabody Museum, Accession Number 10-63, p. 41.

However, after a revisit to the mound produced favourable results, Merwin devoted himself to analysing the building and recording its features. He concluded that Building B was built, demolished, and rebuilt in multiple phases, the final phase being a large, pyramid-shaped superstructure that was constructed to completely cover all earlier temples and building works.[24] This Russian doll-type of building is quite common in Maya urban construction. Merwin completely removed this superstructure to find a well-preserved vaulted stone building that was decorated with painted stucco. Inside he found multiple rooms filled with around twenty interments. Digging downwards into previous incarnations of the building, Merwin found several other chambers with more human burials and corresponding grave goods.[25]

As time and resources were limited, Merwin was forced to halt excavations before he felt that work at Building B was finished. At the end of his account of excavations, Merwin's own field notes implore the reader to 'see other notes as this [further features in Building B] will be examined later',[26] yet these other notes do not exist. Merwin was able to take the portable artefacts that he removed from Building B (i.e. human bones, pottery, and other grave goods) out of the jungle, out of Guatemala, and back to Harvard, where they remain. As for Building B itself, Merwin backfilled some of his artificial trenches but left the rooms and burial chambers that he excavated unfilled. The structure was left as an open and empty shell (see Figure 10.2).

After obtaining his Ph.D. in 1913, Merwin paid a very short visit to Holmul in February of 1914 and then never visited the site again.[27] By 1915 his health was deemed too poor to allow for further excursions into Central America. After a long decline, Merwin died in 1928, having never finished his official report of excavations at Holmul.[28]

VI

Nearly two decades after the excavation of Holmul, Dr Raymond E. Merwin was dead and there was no published report of the site. This was an unacceptable situation to the archaeologists of the first half of the twentieth century, especially with regard to the Holmul excavations. First, at the time, the Maya

---

[24] Raymond E. Merwin, *Field notebooks 1, 2 and 4, 1910/11*, Peabody Museum Accession Number 11-16; Raymond E. Merwin and George C. Vaillant, *The ruins of Holmul, Guatemala* (Cambridge, MA, 1932).

[25] Ibid.

[26] Merwin, *notebook 2*, 1909/10.

[27] Raymond E. Merwin, *Field notebook 5, 1913/14*, Peabody Museum, Accession Number 14-64, p. 2.

[28] Tozzer, preface in Merwin and Vaillant, *The ruins of Holmul*.

Figure 10.2:   Current state of one of Merwin's 1911 excavations. Like Building B, this excavation was left open and exposed, compromising the structure. Photo by Alexandre Tokovinine.

late Preclassic and Early Classic were little understood and the Holmul
Building B artefacts comprised the single largest collection from this time
period. Vaillant considered the Holmul material to be 'the finest collection of
Maya ceramics ever assembled for a single site'.[29] Without proper documentation to accompany the objects from Building B, the artefacts were of little use
as a comparative collection.

Second, during the first half of the twentieth century it seemed unlikely
that anyone else would work at Holmul in the foreseeable future. The logistical
difficulties involved in conducting scientific archaeological work at Holmul
and other such sites were well known. According to Vaillant:

> The unfavourable natural conditions, also, restricted research to temples and
> monuments, since the *almost impenetrable forests* concealed surface indications
> of the rubbish beds on which stratification depends.[30]

Not only was the site remote, but by virtue of it having been investigated once
Holmul was likely to be passed over in favour of the many recently discovered
unexcavated sites. Indeed, archaeological excavations did not resume at
Holmul until nearly ninety years after Merwin's initial work.

Finally, by the time of his death, Merwin's work at Holmul was being
talked about in archaeological circles as the first real 'scientific' inquiry into
the Maya. That is, the Maya archaeologists of the 1930s felt that 'Merwin
has the honour of having provided the first stratigraphical study of a Maya
ruin'.[31] Stratigraphy is held as the hallmark of archaeological modernity and
thus the Holmul excavations were a significant milestone. Vaillant, seeking to
'summarize the significance of Merwin's work at Holmul', wrote:

> [Merwin] made one of the first scientific studies of a Maya site and built a foun-
> dation for field archaeology in the Peten region by architectural and ceramic
> stratification which he discovered. He showed the necessity for a material cul-
> ture sequence in the Maya area since no dated monuments survived at Holmul.
> He collected one of the most historically and artistically significant bodies of
> material ever found in the Maya area. It is a pleasure to give honor where honor
> is due.[32]

The excavation of Holmul, as a pivotal moment in the study of the ancient
Maya, required commemoration and preservation. Several years after
Merwin's death, Tozzer and Vaillant felt that 'the publication of this report
could be delayed no longer'.[33]

---

[29] Merwin and Vaillant, *The ruins of Holmul*.
[30] Ibid., emphasis added.
[31] Tozzer, preface in Merwin and Vaillant, *The ruins of Holmul*.
[32] Merwin and Vaillant, *The ruins of Holmul*, p. 4.
[33] Ibid.

Having emerged as the practitioners of a newly institutionalized discipline, the Mayanists of the 1930s were concerned with their own professional history. To leave Holmul unpublished would be akin to striking a defining disciplinary moment from the record. Vaillant lamented that '[h]ad Dr. Merwin's discoveries been published at the time at which they were made, they would have been unique as developing the only stratigraphy hitherto encountered in the course of Maya archaeology', going on to say that 'the lustre of Dr Merwin's accomplishment ... still remains the first ceramic stratigraphy established in the Maya field'.[34]

And thus Vaillant produced a Holmul excavation report complete with an explanatory introduction by Tozzer. Recall that Tozzer visited the site of Holmul for less than a week and did not participate in the excavation of the site. Vaillant completed a ceramic study of the Holmul collection at Harvard but never visited the site itself. The volume was published in 1932, four years after Merwin's death and twenty-one years after his excavations at Holmul. For the sake of transparency Vaillant placed his initials below paragraphs in the text that contained his own conclusions and Merwin's below conclusions that supposedly came from the late excavator's own writings. This method was repeated a year later by Jens Yde, who produced a similar but unpublished report of Merwin's excavations in Quintana Roo, Mexico, 'carrying [Merwin's] work through' because he had been unable to bring said work 'into a state which was fit for publication'.[35] Suffice to say, Merwin's initials do not appear very often in either of these texts.

The Holmul volume, billed as by 'Merwin and Vaillant', became an important reference work for the study of Early Classic architecture, ceramics, and burial practice. It allowed Harvard's Holmul collection to be used for contextualized comparative study and inspired a number of museum displays complete with models of Building B (Figure 10.3). One such model, along with oversized stratigraphic section drawings from the Merwin and Vaillant text, remains on display at Harvard's Peabody Museum. Thus, for both specialist study and for the public museum-style experience, this volume has become the preserved site of Holmul.

VII

In the summer of 2003 I revisited Building B at Holmul. My original plan was to clean inside the deeper burial chambers within the structure, in search of

[34] Ibid., p. 1.
[35] Jens Yde, 'Architectural remains along the coast of Quintana Roo; a report of the Peabody Museum expedition, 1913–14; compiled from the field notes of Raymond E. Merwin' (1933), unpublished report in the Tozzer Library, Harvard University.

Figure 10.3: Model of a fancifully restored Building B, here referred to as the 'Temple of the Royal Sepulchre'. This model, photographed in 1941 in the Brooklyn Museum, is one of several that present Building B based on its depiction in the Merwin and Vaillant text. Photo from the collection of the Brooklyn Museum.

any human remains that Merwin may have neglected to collect. Sadly, Building B was in such a poor state that my work within the deeper chambers was likely to cause an internal collapse. Before the local workman performed a mime showing me being crushed to death, and advised me to get out, I was able to make an interesting observation inside the structure. The accepted section drawing of the building, the one on display at the Peabody Museum that is the supposed record of the first use of archaeological stratigraphy in the Maya region, was incorrect. I decided that a fresh inquiry into the architectural sequence at Building B was both warranted and feasible.

While cleaning the front room of the structure I discovered the remains of a rectangular-shaped archaeological trench that was not recorded in the Merwin and Vaillant publication. From this trench I recovered artefacts from Merwin's work including two tin cans and a fragmentary shovel. At a depth of around 1.5 metres I encountered another intact Early Classic tomb, complete with burial goods. It appeared as if Merwin detected the burial at the bottom of his trench, as two of the stone slabs that sealed the tomb were missing (see Figure 10.4). This tomb is located in precisely the spot recorded in Merwin's notebook as 'will be examined later'. My best guess is that Merwin made unrecorded cursory excavations, detected the tomb, and was unable to

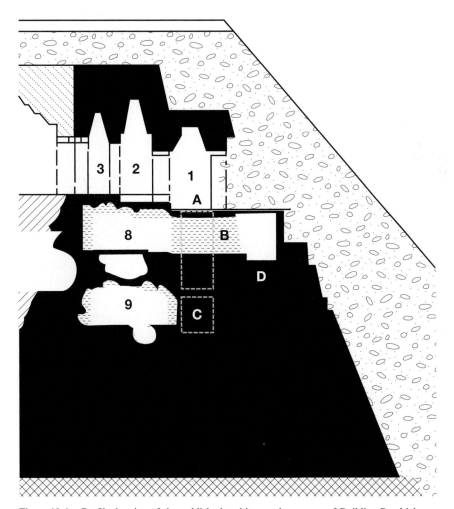

Figure 10.4: Profile drawing of the published architectural sequence of Building B, which was adapted from a sketch in Merwin's notebook. A indicates where I detected one of Merwin's undocumented trenches. B marks layers of cut stones added by Vaillant that were not in Merwin's original sketch. C marks the location of the tomb that was discovered by Merwin in 1911 but was omitted from the 1932 text. D marks the location where Vaillant imagined Merwin searched for but did not find a tomb. Adapted from Merwin and Vaillant, *The ruins of Holmul, Guatemala* (Cambridge, MA, 1932.

follow up on what he found. By not publishing his own notes, this tomb was lost and forgotten.

To make matters worse, Vaillant based his much-reproduced cross-section drawing of the temple (see Figure 10.5) on a very rough sketch from within Merwin's notebook,[36] not on a scaled and detailed architectural plan. Depending on how one interprets this sketch, Merwin's drawing may actually record the presence of the tomb that he found (and I refound) in a location that he wished to revisit at a later date. Yet Vaillant specifically notes that:

> The construction of the front face masonry suggested one or more sealed burial vaults behind it but a rather hasty examination due to the limited time at our disposal, did not reveal such interior chambers.[37]

It seems that, due to fragmentary field notes, the death of the excavator, and the passing of a decade, Vaillant translated a clearly intact burial chamber located below the *front room* of Building B into the failed possibility of a burial chamber behind the building's *front face masonry*. For this and other

Figure 10.5: The logistics of deep jungle archaeology contribute to preservational difficulties. The living conditions of the modern archaeologists working at Holmul seen here hint at what Merwin must have faced. Photo by Alexandre Tokovinine.

[36] Merwin, *notebook 4*, 1910/11, drawing 1.
[37] Merwin and Vaillant, *The ruins of Holmul*.

reasons, conclusions drawn from the presentation of Building B in the Merwin and Vaillant text are likely to be flawed. Despite good intentions, Holmul was not completely preserved via text.

VIII

Archaeologists still imbue the texts that followed early work with an aura of moderate believability, despite examples such as Holmul. Why? Because these texts are what was preserved of the sites. To reject a 'scientific' archaeological text as preservational stand-in for an inaccessible site is to assert that archaeological professionalism, sound methodology, and extended off-site study of recovered materials do not produce a suitable record of the past.

Indeed archaeologists, faced with the inability to re-create any 'archaeological experiment', must routinely have faith in the professional recording methods of others. Seemingly to assure the professional reader that Merwin's death did not result in the loss of the preserved site, Tozzer wrote in his preface to the Holmul report:

> Merwin and I travelled and lived for five months in the tropical bush. Such an association is perhaps the strongest test of character and forbearance. Merwin was an ideal companion in every way. His willingness and good temper were unfailing, his archaeological work was of a very high order, *his methods of record excellent.*[38]

Tozzer personally vouched for Merwin's recording methods and assured the reader that what was presented in the volume should be believed.

Vaillant admits that 'Dr. Merwin was not spared to coordinate the text and to formulate his conclusions', and that the one time he met Merwin in person he 'could not ascertain what his final ideas were on the results of the excavations'. However, he assures the reader that 'Merwin left in the course of his work very full notes and had completed his plans and selected his drawings'.[39] The field notebooks and sketches in the Peabody Museum Archives do not support this claim. Specifically, no completed plans are among Merwin's field notes. While it is possible that Vaillant was working from material that is not housed in the Peabody Museum, his plans are nearly identical to the rough sketches present in Merwin's notebooks. Merwin does appear to have 'selected his drawings' but had not converted them into a polished, professional 'completed' form. It is not surprising that Vaillant overstated the completeness of Merwin's text as he was effectively arguing that archaeological

---

[38] Tozzer, preface in Merwin and Vaillant, *The ruins of Holmul*, emphasis added.
[39] Merwin and Vaillant, *The ruins of Holmul*, p. 4.

field notes could be used to reproduce an archaeological site for public consumption, even without the presence of the original excavator.

While playing down his own involvement, Vaillant asserted that his own personal commentaries within the text 'were so obvious that [Merwin] would in all probability have reached the same conclusions'.[40] This statement is startling to say the least and challenges the very idea of Holmul as being accurately preserved via text. Even shortly after the Holmul report was published it was clear to interested scholars that 'the volume itself is Vaillant's'.[41] Yet this fact was not considered particularly problematic as readers felt that 'the archaeology is soundly presented and the record of the stratigraphy is very clear'.[42] Vaillant's own conclusions were said to 'thoroughly cover the entire situation at Holmul'.[43]

IX

If anything, Holmul is more remote today than it was in Merwin's time. Tozzer refers to a place called Yalloch or Yaloch, an inhabited *chiclero* camp, being about a two hour and fifty minute ride from Holmul, presumably on muleback.[44] Currently, the closest settlement to Holmul is the border town of Melchor de Mencos. The route from Melchor to the site consists of a several-hour truck ride that is significantly lengthened during the height of the rainy season (see Figure 10.5).

As for Building B, it is important to remember that Merwin stripped away both the jungle flora and the later Maya superstructures, exposing an older, more fragile building that had not seen the light of day for centuries. These protective layers are what preserved Building B's delicate stucco decoration. Merwin made no attempt to protect and preserve this inner building and ninety years of exposure have taken their toll. The red paint that Merwin documented on parts of the building is now entirely gone and the stucco itself is badly damaged.

Several structural components of the building display large cracks that are not evident in Merwin's photographs. Merwin's notebooks record that a number of the rooms in Building B had been filled, floor to ceiling, by the Maya, and the structure has not fared well without that additional support. Several parts of the building may be near collapse.

[40] Merwin and Vaillant, *The ruins of Holmul*, p. 5.
[41] Lawrence Roys, 'Review of the ruins of Holmul, Guatemala', *American Anthropologist*, 36 (1934), pp. 297–300.
[42] Ibid.
[43] Ibid.
[44] Tozzer, *notebook 1*, 1909/10, p. 8.

Looting has taken the greatest toll on Holmul (see Figure 10.6). While some degree of illicit artefact hunting was noted at Maya sites as early as the mid-nineteenth century, it was in the 1960s that the collection of Maya antiquities became extremely popular, and by the 1980s the looting of the Petén sites was devastating.[45] Holmul appears to have been a particular target for US-financed illegal looting enterprises in the late 1980s and 1990s, partly because the site was too remote to be monitored by Guatemalan authorities but mostly because of the fame of Merwin's artefact collection.

Holmul has a reputation of producing museum-quality pieces, particularly pottery of a particular iconographic tradition, known as the Holmul Dancer style from a type pot found during Merwin's excavations. Looters' trenches and dynamite have damaged nearly every building at Holmul. In a certain sense, the very publication that was meant to preserve Holmul actually inspired its physical destruction. Ironically, Building B appears to have been left untouched by looters. This is most likely because Merwin's excavations left the building looking like an empty shell, already cleared of any marketable antiquities.

Figure 10.6: Modern looters' trenches into a jungle-covered structure at Holmul. Photo by Alexandre Tokovinine.

[45] See Clemency C. Coggins, 'Illict traffic of pre-Columbian antiquities', *Art Journal*, 29 (1969), pp. 94–8; and Elizabeth Gilgen, 'Looting and the market for Maya objects', in Neil Brodie, Jennifer Doole, and Colin Renfrew, eds., *Illicit antiquities: the destruction of the world's archaeological heritage* (Cambridge, 2001), pp. 73–88.

X

It is easy for archaeologists to deify early academic texts to some extent, even if we know their limitations. Perhaps it is because we like to imagine bits of ourselves in these adventurer academics who brazenly breached the jungle barrier, slinging their hammocks on ruined edifices while laying the foundations of the discipline that we love. I too went to work under the assumption that the sections and plans presented in Merwin and Vaillant would be more or less accurate and was surprised to find that they were not. Archaeologists want the information presented in older publications to be factual or else we have to deal with a situation where our disciplinary heroes are flawed and whole sites have been lost.

By no means do I wish to criticize the actions of past archaeologists; rather I hope that I have constructed a starting point for discussion of the idea of academic publication as a stand-in for the physical preservation of a site or monument in a remote location. And, indeed, text alone was not the sole preservational stand-in employed by the early Mayanists to combat a forbidding landscape. Outside of the purview of this chapter are the extensive plaster moulds of Maya architectural features that were carted out of the jungle on mule-back and into the major museums of the world, particularly at the end of the nineteenth century.[46] While casts and other physical reproductions have inspired much discussion within the academic study of preservation and heritage studies, the use of text itself as a replacement for a lost or distant site has not.

As an archaeologist trained in the American tradition, I find this academic focus on only physical preservation to be quite surprising. We archaeologists are taught that proper site recording, followed by the wide dissemination of the textual results of our work, is our sacred duty. Archaeological codes of ethics mandate timely publication. For example, the Archaeological Institute of America Code of Professional Standards holds that 'Archaeologists should make public the results of their research in a timely fashion';[47] the Code of Ethics of the American Anthropological Institute urges members to 'disseminate their findings to the scientific and scholarly community';[48] and the Society for American Archaeology Principles of Archaeological Ethics[49] says 'the knowledge archaeologists gain from investigation of the archaeological record must be presented in accessible form (through publication or other means)'.

---

[46] See Graham, *Alfred Maudslay and the Maya*, for a discussion of Maudslay's mould-making.
[47] Archaeological Institute of America, *Code of Professional Standards*, 1994,<http://www.archaeological.org/pdfs/AIA_Code_of_Professional_StandardsA5S.pdf>.
[48] American Anthropological Association, *Code of Ethics*, 1998.
[49] Society for American Archaeology, *Principles of Archaeological Ethics*, 1996, <http://www.aaanet.org/committees/ethics/ethicscode.pdf>.

Those archaeologists who develop a reputation for sitting on excavation reports are scorned. Archaeologists are taught that excavation itself is destruction. We destroy a preserved site by excavating it and we can never re-excavate what we have removed from the ground. Thus our written site records become—to the archaeologists and public who will never visit the actual location—the preserved site.

The first excavation at Holmul occurred at the time when the concept of obligatory publication hit archaeology. While Holmul may represent an extreme case of publication as a replacement for preservation, to the archaeologists of the day the production of the site report was a necessary evil meant to right a disciplinary wrong. The archaeologists of the late nineteenth and early twentieth centuries experienced a fresh ancient Maya. Unlike the classical and Near Eastern archaeologists of the day, the early Maya archaeologists had no back corpus of material to draw upon. Everything they saw was new and informative and they created a science to study it: a science that required supporting texts. These archaeologists did not foresee a future where tourists would easily visit jungle sites, and certainly could not predict that the structural integrity of previously excavated remote sites would ever provoke public concern. The archaeologists were genuinely trying to preserve the ancient Maya for posterity despite massive logistical barriers. Text as a stand-in for true physical preservation was the only available option.

11

Plunder or Preservation? Negotiating an Anglo-American Heritage in the Later Nineteenth Century in the Old World and the New: Shakespeare's Birthplace, Niagara Falls, and Carlyle's House*

MELANIE HALL

A SIGNIFICANT CATALYST for British preservation efforts during the second half of the nineteenth century was the threat of being plundered by Americans, who saw Britain's heritage as their own and were keen to acquire it. A catalytic event came when show-business entrepreneur Phineas Barnum aspired, in 1847, to acquire Shakespeare's Birthplace from Stratford-upon-Avon and transport it to New York. The proposed purchase by a travelling-circus owner had, for opponents, connotations of the 'plunder' of a significant symbol of England's heritage and English literature. To them, this represented an attempt to take a site of national memory to the United States for sensationalist purposes and commercial gain.[1] The significance of Shakespeare's Birthplace was not limited to England or the United States. However, in Stratford-upon-Avon it formed part of a visual and experiential narrative of associated sites of the 'motherland' of the English-speaking empire, made available through tourism, art, and print media. The prospect of plunder at the Birthplace proved to be a portent of things to come as America entered its 'gilded age'. With this, an international and, indeed, transnational chapter in museum discourse began, whereby 'preservation' was a response to the 'plunder' of sites

* Several people have read and commented on this chapter and I am grateful to them all. Thanks are due to Peter Mandler, Erik Goldstein, John Walton, and Keith Morgan. My particular thanks go to Astrid Swenson for suggesting the theme and organizing the conference where this chapter was begun.
[1] Pierre Nora, *Realms of memory: rethinking France*, trans. Arthur Goldhammer (New York, 1992), pp. 1–22.

of literary and artistic association.[2] This new type of 'plunder' was associated with a modernizing form of preservation, which privileged place.[3]

The second place of catalytic Anglo-American interest (*c*.1869–85) was the area around Niagara Falls, a boundary site between what was then the Dominion of Canada, for which Britain still spoke in matters of foreign policy, and the United States. Any preservation attempt required United States, British, and Canadian interest groups to come together. Here were potentially multiple layers of 'plunder'. Preserved sites often have a quasi-sacral significance to advocates, and it is not only the site but its significance that 'plunder' threatens and 'preservation' reinterprets. This site was also sacred to the Iroquois tribe, who still inhabited the area on both sides of the new border. There are several phases of preservation at Niagara Falls. In this initial phase powerful interest groups backed up by state agencies aspired to 'preserve' the scenery of the Falls by 'reserving' the area for wonder-filled sightseeing, and from 'despoilment' by rogue elements such as Barnum and the 'democratic amusement', commercial spectacle, Indian sideshows, and lack of social order with which he was associated.[4] When Barnum proposed to cover one of the island viewing-platforms in the middle of the Falls with his big top, thus removing it from sight, its preservation became a campaign for the cultural and commercial identity of the North America polity. This phase was more concerned with use of land, and pre-dates efforts to restrict the extraction of water from the Falls. Here, in an increasingly international milieu, the Anglo-American approach to civil society and land proprietorship was on display. Hegemonic American and British cultural, educational, publishing, and political interest groups joined forces to retain—for what they termed 'higher civilization'—the aesthetic, literary, and high-minded associations of the waterfalls against new forms of commerce and spectacle that were despoiling their new world order.[5]

---

[2] I am using the term 'museum' to indicate buildings as well as areas of landscape that are set aside as institutions for viewing and education. Thus it can be associated both with architecture and landscape architecture, though the latter is often overlooked. A more useful term to incorporate both and indicate site-specific associations is 'site-museum'.

[3] The idea of a place as a museum was expressed by Quatremère de Quincy who described Rome as a 'veritable museum' where monuments, memories, geographical features, and customs were all part of the 'only true museum', in response to the peace treaty of Tolentino (1797), which obliged Pius VI to send art and antiquities for the new Musée Napoleon. See Jukka Jokilehto, *History of architectural conservation* (Oxford, 2001), pp. 72–5; Sylvia Lavin, *Quatremère de Quincy and the invention of a modern language of architecture* (Cambridge, MA, 1992), pp. 156–7.

[4] James W. Cook, 'Mass marketing and cultural history: the case of P. T. Barnum', *American Quarterly*, 51 (1999), pp. 175–86, especially p. 182; Tony Tanner, *The reign of wonder* (Cambridge, 1965), pp. 1–25.

[5] Clara Marburg Kirk, *W. D. Howells and art in his time* (New Brunswick, NJ, 1965), pp. 252–67; Francis R. Kowsky, 'Municipal parks and city planning: Frederick Law Olmsted's Buffalo Park and parkway system', *Journal of the Society of Architectural Historians*, 46 (1987), pp. 49–64.

A third example of significant Victorian Anglo-American preservation interest was the London house of Thomas Carlyle (1894). While this effort had a far more limited social and cultural reach than that at Niagara Falls, it provided a further step towards Anglo-American cooperation in preservation. Carlyle was the vitriolic, sermonizing spokesman of a generation coming to terms with enormous change. Change induced concern about social instability, as well as commercial mayhem, which might be mitigated by education, strong leadership in both countries, and cooperation. Preservation offered a buffer against this rising tide.[6] Carlyle's home, acquired through British, American, and other voluntary subscriptions, was utilized as a site of cultural diplomacy. Carlyle's work was read in both countries; his essay, 'Shooting Niagara: and after?' (1867), written on the eve of Disraeli's Reform Bill to begin to extend the franchise to the working class, evoked the 'Niagara leap' as an analogy for (American-style) 'completed democracy', religious deliquescence, and economic and cultural change towards a 'cheap and nasty' grasping materialism and a continuous search for novelty which, for some, Barnum personified. Carlyle juxtaposed this with a sense of the 'eternal' and his conviction of the need for wise governance by men of genius and a good, educated citizenry. Although not quite a co-owned international site, the Carlyle House Museum was a step in that direction.

Cultural, sub-political, and economic factors combined to motivate preservation activists. The second half of the nineteenth century was one of extraordinary change within Britain, the Dominion of Canada, and the United States, as well as for the international relations between the two imperial powers. Britain was reaching the apogee of empire by the end of the nineteenth century; the United States was emerging as a fast-growing new imperial power and economic force on the world stage, particularly after its Civil War. The United States shared a long land border with the Dominion of Canada, a part of the British empire. Canadian Confederation (1867) made that country a more effective economic and political unit, though Britain still spoke for Canada in matters of foreign policy. These countries had complex ties that included history and language, family, friendship, religion, and economics. Institutional links in some areas (such as the churches and universities) had deep roots. International relations were made more flexible by modern forms of communication. As the United States began its rise as a major economic, military, and political power, arbitration rather than war was used as a tool for resolving Anglo-American disputes, indicating the increasing recognition of their parity and a desire for amity. The so-called 'Alabama Incident' during the American Civil War soured relations, but was settled by the 1871 Treaty of Washington and the subsequent arbitration case

---

[6] Robert H. Wiebe, *The search for order, 1877–1920* (New York, 1967), pp. 57–9, 60–6.

at Geneva. Britain paid reparations in respect of the United States' claims for losses to shipping caused by the British-built, Confederate commerce raider, CSS *Alabama*. Although some in the United States considered the nation's 'manifest destiny' was to incorporate the continent, others, particularly among the old settler communities in New England (who are important for Anglo-American preservation), eschewed imperialist ambitions. Nevertheless, by 1900 the United States had overtaken Britain in industrial production and was becoming the hegemon of the Western hemisphere. The altering power and economic relationships between the two were (remarkably) managed without acrimony. Print media and publishing provided one of the substructures of diplomatic efforts; cooperative preservation efforts were another.[7]

Cooperative preservation was facilitated by several factors, not least of which was the reality of overlapping economic, political, and societal interests in North America. From around the 1860s, W. E. Gladstone sought to include the United States in an imagined community of 'English-speaking peoples'.[8] This was, as Francis Herrick explains, 'basically a liberal view of a possibility of understanding through a common language, and a hopeful projection of future growth ... [and] presumed that shared moral purposes justified special personal relationships'.[9] Other, more self-selecting imagined communities grouped around sightseeing and tourism, including literary tourism, which was facilitated by steam and rail travel, and elements of the publishing industry.[10] Tourism required sites—and sights—as points of reference and comparison. Such sites gained further audiences through print media, particularly as illustrations became more readily available with advances in reproductive technology during the 1870s.[11] Sight-seeking tourism joined a burgeoning culture of spectacle. The impact on valued sites by a new, brash culture of individualism and display—personified at one extreme by Barnum—motivated and made possible cooperation and unity among transatlantic groups. These groups, often with close ties to government, wished to preserve indicative site-museums for orderly, educative social rituals and the interests of the state, including its internationalizing interests, as representational of their expanding civilization and sites of memory.

[7] Bradford Perkins, *The great rapprochement, England and the United States, 1895–1914* (London, 1969), pp. 130–7.
[8] Hugh Tulloch, *James Bryce's American commonwealth, the Anglo-American background* (Royal Historical Society, Studies in History, 54, 1988), pp. 7, 10.
[9] Francis H. Herrick, 'Gladstone and the concept of the "English-Speaking Peoples"', *Journal of British Studies*, 12 (1972), pp. 150–1.
[10] Eric Hobsbawm and Terence Ranger, eds., *The invention of tradition* (Cambridge, 1983); Benedict Anderson, *Imagined communities: reflections on the origin and spread of nationalism* (London, 1983).
[11] Christopher Mulvey, *Anglo-American landscapes, a study of nineteenth-century Anglo-American travel literature* (Cambridge, 1983).

I

The question of language presents problems for anyone writing about plunder and preservation in Britain and the United States. While the two ostensibly share the English language its usage was subject to change and difference. 'Plunder' has particularly complex meanings; as it is most anciently understood (and particularly in Britain) it has connotations of theft and looting, or acquisition by questionable methods. It can mean the despoilment of a site, and has a more immaterial, Miltonian sense of the removal of liberties or honour, and (somewhat archaically) peace. Interestingly, through an additional layer of meaning accrued by the 1890s, it can imply taking 'material from (literature or academic work, etc.) for one's own purposes'.[12] More benign meanings that inverted earlier definitions developed in the United States. These included an innocent, boyish gathering of nature's harvest; equipment used for camping; and goods acquired legitimately through trade.[13] Structural, cultural, economic, and legal issues also had an impact on the very idea of 'plunder'.

The term 'preservation' is also problematical as it is used differently in Britain and America, and its meaning has altered over time. Nevertheless, as plunder and preservation were among the motivating couplings used in the nineteenth century, meanings of preservation, too, need clarification.[14] Preservation (or preservationism) can be more clearly understood in terms of the institutional protection of certain properties rather than as a generic 'movement'. In the United States 'preservation' has a direct association with the law, and the concept is included in the constitutional oath. Things or places can, then, be preserved in the interests of the nation; this is further complicated by the idea of 'state' represented in the nation's nomenclatures. While a state is both a definite place, and a part of a union in the United States, 'the state', as it is understood in broader political parlance, refers to national governments and subsidiary government units. England, by contrast, has a greater emphasis on the concept of 'heritage' as something that has been handed down (and, sometimes, handed over) as part of its practices of state. In both countries today the term 'preservation' is used to denote the protection of

---

[12] *Oxford English Dictionary* definition.

[13] *Webster's Dictionary* definition.

[14] Contrasts were topical throughout the nineteenth century, often underpinning ways in which Victorians conceptualized their world. Contrasts were particularly useful when an ideal world was being advocated. Plunder and preservation, and despoilment and reservation were among the oppositional constructs that came to be invoked by preservation advocates. However, these constructs were subject to changes as thinking about 'preservation' issues developed, and their nuances need to be better understood. See Raymond Williams, *The country and the city* (New York and Oxford, 1973).

historic buildings, but in England it also refers to landscapes, as in the
Commons Preservation Society (founded 1865); preserving customary and
common use and enjoyment of the resource can also be implied. In the United
States, the term 'conservation' is more often applied to landscape protection,
a term which in Britain has a long usage for buildings; this tends to obscure
the intervening phase of landscape preservation in the United States.
Conservation can be better understood as a maintenance and management
philosophy and process, sometimes taking place within preserved landscapes.[15]
During the nineteenth century, landscapes as well as buildings in both countries
were 'preserved', 'reserved', 'protected', or held in 'trust'.

II

Issues of plunder and preservation came together in 1847 at 'Shakespeare's
Birthplace' in Stratford-upon-Avon (Figure 11.1), with news that P. T. Barnum
wanted to remove the 'shrine' from the town. Shakespeare was a useful agent
for Britain's imperial venture; the United States also appropriated the Bard
'in the interests of its own national and imperial project'.[16] Steamboats and
railways, literature and other print media, religion, and migration were all
ways in which national boundaries were transcended; all helped facilitate
international interest in destination places. Many tourist sites were experienced in print or as sightseeing destinations viewed from the outside, access to
which was at the discretion of a private owner. Invariably invested with literary, artistic, or other associations, they were of interest both to established
society and popular leisure entrepreneurs.[17] As material evidence of people's
lives and works gained importance for educational and leisure activities,
Shakespeare associations placed Stratford on the tourist maps of English literature and biography. The 'Birthplace' had long attracted important visitors,
and its proper preservation gained significance in the United States as a mark

---

[15] For a discussion of conservation and landscape see Samuel P. Hays, *Conservation and the
gospel of efficiency, the progressive conservation movement, 1890–1920* (Cambridge, MA, 1969),
pp. 125–33, 189–98; for buildings see Jokilehto, *History of architectural conservation*, pp. 72–5.
Such terms as conservation and restoration are loaded with cultural values as well as practical
applications; in landscape, in the United States, 'conservation' often defines a more scientific
approach to the management of resources; in Britain, it is used to indicate a minimal interventionist
approach to historic buildings and, indeed, town schemes.
[16] Michael Dobson, *The making of the national poet: Shakespeare, adaptation and authorship,
1660–1769* (Oxford, 1992), pp. 227–9.
[17] The relationship between literature, tourism, and 'cultures' is discussed in James Buzard, *The
beaten track, European tourism, literature and the ways to 'culture', 1800–1918* (Oxford, 1993),
pp. 19–154; for Stratford see Ian Ousby, *The Englishman's England: travel, taste and the rise of
tourism* (Cambridge, 1990), pp. 33–57; Mulvey, *Anglo-American landscapes*, pp. 74–92.

of England's civic governance. American 'founding fathers' Thomas Jefferson and John Adams had disparaged the lack of preservation of Shakespeare sites in Stratford during their 1786 tour.[18] Adams used his 'tour' for his country's (and his own) propagandistic purposes; while declaring Shakespeare's universal transcendence of place he pointed out Stratford's negligence in protecting material evidence of his existence: 'There is nothing *preserved* of this great genius which is worth knowing: nothing which might inform us what education, what company, what accident turned his mind to the drama. His name is not even on his gravestone. An ill-sculptured head is set up by his wife, by the side of his grave in the church.'[19] This gave powerful voice to a tension about who owned the legacy of Shakespeare and what that legacy might be.

Figure 11.1: Shakespeare's Birthplace, Henley Street, Stratford-upon-Avon, *c.*1850. By Permission of the Shakespeare Birthplace Trust.

---

[18] Christian Deelman, *The great Shakespeare jubilee* (London, 1964); Dobson, *The making of the national poet*, p. 227.

[19] John Adams, *The works of John Adams, second president of the United States (1851)* (6 vols. repr. New York, 1971), iii, p. 393, cited in Michael Bristol, *Shakespeare's America, America's Shakespeare* (New York, 1990), pp. 53–4 and in Dobson, *The making of the national poet*, p. 229. My italics.

As Shakespeare's plays were becoming part of the American educational and leisure experience, Stratford was becoming identified as Shakespeare's town. Sites associated with the Bard included his school, his monument in the parish church, and homes of family members; additional sites were associated with his plays.[20] American publicity added fuel to Stratford's reputation for dubious care of Shakespeare's places; Washington Irving's popular *The sketch book of Geoffrey Crayon* (1819–20) exposed the propagation of myth and satirized the selling of bogus relics.[21] Irving thought some sites associated with Shakespeare's youth to have been fabricated and even cast doubt on the authenticity of his place of birth. The market for *The sketch book* included wealthy Americans, for whom Stratford was becoming a stop on their European tour, and others who read at home. This transatlantic market had advantages and disadvantages for the author; a lack of adequate American copyright laws or treaties between the two countries impelled Irving to publish editions regularly in both Britain and the United States.[22] Efforts to resolve this tension intersected with attempts to protect literary sites.

Shakespeare's plays enjoyed popularity on both sides of the Atlantic. In the United States the most famous scenes were appropriated by vaudeville acts for farce, buffoonery, and ridicule with pantomime-style audience participation.[23] Interest in preserving the Bard's birthplace for national, high-culture purposes was paralleled by interest in protecting his reputation in authentic prose and verse. By the 1830s, members of the Royal Shaksperean Club were concerned to preserve the Birthplace as part of their desire to protect the reputation of the Bard, and to promote legitimate editions of his works. In 1835 a committee formed within the Club 'for the preservation of the Tomb and Monument of Shakspere, one object of which was "to extend their care to the preservation of the House in which Shakspere's Father resided in Henley Street, the Birth place of Shakspere".'[24]

As nationalism and imperialism amplified religion as a socially binding agent, places associated with artists and poets who were considered to be creative geniuses were regarded as quasi-secular 'shrines'. Shakespeare came to be seen by some as the equivalent of an English saint (his birthday coincides with St George's Day) and his birthplace acquired a shrine-like status; his

---

[20] Roger Pringle, 'The rise of Stratford as Shakespeare's town', in Robert Bearman, ed., *The history of an English borough: Stratford-upon-Avon, 1196–1996* (Stroud and Stratford, 1977), pp. 160–5.
[21] Washington Irving, *The sketch book of Geoffrey Crayon* (New York, and Boston, MA, 1848), pp. 266–87.
[22] W. S. Tryon, 'Nationalism and international copyright: Tennyson and Longfellow in America', *American Literature*, 24 (1952), pp. 301–9.
[23] Louis Levine, *Highbrow lowbrow: the emergence of cultural hierarchy in America* (Cambridge, MA, 1988), pp. 13–81.
[24] Minutes of the committee of the Royal Shaksperean Club, 22 July 1847, Stratford-upon-Avon, Shakespeare Centre Library and Archive (SCLA), Letters, TR 10/2/2/1.

works gained recognition comparable only with the Bible in and beyond the English-speaking world. Stratford's, indeed, England's, custodianship of Shakespeare's historical memory could thus assume quasi-religious—and supra-national—implications for England's legitimacy to act as custodian of English history and literature, and of its subjects.[25] By the time of the sale of Shakespeare's Birthplace, Thomas Carlyle, the London-based Scot, had added to Shakespeare's status as a national hero in his famous essay, *On heroes, hero-worship and the heroic in history* (1842). The fame of 'Shakespeare's Birthplace' as a tourist attraction had determined its value so much that, in 1847, an auction was held in London, well beyond the Stratford marketplace (Figure 11.2). The auction presented a potentially unstable interface between Stratford's civic–leisure interests and uncontrolled commercial interests from maverick elements. Indeed, the house was threatened with 'plunder' from New York showman P. T. Barnum, for whom England's heritage was a resource for popular entertainment in the United States. Barnum wanted to exhibit the house in one of his 'museums'.[26] The first show-business millionaire, Barnum's posthumous fame derives from his travelling circus. However, he had large-scale, popular commercial museums in Philadelphia and New York City. His New York premises, known as the 'American Museum', combined a zoo, so-called 'freak show', and theatre, where the entertainments included vaudeville-style adaptations and the lampooning of famous scenes from Shakespeare's plays.[27]

Barnum's proposition to transport the literary hero's house to New York helped to galvanize support for its retention in situ. As the building's value as an ornament of Stratford's and England's honour was enhanced so, too, was the sense of plunder of Shakespeare's works and reputation. Issues of ownership and stewardship surrounded the Birthplace sale as the building's uses for civic–national and literary purposes were contrasted with the prospect of its exploitation for American spectacle and use as a temporary, touring exhibit alongside exotica and vaudeville acts. Although acquiring this symbol of Englishness had alternative resonances for identity-building in the young United States, representing literary achievement as show-business entertainment was undesirable to more highbrow educated elites. Preserving the homes of heroes as museums to inspire patriotic admiration was becoming topical in the United States, where well-connected voluntarist interests (including

---

[25] Roland Quinault, 'The cult of the centenary, c.1784–1914', *Historical Research*, 71 (1998), pp. 303–23.

[26] Phineas T. Barnum, *The life of P. T. Barnum, written by himself* (New York, 1855), p. 345; Levi Fox, *The Shakespeare Birthplace Trust, a personal memoir* (Norwich, 1997), pp. 3–6; Pringle, 'The rise of Stratford', in Bearman, ed., *The history of an English borough*, p. 171; *Illustrated London News*, 25 Sept. 1847, p. 208.

[27] A. H. Saxon, *P. T. Barnum: the legend and the man* (New York, 1989), p. 105.

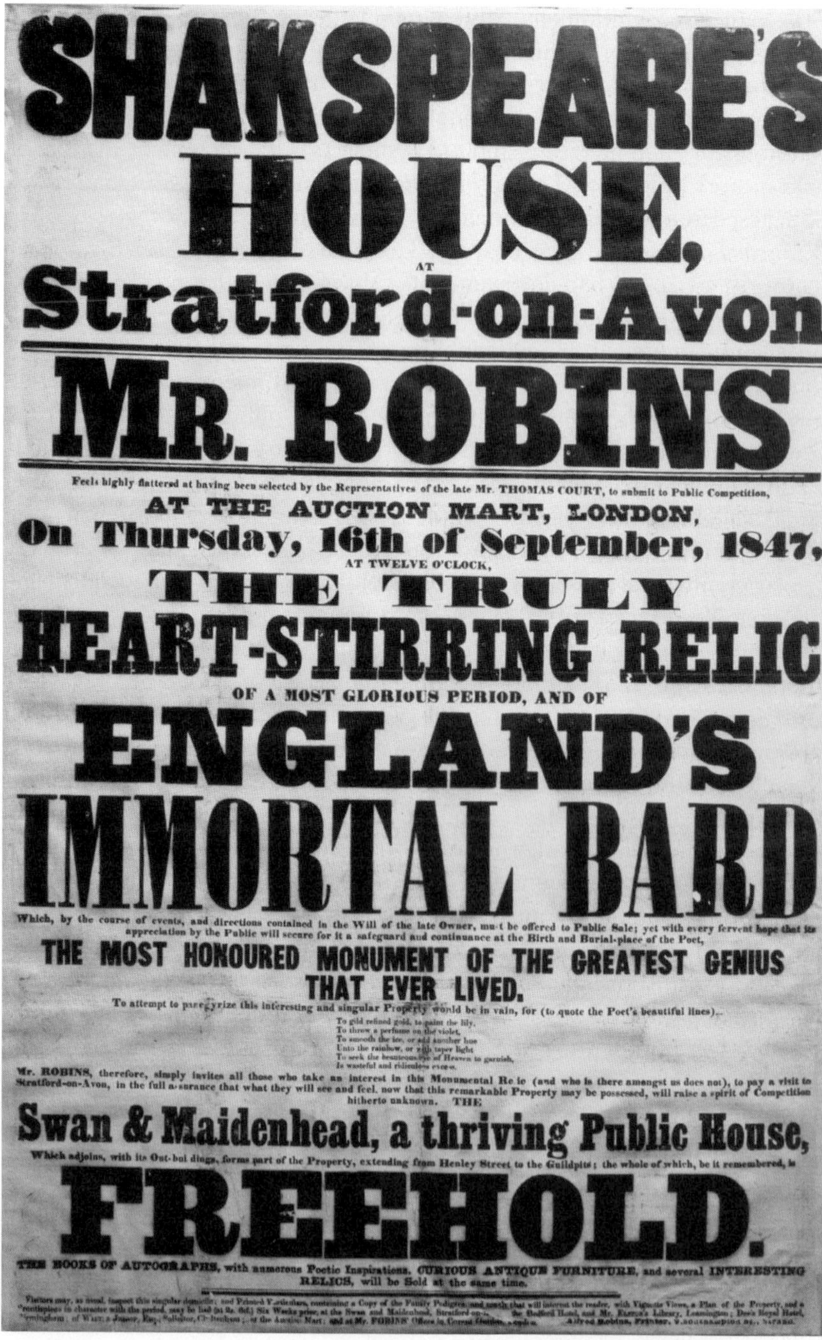

Melanie Hall

Figure 11.2: Auction poster, 1847. By Permission of the Shakespeare Birthplace Trust.

Washington Irving) were beginning attempts to preserve Hasbrouck House, George Washington's upstate New York Revolutionary War headquarters, and, more famously, Mount Vernon, Washington's Virginia estate.[28] Issues of class, taste, seemliness, and domicile gained importance in the preservation campaign.

Barnum's interest spurred attempts to make preserving the Birthplace a *national* concern. Birthplace acquisition committees were established in Stratford and London, comprising members of the Shakespeare Society— mostly concerned with publishing, scholarship, antiquarianism, and the arts— and local philanthropists. Prominent among these were John Payne Collier, the well-known literary editor and scholar of somewhat dubious reputation; James Orchard (later Orchard-Halliwell); the artist and antiquary Frederick W. Fairholt; and publisher and writer Charles Knight. Local representatives included Edward Fordham Flower, the brewer and banker, several times Stratford's mayor, and, subsequently, chairman of the Shakespeare Birthplace Trust.[29] The Committee approached Lord Morpeth, Chief Commissioner of Woods and Forests, who was initially supportive of acquiring the house 'as a just object of national care', but negotiations stalled.[30]

With Barnum's agents waiting to bid at the London auction, national reputation was at stake. *The Times* exposed 'the desecrating grasp of those speculators who are said to be desirous of taking [the Birthplace] from its foundations, and trundling it about on wheels like a caravan of wild beasts, giants, or dwarfs, through the United States of America'.[31] Help was needed not only to 'secure it against being exposed at any future time to the chances of desecration, destruction or removal', but to ensure that the house 'of our greatest poet' be 'preserved ... from persons, either native or foreign, who would treat it merely as a means of making money, and whose purchase ... would afford no guarantee [of suitable use] when its capabilities of yielding a large profit as an exhibition ... should show symptoms of exhaustion'.[32] The Shakespeare Society, actors, Charles Dickens, and eminent Stratfordians harnessed national pride and public subscriptions led by Prince Albert, which enabled them to pay an exorbitant £3,000 secure the house in Stratford.[33]

---

[28] Levine, *Highbrow, lowbrow*, pp. 13–33, 69–81; Charles B. Hosmer, Jr., *Presence of the past* (New York, 1965), p. 41; Patricia West, *Domesticating history, the political origins of America's house museums* (Washington, DC, 1999), pp. 1–38.

[29] Fox, *The Shakespeare Birthplace Trust*, pp. 4, 17.

[30] Minutes of the proceedings of the Shakspeare's Birthplace Committee at Stratford-upon-Avon, 22 July 1847; 19 March 1851, SCLA, TR 2/1/1.

[31] *The Times*, 2 July 1847, qu. in Fox, *The Shakespeare Birthplace Trust*, p. 3.

[32] Ibid.

[33] Frederick W. Fairholt, 'Shakespeariana, consisting of portraits of the poet, views at Stratford-on-Avon, autographs, and miscellaneies connected with the sale of his Birthplace in 1847', vol. 3, SCLA, ER1/112, p. 22; Fox, *The Shakespeare Birthplace Trust*, pp. 3–6.

Negotiations resumed with the Office of Woods and Forests; Morpeth, no longer in charge, attempted to assuage the concerns of his successor, Lord Seymour, who was worried that accessioning the Birthplace would set a precedent: 'As to entailing the custody of other houses upon you, England and the World have only one Shakespeare.'[34] A Bill to make the house a national property was posted in *The London Gazette* early in 1853.[35] A change of administration scuppered the prospect, and the Birthplace remained a matter for Stratford, not a national matter. However, this prospect established a precedent for including historic buildings in the concept of national heritage that was slowly developing during the nineteenth century in Britain.[36]

When the question arose of how to institutionalize, preserve, and present the house as a museum, the Birthplace Committee sought advice from learned societies, including the Society of Antiquaries, the (Royal) Archaeological Institute, and the Royal Society of Literature. To affirm both charitable and literary sentiments these 'noblemen and gentlemen known as men of letters' proposed that 'some decayed literary person' act as guide, and that any profits go 'to the relief of distressed authors'.[37] Architect Edward M. Barry drew up plans for 'a roof of iron and glass' to better preserve the ancient house.[38] Had this been implemented, the perception of the Birthplace as an historical *exhibit* for modern-day consumption would have been enhanced. Barry's 'glass covered Hall', reminiscent of the Crystal Palace, was considered too expensive, and his more conservative proposals for removing 'those excrescences which are decidedly the result of modern innovation', or which were considered fire hazards, were undertaken as funds permitted.[39] Thus, gradually, an appearance of 'authenticity' was invented at this site-museum. A local custodian, rather than an author, was appointed to show visitors around and take entrance fees.

Showmanship spectaculars already coexisted with establishment museums in a sometimes difficult relationship, as they often desired the same

[34] Carlisle to Seymour, 6 Nov. 1850, Cumbria, Muncaster Castle, Muncaster MSS. Morpeth had become earl of Carlisle. I am grateful to Peter Mandler for this reference.
[35] Minutes of the Shakspeare's Birthplace committee, 23 Apr. 1853, SCLA, TR2/1/1.
[36] This episode seems to have been hitherto overlooked. See, for example, Michael Hunter, 'The fitful rise of British preservation', in M. Hunter, ed., *Preserving the past, the rise of heritage in modern Britain* (Stroud, 1996), pp. 1–8; Melanie Hall, 'Affirming community life: preservation, national identity and the state, 1900', in Chris Miele, ed., *From William Morris: building conservation and the Arts and Crafts cult of authenticity, 1877–1939* (New Haven, CT, 2005), pp. 129–57.
[37] Fairholt, 'Shakespeariana', vol. 3, SCLA, ER1/112, p. 22.
[38] Barry to Dr Thomson, 29 June 1857, SCLA, W.O. Hunt Correspondence, vol. 1, 1856–71, ER 1/45/3 f., pp. 138–42.
[39] Ibid.

resources but for different purposes.[40] While this distinction may seem self-evident, it was indicative of a set of increasingly complex and competing visions for the way cultural resources were utilized, valued, and transmitted.[41] When the Birthplace became a deeded museum and library in 1866, its trustees included ex officio the borough mayor, aldermen, and burgesses; the building became an historic–period exhibition case for objects relating to Shakespeare and his works, and a repository for 'Ancient Records of the Borough', which, in turn, added a layer of civic legitimacy to the site.[42] Increasingly, influential interest groups became concerned with retaining museums as places of 'wonder' and 'values' that evoke a sense of admiration derived both from the inherent qualities of the object and its construction (such as beauty or technical virtuosity or age), and from its associations (such as biography or history), which are further connected to systems of social, political, educational, and economic values.[43] The Birthplace Museum was not a public institution run with public money but was dependent on philanthropy and entrance fees; however, it received public funding indirectly as the council refurbished the archive rooms and paid an annual rent from 1862.[44] When establishment groups lay claim to these resources in the name of civic–nationalism they invariably invoke ideal values of civic order and stable community life. In Barnum's world a different, even antithetical order of 'wonders' was expressed in terms of physical skills, social and racial outsiders, 'high culture' highlights, humbug, entrepreneurial individualism, and mobility. He was clearly, also, no respecter of prevailing sensibilities of hierarchy and place. Hence, to some he epitomized moral decline, disorder, unregulated trades, and the commercialization, potential despoilment, and disposability of cultural resources.[45] In short, his travelling museum and circus represented plunder against the interests of community and, sometimes, against the interests of the state.

Increasingly, Britain's heritage houses (and other resources) were becoming targets of opportunity for Americans who also saw this heritage as their

[40] Susan Pearce, 'Antiquaries and the interpretation of ancient objects, 1770–1820', in Susan Pearce, ed., *Visions of antiquity: the Society of Antiquaries of London, 1707–2007* (London, 2007), pp. 161–6.

[41] Anne Goldgar, 'The British Museum and the virtual representation of culture in the eighteenth century', *Albion*, 32 (Summer 2000), pp. 195–231, argues that the British Museum should be understood in similar terms. The situation becomes more complex in Stratford where the house is part of the townscape as well as a museum.

[42] Fox, *The Shakespeare Birthplace Trust*, p. 17. This combination of objects and manuscripts reflected the original collection of the British Museum; Goldgar, 'British Museum', p. 199.

[43] For the different genres of museums see Giles Waterfield, *Palaces of art: art galleries in Britain, 1790–1990* (London, 1991), pp.121–34, 145–56, 159–70.

[44] Minutes of the Birthplace Committee meeting, 31 Dec. 1862, SCLA, TR2/1/1.

[45] Neil Harris, *Humbug: the art of P. T. Barnum* (Chicago, 1973), pp. 189–90.

own.[46] The prospect of collecting and exhibiting complete *houses* from one country in another country was new; this further undermined connotations of *place* in Britain, where the idea of moving houses between locations is less familiar. The wealthy British, more used to collecting than being collected, preferred their houses in situ, framed within (invariably picturesque) landscaped estates, and as exhibitionary repositories for cultural objects—including architectural *fragments*—from other cultures; acquisitions and display were under their own control as interlayered statements of heritage, inheritance, and power.[47] Developments in transport facilitated the possibility that an entire house might become a transportable commodity as well as an exhibitionary display case for an alternative, *American* vision of the Englishman's home. This prospect was increasingly presented to the British, as American wealth and world fairs placed further demands on heritage resources, as we shall see.

III

The plunder and the preservation of cultural and natural resources are often treated as separate and distinct issues; nevertheless, in literature and art, as on grand estates, such distinctions are less easy to make. The initial impetus for preservation at Niagara Falls came from the plunder and despoliation, as some saw it, of the setting, during the phase when the waterfalls were considered to be an iconic *monument* of the North American continent and, for New York, that state, and before riparian rights had been established by treaty. In Ontario, scenic identity at the Falls had not developed greatly. Niagara Falls was a liminal site where issues of identity were complex and changing. Establishing site-museums at the Falls was a means of expressing general and specific identities, as well as order and the possibility of peaceful cooperation between two imperial powers at a spectacular point on this border. In addition to national, state, or imperial identities, another identity lingered. The name Niagara or Onguiaahra, meaning 'thundering water', is attributed to early Iroquois inhabitants, for whom the Falls were a sacred site. Issues of plunder at the Falls have a deeper, British and French colonial history prior to the nineteenth-century United States, British, and Canadian histories. Since

---

[46] Peter Mandler, *The fall and rise of the stately home* (New Haven, CT, and London, 1997), pp. 124–6, 179–80, 184–5; John Harris, *Moving rooms, the trade in architectural salvages* (New Haven, CT, and London, 2007), pp. 101–17, 147–218. Also see, Melanie Hall and Erik Goldstein, 'Writers, the Clergy, and the 'Diplomatization' of Culture: Sub-Structures of Anglo-American Diplomacy, 1820–1914', in John Fisher and Antony Best, eds, *On the Fringes of Diplomacy: Influences on British Foreign Policy, 1800–1945* (Aldershot: Ashgate, 2011), pp. 127–54.
[47] Francis Haskell, 'The British as collectors', in Gervase Jackson-Stops, ed., *Treasure houses of Britain* (New Haven, CT, and London, 1985), pp. 50–9.

place also carries with it connotations of socio-political and economic hierarchy and of cultural memory, establishing site-museums also provided a means to express a democratic New World order and the power of the nation state.

For Westerners the Falls had overlapping cultural meanings; between the 1830s and 1870s its symbolism shifted from a wonderful work of God or nature, to a wonder of the world and site of spectacle. Its potential as a secular monument to science and industry was becoming evident.[48] Niagara Falls straddled the boundary between the United States and the Dominion of Canada, part of the British empire. It was, thus, a transnational and international site where legal issues of riparian rights, land ownership, and national identities were underdeveloped. Cultural, political, and social factors converged to assist in preservation efforts and a cooperative, international solution. Complex legal issues, as well as identity claims in New York State and Ontario, prevented intergovernmental Anglo-American cooperation being institutionally represented.[49] With Canadian Confederation in 1867, the United States bordered an increasingly unified and effective unit of the empire to its north, though one where national identities were still subsumed in imperial identities. Nevertheless, this boundary was an unstable interface that attracted rogue elements. The Irish nationalist 'Fenian raids' across the border almost led to confrontation between the two powers. Neither British, Canadian, nor United States' commercial interests were yet regulated along the water's borders, nor were riparian rights established. At issue for preservationists were what representational values might be promoted at the site, and whether cooperative solutions were feasible.

Waterfalls in Western culture had deep meanings as a form of perpetual motion, often carrying religious symbolism. The Falls had accrued propagandistic value as a site of peace and cooperation from writers, clerics, and politicians. Recounting their 1834 North American Congregationalist tour, the Reverends Andrew Reed and Thomas Mattheson declared the Falls did 'not belong to Canada or America' but were 'the property of civilized mankind'.[50] The Falls were associated with peace between English-speaking peoples by Charles Dickens and Harriet Martineau, among others. Although the site retained an international aura, for the United States it provided an opportunity to express national identity as well. The former United States President,

[48] Charles Mason Dow, *Anthology and bibliography of Niagara Falls* (2 vols., Albany, NY, 1921), gives comprehensive coverage to the Falls' many identities.

[49] The extensive literature on Niagara Falls spans different disciplines. The best account of preservation from the American perspective is Gail Edith Hallett Evans, 'Storm over Niagara: a study of the interplay of cultural values, resource politics, and environmental policy, 1670s–1950' (Ph.D. thesis, University of Califonia, Santa Barbara, 1991). For an international perspective see, Melanie Hall, 'Niagara Falls: Preservation and the Spectacle of Anglo-American Accord', in Melanie Hall (ed), *Towards World Heritage: International Origins of the Preservation Movement 1870–1930* (Aldershot: Ashgate, 2011), pp. 23–43.

[50] Qu. in Charles Mason Dow, *The state reservation at Niagara: a history* (Albany, NY, 1914), p. 9.

John Quincy Adams (1825–29), who had served also as minister to Britain, publicly suggested in a speech in Buffalo (1843) that 'Heaven had considered this vast natural phenomenon too great for one nation.'[51] Adams skilfully represented the Falls as a theatre of friendship, as well as asserting national identity. A Canadian identity had not yet developed, and the British continued to see the site as international or continental. Industrial technology provided an alternative, modern symbol of unity to *The Times* (of London), which described the railway bridge constructed in 1848 across the river as 'an iron link of civilization between the two ruling Powers of the world, [which] will never be severed'.[52] Gradually, associations of peace, literature, and nature tourism competed with spectacle, commerce, and emerging technology at the site. By the 1860s *The Times* described the Falls' banks as a modern, urban, industrial, commercial, and somewhat lawless 'pleasure-ground'.[53] Spectacular entertainments attracted a new kind of day tripper alongside the sightseeing tourist, particularly as nearby Buffalo developed as an industrial city and railway hub. Lack of civic regulation reflected poorly on British imperial and United States governance, and Anglo-American civilization.

While nostalgia is often considered to be an underlying sentiment of preservation, creativity can also be a factor; park-making, whether 'wilderness', 'rural', or civic', is a form of landscape architecture.[54] The Falls' fame as an icon for the United States (rather than the North American continent) multiplied by means of a work of art rather than literature—Frederic Church's spectacular *Niagara* (1859)—and it was this representation of stayed motion that catalysed preservation efforts. A clever agent toured the painting around cities in Britain, France, and the United States during the 1860s, enhancing publicity with saleable reproductions. Church's glossy, gilt-framed painting presented a manipulated vision of the Falls to international viewing audiences.[55] It gained fame as the first truly *American* painting, a term that had both continental and national implications; though the painter represented the United States, the painting depicted the Canadian Horseshoe Falls with a

---

[51] Perkins, *Great rapprochement*, pp. 119–31. Dow, *Anthology*, i, p. 233.

[52] *The Times*, 18 Jan. 1848, p. 5; William Irwin, *The new Niagara: tourism, technology and the landscape of Niagara Falls, 1776–1917* (University Park, PA, 1996), pp. 31–61.

[53] *The Times*, 23 Aug. 1859, p. 10. Mulvey, *Anglo-American landscapes*, pp. 187–208; Patrick V. McGreevy, *Imagining Niagara: the meaning and making of Niagara Falls* (Amherst, MA, 1994), pp. 23–40; Irwin, *New Niagara*, pp. 63–72.

[54] For nostalgia and heritage see David Lowenthal, *The past is a foreign country* (Cambridge, 1985). Denis Dutton, *The art instinct, beauty, pleasure and human evolution* (New York, 2009), pp. 13–28 takes a more anthropological approach to human responses to landscape and landscape art.

[55] Jeremy Adamson, 'Frederic Church's Niagara: the sublime as transcendence' (Ph.D. thesis, University of Michigan, 1981), pp. 16–19, 32–49.

Figure 11.3: Frederic Church, *Niagara* (1857). Oil on canvas, 40 x 90.5 inches. Courtesy of The Corcoran Gallery of Art, Washington, DC. Museum Purchase, Gallery Fund. Accession no. 76.15.

view taken from the Canadian side. *The Times* recognized that 'the most defiant of all ... the many scenes which the New World offers' had been mastered, and predicted for the United States 'a new and national development of painting' to complement its industrial development.[56] W. W. Corcoran bought the work from the Paris Exposition Universelle (1867) for his Washington gallery for $12,500, at that time the most yet paid for an American painting.[57] This assisted in the formation of a United States high-culture identity around the Falls, as opposed to a more broadly American identity.

The contrast of the painting with the reality at the Falls brought into focus powerful tides of change. Impetus to create the aura of a museum around the Falls to protect and direct the view came from Church who, as one of the commissioners for New York City's Central Park, also had a practical interest in park planning. Church campaigned in New York City's Century Club, its cultural hub, and in Boston, to preserve the site around Niagara Falls as an appropriate viewing platform for aesthetic appreciation and 'higher civilization'.[58] He was joined by his cousin, the famous landscapist Frederick Law Olmsted (who had designed Central Park), and Charles Eliot Norton, the erudite editor of both the *North American Review* and *The Nation*, and lecturer on 'the History of the Fine Arts as Connected with Literature' at

[56] *The Times*, 7 Aug. 1857, p. 12; 23 Aug. 1859, p. 10. Gail S. Davidson, 'Landscape icons, tourism and land development in the northeast', in Gail S. Davidson, Floramae Mc-Carron-Cates, Barbara Bloemink, Sarah Burns, and Karal Ann Marling, *Frederick Church, Winslow Homer and Thomas Moran: tourism and the American landscape* (New York, 2006), pp. 3–22.
[57] Elizabeth McKinsey, *Niagara Falls, icon of the American sublime* (Cambridge, 1985), p. 249.
[58] Kirk, *W. D. Howells and art in his time*, pp. 252–67; Kowsky, 'Municipal parks and city planning', pp. 49–64.

Harvard College from 1874 (professor of fine arts from the following year). Norton enjoyed friendships with John Ruskin and Thomas Carlyle, and is an overlooked figure in American preservation. Alfred Bierstadt, known for his sublime nature paintings of both the United States and Canada, acted as intermediary between campaigners in New York and Canada's governor-general, the Earl of Dufferin and Ava. Both Dufferin and New York governor Lucius Robinson supported the idea of an *international* park, which would have effectively turned the area into a site-museum.[59]

Within the Falls are several islands, another of Western culture's sites of fascination. Henry James, the noted American author who spent much of his life in England, put the case for acquiring the privately owned Goat Island, which sits between the American Falls and the Horseshoe Falls but is on the American side. Reminding readers, 'We place a great picture, a great statue, in a museum ... and expose it to no ignoble contact,' he proposed that, 'the State buy up the precious acres ... [for which] no price would be too great to pay.'[60] A change of administration occurred before any such suggestion could be implemented, but increasingly United States' interest would focus on this island.

The 'wonder' of the site, far from being a channel to heaven, was a scene of commercial manufactures and entertainments. The natural roar of the waters was robbed by brass bands; the Churchian view across the Falls disrupted by Charles Blondin's famous tightrope walks. The idea of ordered wildness, then synonymous with United States civic–wilderness park-making, was appropriated as popular entertainment in Wild Bill Hickok and Buffalo Bill's Amer-Indian spectaculars, where customary rituals performed for the crowds were also reminders of the site's deeper histories and activities.[61] Well-publicized tourist exploitation, suicides (another form of Niagara leap), and even murders took place.[62] Industry plundered forests from the banks. In Canada concerns about national identity were developing slowly; the idea that the beauties and higher associations of the Falls were being plundered was voiced in 1879. Canadian property owner William O. Buchanan expressed alarm to the governor-general that unregulated 'despoilers' were intruding into this scene of natural beauty and elevated associations, and acting against the state's interests.[63]

[59] 'Address given to the Ontario Society of Artists', 26 Sept. 1878, in William Leggo, *The history of the administration of the Right Honorable Frederick Temple, Earl of Dufferin, K.P., G.C.M.G., K.C.G., K.C.B., F.R.S., late governor-general of Canada* (Montreal, 1878), pp. 822–4. 'Message of Governor Lucius Robinson', 9 Jan.1879, qu. in Dow, *The state reservation*, pp. 14–16.
[60] Henry James, 'Portraits of places', Part I, *The Nation*, 12 Oct. 1871, 13: 328, pp. 238–39, qu. in Dow, *Anthology*, ii, p. 1099.
[61] Irwin, *New Niagara*, pp. 63–72.
[62] George A. Seibel, *Ontario's Niagara parks, one hundred years: a history* (Ontario, 1985), pp. 135–6.
[63] Buchanan to Dufferin, *c.*1878, Belfast, Public Record Office of Northern Ireland, papers of the Marquis of Dufferin and Ava, D1071/H/B/B/864/1-3.

Once again, Barnum provided a catalyst for preservation when he raised the prospect of expanding his show-business empire and purchasing Goat Island as a permanent pitch for his big top in 1880. The showman understood the powerful relationship between metropolitan and peripheral cultural venues; he already had a model of Niagara Falls in his New York City 'American Museum'. He also understood the representational power of the island site. *The New York Times* reported the prospect of a 'monster hippodrome' covering the entire island, removing it from sight, and charged the nation's cultural elite to 'restore the scenery of Niagara', and 'preserve Goat Island in its present natural beauty'.[64] In a cryptic note to Norton about the preservation campaign Olmsted wrote, 'It is so hard to realize the strength of organized public plunder.'[65] Harnessing the beauty of the Falls for a civic–national social order would have also represented that order as 'natural', and as part of a collection of similar federal reserves.[66]

Support for an international (Anglo-American) site focused on ideas of 'civilization'. Placing the Falls 'under the joint guardianship of the two governments' as a contribution to 'education … the order of society … and … the union and peace of nations' gained favour in Britain and the United States as 'a proper concern of the civilized world'. Signatories to this petition (March 1880), which was presented to New York governor Alonzo B. Cornell and Dufferin's successor, Lord Lorne, suggest interconnected sinews of culture, power, and finance. Government leaders and politicians signed it, including two future governors of New York and United States presidents, Grover Cleveland (Democrat) and Theodore Roosevelt (Republican), along with ambassadors, bishops, leading academics, and bankers. Numerous authors, their publishers, and cultural luminaries from the United States, Canada, and Britain also signed, including Thomas Carlyle, John Ruskin, Ralph Waldo Emerson, and Henry W. Longfellow. The appeal requested that 'the Falls of Niagara … be placed under the joint guardianship of the two governments', though it left vague quite *which* branches of government.[67] Once again, a change of administration meant matters stalled.

Reservations, and state and national parks, were new cultural institutions developing in the United States, particularly in newly occupied areas that invariably had indigenous populations and underdeveloped organizational structures. They provided models that were attractive to white settler communities in

---

[64] *New York Times*, 21 Apr. 1880, p. 4.

[65] Olmsted to Norton, 10 Sept. 1881, Washington, DC, Library of Congress, Frederick Law Olmsted papers, 73.60 1996 addition [AC 18, 328]; Olmsted may have been referring to trades unions that were taking over public places in an organized manner.

[66] Evans, 'Storm over Niagara', p. 96.

[67] 'Memorial Addressed to the Governor of New York and the Governor General of Canada', 2 Mar. 1880, qu. in Dow, *The state reservation*, pp. 18–20.

the British empire: Australia, Canada, and New Zealand all soon acquired national parks.[68] These reserves can be understood as new spatial units for purposes of governance and its representation. Individual site-museums could also form part of a national collection of similar reserves, linked by an expanding infrastructure of rail and road, and tourist guidebooks. Some hoped to harness this model as an expression of Anglo-American civilization. More ephemeral ideals of the cultural property of this New World 'higher civilization', at once both wonderful and natural, were expressed and endorsed through literature, painting, photography, and points of cultural reference. Nature reserves had already been established at Yosemite, California, pre-served (1864) by a federal land grant.[69] In a leap of imagination that took him to England, Olmsted, briefly one of Yosemite's commissioners, thought it resembled Shakespeare's Avon valley.[70] Yellowstone followed as a federal reserve and national park in 1872. Designating Yellowstone a federal reserve circumvented the difficulty of it straddling three territories where no appro-priate state or federal systems of authority and protection yet existed, and reserved for federal government purposes an area filled with monumental wonders and rich mineral resources against any other competing land-grab or, indeed, indigenous, claims. There was some precedent for the idea of sce-nic areas as national property in English romantic tourist literature as William Wordsworth had envisaged the Lake District (which also straddles more than one county) as a 'sort of national property'; a campaign for a national park there was to receive support from imperial federationists.[71] More prevalent than Olmsted's Anglophile cultural evocation were images of North America as a continent of *spectacular scenery*, together with the idea that these sites were natural science 'museums'.[72]

How the United States used and represented federal law in its parks has implications for broader debates about plunder and preservation. The new national parks represented a (federal–)national unity and identity through

---

[68] A national park was established near Sydney, in Australia (1879); Banff National Park, Canada, dates from 1885; Tongariro National Park, New Zealand, from 1887.

[69] Yosemite became a national park in 1890.

[70] Frederick Law Olmsted, 'Yosemite and the Mariposa Grove: a preliminary report, 1865' (Yosemite National Park, CA, Yosemite Association, 1993), <http://www.yosemite.ca.us/library/olmsted/report.html> (accessed 12 September 2012)

[71] William Wordsworth, *A guide through the district of the Lakes in the north of England with a description of the scenery, etc. for the use of tourists and residents* (Kendal, 1835), 2004 edition, issued as William Wordsworth, *Guide to the Lakes*, with a preface by Stephen Gill (London, 2004), p. 93.

[72] *Virginia City Montanian*, 18 Jan. 1872 (reprinting the *Ohio State Journal*), quoted in W. Turrentine Jackson, 'The creation of Yellowstone National Park', *Mississippi Valley Historical Review*, 29 (1942), p. 199.

nature, leisure pursuits, and the rule of law in the western territories, within which past and subsequent issues of 'plunder' could be acculturated. Particularly when underpinned by a myth of 'manifest destiny', the benign and boyish associations of the word 'plunder' are well adapted to such park pursuits as hunting or fishing. A new meaning of legitimate 'plunder', camping plunder, was associated with the famous Lewis and Clark expedition to map the West (1804–06), as equipment taken to a site, rather than something taken from it. These natural, wilderness site-museums were linked to metropolitan parks and museums figuratively and literally by railways and, increasingly, visual exhibits; although they had a broadening reach, most were physically accessible only to wealthy tourists or locals.[73]

In international relations, for a joint venture to work between two or more countries both cooperation and coordination are necessary. At Niagara Falls regional interests and international practicalities intervened. Local political support and jurisdiction could not be roused for an international project on either bank. A New York State Reservation on Goat Island (1885, landscaped by Olmsted) set a precedent where the aim of the commissioners was 'Preserving ... and restoring the scenery to its natural condition' by creating a 'reservation' of the area in and around Niagara Falls.[74] On the Canadian side, where national and regional identities were still subsumed by imperial identities, a Queen Victoria Jubilee Park followed (opened 1888).[75]

Plunder and despoliation at Niagara Falls—in the sense of the removal of honour and its 'higher' cultural associations—caused government intervention to preserve the site for leisure tourism and scenic propaganda. That a measure of cooperation was achieved and some kind of site-museum imposed on either side and between the Falls undoubtedly facilitated further cooperation from the 1880s onwards when Anglo-American hydroelectric companies, a far more powerful economic force, sought to 'plunder' the waters of the Falls for commercial hydroelectricity. Conservation not preservation would provide the solution. Simultaneously, additional meanings of 'plunder' were coming into use; these were the plunder of intellectual goods (such as literature) not yet protected in international treaties and, in the United States, meanings of shopping-plunder associated with purchasing power.

---

[73] Richard Grusin, *Culture, technology, and the creation of America's national parks* (Cambridge, 2004), pp. 1–15, 54–101. Paintings of American western landscapes often relied on photographic innovations such as stereoscopy to achieve more spectacular effects. Floramae McCarron Cates, 'The best possible view: pictorial representation in the American West', in Davidson, et al., *Frederick Church*, pp. 74–115.

[74] Dow, *The state reservation*, p. 26.

[75] Ibid., pp. 21–3; Evans, 'Storm over Niagara', p. 220.

IV

During the 1880s and early 1890s issues of plunder and preservation in Britain were again influenced by interests from the United States. However, between these two powers the dialectic of plunder and preservation was being renegotiated. Export of Britain's heritage resources by Americans gained momentum as the United States surpassed Britain as an economic power during the 1890s. Support for preserving a site-museum to Thomas Carlyle in London as a meeting ground for a more broadly imagined Anglo-American literary community among educated, literary circles in the United States also demonstrated friendship and affirmed certain sites as authenticating significant memories of the nation state.

Plunder of British heritage resources in the sense of 'shopping-plunder' by wealthy Americans gave rise to the National Art Collections Fund (founded 1903), which attempted to mitigate this by purchasing works for national collections.[76] This came together with 'plunder' in the earlier, Miltonian sense of removal of the 'honour' (or sites of admiration) of the nation in 1887, when an 'American showman' (doubtless Barnum) attempted to acquire for export Milton's cottage in Chalfont St Giles. This, in turn, stimulated local efforts, led by the vicar, to preserve the house in situ and, once again, retain a site for authenticating literary associations of the English-speaking world.[77] Barnum was then exporting animals from Europe to his circus; two years later he brought to London his 'Greatest Show on Earth', which invoked an alternative heritage of empire. Advertising itself as 'a stupendous mirror of departed empires', it purported to represent the new America, opening with a 'Grand American March' and a parade of 'curiosities' that included bearded ladies, woolly children, giants, dwarfs, and 'armless writers'.[78] The spectacular entertainment was based on the *decline* of the Roman empire; it received praise from the *Morning Post*, which noted that, 'Good things here are not doled out with a grudging hand, they are poured forth in a Niagara-like profusion.'[79]

Issues of identity, as well as morality, nostalgia, education, an ideal of civilization, and notions of authenticity are associated with ideas of preservation, plunder, and despoliation of sites; so, also, is *admiration*, and notions of

---

[76] As the American government placed an import tax on works of art many collectors chose to keep their collections in Europe; however, the tax was lifted in 1909. Harris, *Moving rooms*, p. 111.

[77] Rev. Phipps to the editor, *Daily News*, 3 May 1887, p. 3. *New York Times*, 15 May 1887. P. H. Ditchfield and Fred Roe, *Vanishing England* (1910, repr. London, 1993), p. 88. Bluford Adams, *E. Pluribus Barnum: the great showman and the making of United States popular culture* (Minneapolis, MN, 1997), p. 188.

[78] *Lloyds Weekly Newspaper*, 3 Nov. 1889, p. 5; *Morning Post*, 12 Nov. 1889, p. 6.

[79] *Morning Post*, 12 Nov. 1889, p. 6.

the future (if not quite eternity) as well as a growing concept of international cooperation. Although Barnum may have subverted Carlyle's model of Niagara's profusion, in 1894 an opportunity arose to preserve Carlyle's Chelsea home from 'degradation' by its use as 'a kind of home for dogs and cats'.[80] It was viewed by many as 'A Desecrated Shrine', which James Froude, Carlyle's intellectual 'disciple' and biographer, with hindsight considered 'ought to have been made national property' or, according to the *Pall Mall Gazette*, 'a national relic'.[81] An appeal to the House of Commons was rejected; Carlyle did not have the same importance as Shakespeare.[82] Instead, preservation advocates sought support from 'the scattered readers of Carlyle'.[83]

Preserving homes of heroes as an agent of civic order and community life was topical in both Britain and the United States.[84] They helped to give historical 'authenticity' to places of literary and biographical memory. In Britain, Robert Burns's cottage, in Alloway, was preserved in 1881; John Milton's cottage, in Chalfont St Giles, in 1887; Hugh Miller's birthplace in Cromarty, and Wordsworth's Dove Cottage, Grasmere, became museums in 1890. Carlyle's Ecclefechan birthplace was open to visitors from at least 1883, when his niece acquired it.[85] The preservation of some of these houses had an American dynamic, which either acted as a catalyst (in the case of Milton's cottage) or, as with Dove Cottage, came in the form of financial support. Appreciation of American literature in Britain and the empire had helped popularize Anglo-American friendship in the States. Publishing interests, too, began to respect authentic claims to authorship. America's Copyright Act of 1891 represented an attempt to prevent future plunder of intellectual property by making it illegal to pirate the work of foreign authors, and was well received by British publishers, authors, and politicians. Though Carlyle had never visited the United States, he was known for his friendship with Emerson, who had collected and sent Carlyle royalties; Carlyle had given his papers to Charles Eliot Norton at Harvard University to edit.

Efforts 'to preserve' Carlyle's Chelsea home brought together British and American voluntarist–subscriber and philanthropic interests.[86] The effort gained sub-diplomatic endorsement and high-level support. Lord Rosebery, the prime minister, gave £50, the highest individual amount, and joined the

---

[80] *Illustrated memorial volume of the Carlyle's House purchase fund committee with catalogue of Carlyle's books and furniture exhibited therein, 1895* (repr. London, 1995), pp. 5–6, 23.

[81] Ibid., p. 3; *Daily Chronicle*, 5 Sept. 1893; *Pall Mall Gazette*, 21 July 1892, p. 6.

[82] *Standard*, 6 Sept. 1894, p. 2.

[83] *Leeds Mercury*, 7 Sept. 1894, p. 3.

[84] Michael Holleran, *Boston's 'changeful times': origins of preservation and planning in America* (Baltimore, MD, 1998), pp. 15–64.

[85] *Dundee Courier and Argus and Northern Warder*, 27 Feb. 1883.

[86] *Illustrated Memorial* (1895, 1995), p. 25.

purchase fund committee along with the American ambassador, Thomas Bayard.[87] Americans gave so generously to the Carlyle House Museum fund, providing around a quarter of the cost, that Ambassador Bayard was offered and accepted the chairmanship of the museum board; several of his successors also served as either chair or as board members.[88] It is unlikely this event took place without government approval. Although this did not represent joint ownership of a site-museum in law, it was an example of cooperative international preservation among voluntarist high-minded idealists with political backing. The house provided a stable and secular reminder of literary and domestic values, and the achievements of literary men. Preserving the house demonstrated the possibilities of group activity at a time that saw the fast-flowing change and excessive individualism which Carlyle sought to mitigate.

International cooperation, shared concerns, the possibility of Anglo-American collaboration, and an acknowledgement of the rising power of the United States were represented in a symbolic gesture when the deeds to Carlyle's House were handed over at the US Embassy (1894) and deposited there for safe keeping.[89] In addition to recognition, the American gift required reciprocity, and for it to be a successful act of diplomacy any return gift had to take 'the correct dialectical form'. The British reciprocal gift adroitly inserted diplomacy (as the art of both collecting and organizing archives, and an understanding of 'the history of international negotiations') into the context of the plunder and preservation dialectic.[90] In a culturally diplomatic exchange, the ambassador returned to Boston with the so-called 'Bradford Manuscript' for display in the Massachusetts State House Museum as part of the 1897 Jubilee celebrations, resolving an American campaign for its return waged over thirty years. Governor Bradford's account of the *Mayflower* voyage and 'history of the "Plimouth plantation"' had been 'preserved' in Fulham Palace library since the War of Independence.[91] British troops had taken the manuscript with them as they withdrew. Some might consider this to have been an act of 'plunder', while others perceive it as a legitimate removal. The diplomatic gesture was regarded by the *Boston Evening Transcript* as a 'gracious act of international courtesy'.[92]

[87] *Illustrated Memorial* (1895, 1995), p. 141; *New York Times*, 30 Nov. 1894, p. 5; *Aberdeen Weekly Journal*, 1 Dec. 1894, p. 5.
[88] *Illustrated Memorial* (1895, 1995), pp. 19, 1154–56. *Boston Globe*, 23 Apr. 1896.
[89] Minutes of First Meeting of (Provisional) Committee of Management, 4 Dec. 1895, London, Carlyle's House Museum Archives.
[90] Harold Nicholson, *Diplomacy* (London, 1950), pp. 23–8, 106.
[91] London, The National Archive, FO 5/2333, Despatches from the Consul at Boston, Sir Dominic Colnaghi, 27 May 1897.
[92] Ibid., from *Boston Evening Transcript*, 26 May 1897.

Complex issues surround considerations of plunder and preservation during the second half of the nineteenth century. In the context of the Anglo-American relationship such issues have an unusually complex texture to them because of shared history, literature, and land. These complexities contributed to redefinitions of the dialectic and of the concepts themselves, as the two great imperial powers negotiated their new diplomatic relationship and came to represent themselves as stewards, rather than plunderers, of culture and nature. Underpinning factors in these redefinitions included the expansion of entrepreneurial capitalist empires, particularly in the New World, with increasingly international reaches; the ability of certain interest groups to act collectively and, if necessary, internationally to protect and represent their political and cultural interests; and the desire of two powerful, democratic empires to represent their presence both physically and culturally by designating specific sites as places of memory for the nation that also had meaning as internationalizing site-museums. New significance came to be associated with notions of *place* and its related hierarchies and power structures, not only through literature and art, or because of changes brought about by industrialization, but as developments in transportation allowed the removal of entire buildings from the 'Old World' to the New. Additionally, in the 'new world' the removal of land from the property register by the nation state for its own (albeit democratic) purposes gave emphasis to specific sites as part of the national heritage.

As 'plunder' was renegotiated in the context of preserving the Anglo-American relationship, regulating alternative internationalizing commercial empires was a consideration, as was preserving peaceful diplomatic relations and stable democracies with fixed reference points. Cooperative preservation of cultural sites indicative of shared interests arguably facilitated cooperation in more contentious political, diplomatic, and economic areas, and helped to ameliorate the consequences of the 'Niagara leap'.

12

Dying Americans:
Race, Extinction, and
Conservation in the New World

SADIAH QURESHI

LAMENTING THE PREDICAMENT of dying races became an increasingly prominent preoccupation in the long nineteenth century. Novelists, painters, scientists, politicians, poets, travel writers, and missionaries all contributed to
creating and perpetuating the sense that some peoples were doomed, perhaps
even providentially predestined, to a speedy extinction. Early modern writers
had long noted the apparent decimation of some indigenous peoples; however, such discussions took on a new and urgent form in the nineteenth century. Although many scholars have explored the notion of dying races in
histories of settler colonialism, modern land rights, or genocide, many have
overlooked the new epistemological status of extinction as a mechanism for
explaining natural change.

Whilst early modern writers mourned the remnants of past peoples, in the
1800s commentators were able to appeal to a new scientific understanding of
extinction: that is to say, a view of the natural world in which extinction was
not only plausible but was often viewed as an endemic feature of natural
change. Once established, the reality of extinction quickly informed how the
relationship between humans and their environment was conceived and
underpinned choices about what or who should be privileged enough to be
conserved. In some cases, the perceived threat mobilized campaigners to petition for conservation measures to protect indigenous peoples. Yet others cast
endangered peoples as the necessary victims of human racial competition, in
which case their expected demise was both mourned and celebrated, and
sometimes actively pursued. This chapter explores how this new understanding of human endangerment became combined with notions of wilderness in
the American context to rationalize policies of Indian dispossession, forced
removal from their traditional homelands, and the establishment of the world's
first national parks. Starting with the shifting epistemological status of extinction in the early decades of the 1800s, the chapter highlights how extinction

Proceedings of the British Academy, **187**, 267–286. © The British Academy 2013.

came to be used to explain the nature of intercultural contact, its relationship to shifting federal Indian policy, and the foundation of the national parks. In doing so, it suggests that humans need to be reintegrated into histories of heritage as both the agents and subjects of environmental change. After all, this was a period during which indigenous peoples shifted from being seen as elements of the natural environment to being characterized as its destroyers. Revealingly, in conservationist circles the emphasis shifted from protecting endangered peoples within their homelands to excluding them in order to privilege flora and fauna. This approach builds on a considerable body of work in which each of these themes is well known; however, in bringing them together, the intention is to highlight fruitful directions for future histories of heritage, endangerment, and conservation.

I

The notion that colonized societies were somehow dying out in the face of contact with white settlers was well established before the nineteenth century. Thomas Jefferson's well-known *Notes on the state of Virginia*, first written in 1781 but only publicly circulated in revised form in 1787, speculated:

> What would be the melancholy sequel of their [Indian] history, may however be argued from the census of 1669; by which we discover that the tribes therein enumerated were, in the space of 62 years, reduced to about one-third of their former numbers. Spirituous liquors, the small-pox, war and an abridgement of territory, to a people who lived principally on the spontaneous productions of nature, had committed terrible havock among them, which generation, under the obstacles opposed to it among them, was not likely to make good.[1]

Jefferson's statistics exaggerated the depletion, since the census he used only included warriors, not the entire population.[2] Nonetheless, in many senses, the fear of imminent loss was well founded, as numerous human societies found themselves ravaged by the new diseases, territorial dispossession, warfare, and genocide due to violent intercultural contact and imperial ambition, particularly expansive settler colonialism.[3] Significantly, the explanatory causes invoked

---

[1] Thomas Jefferson, *Notes on the state of Virginia* (3rd edn., New York, 1801), pp. 139–40 and Anthony F. C. Wallace, *Jefferson and the Indians: the tragic fate of the first Americans* (Cambridge, MA, 1999). In Britain, 'Native American' has long been the preferred term; however, in some American contexts, the term 'Indian' has been reappropriated, as in the National Museum of the American Indian, and so is used in this chapter.
[2] Wallace, *Jefferson and the Indians*, pp. 89–90.
[3] On settler colonialism see James Belich, *Replenishing the earth: the settler revolution and the rise of the Anglo-world, 1783–1939* (Oxford, 2009).

in discussions of human endangerment changed as naturalists' understandings of extinction were transformed in the early decades of the nineteenth century.

Although the disappearance of flora and fauna was hardly unknown, these had been caused by human actions; explaining the loss of species within the context of endemic natural change proved more difficult. Most infamously, the case of the Mauritian dodo, a flightless bird exterminated through hunting in the seventeenth century, indicated the potential for human devastation. However, accepting extinction as a feature of the natural world posed several difficulties throughout the eighteenth century. For many theists and deists alike, the possibility of extinction appeared to undermine the perfection one might expect of a natural world designed by a Supreme Being. Moreover, it contradicted the notion of natural plenitude: the widely accepted proposition that all possible forms of existence, whether living or not, had existed and would continue to do so in order to assure that Creation exhibited the full range of its diversity at any given moment. Accepting, or claiming, that extinction was an endemic feature of natural change 'could therefore seem tantamount to supporting an atheistic view of the world, in which there was no providence, no design, and no plenitude'.[4]

For those unconcerned by the theological ramifications, migration and transmutation appeared to provide plausible explanatory mechanisms for extinction. Naturalists were fundamentally aware that much of the world's flora and fauna remained uncatalogued or even undiscovered. Thus it seemed entirely possible that animals that appeared to be extinct, such as fossilized megafauna, might roam in as yet untrodden lands or in the depths of the oceans. (After all, Jefferson's *Notes on the state of Virginia* famously proposed that megafauna might yet be found wandering in the western terra incognita.) Although much more rarely relied upon, the final option offered the possibility that, rather than disappearing, natural forms had transmuted into their present form. Thus, in the early nineteenth century, the 'three explanations were treated as alternatives, as it were on a par with one another'. Extinction, migration, and transmutation (or, in modern parlance, evolution) all provided viable alternatives, and none was 'obviously more plausible than the others. Each entailed grave difficulties and further problems.'[5]

As an explanation of natural change, extinction gained considerable ground in the late eighteenth and early nineteenth centuries in light of the work of the French comparative anatomist Georges Cuvier. Appointed in the wake of the French Revolution to the newly formed Musée d'histoire naturelle in Paris, Cuvier quickly established himself as the premier authority on fossils

---

[4] Martin Rudwick, *Bursting the limits of time: the reconstruction of geohistory in the age of revolution* (Chicago, 2005), p. 244.
[5] Rudwick, *Bursting the limits of time*, p. 243.

and functionalist comparative anatomy. Most famously, he developed the notion of the 'correlation of parts' to argue that animals' internal assemblages were interdependent; thus, even with fragmentary empirical evidence in hand, such as a handful of bones, Cuvier felt able to make educated guesses regarding the overall structure of the entire animal. Based on this method, in 1796 Cuvier published a paper comparing the remains of a fossil elephant to living examples of both Asian and African elephants, and suggested that the fossil elephant was both a distinct species and extinct.[6] The paper became the first of several examining fossilized remains, including a second look at elephants and an offering on the mastodon in 1806.[7] Such detailed research increasingly appeared irrefutable and thus helped establish extinction as a reality.

Accepting extinction as an endemic natural process had significant repercussions for discussions of intercultural encounter, since theories of extinction were quickly used to explain, and even rationalize, human population decimations. For instance, eighteenth- and nineteenth-century stadial theories of human development proposed that humanity passed from 'savagery' to 'civilization' based on changes in modes of subsistence; four distinctive stages, usually defined by hunting, pasturage, agriculture, and, finally, commerce, were each associated with given practices of social, political, and civil organization as well as manners and morals.[8] In these schemes, indigenous societies would inevitably disappear as people were assimilated into settler society and so progressed onto ostensibly higher stages of human development. Alternatively, some argued indigenous peoples were fixed in their nature or so closely tied to the environments in which they lived that they were incapable of improvement and, unless removed or protected, would inevitably fall by the wayside.[9]

Over the course of the nineteenth century it became increasingly expedient to explain the fate of peoples identified as doomed in terms of racialized differences; in this guise, extinction became a necessary by-product that would be observed wherever different human varieties met, and might even be pursued through attempts at active extermination. For instance, in 1864 the anthropologist Richard Lee presented a paper for the Anthropological Society of London (f. 1863) in which he argued that:

> The rapid disappearance of aboriginal tribes before the advance of civilisation is one of the many remarkable incidents of the present age. In every new country, from America to New Zealand, from Freemantle to Honolulu, it is observable, and seems to be a *necessary result of an approximation of different races,*

[6] Mark V. Barrow, Jr, *Nature's ghosts: confronting extinction from the age of Jefferson to the age of ecology* (Chicago, 2009), pp. 39–42.
[7] Barrow, *Nature's ghosts*, p. 370, n. 103.
[8] Ronal Meek, *Social science and the ignoble savage* (Cambridge, 1976) and Roxann Wheeler, *The complexion of race: categories of difference in eighteenth-century culture* (Philadelphia, PA, 2000).
[9] Ronald N. Satz, *American Indian policy in the Jacksonian era* (Lincoln, NE, 1975).

peculiar, however, in degree, at least, *to this portion of the world's history*. It has been estimated that the Hawaiians have been reduced as much as eighty-five per cent during the last hundred years. The natives of Tasmania are almost, if not quite, extinct. The Maories are passing away at the rate of about twenty five per cent every fourteen years, and in Australia, as in America, whole tribes have disappeared before the advance of the white man.[10]

Lee's 'The extinction of races' illustrates that, in some circles, the population depletions seen in settler colonies were quickly being naturalized as the endemic process of human extinction, rather than the outcome of policies many now see as genocidal.[11] His chilling list of colonialism's casualties and his hypothesis that such destruction was an apparently 'necessary' feature of 'different races' coming into contact effectively sought to rationalize human endangerment as an inevitable feature of global human contact, even as he noted its prevalence in the 'present' age.

Perhaps most famously, in 1871 Charles Darwin's *Descent of man* proposed that when 'civilised nations come into contact with barbarians the struggle is short, except where a deadly climate gives its aid to the native race'. Expanding further on the consequences of his evolutionary theory for human history, he noted:

> Extinction follows chiefly from the competition of tribe with tribe, and race with race. Various checks are always in action ... which serve to keep down the numbers of each savage tribe,—such as periodical famines, the wandering of the parents and the consequent deaths of infants, prolonged suckling, the stealing of women, wars, accidents, sickness, licentiousness, especially infanticide, and, perhaps, lessened fertility from less nutritious food, and many hardships. If from any cause any one of these checks is lessened, even in a slight degree, the tribe thus favoured will tend to increase; and when one of two adjoining tribes becomes more numerous and powerful than the other, the contest is soon settled by war, slaughter, cannibalism, slavery, and absorption. Even when a weaker tribe is not thus abruptly swept away, if it once begins to decrease, it generally goes on decreasing until it is extinct.[12]

Darwin essentially recast intercultural encounters and conflict as a form of human selection that functioned at a group level (whether of nations, races, or tribes): wherever different peoples came into contact, and thus competed for resources, their respective degrees of social and cultural development were

---

[10] Richard Lee, 'The extinction of races', *Journal of the Anthropological Society of London*, 2 (1864), pp. xcv–xcix, my emphasis.

[11] See the treatment of such colonial activity in Ben Kiernan, *Blood and soil: a world history of genocide and extermination from Sparta to Darfur* (Princeton, NJ, 2007) and A. Dirk Moses, ed., *Empire, colony, genocide: conquest, occupation, and subaltern resistance in world history* (Oxford, 2008).

[12] Charles Darwin, *The descent of man, and selection in relation to sex* (London, 1871), p. 238.

argued to determine who would shortly outlive their rivals. Thus, in Darwin's view, an inhospitable climate remained the only hope for the ostensibly uncivilized or weaker peoples. Such views gained further purchase as some peoples were argued to have become genuinely extinct. Notoriously, in 1869 William Lanney, widely perceived as the last Tasmanian man, and, in 1876 Trugernanner, reported to be the last Tasmanian woman, passed away.[13]

Prophesied doom did not go unchallenged. Thomas Bendyshe, who translated the *Anthropological treatise of Johann Friedrich Blumenbach* (1865), presented an alternative explanation at the same meeting of the Society at which Lee had spoken. Deeply dismissive of those who claimed human extinction was Providential will, he acknowledged that human populations were declining in numerous colonized lands, including North America; nonetheless, he insisted that predestined extinction had been predicted with 'some unphilosophical haste' since it had yet to be established as a 'fact'. In contrast, he proposed the 'more reasonable view' that 'races have only been, or brought to the verge of extinction' when other peoples occupied their land at the same time as their 'number was in the process of diminution through the operation of the same causes to which all races are periodically subject'.[14] Thus, according to Bendyshe, if favourable conditions were able to re-emerge, through natural change or artificial encouragement, endangered peoples would be able to recover from the demographic depletion.

American writers contributed heavily to the creation and promotion of a naturalized view of human extinction. Theodor Waitz's *Introduction to anthropology* (1863), for instance, observed that craniometrist Samuel Morton, Harvard-based natural historian Louis Agassiz, and their followers had created an 'American School' which promoted the view that since the extinction of the 'lower races is predestined by nature ... it would appear that we must not merely acknowledge the right of the white American to destroy the red man, but perhaps praise him that he has constituted himself the instrument of Providence in carrying out and promoting this law of destruction. The pious manslayer thus enjoys the consolation that he acts according to the laws of nature which govern the rise and extinction of races.'[15] Although not convinced by these claims, Waitz's work, originally published in Germany in 1859, indicates how American theorists were becoming internationally associated with rationalizing exterminationist political policies by promoting human

---

[13] Patrick Bratlinger, *Dark vanishings: discourse on the extinction of primitive races, 1800–1930* (Ithaca, NY, and London, 2003) and Lyndall Ryan, *The aboriginal Tasmanians* (St Lucia, 1981).
[14] T[homas] Bendyshe, 'On the extinction of races', *Journal of the Anthropological Society of London*, 2 (1864), pp. xcix–cxii, at xcix and ci–cii. See also Brian Dippie, *The vanishing American: white attitudes and U.S. Indian policy* (Lawrence, KA, 1982), pp. 122–38.
[15] Theodor Waitz, *Introduction to anthropology*, ed. J. Frederick Collingwood (London, 1863), p. 351.

extinction as desirable and an inevitable by-product of intercultural contact (long before Darwin's own work on human evolution). As the notion of human extinction became entrenched within the sciences, anthropologists increasingly sought to catalogue, classify, and preserve dying races before they disappeared entirely. Like museum relics, some humans were increasingly likely to be seen as remnants of the human past.[16] Meanwhile, by direct appeal or implication, notions of human endangerment underpinned changing political policies on indigenous peoples' futures.

II

In the American context, it has been argued that in the early nineteenth century the idea of vanishing Indians was nurtured by nationalist writers who incorporated it into an epic tale of America's progressive civilization and progress. In this epic, Native Americans became ancient inhabitants who were doomed to disappear in the face of presumed progress, much as the ancient Britons had in Britain.[17] One of the best-known uses of this kind of narrative is to be found in the work of painter and collector George Catlin. Although well known, Catlin's career is worth considering because he provides an excellent example of how closely entangled were notions of wilderness, endangerment, and conservation in the early to mid-nineteenth century, and provides a contrast with the later period. In the 1830s, Catlin spent six years wandering the plains and Rocky Mountains of North America in an effort to document its inhabitants, whilst also amassing an enormous collection of artefacts from the various First Nations amongst whom he found hospitality. Ultimately, Catlin hoped to make his mark and fortune by selling the entire collection to the American government as a comprehensive record of its vanishing people. When this venture failed, Catlin toured the British, European, and American lecture circuits in the 1840s, accompanied by three groups of Anishinabe and Bakhoje. Catlin's shows publicized the plight of peoples whom he believed were in danger of either being wiped out entirely or, to their profound detriment, losing their cultural identity by becoming assimilated into urban American life.[18]

---

[16] Jacob Gruber, 'Ethnographic salvage and the shaping of anthropology', *American Anthropologist*, 72 (1970), pp. 1289–99.

[17] A. von Riper, *Men among the mammoths: Victorian science and the discovery of human prehistory* (Chicago, 1993).

[18] Kate Flint, *The Transatlantic Indian, 1776–1930* (Princeton, NJ, 2009) and Sadiah Qureshi, *Peoples on parade: exhibitions, empire and anthropology in nineteenth-century Britain* (Chicago, 2011).

Significantly, Catlin set out on his trek precisely because, like many others, he was utterly persuaded that the Indians and the pristine wilderness in which they lived were endangered.[19] His sense of urgency was aided by the fact that he set off on his trek in the wake of significant shifts in federal Indian policy.[20] In 1830, under the presidency of Andrew Jackson, the United States passed legislation that came to be known as the Indian Removal Act and which, for the first time, legalized the forced removal of peoples east of the Mississippi to the west. Suggested by Jefferson and James Monroe, but enforced by Jackson, the legislation was publicly rationalized by the claim that, if nothing was done, the spectre of certain extinction hovered over the eastern nations. Infamously, in 1829 Jackson's first Annual Message to Congress had claimed that:

> Our ancestors found them [Indians] the uncontrolled possessors of these vast regions. By persuasion and force, they have been made to retire from river to river, and from mountain to mountain; until some of the tribes have become extinct, and others have left but remnants, to preserve, for a while, their once terrible names. Surrounded by the whites, with their arts of civilization, which, by destroying the resources of the savage, doom him to weakness and decay; the fate of the Mohegan, the Narragansett, and the Delaware, is fast overtaking the Choctaw, the Cherokee, and the Creek. That this fate surely awaits them, if they remain within the limits of the States, does not admit of a doubt. Humanity and national honor demand that every effort should be made to avert such a great calamity.[21]

Bitterly fought over, the legislation eventually passed with a majority of just one vote.[22] Jackson's development of and commitment to the policy, especially in the face of such vigorous opposition, suggests how in some circles the prospects for assimilation, the other available option, were deemed either practically unfeasible or impossible. Instead, since westward expansion could not be halted (or willingly and easily contemplated), its effects on indigenous populations could be alleviated, Jackson expediently argued, only by enforced relocation to a designated territory of the government's choosing. Catlin began his travels up the Missouri River in the wake of these policy shifts and in full expectation of the impending disappearance of his subjects.[23] As a

---

[19] John Hausdoerfer, *Catlin's lament: Indians, manifest destiny and the ethics of nature* (Lawrence, KA, 2009).

[20] S. Lyman Tyler, *A history of Indian policy* (Washington, DC, 1973); Francis Paul Prucha, *The Great Father: the United States government and the American Indians* (2 vols. combined, Lincoln, NE, 1995).

[21] Andrew Jackson, 'First annual message, Dec. 8 1829', in N. H. Concord, ed., *Messages of Gen. Andrew Jackson with a short sketch of his life* (Boston, MA, 1837), pp. 39–68, at p. 61.

[22] Satz, *American Indian policy*. See also R. Douglas Hurt, *The Indian Frontier, 1763–1846* (Albuquerque, NM, 2002).

[23] Hausdoerfer, *Catlin's lament*; Mark David Spence, *Dispossessing the wilderness: Indian removal and the making of the national parks* (Oxford, 1999); Kathryn S. Hight, '"Doomed to perish": George Catlin's depictions of the Mandan', *Art Journal*, 49 (1990), pp. 119–24.

result of these kinds of discussion and romantic idealization, in the early to mid-nineteenth century 'real Indians' come to be thought of as either belonging to the past when their populations were more abundant, or west of the (as yet uncolonized) Mississippi River. Eastern Indians were often argued to have been deeply corrupted by their contact with settlers, practically non-existent, or in desperate need of paternalistic protection from possible extinction.[24] Moreover, Jackson simultaneously argued that the policy would protect the relocated peoples whilst presiding over an Act that made provision for future Indian extinction by stating that the 'United States will forever secure and guaranty to them [removed Indians], and their heirs or successors, the country so exchanged with them ... *Provided always*, That such lands shall revert to the United States, if the Indians become extinct, or abandon the same.'[25] In doing so, the Act reinforced the expectation that extinction was not only possible, but should be pre-emptively written into national legislation.

The 1840s and 1850s witnessed significant westward expansion, increasing pressure to acquire Indian lands, and a shift in Indian policy from removal to confinement on reservations.[26] For instance, between 1845 and 1850, the Union expanded as Texas, California, and Oregon either gained statehood or came under US control, and Mexico ceded a vast southwestern territory after the Mexican–American War.[27] 'It was not long, however, before the idea of moving a *few* Indians out of the way became a policy of confining *all* Indians in the out-of-the-way places.'[28] Reservations differed from previous Indian territories by allowing for rather more than the enforced relocation of numerous groups into more colonially convenient locations; instead, they were tied to paternalistic attempts to control and assimilate indigenous peoples. It has been suggested that the reservation system, as set up in California, was modelled on the use of asylums in broader contexts to isolate problematic individuals in special environments in order to correct perceived shortcomings.

[24] Dippie, *The Vanishing American*.
[25] Indian Removal Act, 28 May 1830, repr. in Francis Paul Prucha, ed., *Documents of United States Indian policy* (Lincoln, NE, 1975), pp. 52–3.
[26] On the development of reservations see Joel R. Hyer, *'We are not savages': Native Americans in southern California and the Pala Reservation, 1840–1920* (East Lansing, MI, 2001); George Harwood Phillips, *Indians and Indian agents: the origins of the reservation system in California, 1849–1852* (Norman, OK, 1997); Jane F. Lancaster, *Removal aftershock: the Seminoles' struggles to survive in the West, 1836–1866* (Knoxville, TN, 1994); Brad Asher, *Beyond the reservation: Indians, settlers, and the law in Washington Territory, 1853–1889* (Norman, OK, 1999); Richard J. Perry, *Apache reservation: indigenous peoples and the American state* (Austin, TX, 1993); and David J. Wishart, *Unspeakable sadness: the dispossession of the Nebraska Indians* (Lincoln, NE, 1994).
[27] See Robert M. Utley, *The Indian frontier, 1846–1890* (Albuquerque, NM, 1984) and Ned Blackhawk, *Violence over the land: Indians and empires in the early American West* (Boston, MA, 2006) for broader shifts in this period.
[28] Phillips, *Indians and Indian agents*, p. 4.

Moreover, since the reservation had been 'designed as a movable asylum, both keepers and inmates came to see the reserve as a transient institution'.[29] Paradoxically, supporters argued that such confinement and segregation was essential to eventual assimilation; in effect, reservations were intended to function as an intermediate zone (temporal and spatial) between colonial encroachment and future citizenship.

By 1865, suspected governmental corruption and inefficiency within the Bureau of Indian Affairs, tensions between settlers and Indians following the Civil War, and events such as the Sand Creek massacre of 1864 prompted a congressional investigation into Indian affairs.[30] Senator Doolittle's subsequent report on the *Condition of the Indian tribes* (1867) summarized the responses to a questionnaire initially circulated to politicians, army officers, agents, and missionaries. Although predominantly concerned with how to improve the Indian service and the future of the Bureau of Indian Affairs (the report recommended it remain with the Department of the Interior rather than be moved to the War Department), it also collated information on the state of indigenous populations and the best way to tackle any perceived problems. Significantly, twenty of the twenty-seven respondents felt that Indian populations were decreasing, whilst only one observed an increase. The demise was attributed to factors as diverse as 'Providence, the encroachment of the white man, civilization in all its forms, inefficient and unfaithful agents, injustice and abuse, want of proper judicious attention—all these cause the extinction of the Indian race.'[31] The remedial measures proposed ranged from 'there is none' to 'the only practical remedy to prevent the total extinction of the Indian tribes, is to separate them entirely from the white race'.[32] Ultimately, the committee suggested that as traditional 'hunting grounds are taken away, the reservation system, which is the only alternative to their extermination, must be adopted'.[33] The extensive report provides a fascinating insight into mid-century perceptions of decline. Crucially, it also suggests how the notion of human endangerment contributed to discussions on the future of federal Indian policy and the reform of the Indian service. After all, one of the professed roles of the service was to protect the indigenous populations as best they could until they were either entirely assimilated or extirpated.

---

[29] John M. Findlay, 'An elusive institution: the birth of Indian reservations in gold rush California', in George Pierre Castile and Robert L. Bee, eds., *State and reservation: new perspectives on federal Indian policy* (Tucson, AZ, 1992), pp. 19–21, at p. 19.

[30] Donald Chaput, 'Generals, Indian agents, politicians: the Doolittle survey of 1865', *Western Historical Quarterly*, 3 (1972), pp. 269–82. See also Blackhawk, *Violence over the land*.

[31] US Congress, Senate, *Condition of the Indian tribes: report of the joint special committee appointed under joint resolution of March 3, 1965* (Washington, DC, 1867), p. 428. Better known as the Doolittle report.

[32] Ibid., pp. 472 and 440 respectively.

[33] Ibid., p. 7.

In the 1880s, federal Indian policy shifted again in an interventionist attempt to transform Indian subsistence through the use of allotment. In 1887, Senator Henry Dawes guided the General Allotment Act into the statute books. Coupled with mission schools and industrial training, the period witnessed an aggressive push towards assimilation, which continued until 1934 when Franklin Roosevelt's Indian New Deal abolished allotment and attempted to restore Indian self-government.[34] Essentially, the Act legalized the partition of reservations into small holdings that were owned by individual Indians, rather than held in common by a tribe, and also conferred citizenship upon holders of allotted land. Significantly, by stipulating how much land individuals needed, the Dawes Act effectively endorsed the federal redistribution of 'surplus' land for purchase by settlers and commercial development, particularly by railway companies. Intended to create a nation dependent on farming, its supporters hoped that it would free up valuable, and currently 'wasted', lands. Spurred on by the conviction that hunting and gathering was fundamentally inefficient when compared to an agrarian subsistence, supporters of allotment consistently argued that Indians must be 'civilized' for the good of both the nation and themselves.[35] In this sense, reformers followed in the vein of Jefferson, who had dreamed of transforming Indians into yeoman farmers.[36] Meanwhile, as noted by its original Indian 'beneficiaries' and subsequent historians, the Act implicitly depended upon the notion of human extinction, since it made no provision for a future increase in Indian populations.[37] Meanwhile, just as the notion of human endangerment underpinned shifts in federal Indian policy throughout the nineteenth century, by the late 1800s it had simultaneously become associated with new conservationist agendas in the formation of the national parks.

III

In 1832, as part of Catlin's campaign to promote the protection of Indians, he envisioned a future in which 'by some great protecting policy of government', the nation's realms would be

> preserved in their pristine beauty and wilderness, in a *magnificent park*, where the world could see for ages to come, the native Indian in his classic attire, galloping with his wild horse, with sinewy bow, and shield and lance, amid the

[34] Tyler, *A history of Indian policy*.
[35] Philip Burnham, *Indian country, God's country: Native Americans and national parks* (Washington, DC, 2002), pp. 35–9.
[36] Wallace, *Jefferson and the Indians*.
[37] Dippie, *The vanishing American*; Burnham, *Indian country, God's country*.

fleeting herds of elks and buffaloes. What a beautiful and thrilling specimen for America to preserve and hold up to the view of her refined citizens and the world, in future ages! A *nation's Park*, containing man and beast, in all the wild and freshness of their nature's beauty.[38]

Catlin's well-known dream has often led to him being credited with inventing the notion of a national park. Whether one chooses to accept this genealogy or not, it is particularly pertinent that his vision emerged out of a sense that parks might prevent Indian extermination. Moreover, he not only included Indians within park boundaries, but expected them to continue using the land in their customary ways. Yet, as the century wore on, the land's ancestral inhabitants were increasingly likely to be literally and figuratively excised from their homelands. Catlin's American landscapes usually included Indians as a means of indicating his subjects' pristine and untouched nature. Likewise, Thomas Cole, founder of the Hudson River School of American landscape painting, often used such figures to indicate 'wildness' in a way that was consistent with romantic notions of a once noble, but now doomed, race. In contrast, by the mid-century wilderness has been redefined as natural landscape that was both untouched and uninhabited by humans. Thus, images such as Thomas Moran's *Mountain of the Holy Cross* (1875) or Charles M. Russell's painting *When the land belonged to God* (1914) relied upon using nature's sublime quality to help establish wilderness as the pristine creation of Providence and protected from human interference.[39] Ultimately, this notion of wilderness underpinned a new way of furthering forced relocation and progressive territorial dispossession.

National parks, the crown jewels of American environmental heritage, both created and perpetuated a vision of wilderness in which the nation's landscapes were devoid of continued human presence. Whilst California's Yosemite was established as the first state park in 1864, Yellowstone became the world's first national park in 1872.[40] Over the century, a variety of arguments were proposed in favour of creating this new heritage solution. In the earliest campaigns, they were often justified as a means of creating national monuments. Whilst campaigners regularly argued that the parks were areas of unmatched natural splendour, they consistently reiterated their agricultural or commercial worthlessness. Meanwhile, powerful corporations such as the railway companies lent their support to the movement in an effort to secure the custom of future tourists.[41] As has been acknowledged, these cam-

---

[38] George Catlin, *Letters and notes on the manners, customs and condition of the North American Indians* (2 vols., London, 1841), i, p. 262.

[39] This discussion draws heavily from Spence, *Dispossessing the wilderness*.

[40] Burnham, *Indian country, God's country*, p. 20.

[41] Ibid., p. 19.

paigns ironically began promoting the virtues of communal ownership in an era when the Dawes Act sought to remedy the 'problem' of tribal ownership because it was seen as uncivilized and as perpetuating 'heathen' forms of 'socialism' or 'communism'.[42] In later years, as the concern regarding the extinction of flora and fauna gained ground, the arguments shifted to favour conservationist agendas, with campaigners arguing that the parks offered a sanctuary for endangered species.[43]

In recent years, there has been considerable interest in traditional uses of national parkland. Such work has drawn attention to the ways in which Indian uses of their homelands were consistently misunderstood and suppressed in order to create the national parks.[44] In most cases, the parks were cobbled together from First Nations' lands, which sometimes became entirely enclosed within the newly established reservations, and their ownership transferred to the United States of America. For example, Yellowstone (f. 1872) had been used regularly by Sheepeater, Crow, Shoshone, Nez Perce Bannock, Flathead, Blackfeet, and Tukedeka groups; Yosemite (made national in 1890) was home to Miwok groups; Mesa Verde (f. 1906) was associated with the Utes and Anasazi; Glacier National Park (f. 1910) was home to the Blackfeet; whilst the Grand Canyon (f. 1919) was used by the Hopi and Navajo. In creating parks, the government often insisted on transferring land into national ownership and extinguishing subsistence rights to activities such as hunting or timber use. Moreover, the establishment of the parks frequently involved coercive land transfer and owed much to successful lobbying from corporations.[45] Simultaneously, in the earliest park campaigns, park officials argued that they needed to rid the park of Indian inhabitants in case they scared visitors and therefore spoiled their enjoyment of the parks.[46] Later in the century, traditional uses of the land came to be seen as environmentally ignorant and so provided new grounds for rationalizing indigenous exclusion in favour of federal management. For instance, officials began arguing that Indians must be removed because their ostensibly ignorant behaviour, such as hunting and lighting fires, was damaging the pristine nature of the American wilderness and possibly causing the extinction of flora and fauna. In this context, Indians became seen as the destroyers of wilderness. Thus, it has been argued that the removal undertaken at the park's set-up has to be seen within the context of the 'American Wonderland' and fears that Indians might stop tourists from enjoying the park's pleasures, rather than an immediate concern with environmental protection.

[42] Ibid., p. 37.
[43] Barrow, *Nature's Ghosts*; Spence, *Dispossessing the wilderness*.
[44] Spence, *Dispossessing the wilderness*; Burnham, *Indian country, God's country*, and Michael F. Turek, *American Indians and national parks* (Tuscon, AZ, 1998).
[45] Burnham, *Indian country, God's country*, p. 9 and pp. 16–19.
[46] Spence, *Dispossessing the wilderness*, pp. 54–6.

National parks were routinely promoted as untouched wildernesses; however, maintaining this 'wilderness' usually involved considerable effort: customary uses of the land were denied or suppressed and traditional uses of parkland had to be policed. For instance, Nathaniel Langford's *Diary of the Washburn expedition to Yellowstone and Firehole rivers* (1905) alleged that the notion of establishing Yellowstone as a national park had occurred to a group of Montana men with whom he was trekking and camping in the areas basins in the summer of 1870. One evening, around the campfire, they discussed the best means of publicizing their adventures. Some proposed that they should lay claim to the land, divide it between them, and then profit from the tourists who would inevitably follow when the public learned of the wonders they had seen. One man, Cornelius Hedges, vehemently disagreed, saying that the whole area ought to be set aside as a national park. Quickly converted, they agreed to try and establish the park as soon as possible.[47] In their later campaigns to establish the park, the group would later claim that the land was no longer used by Indians (falsely claiming that they were scared of the geysers) and so was available for the nation; however, as recent histories of the American conservation movement show, despite their claims, these campaigners were well aware of the Indian presence. For instance, they not only requested a military escort to offer them protection from the Indian populations but they met bands of Crow passing through the area. They also saw several abandoned camps on their travels through the landscape. Instead of recognizing them as seasonal dwellings that were temporarily out of use, the group dismissed them as marks made by ancient inhabitants rather than contemporary populations or, in the case of the Crow whom they saw whilst trekking, plains Indians anomalously seeking refuge in mountains.[48]

The measures taken to suppress Indian use overlooked the fact that much of the environments the parks sought to preserve had been created by human intervention. For example, in Yellowstone, hunting had led to the extinction of ancient varieties of animal such as the horse, bison, and camel in this region. With their disappearance, subsistence patterns changed to incorporate the area's plants and smaller animals and continued into the late nineteenth century. Indians used the thermal properties of the park's geysers to prepare food, aid healing, and as sites for religious worship. Meanwhile, the area contained ancient campsites, formed part of a trade network in obsidian, and was marked with a trail system, which is still followed by modern park highways. Crucially, fires were regularly lit to manage the undergrowth and

[47] Keller and Turek, *American Indians and national parks*, p. 23; Spence, *Dispossessing the wilderness*.
[48] Spence, *Dispossessing the wilderness*, pp. 41–54; Keller and Turek, *American Indians and national parks*, pp. 24–6.

help promote the flora and fauna on which Indians subsisted.[49] By promoting a vision of wilderness in which human usage was either systematically erased or denied, the national parks contributed to a broader current that has continued to hold sway in some conservationist circles. Yet, as environmental historians have consistently argued, this presents considerable problems for both historians and policy-makers. By effectively denying human intervention, use, and management of nature as legitimate or desirable, this narrow vision of wilderness creates a bipolar bind in which the 'natural' and 'artificial' vie against each other.[50]

Although the use of national parkland remains heavily contested to the present by many First Nations, ultimately, the park officials managed to win a victory of sorts. In Yosemite, Miwok villages were strategically razed to the ground whilst the peoples were starved or froze.[51] In Yellowstone, treaty-making progressively ceded ever larger portions of Indian territory to the nation. In 1886 park grounds received military protection, and in 1894 hunting was criminalized in park grounds.[52] These kinds of protectionist activity systematically redefined customary uses of the land as 'poaching' or criminal damage. The measures taken in Yellowstone were successful enough for George Wingate to gloat, 'The Indian difficulty has been cured, the Indians have been forced back on their distant reservations, and the traveller in the park will see or hear no more of them than if he was in the Adirondacks or White Mountains.'[53] Thus, as parks were established and lands ceded, reservations, the parks' human corollaries, became home to ever more people. However, despite Wingate's assertions, considerable tensions were caused as Indians continued to cross parklands and make use of the land away from the tourist trails. Such persistent resistance left many early conservationists clamouring for a more effective means of ensuring that Indians remained on their allotted reservations and off parkland.[54] In this sense, reservations gained a new role in both perpetuating Indian dispossession and the protecting of the environment. Crucially, Yellowstone set precedents that were followed when further national parks were created, such as the National Glacier Park and at Yosemite.[55]

Whilst for Catlin a national park would provide a means of protecting vanishing Indians, by the time the parks were established they became associated with a new vision of wilderness that implicitly came to promote the

[49] Keller and Turek, *American Indians and national parks*, p. 22.
[50] William Cronon, 'The trouble with wilderness; or, getting back to the wrong nature', in idem, ed., *Uncommon ground: rethinking the human place in nature* (New York, 1995), pp. 69–90. Reprinted in *Environmental History*, 1 (1996), pp. 7–28.
[51] Keller and Turek, *American Indians and national parks*, p. 21.
[52] Spence, *Dispossessing the wilderness*, pp. 55–70.
[53] George W. Wingate, *Through the Yellowstone park on horseback* (New York, 1886), p. 140.
[54] Spence, *Dispossessing the wilderness*, pp. 62–70.
[55] Ibid.

notion of Indians as belonging to the past. For early tourists the Indian presence was usually either absent, minimal, or heavily stage-managed. For example, many Indians began to retreat from the tourist trails, coerced by the official move to curtail their activities.[56] Meanwhile, Indians such as the Blackfeet at Glacier National Park sometimes worked as tour guides or performed set pieces designed to showcase their lifestyles to the paying public. In this sense, they provided entertainment as exemplars of America's earliest peoples, or '"past-tense" Indians', rather than the present-day dispossessed.[57] Moreover, in 1906 Congress introduced legislation known as the Antiquities Act, which allowed the removal of land from public sale if it was deemed of sufficient historical significance. Partly introduced to preserve Indian relics, the Act nonetheless celebrated '*ancient* Indian peoples, not contemporary' groups.[58] Such attention to preserving Indian antiquities, especially in park grounds, further contributed to the sense that the land was no longer inhabited by humans; yet, it simultaneously undermined the very notion of wilderness that park officials were attempting to stage-manage in conservationist circles. Thus, as historians of the parks have argued, 'With newcomers believing that the land was virgin or that native populations would soon disappear, early park experiences seemed to confirm this bias.'[59] Meanwhile, America's parks provided a global model for the emergence of protected natural landscapes for both the later nineteenth and early twentieth centuries.

IV

America was home to the world's first national parks, but its earliest conservation ventures, such as Yellowstone, set precedents that were quickly repeated worldwide. Other former British possessions quickly took up the 'American experiment' including Canada (1887), Australia (1879, 1891, and 1915), and New Zealand (1894). In particular, the use of military personnel in park management, the growing importance attached to environmental conservation (often equating to an advocacy of wilderness), and the development of both a national and international tourist trade became common features. In Britain, the campaigning for national parks began early in the twentieth century but failed to see fruition until after the Second World War. Meanwhile, significant conservationist efforts were expended in Africa with the establishment of Kenya's Kruger Park in 1926, and Tanzania's Serengeti Park in 1948. In the

[56] Burnham, *Indian country, God's country.*
[57] Spence, *Dispossessing the wilderness*, pp. 71–82, at p. 71, and Keller and Turek, *American Indians and national parks*, pp. 56–64.
[58] Burnham, *Indian country, God's country*, pp. 48–59, at p. 49.
[59] Keller and Turek, *American Indians and national parks*, p. 20.

mid-twentieth century, American interest turned towards addressing the issue of conservation globally, rather than nationally, as the campaign to establish the first international inventory of extinction flourished.[60]

Of these sites, Kenya, formerly British East Africa Protectorate, provides one of the most instructive counterparts in terms of territorial dispossession, environmental conservation, and modern political significance through the case of the Maasai.[61] In 1904, in order to clear the way for white settlement, the British relocated the nomadic Maasai from their favoured grazing grounds to two reserves, on the promise that they would retain their right to these areas 'so long as the Masai as a race shall exist'.[62] Yet, between 1911 and 1913, over 20,000 northern Maasai were moved at gunpoint to a new southern reserve, which they considered to be of inferior quality, resulting in a loss of land estimated at between 50 and 70 per cent. In 1913, a group of Maasai launched an ultimately unsuccessful attempt to legally challenge the territorial dispossession.

The relocation of the Maasai presents several *thematic* parallels to the American formation of the national parks. For instance, Lord Cranworth's *A colony in the making* (1912) presents a history of British East Africa in which white settlers arrived to find 'large tracts of splendid grazing land, apparently not occupied at all, certainly not utilised' that they aspired to cultivate. Such aspirations left the Maasai in 'danger of degeneration if not of extermination' unless a 'reserve large enough to allow them to carry on their own mode of wandering life' was created or they 'abandon[ed] their habits and gradually' became 'useful members of society by curtailing their area and interspersing it with European farms and settlements'.[63] In this sense, the notion of endangerment played an important role in rationalizing the choice to relocate and, as the original treaty suggests, the possible future extinction of the Maasai was anticipated. Moreover, the relocation was not originally undertaken for the purposes of environmental conservation, but to open up land for settlement; only later did it become associated with conservationist agendas and the protection of flora and fauna. Likewise, modern political activists have consistently sought to reassert their ownership and seek restitution in debates that play an important role in determining ethnic identity. Whilst these claims

---

[60] William M. Adams, *Against extinction: the story of conservation* (London, 2004), pp. 67–100, at p. 78. On the international conservation movement in relationship to animals see Barrow, *Nature's ghosts*, especially pp. 135–67.
[61] See the excellent Lotte Hughes, 'Rough time in paradise: claims, blames and memory making around some protected areas in Kenya', *Conservation and Society*, 5 (2007), pp. 307–30, and idem, 'Malice in Maasailand: the historical roots of current political struggles', *African Affairs*, 104 (2005), pp. 202–24.
[62] Cited in Hughes, 'Rough time in paradise', p. 310.
[63] Lord Cranworth, *A colony in the making: or sport and profit in British East Africa* (London, 1912), pp. 35–6.

clearly have a strong historical basis, activists erase the use of the land by other groups such as the Kikuyu, and inaccurately argue that the Maasai actively fought to save their land in 1904, as they seek to reconcile their desire to return with the historical act of departure.[64] It is beyond the scope of this chapter to argue for a direct genealogical relationship between the American and African examples discussed here and it is crucial that comparative studies remain alert to regional specificities.[65] Nonetheless, the similarities are instructive as they indicate the rich potential for both a global history of human endangerment and new opportunities for historians of heritage.

V

It has been beyond the scope of this chapter to provide anything but the briefest sketch of how science was mobilized in debates over human endangerment and conservationism; however, examining the notion of endangered peoples, particularly within the formative American context, raises issues that are of considerable relevance for broader histories of heritage.

Exploring human endangerment presents valuable opportunities to make histories of the environment and heritage more balanced, by reintegrating humans within these histories as both the subjects and agents of conservation policy. Many studies of heritage and environmental conservation not only focus on campaigns in favour of conservation, but tend to focus on large mammals, such as the tiger or the World Wildlife Fund's iconic panda; buildings; and special, often aesthetically spectacular, sites such as the Taj Mahal, Stonehenge, or Yellowstone. By contrast, human endangerment is often discussed in separate literatures, for example within the context of land rights, the emergence of the reservation system, or genocide.[66] Yet, these separate histories often take for granted a potentially anachronistic distinction between humans and their natural environment. Throughout the nineteenth century, but especially in the early 1800s, natural history was a broadly defined field in

---

[64] Hughes, 'Rough time in paradise' and idem, 'Malice in Maasailand'.

[65] For instance, in Canada's Banff National Park, aboriginal peoples' exclusion was rationalized primarily in order to preserve game (rather than wildlife more broadly), stimulate hunting tourism, and promote assimilation rather than to promote the notion of wilderness. Significantly, in the Canadian context, this exclusion occurred in a period when human inhabitation was both common and not subject to the same forms of exclusion seen in the American context. Theodore Binnema and Melanie Niemi, '"Let the line be drawn now": wilderness, conservation, and the exclusion of aboriginal people from Banff National Park', *Environmental History*, 11 (2006), pp. 724–50.

[66] In addition to the material already cited see David Maybury-Lewis, 'Genocide against indigenous peoples', in Alexander Laban Hinton, ed., *Annihilating difference: the anthropology of genocide* (Berkeley, CA, 2002), pp. 41–53 and Kiernan, *Blood and soil*.

which humans, animals, and plants were equally legitimate objects of study. As such, the study of human varieties was intimately bound to the broader environment. Recognizing and exploring these historical associations does not require historians to promote the rather offensive assumption that indigenous peoples are, in any sense, just another element of natural environments. Rather, it pushes them to acknowledge and take account of how the shifting relationships between humans and the environment had significant repercussions for the later debates on how land ought to be used and by whom, most obviously with the establishment of the national parks.

A consideration of the debates on human endangerment and the preservation of wilderness also highlights how, despite appearances, the whole notion of wilderness is fundamentally problematic, in that it often denies, or seeks to erase, human presence or historical usage. The birth of the park system helped to both create and promote a vision of wilderness that continues to remain powerful and which has complicated associations with the notion of dying races. Most obviously, and in many senses, this has potential parallels in the debates over restoration and what counts as authentic or the most appropriate object of conservationist agendas. Meanwhile, it also raises the politically critical and unresolved issue of land rights for dislocated, often formerly colonized, peoples, created by the emergence of protected areas; for instance, one recent survey offered the provisional, and likely underestimate, of 'just under 250 reports on relocations from 180 protected areas', which provided 'substantial evidence of the harm done by eviction' in terms of both economic, social, and territorial terms.[67] Indigenous resistance to such dispossession has long been manifest in intense inter-ethnic conflict within settler societies; after all, would-be colonists had to fight, with guns and treaties, to forcibly relocate many peoples. Yet, in their contemporary guises, such campaigns for the recognition and protection of indigenous rights stem from, and are relevant to, broader developments in the aftermath of the Second World War, such as the move to reject racism and recognize universal human rights, and the struggle to secure self-rule during decolonization.[68] More recently, during the 1860s and 1870s, the establishment of politically active non-governmental organizations (NGOs) such as Survival International (f. 1969), which focused exclusively on indigenous rights and the mobilization of aboriginal political organizations, have further highlighted the attempts of formerly marginalized communities to obtain some form of redress. Thus, the notion of wilderness,

[67] Daniel Brockington and James Igoe, 'Eviction for conservation: a global overview', *Conservation and Society*, 4 (2006), pp. 424–70, at pp. 427–8. It should be added that the numbers of people evicted in these reports are often omitted; however, where included they ranged from 'five families … to tens of thousands of people', p. 437.
[68] Ken S. Coates, *A global history of indigenous peoples: struggle and survival* (Basingstoke, 2004), pp. 232–63.

and thereby its conservation, is fundamentally rooted in coerced and collaborative dispossession and in the trope of human endangerment, creating a
complicated and rich history that is worth revisiting. Ultimately, regarding
humans as both agents and subjects in discussions on environmental change
offers the possibility of integrating currently separate literatures, offering a
balanced perspective on the notion of heritage and opportunities to craft
histories that treat human dispossession as more than a contextualizing 'touch
of history'.[69]

---

[69] Mahesh Rangarajan and Ghazala Shahabuddin, 'Displacement and reolcation from protected
areas: towards a biological and historical synthesis', *Conservation and Society*, 4 (2006),
pp. 359–78.

Index

Morocco 18
Morpeth, George Howard, Lord 251, 252
Morris, William 3, 4, 5, 17, 18, 24, 25, 121,
  127n51, 132, 143, 184
Morton, Samuel 272
mosques, preservation of Indian 177–8, 183,
  185
Mount Vernon, Virginia 251
Mubarak, Ali 101, 210, 211, 212
Mughal architecture 16, 67, 172, 177, 180–
  1n24
Mughal empire 172, 177, 178
Muhammad Ali, Viceroy of Egypt 192
Musawwarat, Great Enclosure 67, 68
Museum of Sudanese History, Khartoum 76,
  82
museums
  disregard for interests of 114
  homes of heroes preserved as 249–51, 252,
    253, 263–4, 265
  Niagara Falls site 254–5, 257, 258, 261
  places as 241–2, 265
  ransacking and destruction of 15, 33, 43–4,
    47
  removal of objects to 25, 228
  scenery as natural science museums 260
  site museums at reserves 260
  wilderness sites 261
  see also specific museums by name
Muslims *see* Islam
Muthesius, Hermann 21
Myanmar *see* Burma
Mycenaeans 81
mythology 164

Naga-ed-Deir 112
Napier, Sir Charles 44
Napoleon I, Emperor *see* Bonaparte,
  Napoleon
Napoleon III, Emperor 189n5, 193
Nasser, Gamal Abdel 213
The Nation 257
National Art Collections Fund 262
National Gallery 106
national heritage 8–9, 248–9, 251, 252
national parks 259–61
  and indigenous people 267–8, 277–82, 285
National Trust 132n56
  American Council 4
  foundation of 4, 9
  interests beyond British Isles 4
nationalism
  Arab 91, 126
  and art 188
  competitive building projects in Jerusalem
    120
  in Egypt 213, 214
  heritage claimed by anti-colonial 7, 17, 147

and Holy Land 91
Irish 255
missionary 91
and perpetuation of imperial refashioning
  of heritage 147
postcolonial 17
and roots of 'heritage obsession' 8
the 'native'
  connotations of 149
  detachment, disparagement and
    segregation 170
  and history-writing 164
  ideas of 147, 149–51, 158, 165, 169, 170
  recasting from noble to inferior civilization
    150, 170
  role in comparative and global schemes
    170
  as separable and naturalistic 158
  see also indigenous people
Native Americans
  antiquities of 282
  depletion of 268, 272, 273, 275, 276
  dispossession of 267–8, 274, 277, 278, 279,
    280, 282
  ethnography 223
  and national parks 277–82
  reservations 274, 275–7, 279, 281
  sacred sites 242, 254
natural history 151, 165–9, 170, 269, 284–5
natural world
  as heritage 215
  preservation of 242, 246, 254–61
nature reserves 260
navigational techniques, Pacific islanders' 152,
  157, 158
Naville, Edouard 100
Nebuchadnezzar II, King of Babylon 116
Nekhbet 198
Nelson, Admiral Horatio 103n26, 189
New Delhi 66, 67
New Hebrides 153
New World 20, 215–86
New York
  Central Park 257
  Egyptian obelisk in 192, 193, 205
  plan to bring Maya temple to 24, 219
  plan to bring Shakespeare's Birthplace to
    27, 241, 246, 249, 251
The New York Times 259
New Zealand 53
  Cook in 155, 157
  Maoris 155, 157, 270, 271
  national parks 260, 282
  Polynesian exploration and settlement 152,
    153
Niagara (Church) 256–7
Niagara Falls 27, 242, 254–61
Nile, Battle of the 103